The Outsider

Dissent and Alienation in America

edited by

Sam B. Girgus
Michele Conte
Anthony Piccolo
The University of Oregon

KENDALL/HUNT
PUBLISHING COMPANY
Dubuque, Iowa

B
808.2
.O98
1988

Cover photos by Judith Scot-Smith Girgus at Jo Federigo's Cafe and Bar, Eugene, Oregon

Illustrations by Shane Kessler.

Excerpts from AMERICA IN THE HEART by Carlos Bulosan, copyright 1943, 1946 by Harcourt Brace Jovanovich, Inc., reprinted by permission of the publisher.

Copyright © 1988 by Kendall/Hunt Publishing Company

Library of Congress Catalog Card Number: 88–82428

ISBN 0-8403-5044-9

All rights reserved. No part of this publication may be reproduced, stored in a retrieval system, or transmitted, in any form or by any means, electronic, mechanical, photocopying, recording, or otherwise, without the prior written permission of the copyright owner.

Printed in the United States of America
10 9 8 7 6 5 4 3 2 1

Contents

Introduction   v

   I.   Sources of Alienation: The Divided Modern Self   1
- 1. Repression and the Unconscious, Sigmund Freud   1
- 2. Thoughts for the Times on War and Death, Sigmund Freud   9
- 3. Alienation and Labor, Karl Marx   24
- 4. Economics and Ideology, Karl Marx   27
- 5. Oregon's Romantic Rebels, Edwin R. Bingham   30
- 6. What Pragmatism Means, William James   46
- 7. The Will to Believe, William James   56
- 8. The Radical Individualism of William James   69
- 9. The American Quest for Religious Certainty, Ferenc Szasz   77

  II.   The American Way of Alienation: The Example of Huck   91
- 10. Huck's Sound Heart and Deformed Conscience, Henry Nash Smith   91
- 11. *Huck Finn's* Humor Today, Hamlin Hill   104

 III.   Age of Alienation and Dissent: The 1920s   113
- 12. Introduction to Dewey, John J. Stuhr   113
- 13. The Lost Individual, John Dewey   116
- 14. Why Paris, George Wickes   123

 IV.   Woman as Outsider   129
- 15. Freedom and Desire, Sam B. Girgus   129
- 16. The Blight of Southern Womanhood, Louise Westling   146

  V.   Native Americans   169
- 17. Black Elk Speaks   169
- 18. Chief Joseph   175
- 19. Black Hawk   176

 VI.   Hispanic-Americans   177
- 20. Rudolfo A. Anaya   177

VII. Afro-Americans **185**
- 21. Langston Hughes **185**
- 22. Black Rage, Black Identity, Edwin L. Coleman II **187**

VIII. Asian-Americans **195**
- 23. Jeanne Wakatsuki Houston **195**
- 24. Ruthanne Lum McCunn **200**
- 25. John Okada **203**
- 26. Carlos Bulosan **210**

IX. Jewish-American **215**
- 27. Mira Rothenberg **215**

X. Epilogue **219**
- 28. The American as Radical Outsider **219**

Introduction

The first volume of this text argued that the American experience can be studied in terms of an ideology and myth of renewal and regeneration that provide the basis for an ideological ritual of consensus. According to this theory, the American ideology encourages the creation of a consensus of individuals and nay-sayers who see themselves as exemplifying the American way. Radical individualism defines and forms the foundation for cultural consensus. Seen in this way, America becomes a nation of loners and outsiders, a community of permanent aliens who thrive and prosper on the fringes and margins of established society and conventional behavior. In their own ways the radical Puritans, the revolutionaries, Thoreau and a long tradition of writers, thinkers and historical figures epitomize and dramatize this tradition. It is the purpose of this second volume to reconsider this thesis by challenging and questioning it. This volume wonders if our understanding of modern alienation and our insights into the nature of contemporary society have undermined and vitiated the sources and capacity for achieving consensus. In other words, does modern culture condemn consensus to irrelevance? Does recent social and intellectual history suggest that consensus has existed for some rugged individuals but not for all? Certainly, by the beginning of this century there already existed a major body of work and thought that proffered visions of the individual in society and culture that were based on alienation and fragmentation. Freud spoke of a form of internal alienation in which the individual is always separated and divided from himself. For Marx and his followers alienation grew out of the individual's separation from his own labor. This modern perspective on the nature of the individual in society represents a sharp challenge to the hope of achieving consensus. At the same time, in more recent decades the idea of consensus has been faced with additional social and cultural challenges. Forces of ethnicity, race and gender question the relevance and ability of the old ritual of consensus to change quickly and profoundly enough to accommodate the needs and aspirations of people and groups who have felt themselves to be historically outside of the ideology of renewal. For these people, alienation has meant exclusion from the democratic processes of individual regeneration and cultural transformation. For them, our age has been one not of consensus but of dissensus. Accordingly, the following volume attempts to explore the question of what this kind of dissent and alienation has to say about the future prospects of the ideological ritual of consensus as we move toward a new century.

Sam B. Girgus

I
Sources of Alienation
The Divided Modern Self
1
Repression and the Unconscious
Sigmund Freud

The concepts of repression and the unconscious constitute the heart of Freud's theory of psychoanalysis. These brief excerpts from Freud's seminal essays, "Repression" and "The Unconscious," are part of his "Papers on Metapsychology" that appeared in 1915. For much of his mature life, Freud developed and advanced these ideas. In the following excerpt Freud defines the concept of repression as the diversion from consciousness of psychical forces that cause discomfort and pain. This idea of repression is related to and supports his theory of the unconscious which explains, for Freud, not only important gaps in consciousness but also many other mental processes and acts.

Repression

One of the vicissitudes an instinctual impulse may undergo is to meet with resistances which seek to make it inoperative. Under certain conditions, which we shall presently investigate more closely, the impulse then passes into the state of 'repression' [*'Verdrängung'*]. If what was in question was the operation of an external stimulus, the appropriate method to adopt would obviously be flight; with an instinct, flight is of no avail, for the ego cannot escape from itself. At some later period, rejection based on judgement *(condemnation)* will be found to be a good method to adopt against an instinctual impulse. Repression is a preliminary stage of condemnation, something between flight and condemnation; it is a concept which could not have been formulated before the time of psycho-analytic studies.

It is not easy in theory to deduce the possibility of such a thing as repression. Why should an instinctual impulse undergo a vicissitude like this? A necessary condition of its happening must clearly be that the instinct's attainment of its aim should produce unpleasure instead of pleasure. But we cannot well imagine such a contingency. There are no such instincts: satisfaction of an instinct is always pleasurable. We should have to assume certain peculiar circumstances, some sort of process by which the pleasure of satisfaction is changed into unpleasure.

Sigmund Freud Copyrights Ltd, The Institute of Psychoanalysis and The Hogarth Press for permission to quote from THE STANDARD EDITION OF THE COMPLETE PSYCHOLOGICAL WORKS OF SIGMUND FREUD translated and edited by James Strachey.

In order the better to delimit repression, let us discuss some other instinctual situations. It may happen that an external stimulus becomes internalized—for example, by eating into and destroying some bodily organ—so that a new source of constant excitation and increase of tension arises. The stimulus thereby acquires a far-reaching similarity to an instinct. We know that a case of this sort is experienced by us as *pain*. The aim of this pseudo-instinct, however, is simply the cessation of the change in the organ and of the unpleasure accompanying it. There is no other direct pleasure to be attained by cessation of pain. Further, pain is imperative; the only things to which it can yield are removal by some toxic agent or the influence of mental distraction.

The case of pain is too obscure to give us any help in our purpose.[1] Let us take the case in which an instinctual stimulus such as hunger remains unsatisfied. It then becomes imperative and can be allayed by nothing but the action that satisfies it;[2] it keeps up a constant tension of need. Nothing in the nature of a repression seems in this case to come remotely into question.

Thus repression certainly does not arise in cases where the tension produced by lack of satisfaction of an instinctual impulse is raised to an unbearable degree. The methods of defence which are open to the organism against that situation must be discussed in another connection.[3]

Let us rather confine ourselves to clinical experience, as we meet with it in psycho-analytic practice. We then learn that the satisfaction of an instinct which is under repression would be quite possible, and further, that in every instance such a satisfaction would be pleasurable in itself; but it would be irreconcilable with other claims and intentions. It would, therefore, cause pleasure in one place and unpleasure in another. It has consequently become a condition for repression that the motive force of unpleasure shall have acquired more strength than the pleasure obtained from satisfaction. Psycho-analytic observation of the transference neuroses, moreover, leads us to conclude that repression is not a defensive mechanism which is present from the very beginning, and that it cannot arise until a sharp cleavage has occurred between conscious and unconscious mental activity—that *the essence of repression lies simply in turning something away, and keeping it at a distance, from the conscious.*[4] This view of repression would be made more complete by assuming that, before the mental organization reaches this stage, the task of fending off instinctual impulses is dealt with by the other vicissitudes which instincts may undergo—e.g. reversal into the opposite or turning round upon the subject's own self [cf. pp.126–7].

It seems to us now that, in view of the very great extent to which repression and what is unconscious are correlated, we must defer probing more deeply into the nature of repression until we have learnt more about the structure of the succession of psychical agencies and about the differentiation between what is unconscious and conscious. [See the following paper, p. 180 ff.] Till then, all we can do is to put together in a purely descriptive fashion a few characteristics of repression that have been observed clinically, even though we run the risk of having to repeat unchanged much that has been said elsewhere.

We have reason to assume that there is a *primal repression*, a first phase of repression, which consists in the psychical (ideational) representative of the instinct[5] being denied entrance into the conscious. With this a *fixation* is established; the representative in question persists unaltered from then onwards and the instinct remains attached to it. This is due to the properties of unconscious processes of which we shall speak later [p. 187].

The second stage of repression, *repression proper*, affects mental derivatives of the repressed representative, or such trains of thought as, originating elsewhere, have come into associative connection with it. On account of this association, these ideas experience the same fate as what was primally repressed. Repression proper, therefore, is actually an after-pressure.[6] Moreover, it is a mistake to emphasize only the repulsion which operates from the direction of the conscious upon what is to be repressed; quite as important is the attraction exercised by what was primally repressed upon everything with which it can establish a connection. Probably the trend towards repression would fail in its purpose if these two forces did not cooperate, if there were not something previously repressed ready to receive what is repelled by the conscious.[7]

Under the influence of the study of psychoneuroses, which brings before us the important effects of repression, we are inclined to overvalue their psychological bearing and to forget too readily that repression does not hinder the instinctual representative from continuing to exist in the unconscious, from organizing itself further, putting out derivatives and establishing connections. Repression in fact interferes only with the relation of the instinctual representative to *one* psychical system, namely, to that of the conscious.

Psycho-analysis is able to show us other things as well which are important for understanding the effects of repression in the psychoneuroses. It shows us, for instance, that the instinctual representative develops with less interference and more profusely if it is withdrawn by repression from conscious influence. It proliferates in the dark, as it were, and takes on extreme forms of expression, which when they are translated and presented to the neurotic are not only bound to seem alien to him, but frighten him by giving him the picture of an extraordinary and dangerous strength of instinct. This deceptive strength of instinct is the result of an uninhibited development in phantasy and of the damming-up consequent on frustrated satisfaction. The fact that this last result is bound up with repression points the direction in which the true significance of repression has to be looked for.

Reverting once more, however, to the opposite aspect of repression, let us make it clear that it is not even correct to suppose that repression withholds from the conscious *all* the derivatives of what was primarily repressed.[8] If these derivatives have become sufficiently far removed from the repressed representative, whether owing to the adoption of distortions or by reason of the number of intermediate links inserted, they have free access to the conscious. It is as though the resistance of the conscious against them was a function of their distance from what was originally repressed. In carrying out the technique of psycho-analysis, we continually require the patient to produce such derivatives of the repressed as, in consequence either of their remoteness or of their distortion, can pass the censorship of the conscious. Indeed, the associations which we require him to give without being influenced by any conscious purposive idea and without any criticism, and from which we reconstitute a conscious translation of the repressed representative—these associations are nothing else than remote and distorted derivatives of this kind. During this process we observe that the patient can go on spinning a thread of such associations, till he is brought up against some thought, the relation of which to what is repressed becomes so obvious that he is compelled to repeat his attempt at repression. Neurotic symptoms, too, must have fulfilled this same condition, for they are derivatives of the repressed, which has, by their means, finally won the access to consciousness which was previously denied to it.[9]

We can lay down no general rule as to what degree of distortion and remoteness is necessary before the resistance on the part of the conscious is removed. A delicate balancing is here taking place, the play of which is hidden from us; its mode of operation, however, enables us to infer that it is a question of calling a halt when the cathexis of the unconscious reaches a certain intensity—an intensity beyond which the unconscious would break through to satisfaction. Repression acts, therefore, in a *highly individual* manner. Each single derivative of the repressed may have its own special vicissitude; a little more or a little less distortion alters the whole outcome. In this connection we can understand how it is that the objects to which men give most preference, their ideals, proceed from the same perceptions and experiences as the objects which they most abhor, and that they were originally only distinguished from one another through slight modifications. [Cf. p. 93.] Indeed, as we found in tracing the origin of the fetish,[10] it is possible for the original instinctual representative to be split in two, one part undergoing repression, while the remainder, precisely on account of this intimate connection, undergoes idealization.

The same result as follows from an increase or a decrease in the degree of distortion may also be achieved at the other end of the apparatus, so to speak, by a modification in the condition for the production of pleasure and unpleasure. Special techniques have been evolved, with the purpose of bringing about such changes in the play of mental forces that what would otherwise give rise to unpleasure may on this occasion result in pleasure; and, whenever a technical device of this sort comes into operation, the repression of an instinctual representative which would otherwise be repudiated is removed. These techniques have till now only been studied in any detail in jokes.[11] As a rule the repression is only temporarily removed and is promptly reinstated.

Observations like this, however, enable us to note some further characteristics of repression. Not only is it, as we have just shown, *individual* in its operation, but it is also exceedingly *mobile*. The process of repression is not to be regarded as an event which takes place *once*, the results of which are permanent, as when some living thing has been killed and from that time onward is dead; repression demands a persistent expenditure of force, and if this were to cease the success of the repression would be jeopardized, so that a fresh act of repression would be necessary. We may suppose that the repressed exercises a continuous pressure in the direction of the conscious, so that this pressure must be balanced by an unceasing counter-pressure.[12] Thus the maintenance of a repression involves an uninterrupted expenditure of force, while its removal results in a saving from an economic point of view. The mobility of repression, incidentally, also finds expression in the psychical characteristics of the state of sleep, which alone renders possible the formation of dreams.[13] With a return to waking life the repressive cathexes which have been drawn in are once more sent out.

Finally, we must not forget that after all we have said very little about an instinctual impulse when we have established that it is repressed. Without prejudice to its repression, such as impulse may be in widely different states. It may be inactive, i.e. only very slightly cathected with mental energy; or it may be cathected in varying degrees, and so enabled to be active. True, its activation will not result in a direct removal of the repression, but it will set in motion all the processes which end in a penetration by the impulse into consciousness along circuitous paths. With unrepressed derivatives of the unconscious the fate of a particular idea is often decided by the degree of its activity or cathexis. It is an everyday occurrence that such a derivative remains unrepressed so long as it represents only a small amount of energy, although its content would be calculated to give rise to a conflict with what is dominant in consciousness. The quantitative factor proves decisive for this conflict: as soon as the basically obnoxious idea exceeds a certain degree of strength, the conflict becomes a real one, and it is precisely this activation that leads to repression. So that, where repression is concerned, an increase of energic cathexis operates in the same sense as an approach to the unconscious, while a decrease of that cathexis operates in the same sense as remoteness from the unconscious or distortion. We see that the repressive trends may find a substitute for repression in a weakening of what is distasteful.

Notes

1. [Pain and the organism's method of dealing with it are discussed in Chapter IV of *Beyond the Pleasure Principle (1920g)*, *Standard Ed.*, *18*, 30. The subject is already raised in Part I, Section 6, of the 'Project' (1950a [1895]).]
2. [In the 'Project' (1950a[1895]), Part I, Section 1, this is termed the 'specific action'.]
3. [It is not clear what 'other connection' Freud had in mind.]
4. [A modification of this formula will be found below on p. 203.]

5. [See the Editor's Note to the previous paper, p. 111 ff.]
6. ['*Nachdrägen.*' Freud uses the same term in his account of the process in the Schreber analysis (see next footnote), and also in his paper on 'The Unconscious' (see below, pp. 180 and 181). But, on alluding to the point more than twenty years later in the third section of 'Analysis Terminable and Interminable' (1937*c*), he uses the word '*Nachverdrängung*' (after-repression').]
7. [The account of the two stages of repression given in the last two paragraphs had been anticipated by Freud four years earlier (though in a somewhat different form) in the third section of the Schreber analysis (1911*c*), and in a letter to Ferenczi of December 6, 1910 (Jones, 1955, 499). See also *Standard Ed.,* **5**, 547 *n.*, and ibid. **7**, 175-6 *n.*]
8. [What follows in this paragraph is discussed at greater length in Section VI of 'The Unconscious' (below, p. 190 ff.).]
9. [In the German editions before 1924 the latter part of this sentence read: 'Welches sich . . . den ihm versagten Zugang vom Bewusstsein endlich erkampft hat'. This was translated formerly 'which has finally . . . wrested from consciousness the right of way previously denied it'. In the German editions from 1924 onwards the word '*vom*' was corrected to '*zum*', thus altering the sense to that given in the text above.]
10. [Cf. Section 2 (A) of the first of Freud's *Three Essays* (1905*d*), *Standard Ed.,* **7**, 153-4.]
11. [See the second chapter of Freud's book on jokes (1905).]
12. [This is discussed further on p. 180 f. below.]
13. [Cf. *The Interpretation of Dreams* (1900a), Chap. VII (C), *Standard Ed.,* **5**, 57-8. *See also below, p. 225.*]

The Unconscious

We have learnt from psycho-analysis that the essence of the process of repression lies, not in putting an end to, in annihilating, the idea which represents an instinct, but in preventing it from becoming conscious. When this happens we say of the idea that it is in a state of being 'unconscious,' and we can produce good evidence to show that even when it is unconscious it can produce effects, even including some which finally reach consciousness. Everything that is repressed must remain unconscious; but let us state at the very outset that the repressed does not cover everything that is unconscious. The unconscious has the wider compass: the repressed is a part of the unconscious.

How are we to arrive at a knowledge of the unconscious? It is of course only as something conscious that we know it, after it has undergone transformation or translation into something conscious. Psycho-analytic work shows us every day that translation of this kind is possible. In order that this should come about, the person under analysis must overcome certain resistances—the same resistances as those which, earlier, made the material concerned into something repressed by rejecting it from the conscious.

I. Justification for the Concept of the Unconscious

Our right to assume the existence of something mental that is unconscious and to employ that assumption for the purposes of scientific work is disputed in many quarters. To this we can reply that our assumption of the unconscious is *necessary* and *legitimate*, and that we possess numerous proofs of its existence.

It is *necessary* because the data of consciousness have a very large number of gaps in them; both in healthy and in sick people psychical acts often occur which can be explained only by presupposing other acts, of which, nevertheless, consciousness affords no evidence. These not only include parapraxes and dreams in healthy people, and everything described as a psychical symptom or an obsession in the sick; our most personal daily experience acquaints us with ideas that come into our head we do not know from where, and with intellectual conclusions arrived at we do not know how. All these conscious acts remain disconnected and unintelligible if we insist upon claiming that every mental act that occurs in us must also necessarily be experienced by us through consciousness; on the other hand, they fall into a demonstrable connection if we interpolate between them the unconscious acts which we have inferred. A gain in meaning is a perfectly justifiable ground for going beyond the limits of direct experience. When, in addition, it turns out that the assumption of there being an unconscious enables us to construct a successful procedure by which we can exert an effective influence upon the course of conscious processes, this success will have given us an incontrovertible proof of the existence of what we have assumed. This being so, we must adopt the position that to require that whatever goes on in the mind must also be known to consciousness is to make an untenable claim.

We can go further and argue, in support of there being an unconscious psychical state, that at any given moment consciousness includes only a small content, so that the greater part of what we call conscious knowledge must in any case be for very considerable periods of time in a state of latency, that is to say, of being psychically unconscious. When all our latent memories are taken into consideration it becomes totally incomprehensible how the existence of the unconscious can be denied. But here we encounter the objection that these latent recollections can no longer be described as psychical, but that they correspond to residues of somatic processes from which what is psychical can once more arise. The obvious answer to this is that a latent memory is, on the contrary, an unquestionable residuum of a *psychical* process. But it is more important to realize clearly that this objection is based on the equation—not, it is true, explicitly stated but taken as axiomatic—of what is conscious with what is mental. This equation is either a *petitio principii* which begs the question whether everything that is psychical is also necessarily conscious; or else it is a matter of convention, of nomenclature. In this latter case it is, of course, like any other convention, not open to refutation. The question remains, however, whether the convention is so expedient that we are bound to adopt it. To this we may reply that the conventional equation of the psychical with the conscious is totally inexpedient. It disrupts psychical continuities, plunges us into the soluble difficulties of psycho-psychical parallelism,[1] is open to the reproach that for no obvious reason it over-estimates the part played by consciousness, and that it forces us prematurely to abandon the field of psychological research without being able to offer us any compensation from other fields.

It is clear in any case that this question—whether the latent states of mental life, whose existence is undeniable, are to be conceived of as conscious mental states or as physical ones—threatens to resolve itself into a verbal dispute. We shall therefore be better advised to focus our attention on what we know with certainty of the nature of these debatable states. As far as their physical characteristics are concerned, they are totally inaccessible to us: no physiological concept or chemical process can give us any notion of their nature. On the other hand, we know for certain that they have abundant points of contact with conscious mental processes; with the help of a certain amount of work they can be transformed into, or replaced by, conscious mental processes, and all the categories which we employ to describe conscious mental acts, such as ideas, purposes, resolutions and so on, can be applied to them. Indeed, we are obliged to say of some of these latent states that the only respect in which they differ from conscious ones is precisely in the absence of consciousness. Thus we shall not hesitate to treat them as objects of psychological research, and to deal with them in the most intimate connection with conscious mental acts.

The stubborn denial of psychical character to latent mental acts is accounted for by the circumstance that most of the phenomena concerned have not been the subject of study outside psycho-analysis. Anyone who is ignorant of pathological facts, who regards the parapraxes of normal people as accidental, and who is content with the old saw that dreams are froth [*'Träume sind Schäume'*] has only to ignore a few more problems of the psychology of consciousness in order to spare himself any need to assume an unconscious mental activity. Incidentally, even before the time of psycho-analysis, hypnotic experiments, and especially post-hypnotic suggestion, had tangibly demonstrated the existence and mode of operation of the mental unconscious.[3]

The assumption of an unconscious is, moreover, a perfectly *legitimate* one, inasmuch as in postulating it we are not departing a single step from our customary and generally accepted mode of thinking. Consciousness makes each of us aware only of his own states of mind; that other people, too, possess a consciousness is an inference which we draw by analogy from their observable utterances and actions, in order to make this behaviour of theirs intelligible to us. (It would no doubt be psychologically more correct to put it in this way: that without any special reflection we attribute to everyone else our own constitution and therefore our consciousness as well, and that this identification is a *sie qua non* of our understanding.) This inference (or this identification) was formerly extended by the ego to other human beings, to animals, plants, inanimate objects and to the world at large, and proved serviceable so long as their similarity to the individual ego was overwhelmingly great; but it became more untrustworthy in proportion as the difference between the ego and these 'others' widened. To-day, our critical judgement is already in doubt on the question of consciousness in animals; we refuse to admit it in plants and we regard the assumption of its existence in inanimate matter as mysticism. But even where the original inclination to identification has withstood criticism—that is, when the 'others' are our fellow-men—the assumption of a consciousness in them rests upon an inference and cannot share the immediate certainty which we have of our own consciousness.

Psycho-analysis demands nothing more than that we should apply this process of inference to ourselves also—a proceeding to which, it is true, we are not constitutionally inclined. If we do this, we must say: all the acts and manifestations which I notice in myself and do not know how to link up with the rest of my mental life must be judged as if they belonged to someone else: they are to be explained by a mental life ascribed to this other person. Furthermore, experience shows that we understand very well how to interpret in other people (that is, how to fit into their chain of mental events) the same acts which we refuse to acknowledge as being mental in ourselves. Here some special hindrance evidently deflects our investigations from our own self and prevents our obtaining a true knowledge of it.

This process of inference, when applied to oneself in spite of internal opposition, does not, however, lead to the disclosure of an unconscious; it leads logically to the assumption of another, second consciousness which is united in one's self with the consciousness one knows. But at this point, certain criticisms may fairly be made. In the first place, a consciousness of which its own possessor knows nothing is something very different from a consciousness belonging to another person, and it is questionable whether such a consciousness, lacking, as it does, its most important characteristics, deserves any discussion at all. Those who have resisted the assumption of an unconscious *psychical* are not likely to be ready to exchange it for an unconscious *consciousness*. In the second place, analysis shows that the different latent mental processes inferred by us enjoy a high degree of mutual independence, as though they had no connection with one another, and knew nothing of one another. We must be prepared, if so, to assume the existence in us not only of a second consciousness, but of a third, forth, perhaps of an unlimited number of states of consciousness, all unknown to us and to one another. In the third place—and this is the most weighty argument of all—we have to take into account the fact that analytic investigation reveals some of these latent processes as having characteristics and peculiarities which seem alien to us, or even incredible, and which run directly counter to the attributes of consciousness with which we are familiar. Thus we have grounds for modifying our inference about ourselves and saying that what is proved is not the existence of a second consciousness in us, but the existence of psychical acts which lack consciousness. We shall also be right in rejecting the term 'subconsciousness' as incorrect and misleading.[4] The well-known cases of *'double conscience'*[5] (splitting of consciousness) prove nothing against our view. We may most aptly describe them as cases of a splitting of the mental activities into two groups, and say that the same consciousness turns to one or the other of these groups alternately.

In psycho-analysis there is no choice for us but to assert that mental processes are in themselves unconscious, and to liken the perception of them by means of consciousness to the perception of the external world by means of the sense-organs.[6] We can even hope to gain fresh knowledge from the comparison. The psycho-analytic assumption of unconscious mental activity appears to us, on the one hand, as a further expansion of the primitive animism which caused us to see copies of our own consciousness all around us, and, on the other hand, as an extension of the corrections undertaken by Kant of our views on external perception. Just as Kant warned us not to overlook the fact that our perceptions are subjectively conditioned and must not be regarded as identical with what is perceived though unknowable, so psycho-analysis warns us not to equate perceptions by means of consciousness with the unconscious mental processes which are their object. Like the physical, the psychical is not necessarily in reality what it appears to us to be. We shall be glad to learn, however, that the correction of internal perception will turn out not to offer such great difficulties as the correction of external perception—that internal objects are less unknowable than the external world.

Notes

1. [Freud seems himself at one time to have been inclined to accept this theory, as is suggested by a passage in his book on aphasia (1891*b*, 56 ff.). This will be found translated below in Appendix B (p. 206).]
2. [Cf. *The Interpretation of Dreams* (1900*a*), *Standard Ed.*, **4**, 133.]
3. [In his very last discussion of the subject, in the unfinished fragment 'Some Elementary Lessons in Psycho-Analysis' (1940*b*), Freud entered at some length into the evidence afforded by post-hypnotic suggestion,]
4. [In some of his very early writings, Freud himself used the term 'subconscious', e.g. in his French paper on hysterical paralyses (1893*c*) and in *Studies on Hysteria* (1895), *Standard E.*, **2**, 69 *n*. But he disrecommends the term as early as in *The Interpretation of Dreams* (1900*a*), *Standard Ed.*, **5**, 615. He alludes to the point again in Lecture XIX of the *Introductory Lectures* (1916-17), and argues it a little more fully near the end of Chapter II of *The Question of Lay Analysis* (1920*e*).]
5. [The French term for 'dual consciousness'.]
6. [This idea had already been dealt with at some length in Chapter VII (F) of *The Interpretation of Dreams* (1900*a*), *Standard Ed.*, **5**, 615-17.]

2
Thoughts for the Times on War and Death
Sigmund Freud

The following essay by Freud is not only important in the development of the psychoanalytical model of the mind, it also represents a provocative piece of social and cultural criticism. The essay tries to explain from a psychoanalytical perspective how it was possible for the advanced civilizations of the West to catapult themselves into the unbelievable destruction of the First World War. It also attempts an explanation of the malaise and disillusionment that this event caused in the Western mind. Freud's essay offers original insights into attitudes toward heroism and death and suggests that many human problems reside in the unconscious ambivalence of our feelings toward our parents and our fear of death. Published in 1915, the essay is in volume 14 of the Standard Edition.

I. The Disillusionment of the War

Swept as we are into the vortex of this war-time, our information one-sided, ourselves too near to focus the mighty transformations which have already taken place or are beginning to take place, and without a glimmering of the inchoate future, we are incapable of apprehending the significance of the thronging impressions, and know not what value to attach to the judgments we form. We are constrained to believe that never has any event been destructive of so much that is valuable in the common wealth of humanity, nor so misleading to many of the clearest intelligences, nor so debasing to the highest that we know. Science herself has lost her passionless impartiality; in their deep embitterment her servants seek for weapons from her with which to contribute towards the defeat of the enemy. The anthropologist is driven to declare the opponent inferior and degenerate; the psychiatrist to publish his diagnosis of the enemy's disease of mind or spirit. But probably our sense of these immediate evils is disproportionately strong, and we are not entitled to compare them with the evils of other times of which we have not undergone the experience.

The individual who is not himself a combatant—and so a wheel in the gigantic machinery of war—feels conscious of disorientation, and of an inhibition in his powers and activities. I believe that he will welcome any indication, however slight, which may enable him to find out what is wrong with himself at least. I propose to distinguish two among the most potent factors in the men-

Sigmund Freud Copyrights Ltd, The Institute of Psychoanalysis and The Hogarth Press for permission to quote from THE STANDARD EDITION OF THE COMPLETE PSYCHOLOGICAL WORKS OF SIGMUND FREUD translated and edited by James Strachey.

tal distress felt by non-combatants, against which it is such a heavy task to struggle, and to treat of them here: the disillusionment which this war has evoked; and the altered attitude towards death which this—like every other war—imposes on us.

When I speak of disillusionment, everyone at once knows what I mean. One need not be a sentimentalist; one may perceive the biological and psychological necessity of suffering in the economics of human life, and yet condemn war both in its means and in its aims, and devoutly look forward to the cessation of all wars. True, we have told ourselves that wars can never cease so long as nations live under such widely differing conditions, so long as the value of individual life is in each nation so variously computed, and so long as the animosities which divide them represent such powerful instinctual forces in the mind. And we were prepared to find that wars between the primitive and the civilized peoples, between those races whom a colourline divides, nay, wars with and among the undeveloped nationalities of Europe or those whose culture has perished—that for a considerable period such wars would occupy mankind. But we permitted ourselves to have other hopes. We had expected the great ruling powers among the white nations upon whom the leadership of human species has fallen, who were known to have cultivated world-wide interests, to whose creative powers were due to our technical advances in the direction of dominating nature as well as the artistic and scientific acquistions of the mind—people such as these we had expected to succed in discovering another way of settling misunderstandings and conflicts of interest. Within each of these nations there prevailed high standards of accepted custom for the individual, to which his manner of life was bound to conform if he desired a share of communal privileges. These ordinances, frequently too stringent, exacted a great deal from him, much self-restraint, much renunciation of instinctual gratification. He was especially forbidden to make use of the immense advantages to be gained by the practice of lying and deception in the competition with his fellow-men. The civilized state regarded these accepted standards as the basis of its existence; stern were its proceedings when an impious hand was laid upon them; frequent the pronouncement that to subject them even to examination by a critical intelligence was entirely impracticable. It could be assumed, therefore, that the state itself would respect them, nor would contemplate undertaking any infringement of what it acknowledged as the basis of its own existence. To be sure, it was evident that within these civilized states were mingled remnants of certain other races who were universally unpopular and had therefore been only reluctantly, and even so not to the fullest extent, admitted to participation in the common task of civilization, for which they had shown themselves suitable enough. But the great nations themselves, it might have been supposed, had acquired so much comprehension of their common interests, and enough tolerance for the differences that existed between them, that 'foreigner' and enemy' could no longer, as still in antiquity, be regarded as synonymous.

Relying on this union among the civilized races, countless people have exchanged their native home for a foreign dwelling-place, and made their existence dependent on the conditions of intercourse between friendly nations. But he who was not by stress of circumstances confined to one spot, could also confer upon himself, through all the advantages and attractions of these civilized countries, a new, a wider fatherland, wherein he moved unhindered and unsuspected. In this way he enjoyed the blue sea, and the gray; the beauty of the snow-clad mountains and of the green pasturelands; the magic of the northern forests and the splendour of the souther vegetation; the emotion inspired by landscapes that recall great historical events, and the silence of nature in her inviolate places. This new fatherland was for him a museum also, filled with all the treasures which the artists among civilized communities had in the successive centuries created and left behind. As he wandered from one gallery to another in this museum, he could appreciate impartially the varied types of perfection that miscegenation, the course of historical events, and the special characteristics of their mother-earth had produced among his more remote compatriots. Here he would find a cool inflexible energy developed to the highest point; there, the gracious art of beautifying existence; elsewhere, the sense of order and fixed law—in short, any and all of the qualities which have made mankind the lords of the earth.

Nor must we forget that each of these citizens of culture had created for himself a personal 'Parnassus' and 'School of Athens'. From among the great thinkers and artists of all nations he had chosen those to whom he conceived himself most deeply indebted for what he had achieved in enjoyment and comprehension of life, and in his veneration had associated them with the immortals of old as well as with the more familiar masters of his own tongue. None of these great figures had seemed to him alien because he had spoken another language—not the incomparable investigator of the passions of mankind, nor the intoxicated worshipper of beauty, nor the vehement and threatening prophet, nor the subtle mocking satirist; and never did he on this account rebuke himself as a renegade towards his own nation and his beloved mother-tongue.

The enjoyment of this fellowship in civilization was from time to time disturbed by warning voices, which declared that as a result of long-prevailing differences wars were unavoidable, even among the members of a fellowship such as this. We refused to believe it; but if such a war indeed must be, what was our imaginary picture of it? We saw it as an opportunity for demonstrating the progress of mankind in communal feeling since the era when the Greek Amphictyones had proclaimed that no city of the league might be demolished, nor its olive-groves hewn down, nor its water cut off. As a chivalrous crusade, which would limit itself to establishing the superiority of one side in the contest, with the least possible infliction of dire sufferings that could contribute nothing to the decision, and with complete immunity for the wounded who must of necessity withdraw from the contest, as well as for the physicians and nurses who devoted themselves to the task of healing. And of course with the utmost precautions for the non-combatant classes of the population—for women who are debarred from war-work, and for the children who, grown older, should be enemies no longer but friends and co-operators. And again, with preservation of all the international undertakings and institutions in which the mutual civilization of peace-time had been embodied.

Even a war like this would have been productive of horrors and sufferings enough; but it would not have interrupted the development of ethical relations between the greater units of mankind, between the peoples and the states.

Then the war in which we had refused to believe broke out, and brought—disillusionment. Not only is it more sanguinary and more destructive than any war of other days, because of the enormously increased perfection of weapons of attack and defence; but it is at least as cruel, as embittered, as implacable as any that has preceded it. It sets at naught all those restrictions known as International Law, which in peace-time the states had bound themselves to observe; it ignores the prerogatives of the wounded and the medical service, the distinction between civil and military sections of the population, the claims of private property. It tramples in blind fury on all that comes in its way, as though there were to be no future and no goodwill among men after it has passed. It rends all bonds of fellowship between the contending peoples, and threatens to leave such a legacy of embitterment as will make any renewal of such bonds impossible for a long time to come.

Moreover, it has brought to light the almost unbelievable phenomenon of a mutual comprehension between the civilized nations so slight that the one can turn with hate and loathing upon the other. Nay, more—that one of the great civilized nations is so universally unpopular that the attempt can actually be made to exclude it from the civilized community as 'barbaric', although it long has proved its fitness by the most magnificent co-operation in the work of civilization. We live in the hope that the impartial decision of history will furnish the proof that precisely this nation, this in whose tongue we now write, this for whose victory our dear ones are fighting, was the one which least transgressed the laws of civilization—but at such a time who shall dare present himself as the judge of his own cause?

Nations are in a measure represented by the states which they have formed; these states, by the governments which administer them. The individual in any given nation has in this war a terrible opportunity to convince himself of what would occasionally strike him in peace-time—that the state has forbidden to the individual the practice of wrong-doing, not because it desired to abolish it, but because it desires to monopolize it, like salt and tobacco. The warring state permits itself every such misdeed, every such act of violence, as would disgrace the individual man. It practices not only the accepted stratagems, but also deliberate lying and deception against the enemy; and this, too, in a measure which appears to surpass the usage of former wars. The state exacts the utmost degree of obedience and sacrifice from its citizens, but at the same time treats them as children by maintaining an excess of secrecy, and a censorship of news and expressions of opinion that renders the spirits of those thus intellectually oppressed defenseless against every unfavourable turn of events and every sinister rumour. It absolves itself from the guarantees and contracts it had formed with other states, and makes unabashed confession of its rapacity and lust for power, which the private individual is then called upon to sanction in the name of patriotism.

Nor may it be objected that the state cannot refrain from wrong-doing, since that would place it at a disadvantage. It is no less disadvantageous, as a general rule, for the individual man to conform to the customs of morality and refrain from brutal and arbitrary conduct; and the state but seldom proves able to indemnify him for the sacrifices it exacts. It cannot be a matter for astonishment, therefore, that this relaxation of all the moral ties between the greater units of mankind should have had a seducing influence on the morality of individuals; for our conscious is not the inflexible judge that ethical teachers are wont to declare it, but in its origin is 'dread of the community' and nothing else. When the community has no rebuke to make, there is an end of all suppression of the baser passions, and men perpetrate deeds of cruelty, fraud, treachery and barbarity so incompatible with their civilization that one would have held them to be impossible.

Well may that civilized cosmopolitan, therefore, of whom I spoke, stand helpless in a world grown strange to him—his all-embracing patrimony disintegrated, the common estates in it laid waste, the fellow-citizens embroiled and debased!

In criticism of his disillusionment, nevertheless, certain things must be said. Strictly speaking, it is not justified, for it consists in the destruction of—an illusion! We welcome illusions because they spare us emotional distress, and enable us instead to indulge in gratification. We must not then complain if now and again they come into conflict with some portion of reality, and are shattered against it.

Two things in this war have evoked our sense of disillusionment: the destitution shown in moral relations externally by the states which in their interior relations pose as the guardians of accepted moral usage, and the brutality in behaviour shown by individuals, whom, as partakers in the highest form of human civilization, one would not have credited with such a thing.

Let us begin with the second point and endeavour to formulate, as succinctly as may be, the point of view which it is proposed to criticize. How do we imagine the process by which an individual attains to a higher plane of morality? The first answer is sure to be: He is good and noble from his very birth, his very earliest beginnings. We need not consider this any further. A second answer will suggest that we are concerned with a developmental process, and will probably assume that this development consists in eradicating from him the evil human tendencies and, under the influence of education and a civilized environment, replacing them by good ones. From that standpoint it is certainly astonishing that evil should show itself to have such power in those who have been thus nurtured.

But this answer implies the thesis from which we propose to dissent. In reality, there is no such thing as 'eradicating' evil tendencies. Psychological—more strictly speaking, psycho-analytic—investigation shows instead that the inmost essence of human nature consists of elemental instincts, which are common to all men and aim at the satisfaction of certain primal needs. These instincts in themselves are neither good nor evil. We but classify them and their manifestations in that fashion, according as they meet the needs and demands of the human community. It is admitted that all those instincts which society condemns as evil—let us take as representatives the selfish and the cruel—are of this primitive type.

These primitive instincts undergo a lengthy process of development before they are allowed to become active in the adult being. They are inhibited, directed towards other aims and departments, become commingled, alter their objects, and are to some extent turned back upon their possessor. Reaction-formations against certain instincts take the deceptive form of a change in content, as though egoism had changed into altruism, or cruelty into pity. These reaction-formations are facilitated by the circumstance that many instincts are manifested almost from the first in pairs of opposites, a very remarkable phenomenon—and one strange to the lay public—which is termed the 'ambivalence of feeling'. The most easily observable and comprehensible instance of this is the fact that intense love and intense hatred are so often to be found together in the same person. Psycho-analysis adds that the conflicting feelings not infrequently have the same person for their object.

It is not until all these 'vicissitudes to which instincts are subject' have been surmounted that what we call the character of a human being is formed, and this, as we know, can only very inadequately be classified as 'good' or 'bad'. A human being is seldom altogether good or bad; he is usually 'good' in certain external circumstances and in others decidedly 'bad'. It is interesting to learn that the existence of strong 'bad' impulses in infancy is often the actual condition for an unmistakable inclination towards 'good' in the adult person. Those who as children have been the most pronounced egoists may well become the most helpful and self-sacrificing members of the community; most of our sentimentalists, friends of humanity, champions of animals, have been evolved from little sadists and animal-tormentors.

The transformation of 'bad' instincts is brought about by two co-operating factors, an internal and an external. The internal factor consists in an influence on the bad—say, the egoistic—instincts exercised by erotism, that is, by the human need for love, taken in its widest sense. By the admixture of *erotic* components the egoistic instincts are transmuted into *social* ones. We learn to value being loved as an advantage for which we are willing to sacrifice other advantages. The external factor is the force exercised by up-bringing, which advocates the claims of our cultural environment, and this is furthered later by the direct pressure of that civilization by which we are surrounded. Civilization is the fruit of renunciation of instinctual satisfaction, and from each newcomer in turn it exacts the same renunciation. Throughout the life of the individual there is a constant replacement of the external compulsion by the internal. The influences of civilization cause an ever-increasing transmutation of egoistic trends into altruistic and social ones, and this by an admixture of erotic elements. In the last resort it may be said that every internal compulsion which has been of service in the development of human beings was originally, that is, in the evolution of the human race, nothing but an external one. Those who are born to-day bring with them as an inherited constitution some degree of a tendency (disposition) towards transmutation of egoistic into social instincts, and this disposition is easily stimulated to achieve that effect. A further measure of this transformation must be accomplished during the life of the individual himself. And so the human being is subject not only to the pressure of his immediate environment, but also to the influence of the cultural development attained by his forefathers.

If we give the name of *cultural adaptability* to a man's personal capacity for transformation of the egoistic impulses under the influence of the erotic, we may further affirm that this adaptability is made up of two parts, one innate and the other acquired through experience, and that the relation of the two to each other and to that portion of the instinctual life which remains untransformed is a very variable one.

Generally speaking, we are apt to attach too much importance to the innate part, and in addition to this we run the risk of overestimating the general adaptability to civilization in comparison with those instincts which have remained in their primitive state—by which I mean that in this way we are led to regard human nature as 'better' than it actually is. For there is, besides, another factor which obscures our judgement and falsifies the issue in too favourable a sense.

The impulses of another person are naturally hidden from our observation. We deduce them from his actions and behaviour, which we trace to motives born of his instinctual life. Such a conclusion is bound to be, in many cases, erroneous. This or that action which is 'good' from the civilized point of view may in one instance be born of a 'noble' motive, in another not so. Ethical theorists class as 'good' actions only those which are the outcome of good impulses; to the others they refuse their recognition. But society, which is practical in its aims, is little troubled on the whole by this distinction; it is content if a man regulates his behaviour and actions by the precepts of civilization, and is little concerned with his motives.

We have seen that the external compulsion exercised on a human being by his up-bringing and environment produces a further transformation towards good in his instinctual life—a turning from egoism towards altruism. But this is not the regular or necessary effect of the external compulsion. Education and environment offer benefits not only in the way of love, but also employ another kind of premium system, namely, reward and punishment. In this way their effect may turn out to be that he who is subjected to their influence will choose to 'behave well' in the civilized sense of the phrase, although no ennoblement of instinct, no transformation of egoistic into altruistic inclinations, has taken place within. The result will, roughly speaking, be the same; only a particular concatenation of circumstances will reveal that one man always acts rightly because his instinctual inclination compels him so to do, and the other is 'good' only in so far and for so long as such civilized behaviour is advantageous for his own egoistic purposes. But superficial acquaintance with an individual will not enable us to distinguish between the two cases, and we are certainly misled by our optimism into grossly exaggerating the number of human beings who have been transformed in a civilized sense.

Civilized society, which exacts good conduct and does not trouble itself about the impulses underlying it, has thus won over to obedience a great many people who are not thereby following the dictates of their own natures. Encouraged by this success, society has suffered itself to be led into straining the moral standard to the highest possible point, and thus it has forced its members into a yet greater estrangement from their instinctual dispositions. They are consequently subjected to an unceasing suppression of instinct, the resulting strain of which betrays itself in the most remarkable phenomena of reaction and compensation formations. In the domain of sexuality, where such suppression is most difficult to enforce, the result is seen in the reaction-phenomena of neurotic disorders. Elsewhere the pressure of civilization brings in its train no pathological results, but is shown in malformations of character, and in the perpetual readiness of the inhibited instincts to break through to gratification at any suitable opportunity. Anyone thus compelled to act continually in the sense of precepts which are not the expression of instinctual inclinations, is living, psychologically speaking, beyond his means, and might objectively be designated a hypocrite, whether this difference be clearly known to him or not. It is undeniable that our contemporary civilization is extraordinarily favourable to the production of this form of hypocrisy. One might venture to say that it is based upon such hypocrisy, and that it would have to submit to far-reaching modifications if people were to undertake to live in accordance with the psychological truth. Thus there are very many more hypocrites than truly civilized persons—indeed, it is a debatable point whether a certain degree of civilized hypocrisy be not indispensable for the maintenance of civilization, because the cultural adaptability so far attained by those living to-day would perhaps not prove adequate to the task. On the other hand, the maintenance of civilization even on so questionable a basis offers the prospect of each new generation achieving a farther-reaching transmutation of instinct, and becoming the pioneer of a higher form of civilization.

From the foregoing observations we may already derive this consolation—that our mortification and our grievous disillusionment regarding the uncivilized behaviour of our world-compatriots in this war are shown to be unjustified. They were based on an illusion to which we had abandoned ourselves. In reality our fellow-citizens have not sunk so low as we feared, because they had never risen so high as we believed. That the greater units of humanity, the peoples and states, have mutually abrogated their moral restraints naturally prompted these individuals to permit themselves relief for a while from the heavy pressure of civilization and to grant a passing satisfaction to the instincts it holds in check. This probably caused no breach in the relative morality within their respective national frontiers.

We may, however, obtain insight deeper than this into the change brought about by the war in our former compatriots, and at the same time receive a warning against doing them an injustice. For the evolution of the mind shows a peculiarity which is present in no other process of development. When a village grows into a town, a child into a man, the village and the child become submerged in the town and the man. Memory alone can trace the earlier features in the new image; in reality the old materials or forms have been superseded and replaced by new ones. It is otherwise with the development of the mind. Here one can describe the state of affairs, which is a quite peculiar one, only by saying that in this case every earlier stage of development persists alongside the later stage which has developed from it; the successive stages condition a co-existence, although it is in reference to the same materials that the whole series of transformations has been fashioned. The earlier mental state may not have manifested itself for years, but none the less it is so far present that it may at any time again become the mode of expression of the forces in the mind, and that exclusively, as though all later developments had been annulled, undone. This extraordinary plasticity of the evolution that takes place in the mind is not unlimited in its scope; it might be described as a special capacity for retroversion—for regression—since it may well happen that a later and higher stage of evolution, once abandoned, cannot be reached again. But the primitive stages can always be re-established; the primitive mind is, in the fullest meaning of the word, imperishable.

What are called mental diseases inevitably impress the layman with the idea of destruction of the life of mind and soul. In reality, the destruction relates only to later accretions and developments. The essence of mental disease lies in a return to earlier conditions of affective life and functioning. An excellent example of the plasticity of mental life is afforded by the state of sleep, which every night we desire. Since we heave learnt to interpret even absurd and chaotic dreams, we know that whenever we sleep we cast off our hard-won morality like a garment, only to put it on again next morning. This divestiture is naturally unattended by any danger because we are paralysed, condemned to inactivity, by the state of sleep. Only through a dream can we learn of the regression of our emotional life to one of the earliest stages of development. For instance, it is noteworthy that all our dreams are governed by purely egoistic motives. One of my English friends put forward this proposition at a scientific meeting in America, whereupon a lady who was present remarked that that might be the case in Austria, but she could maintain for herself and her friends that *they* were altruistic even in their dreams. My friend, although himself of English race, was obliged to contradict the lady emphatically on the ground of his personal experience in dream-analysis, and to declare that in their dreams high-minded American ladies were quite as egoistical as the Austrians.

Thus the transformations of instinct on which our cultural adaptability is based, may also be permanently or temporarily undone by the experiences of life. Undoubtedly the influences of war are among the forces that can bring about such regression; therefore we need not deny adaptability for culture to all who are at the present time displaying uncivilized behaviour, and we may anticipate that the refinement of their instincts will be restored in times of peace.

There is, however, another symptom in our world-compatriots which has perhaps astonished and shocked us no less than the descent from their ethical nobility which has so greatly distressed us. I mean the narrow-mindedness shown by the best intellects, their obduracy, their inaccessibility to the most forcible arguments, their uncritical credulity for the most disputable assertions. This indeed presents a lamentable picture, and I wish to say emphatically that in this I am by no means a blind partisan who finds all the intellectual shortcomings on one side. But this phenomenon is much easier to account for and much less disquieting than that which we have just considered. Students of human nature and philosophers have long taught us that we are mistaken in regarding our intelligence as an independent force and in overlooking its dependence upon the emotional life. Our intelligence, they teach us, can function reliably only when it is removed from the influences of strong emotional impulses; otherwise it behaves merely as an instrument of the will and delivers the inference which the will requires. Thus, in their view, logical arguments are impotent against affective interests, and that is why reasons, which in Falstaff's phrase are 'as plenty as blackberries', produce so few victories in the conflict with interests. Psycho-analytic experience has, if possible, further confirmed this statement. It daily shows that the shrewdest persons will all of a sudden behave like imbeciles as soon as the needful insight is confronted by an emotional resistance, but will completely regain their wonted acuity once that resistance has been overcome. The logical infatuations into which this war has deluded our fellow-citizens, many of them the best of their kind, are therefore a secondary phenomenon, a consequence of emotional excitement, and are destined, we may hope, to disappear with it.

Having in this way come to understand once more our fellow-citizens who are now so greatly alienated from us, we shall the more easily endure the disillusionment which the nations, those greater units of the human race, have caused us, for we shall perceive that the demands we make upon them ought to be far more modest. Perhaps they are reproducing the course of individual evolution, and still to-day represent very primitive phases in the organization and formation of higher unities. It is in agreement with this that the educative factor of an external compulsion towards morality, which we found to be so effective for the individual, is barely discernible in them. True, we had hoped that the extensive community of interests established by commerce and production would constitute the germ of such a compulsion, but it would seem that nations still obey their immediate passions far more readily than their interests. Their interests serve them, at most, as rationalizations for their passions; they parade their interests as their justification for satisfying their passions. Actually why the national units should disdain, detest, abhor one another, and that even when they are at peace, is indeed a mystery. I cannot tell why it is. It is just as though when it becomes a question of a number of people, not to say millions, all individual moral acquirements were obliterated, and only the most primitive, the oldest, the crudest mental attitudes were left. Possibly only future stages in development will be able in any way to alter this regrettable state of affairs. But a little more truthfulness and upright dealing on all sides, both in the personal relations of men to one another and between them and those who govern them, should also do something towards smoothing the way for this transformation.

II. Our Attitude Towards Death

The second factor to which I attribute our present sense of estrangement in this once lovely and congenial world is the disturbance that has taken place in our attitude towards death, an attitude to which hitherto we have clung so fast.

This attitude was far from straightforward. We were of course prepared to maintain that death was the necessary outcome of life, that everyone owes a debt to Nature and must expect to pay the reckoning—in short, that death was natural, undeniable and unavoidable. In realty, however, we were accustomed to behave as if it were otherwise. We displayed an unmistakable tendency to 'shelve' death, to eliminate it from life. We tried to hush it up; indeed we even have the saying, 'To think of something as we think of death'.[1] That is our own death, of course. Our own death is indeed unimaginable, and whenever we make the attempt to imagine it we can perceive that we really survive as spectators. Hence the psychoanalytic school could venture on the assertion that at bottom no one believes in his own death, or to put the same thing in another way, in the unconscious every one of us is convinced of his own immortality.

As to the death of another, the civilized man will carefully avoid speaking of such a possibility in the hearing of the person concerned. Children alone disregard this restriction; unabashed they threaten one another with the eventuality of death, and even go so far as to talk of it before one whom they love, as for instance: 'Dear Mamma, it will be a pity when you are dead but then I shall do this or that.' The civilized adult can hardly even entertain the thought of another's death without seeming to himself hard or evil-hearted; unless, of course, as a physician, lawyer or something of the sort, he has to deal with death professionally. Least of all will he permit himself to think of the death of another if with that event some gain to himself in freedom, means or position is connected. This sensitiveness of ours is of course impotent to arrest the hand of death; when it has fallen, we are always deeply affected, as if we were prostrated by the overthrow of our expectations. Our habit is to lay stress on the fortuitous causation of the death—accident, disease, infection, advanced age; in this way we betray our endeavour to modify the significance of death from a necessity to an accident. A multitude of simultaneous deaths appears to us exceedingly terrible. Towards the dead person himself we take up a special attitude, something like admiration for one who has accomplished a very difficult task. We suspend criticism of him, overlook his possible misdoings, issue the command: *De mortuis nil nisi bene,* and regard it as justifiable to set forth in the funeral-oration and upon the tombstone only that which is most favourable to his memory. Consideration for the dead, who no longer need it, is dearer to us than the truth, and certainly, for most of us, is dearer also than consideration for the living.

The culmination of this conventional attitude towards death among civilized persons is seen in our complete collapse when death has fallen on some person whom we love—a parent or a partner in marriage, a brother or sister, a child, a dear friend. Our hopes, our pride, our happiness, lie in the grave with him, we will not be consoled, we will not fill the loved one's place. We behave then as if we belonged to the tribe of the Asra, who must die too when those die whom they love.

But this attitude of ours towards death has a powerful effect upon our lives. Life is impoverished, it loses in interest, when the highest stake in the game of living, life itself, may not be risked. It becomes as flat, as superficial, as one of those American flirtations in which it is from the first understood that nothing is to happen, contrasted with a Continental love-affair in which both partners must constantly bear in mind the serious consequences. Our ties of affection, the unbearable intensity of our grief, make us disinclined to court danger for ourselves and for those who belong to us. We dare not contemplate a great many undertakings which are dangerous but quite indispensable, such as attempts at mechanical flight, expeditions to far countries, experiments with explosive substances. We are paralysed by the thought of who is to replace the son with his mother, the husband with his wife, the father with his children, if there should come disaster. The tendency to exclude death from our calculations brings in its train a number of other renunciations and exclusions. And yet the motto of the Hanseatic League declared: *'Navigare necesse est, vivere non necesse'!* (It is necessary to sail the seas, it is not necessary to live.)

It is an inevitable result of all this that we should seek in the world of fiction, of general literature and of the theatre compensation for the impoverishment of life. There we still find people who know how to die, indeed, who are even capable of killing someone else. There alone too we can enjoy the condition which makes it possible for us to reconcile ourselves with death—namely, that behind all the vicissitudes of life we preserve our existence intact. For it is indeed too sad that in life it should be as it is in chess, when one false move may lose us the game, but with the difference that we can have no second game, no return-match. In the realm of fiction we discover that plurality of lives for which we crave. We die in the person of a given hero, yet we survive him, and are ready to die again with the next hero just as safely.

It is evident that the war is bound to sweep away this conventional treatment of death. Death will no longer be denied; we are forced to believe in him. People really are dying, and now not one by one, but many at a time, often ten thousand in a single day. Nor is it any longer an accident. To be sure, it still seems a matter of chance whether a particular bullet hits this man or that; but the survivor may easily be hit by another bullet; and the accumulation puts an end to the impression of accident. Life has, in truth, become interesting again, it has regained its full significance.

Here a distinction should be made between two groups—those who personally risk their lives in battle, and those who have remained at home and have only to wait for the loss of their dear ones by wounds, disease, or infection. It would indeed be very interesting to study the changes in the psychology of the combatants, but I know too little about it. We must stop short at the second group, to which we ourselves belong. I have said already that in my opinion the bewilderment and the paralysis of energies, now so generally felt by us, are essentially determined in part by the circumstance that we cannot maintain our former attitude towards death, and have not yet discovered a new one. Perhaps it will assist us to do this if we direct our psychological inquiry towards two other relations with death—the one which we may ascribe to primitive, prehistoric peoples, and that other which in every one of us still exists, but which conceals itself, invisible to consciousness, in the deepest-lying strata of our mental life.

The attitude of prehistoric man towards death is known to us, of course, only by inferences and reconstruction, but I believe that these processes have furnished us with tolerably trustworthy information.

Primitive man assumed a very remarkable attitude towards death. It was far from consistent, was indeed extremely contradictory. On the one hand, he took death seriously, recognized it as the termination of life and used it to that end; on the other hand, he also denied death, reduced it to nothingness. This contradiction arose from the circumstance that he took up radically different attitudes towards the death of another man, of a stranger, of an enemy, and towards his own. The death of the other man he had no objection to; it meant the annihilation of a creature hated, and primitive man had no scruples against bringing it about. He was, in truth, a very violent being, more cruel and more malign than other animals. He liked to kill, and killed as a matter of course. That instinct which is said to restrain the other animals from killing and devouring their own species we need not attribute to him.

Hence the primitive history of mankind is filled with murder. Even to-day, the history of the world which our children learn in school is essentially a series of race-murders. The obscure sense of guilt which has been common to man since prehistoric times, and which in many religions has been condensed into the doctrine of original sin, is probably the outcome of a blood-guiltiness incurred by primitive man. In my book *Totem und Tabu* (1913) I have, following clues given by W. Robertson Smith, Atkinson and Charles Darwin, attempted to surmise the nature of this primal guilt, and I think that even the contemporary Christian doctrine enables us to deduce it. If the Son of God was obliged to sacrifice his life to redeem mankind from original sin, then by the law of the talion, the requital of like for like, that sin must have been a killing, a murder. Nothing else could call for the sacrifice of a life in expiation. And if the original sin was an offence against God the Father, the primal crime of mankind must have been a parricide, the killing of the primal father of the primitive human horde, whose image in memory was later transfigured into a deity.[2]

His own death was for primitive man certainly just as unimaginable and unreal as it is for any one of us to-day. But there was for him a case in which the two opposite attitudes towards death came into conflict and joined issue; and this case was momentous and productive of far-reaching results. It occurred when primitive man saw someone who belonged to him die—his wife, his child, his friend, whom assuredly he loved as we love ours, for love cannot be much younger than the lust to kill. Then, in his pain, he had to learn that one can indeed die oneself, an admission against which his whole being revolted; for each of these loved ones was, in very truth, a part of his own beloved ego. But even so, on the other hand, such deaths had a rightfulness for him, since in each of the loved persons something of the hostile stranger had resided: The law of ambivalence of feeling, which to this day governs our emotional relations with those whom we love most, had assuredly a very much wider validity in primitive periods. Thus these beloved dead had also been enemies and strangers who had aroused in him a measure of hostile feeling.[3]

Philosophers have declared that the intellectual enigma presented to primitive man by the picture of death was what forced him to reflection, and thus that it became the starting-point of all speculation. I believe that here the philosophers think too philosophically, and give too little consideration to the primarily effective motives. I would therefore limit and correct this assertion: By the body of his slain enemy primitive man would have triumphed, without racking his brains about the enigma of life and death. Not the intellectual enigma, and not every death, but the conflict of feeling at the death of loved, yet withal alien and hated persons was what disengaged the spirit of inquiry in man. Of this conflict of feeling psychology was the direct offspring. Man could no longer keep death at a distance, for he had tasted of it in his grief for the dead; but still he did not consent entirely to acknowledge it, for he could not conceive of himself as dead. So he devised a compromise; he conceded the fact of death, even his own death, but denied it the significance of annihilation, which he had had no motive for contesting where the death of his enemy had been concerned. During his contemplation of his loved one's corpse he invented ghosts, and it was his sense of guilt at the satisfaction mingled with his sorrow that turned these new-born spirits into evil dreaded demons. The changes wrought by death suggested to him the disjunction of the individuality into a body and a soul—first of all into several souls; in this way his train of thought ran parallel with the process of disintegration which sets in with death. The enduring remembrance of the dead became the basis for assuming other modes of existence, gave him the conception of life continued after apparent death.

These subsequent modes of existence were at first no more than appendages to that life which death had brought to a close—shadowy, empty of content, and until later times but slightly valued; they showed as yet a pathetic inadequacy. We may recall the answer made to Odysseus by the soul of Achilles:

> Erst in the life on the earth, no less than a god we revered thee,
> We the Achaeans; and now in the realm of the dead as a monarch
> Here dost thou rule; then why should death thus grieve thee, Achilles?
> Thus did I speak: forthwith then answering thus he addressed me,
> Speak not smoothly of death, I beseech, O famous Odysseus,
> Better by far to remain on the earth as the thrall of another;
> E'en of a portionless man that hath means right scanty of living,
> Rather than reign sole king in the realm of the bodiless phantoms. [4]

Or in the powerful, bitterly burlesque rendering by Heine, where he makes Achilles say that the most insignificant little Philistine at Stuckert-on-the-Neckar, in being alive, is far happier than he, the son of Peleus, the dead hero, the prince of shadows in the nether world.

It was not until much later that the different religions devised the view of this after-life as the more desirable, the truly valid one, and degraded the life which is ended by death to a mere preparation. It was then but consistent to extend life backward into the past, to conceive of former existences, transmigrations of the soul and reincarnation, all with the purpose of depriving death of its meaning as the termination of life. So early did the denial of death, which above we designated a convention of civilization, actually originate.

Beside the corpse of the beloved were generated not only the idea of the soul, the belief in immortality, and a great part of man's deep-rooted sense of guilt, but also the earliest inkling of ethical law. The first and most portentous prohibition of the awakening conscience was: Thou shalt not kill. It was born of the reaction against that hate-gratification which lurked behind the grief for the loved dead, and was gradually extended to unloved strangers and finally even to enemies.

This final extension is no longer experienced by civilized man. When the frenzied conflict of this war shall have been decided, every one of the victorious warriors will joyfully return to his home, his wife and his children, undelayed and undisturbed by any thought of the enemy he has slain either at close quarters or by distant weapons of destruction. It is worthy of note that such primitive races as still inhabit the earth, who are undoubtedly closer than we to primitive man, act differently in this respect, or did so act until they came under the influence of our civilization. The savage—Australian, Bushman, Tierra del Fuegan—is by no means a remorseless murderer; when he returns victorious from the war-path he may not set foot in his village nor touch his wife until he has atoned for the murders committed in war by penances which are often prolonged and toilsome. This may be presumed, of course, to be the outcome of superstition; the savage still goes in fear of the avenging spirits of the slain. But the spirits of the fallen enemy are nothing but the expression of his own conscience, uneasy on account of his blood-guiltiness; behind this superstition lurks a vein of ethical sensitiveness which has been lost by us civilized men.[5]

Pious souls, who cherish the thought of our remoteness from whatever is evil and base, will be quick to draw from the early appearance and the urgency of the prohibition of murder gratifying conclusions in regard to the force of these ethical stirrings, which must consequently have been implanted in us. Unfortunately this argument proves even more for the opposite contention. So powerful a prohibition can only be directed against an equally powerful impulse. What no human soul desires there is no need to prohibit;[6] it is automatically excluded. The very emphasis of the commandment *Thou shalt not kill* makes it certain that we spring from an endless ancestry of murderers, with whom the lust for killing was in the blood, as possibly it is to this day with ourselves. The ethical strivings of mankind, of which we need not in the least depreciate the strength and the significance, are an acquisition accompanying evolution; they have then become the hereditary possession of those human beings alive to-day, though unfortunately only in a very variable measure.

Let us now leave primitive man, and turn to the unconscious in our own mental life. Here we depend entirely upon the psycho-analytic method of investigation, the only one which plumbs such depths. We ask what is the attitude of our unconscious towards the problem of death. The answer must be: Almost exactly the same as primitive man's. In this respect, as in many others, the man of prehistoric ages survives unchanged in our unconscious. Thus, our unconscious does not believe in its own death; it behaves as if immortal. What we call our 'unconscious' (the deepest strata of our minds, made up of instinctual impulses) knows nothing whatever of negatives or of denials—contradictories coincide in it—and so it knows nothing whatever of our own death, for to that we can give only a negative purport. It follows that no instinct we possess is ready for a belief in death. This is even perhaps the secret of heroism. The rational explanation for heroism is that it consists in the decision that the personal life cannot be so precious as certain abstract general ideals. But more frequent, in my view, is that instinctive and impulsive heroism which knows no such motivation, and flouts danger in the spirit of Anzengruber's Hans of the Road—Mender: 'Nothing can happen to *me*.' Or else that motivation serves but to clear away the hesitation which might delay an heroic reaction in accord with the unconscious. The dread of death, which dominates us oftener than we know, is on the other hand something secondary, being usually the outcome of the sense of guilt.

On the other hand, for strangers and for enemies, we do acknowledge death, and consign them to it quite as readily and unthinkingly as did primitive man. Here there does, indeed, appear a distinction which in practice shows for a decisive one. Our unconscious does not carry out the killing; it merely thinks it and wishes it. But it would be wrong entirely to depreciate this psychical reality as compared with actual reality. It is significant and pregnant enough. In our unconscious we daily and hourly deport all who stand in our way, all who have offended or injured us. The expression: 'Devil take him!' which so frequently comes to our lips in joking anger, and which really means 'Death take him!' is in our unconscious an earnest deliberate death-wish. Indeed, our unconscious will murder even for trifles; like the ancient Athenian law of Draco, it knows no other punishment for crime than death; and this has a certain consistency, for every injury to our almighty and autocratic ego is at bottom a crime of *lèse-majestè*.

And so, if we are to be judged by the wishes in our unconscious, we are, like primitive man, simply a gang of murderers. It is well that all these wishes do not possess the potency which was attributed to them by primitive men;[7] in the cross-fire of mutual maledictions mankind would long since have perished, the best and wisest of men and the loveliest and airiest of women with the rest.

Psycho-analysis finds little credence among laymen for assertions such as these. They reject them as calumnies which are confuted by conscious experience, and adroitly overlook the faint indications through which the unconscious is apt to betray itself even to consciousness. It is therefore relevant to point out that many thinkers who could not have been influenced by psycho-analysis have quite definitely accused our unspoken thoughts of readiness, heedless of the murder-prohibition, to get rid of anyone who stands in our way. From many examples of this I will choose one very famous one:

In *Le Pére Goriot,* Balzac alludes to a passage in the works of J. J. Rousseau where that author asks the reader what he would do if—without leaving Paris and of course without being discovered—he could kill with great profit to himself, an old mandarin in Peking by a mere act of the will. Rousseau implies that he would not give much for the life of this dignitary. *'Tuer son mandarin'* has passed into a proverb for this secret readiness even on the part of ourselves to-day.

There is as well a whole array of cynical jests and anecdotes which testify in the same sense, such as, for instance, the remark attributed to a husband: 'If one of us dies, I shall go and live in Paris.' Such cynical jokes would not be possible unless they contained an unacknowledged verity which could not be countenanced if seriously and baldly expressed. In joke, as we know, even the truth may be told.

As for primitive man, so also for us in our unconscious, there arises a case in which the two contrasted attitudes towards death, that which acknowledges it as the annihilation of life and the other which denies it as ineffectual to that end, conflict and join issue—and this case is the same as in primitive ages—the death, or the endangered life, of one whom we love, a parent or partner in marriage, a brother or sister, a child or dear friend. These loved ones are on the one hand an inner possession, an ingredient of our personal ego, but on the other hand are partly strangers, even enemies. With the exception of only a very few situations, there adheres to the tenderest and closest of our affections a vestige of hostility which can excite an unconscious death-wish. But this conflict of ambivalence does not now, as it did then, find issue in theories of the soul and of ethics, but in neuroses, which afford us deep insight into normal mental life as well. How often have those physicians who practice psycho-analysis had to deal with the symptom of an exaggeratedly tender care for the well-being of relatives, or with entirely unfounded self-reproaches after the death of a loved person. The study of these cases has left them in no doubt about the extent and the significance of unconscious death-wishes.

The layman feels an extraordinary horror at the possibility of such feelings, and takes this repulsion as a legitimate ground for disbelief in the assertions of psycho-analysis. I think, mistakenly. No depreciation of our love is intended, and none is actually contained in it. It is indeed foreign to our intelligence as also to our feelings thus to couple love and hate, but Nature, by making use of these twin opposites, contrives to keep love ever vigilant and fresh, so as to guard it against the hate which lurks behind it. It might be said that we owe the fairest flowers of our love-life to the reaction against the hostile impulse which we divine in our breasts.

To sum up: Our unconscious is just as inaccessible to the idea of our own death, as murderously minded towards the stranger, as divided or ambivalent towards the loved, as was man in earliest antiquity. But how far we have moved from this primitive state in our conventionally civilized attitude towards death!

It is easy to see the effect of the impact of war on this duality. It strips us of the later accretions of civilization, and lays bare the primal man in each of us. It constrains us once more to be heroes who cannot believe in their own death; it stamps the alien as the enemy, whose death is to be brought about or desired; it counsels us to rise above the death of those we love. But war is not to be abolished; so long as the conditions of existence among the nations are so varied, and the repulsions between peoples so intense, there will be, must be wars. The question then arises: Is it not we who must give in, who must adapt ourselves to them? Is it not for us to confess that in our civilized attitude towards death we are once more living psychologically beyond our means, and must reform and give truth its due? Would it not be better to give death the place in actuality and in our thoughts which properly belongs to it, and to yield a little more prominence to that unconscious attitude towards death which we have hitherto so carefully suppressed? This hardly seems indeed a greater achievement, but rather a backward step in more than one direction, a regression; but it has the merit of taking somewhat more into account the true state of affairs, and of making life again more endurable for us. To endure life remains, when all is said, the first duty of all living beings. Illusion can have no value if it makes this more difficult for us.

We remember the old saying: *Si vis pacem, para bellum.* If you desire peace, prepare for war.

It would be timely thus to paraphrase it: *Si vis vitam, para mortem.* If you would endure life, be prepared for death.

Notes

1. [The German saying is used as an equivalent for 'incredible' or 'unlikely'.—Trans.]
2. Cf. 'Die infantile Wiederkehr des Totemismus', *Totem und Tabu.*
3. Cf. 'Tabu und Ambivalenz', *Totem and Tabu.*
4. *Odyssey,* xi. 484-491; translated by H. B. Cotterill.
5. Cf. *Totem und Tabu.*
6. Cf. the brilliant argument of Frazer quoted in *Totem und Tabu.*
7. Cf. 'Allmacht der Gedanken', *Totem und Tabu.*

3
Alienation and Labor
Karl Marx

Marx's theory of alienation has roots in Hegelian concepts of consciousness and history as well as the social philosophies of many of his contemporaries. His conviction that alienation derives from the individual's estrangement from his own labour and from the economic forces of production is part of Marx's overall understanding of historical materialism. The following is from The Economic and Philosophic Manuscripts of 1844.

Till now we have been considering the estrangement, the alienation of the worker only in one of its aspects, i.e., the worker's *relationship to the products of his labour*. But the estrangement is manifested not only in the result but in the *act of production*—within the *producing activity,* itself. How could the worker come to face the product of his activity as a stranger, were it not that in the very act of production he was estranging himself from himself? The product is after all but the summary of the activity, of production. If then the product of labour is alienation, production itself must be active alienation, the alienation of activity, the activity of alienation. In the estrangement of the object of labour is merely summarized the estrangement, the alienation, in the activity of labour itself.

What, then, constitutes the alienation of labour?

First, the fact that labour is *external* to the worker, i.e., it does not belong to his essential being; that in his work, therefore, he does not affirm himself but denies himself, does not feel content but unhappy, does not develop freely his physical and mental energy but mortifies his body and ruins his mind. The worker therefore only feels himself outside his work, and in his work feels outside himself. He is at home when he is not working, and when he is working he is not at home. His labour is therefore not voluntary, but coerced; it is *forced labour*. It is therefore not the satisfaction of a need; it is merely a *means* to satisfy needs external to it. Its alien character emerges clearly in the fact that as soon as no physical or other compulsion exists, labour is shunned like the plague. External labour, labour in which man alienates himself, is a labour of self-sacrifice, of mortification. Lastly, the external character of labour for the worker appears in the fact that it is not his own, but someone else's, that it does not belong to him, that in it he belongs, not to himself, but to another. Just as in religion the spontaneous activity of the human imagination, of the human brain and the human heart, operates independently of the individual—that is, operates on him as an alien,

From *The Economic and Philosophic Manuscripts of 1844*, translated from the German by Martin Milligan, edited and with an introduction by Dirk J. Struik, New York, 1964, pp. 110–14, reprinted by permission of International Publishers Co., Inc., New York.

divine or diabolical activity—so is the worker's activity not his spontaneous activity. It belongs to another; it is the loss of his self.

As a result, therefore, man (the worker) only feels himself freely active in his animal functions—eating, drinking, procreating, or at most in his dwelling and in dressing-up, etc.; and in his human functions he no longer feels himself to be anything but an animal. What is animal becomes human and what is human becomes animal.

Certainly eating, drinking, procreating, etc., are also genuinely human functions. But abstractly taken, separated from the sphere of all other human activity and turned into sole and ultimate ends, they are animal functions.

We have considered the act of estranging practical human activity, labour, in two of its aspects. (1) The relation of the worker to the *product of labour* as an alien object exercising power over him. This relation is at the same time the relation to the sensuous external world, to the objects of nature, as an alien world inimically opposed to him. (2) The relation of labour to the *act of production* within the *labour* process. This relation is the relation of the worker to his own activity as an alien activity not belonging to him; it is activity as suffering strength as weakness, begetting as emasculating, the worker's own physical and mental energy, his personal life—indeed, what is life but activity?—as an activity which is turned against him, independent of him and not belonging to him. Here we have *self-estrangement*, as previously we had the estrangement of the thing.

We have still a third aspect of *estranged labour* to deduce from the two already considered.

Man is a species being, not only because in practice and in theory he adopts the species as his object (his own as well as those of other things), but—and this is only another way of expressing it—also because he treats himself as the actual, living species; because he treats himself as a *universal* and therefore a free being.

The life of the species, both in man and in animals, consist physically in the fact that man (like the animal) lives on inorganic nature; and the more universal man is compared with an animal, the more universal is the sphere of inorganic nature on which he lives. Just as plants, animals, stones, the air, light, etc., constitute theoretically a part of human consciousness, partly as object of natural science, partly as objects of art—his spiritual inorganic nature, spiritual nourishment which he must first prepare to make palatable and digestible—so also in the realm of practice they constitute a part of human life and human activity. Physically man lives only on these products of nature, whether they appear in the form of food, heating, clothes, a dwelling, etc. The universality of man appears in practice precisely in the universality which makes all nature his *inorganic* body—both inasmuch as nature is (1) his direct means of life, and (2) the material, the object, and the instrument of his life-activity. Nature is man's *inorganic?* body—nature, that is, in so far as it is not itself the human body. Man *lives* on nature—means that nature is his *body*, with which he must remain in continuous interchange if he is not to die. That man's physical and spiritual life is linked to nature means simply that nature is linked to itself, for man is a part his life-activity, estranged labour estranges the *species* from man. It changes for him the *life of the species* into a means of individual life. First it estranges the life of the species and individual life, and secondly it makes individual life in its abstract form the purpose of the life of the species, likewise in its abstract and estranged form.

Indeed, labour, *life-activity, productive life* itself, appears in the first place merely as a *means* of satisfying a need—the need to maintain physical existence. Yet the productive life is the life of the species. It is life-engendering life. The whole character of a species—its species character—is contained in the character of its life-activity; and free, conscious activity is man's species character. Life itself appears only as a *means to life*.

The animal is immediately identical with its life activity. It does not distinguish itself from it. It is *its life activity*. Man makes his life activity itself the object of his will and of his consciousness. He has conscious life activity. It is not a determination with which he directly merges. Conscious life activity distinguishes man immediately from animal life activity. It is just because of this that he is a species being. Or rather, it is only because he is a species being that he is a Conscious Being, i.e., that his own life is an object for him. Only because of that is his activity free activity. Estranged labour reverses this relationship, so that it is just because man is a conscious being that he makes his life activity, his *essential* being, a mere means to his *existence*.

In creating a *world of objects* by his practical activity, in *his work upon* inorganic nature, man proves himself a conscious species being, i.e., as a being that treats the species as its own essential being, or that treats itself as a species being. Admittedly animals also produce. They build themselves nests, dwellings, like the bees, beavers, ants, etc. But an animal only produces what it immediately needs for itself or its young. It produces one-sidedly, whilst man produces universally. It produces only under the dominion of immediate physical need, whilst man produces even when he is free from physical need and only truly produces in freedom therefrom. An animal produces only itself, whilst man reproduces the whole of nature. An animal's product belongs immediately to its physical body, whilst man freely confronts his product. An animal forms things in accordance with the standard and the need of the species to which it belongs, whilst man knows how to produce in accordance with the standard of every species, and knows how to apply everywhere the inherent standard to the object. Man therefore also forms things in accordance with the laws of beauty.

It is just in his work upon the objective world, therefore, that man first really proves himself to be a *species being*. This production is his active species life. Through and because of this production, nature appears as *his* work and his reality. The object of labour is, therefore, the *objectification of man's species life:* for he duplicates himself not only, as in consciousness, intellectually, but also actively, in reality, and therefore he contemplates himself in a world that he has created. In tearing away from man the object of his production, therefore, estranged labour tears from him his *species life*, his real objectivity as a member of the species and transforms his advantage over animals into the disadvantage that his inorganic body, nature, is taken away from him.

The consciousness which man has of his species is thus transformed by estrangement in such a way that the species life becomes for him a means.

Estranged labour turns thus:

(3) *Man's species being,* both nature and his spiritual species property, into a being *alien* to him, into a *means* to his *individual existence*. It estranges man from his own body, as well as external nature and his spiritual essence, his *human* being.

(4) An immediate consequence of the fact that man is estranged from the product of his labour, from his life activity, from his species being is the *estrangement of man from man.* When man confronts himself, he confronts the *other* man. What applies to a man's relation to his work, to the product of his labour and to himself, also holds of a man's relation to the other man, and to the other man's labour and object of labour.

In fact, the proposition that man's species nature is estranged from him means that one man is estranged from the other, as each of them is from man's essential nature.

4
Economics and Ideology
Karl Marx

The following selection from *The German Ideology* (1846) succinctly summarizes Marx's belief in the economic basis of all ideologies. For Marx ideologies and cultural institutions comprised a superstructure that was determined by and built upon the economic conditions of existence.

In direct contrast to German philosophy, which descends from heaven to earth, here we ascend from earth to heaven. That is to say, we do not set out from what men say, imagine, conceive, nor from men as narrated, thought of, imagined, conceived, in order to arrive at men in the flesh. We set out from real, active men, and on the basis of their real life process we demonstrate the development of the ideological reflexes and echoes of this life process. The phantoms formed in the human brain are also, necessarily, sublimates of their material life process, which is empirically verifiable and bound to material premises. Morality, religion, metaphysics, all the rest of ideology and their corresponding forms of consciousness, thus no longer retain the semblance of independence. They have no history, no development; but men, developing their material production and their material intercourse, alter, along with this, their real existence, their thinking, and the products of their thinking. Life is not determined by consciousness, but consciousness by life. In the first method of approach the starting point is consciousness taken as the living individual; in the second it is the real, living individuals themselves, as they are in actual life, and consciousness is considered solely as *their* consciousness.

This method of approach is not devoid of premises. It starts out from the real premises, and does not abandon them for a moment. . . .

Our conception of history depends on our ability to expound the real process of production, starting out from the simple material production of life, and to comprehend the form of intercourse connected with this and created by this (i.e., civil society in its various stages), as the basis of all history; further, to show it in its action as state, and so, from this starting point, to explain the whole mass of different theoretical products and forms of consciousness, religion, philosophy, ethics, etc., and trace their origins and growth, by which means, of course, the whole thing can be shown in its totality (and therefore, too, the reciprocal action of these various sides on one another). It has not, like the idealistic view of history, in every period to look for a category, but remains constantly on the real ground of history; it does not explain practice from the idea, but explains the formation of

From *The German Ideology*, ed. R. Pascal and translated from the German by W. Lough and C.P. Magill, London, 1938, pp. 14–15, 28–32; reprinted by permission of International Publishers, Co., Inc.

ideas from material practice, and accordingly it comes to the conclusion that all forms and products of consciousness cannot be dissolved by mental criticism, by resolution into "self-consciousness" or transformation into "apparitions," "specters," "fancies," etc., but only by the practical overthrow of the actual social relations which gave rise to this idealistic humbug; that not criticism but revolution is the driving force of history, also of religion, of philosophy, and all other types of theory. It shows that history does not end by being resolved into "self-consciousness" as "spirit of the spirit" but that in it at each stage there is found a material result: a sum of productive forces, a historically created relation of individuals to nature and to one another, which is handed down to each generation from its predecessor; a mass of productive forces, different forms of capital, and conditions, which, indeed, is modified by the new generation on the one hand, but also on the other prescribes for it its conditions of life and gives it a definite development, a special character. It shows that circumstances make men just as much as men make circumstances.

This sum of productive forces, forms of capital, and social forms of intercourse, which every individual and generation finds in existence as something given, is the real basis of what the philosophers have conceived as "substance" and "essence of man," and what they have defied and attacked: a real basis which is not in the least disturbed, in its effect and influence on the development of men, by the fact that these philosophers revolt against it as "self-consciousness" and "the unique." These conditions of life, which different generations find in existence, decide also whether or not the periodically recurring revolutionary convulsion will be strong enough to overthrow the basis of all existing forms. And if these material elements of a complete revolution are not present (namely, on the one hand the existence of productive forces, on the other the formation of a revolutionary mass, which revolts not only against separate conditions of society up till then, but against the very "production of life" till then, the "total activity" on which it was based),then, as far as practical development is concerned, it is absolutely immaterial whether the "idea" of this revolution has been expressed a hundred times already, as the history of communism proves.

In the whole conception of history up to the present this real basis of history has been either totally neglected or else considered as a minor matter, quite irrelevant to the course of history. History must therefore always be written according to an extraneous standard; the real production of life seems to be beyond history, while the truly historical appears to be separated from ordinary life, something extra-superterrestrial. With this the relation of man to nature is excluded from history, and hence the antithesis of nature and history is created. The exponents of this conception of history have consequently been able to see in history only the political actions of princes and states, religious and all sorts of theoretical struggles, and in particular in each historical epoch have had to share the *illusion of that epoch*. For instance, if an epoch imagines itself to be actuated by purely "political" or "religious" motives, although "religion" and "politics" are only forms of its true motives, the historian accepts this opinion. The "idea," the "conception" of these conditioned men about their real practice is transformed into the sole determining, active force, which controls and determines their practice. When the crude form in which the division of labor appears with the Indians and Egyptians calls forth the caste system in their state and religion, the historian believes that the caste system is the power which has produced this crude social form. While the French and the English at least hold by the political illusion, which is moderately close to reality, the Germans move in the realm of the "pure spirit" and make religious illusion the driving force of history.

The Hegelian philosophy of history is the last consequence, reduced to its "finest expression," of all this German historiography, for which it is not a question of real, or even of political, interests, but of pure thoughts, which inevitably appear, even to St. Bruno, as a series of "thoughts" that devour one another and are finally swallowed up in "self-consciousness." And equally inevitably and more logically, the course of history appears to the blessed Max Stirner, who knows not a thing about real history, as a mere tale of "knights," robbers, and ghosts, from whose visions he can, of course, save himself only by "unholiness." This conception is truly religious: it postulates religious man as the primitive man, and in its imagination puts the religious production of fancies in the place of the real production of the means of subsistence and of life itself. This whole conception of history, together with its dissolution and the scruples and qualms resulting from it, is a purely *national* affair of the Germans and has only *local* interest for the Germans, as for instance the important question treated several times of late: how really we "pass from the realm of God to the realm of man"—as if this "realm of God" has ever existed anywhere save in the imagination, and the learned gentlemen, without being aware of it, were not constantly living in the "realm of man," to which they are now seeking the way; and as if the learned pastime (for it is nothing more) of explaining the mystery of this theoretical bubble-blowing did not, on the contrary, lie in demonstrating its origin in actual earthly conditions.

Always, for these Germans, it is simply a matter of resolving the nonsense of earlier writers into some other freak, i.e., of presupposing that all this nonsense has a special meaning which can be discovered; while really it is only a question of explaining this theoretical talk from the actual existing conditions. The real, practical dissolution of these phrases, the removal of these notions from the consciousness of men, will, as we have already said, be effected by altered circumstances, not by theoretical deductions. For the mass of men, i.e., the proletariat, these theoretical notions do not exist, and hence do not require to be dissolved, and if this mass ever had any theoretical notions, e.g., religion, etc., these have now long been dissolved by circumstances.

5
Oregon's Romantic Rebels John Reed and Charles Erskine Scott Wood

Edwin R. Bingham

The following essay by Edwin R. Bingham, Professor Emeritus of History at the University of Oregon, dramatically shows the influence of modern radicalism and Marxism upon figures who are important to both regional and national history.

The lives of John Reed and Charles Erskine Scott Wood were curiously like their names. The one, short and explosive, ended abruptly before it was well under way; the other, long and sustained, threatened not to end at all. Although contemporaries for a time, Wood and Reed were of separate generations. When John Reed was born, in 1887, C. E. S. Wood was thirty-four, an age Reed never attained. When Reed died in 1920, at thirty-two, Wood had just entered a new, and in some respects the richest, phase of his ninety-one-year career.

For a substantial period, each man was closely identified with Oregon. Reed lived in Portland for the first half of his life, and Wood spent nearly forty years there. Jack Reed was the sometime companion of Wood's younger sons and was influenced by their father, although probably not profoundly. Both men left the Pacific Northwest permanently, and Reed repudiated Portland; yet the region left its mark on them both, and Wood, at least, reciprocated. Both men thought of themselves first of all as poets, although each achieved his greatest distinction through prose. Wood cannot match Reed in national and international reputation, but some of the writing of each has had currency abroad through German, Russian, and Danish translations. Both men were rebels, and, where they are known, they still stir controversy and arouse conjecture.

Charles Erskine Scott Wood, born in Erie, Pennsylvania, early in the tense decade of the 1850s, was a schoolboy during the Civil War, and his early memories were of that era, reinforced by stories his father told of duty as a navy surgeon with the Atlantic blockading squadron. After the war the family moved to Rosewood Glen, a farm on the outskirts of Baltimore. Wood remembered the years on the Maryland farm as an idyllic period for the most part. The house was an old colonial brick, rising from a shallow slope crowned by great oaks. A swift stream flowed through the property, threading the nearby stands of hickory, maple, and red gum. In the autumn the trees were hung

Edwin R. Bingham, "Oregon's Romantic Rebels: John Reed and Charles Erskine Scott Wood," *Pacific Northwest Quarterly*, L (July 1959), 77–90.

with purple clusters of fox grapes; and spring brought trailing arbutus, spangling the ground with pink stars, and laurel, wild honeysuckle, and azaleas sweetened the woods. At Rosewood Glen, Erskine learned to swing the scythe, to hunt coon and possum, to pick eggs; and here his speech took on the suggestion of a drawl that it never lost. His formal education was as a day scholar in a small private school adjoining his father's property.

Wood also remembered and resented the taut household his father ran, wherein naval discipline was imposed upon Erskine and his five brothers. The military rigor of the Wood ménage was eased by the fact that the boys had access to their father's extensive library. Indeed, the elder Wood was himself the author of several competent and colorful accounts of his experiences in the Caribbean and China seas, and Erskine, his second son, gave evidence early of a literary bent. All in all, C. E. S. Wood grew up in a conservative, upper-middle-class environment, where duty, courtesy, order, and propriety were considered cardinal virtues.

John Reed's boyhood was spent in the quiet backwaters of Portland. The war of his youth, the one with Spain, did not amount to much. Like Wood, he came from a secure and privileged home. His maternal grandmother, Charlotte Green, widow of a pioneer in Portland industry, entertained grandly in her West Hill mansion, where on summer evenings guests danced on the lawn, casting grotesque shadows in the flaring light of natural gas piped to jets in the tops of Douglas firs. Reed's reluctance to conform stemmed in part, perhaps, from the example set by this spirited lady who went her own way.

John Reed's father was not so conspicuously successful as were the Greens, but John and his younger brother, Harry, lacked for little in a material way and enjoyed the sense of ease and place that belongs to the well off and the well born. Jack Reed, too, had a private school education, first in the Portland Academy and then at Morristown, New Jersey, in preparation for Harvard. His interest in writing developed early, and in his mid-teens Reed was publishing verse in the *Morristonian* and the *Pacific Monthly*. In this first stage of his writing career, Jack Reed had some contact with C. E. S. Wood, but if the older man contributed to the boy's drift into radicalism, Reed failed to mention it in his autobiographical sketch entitled "Almost Thirty."

The experiences of the two men with higher education were sharply different. Wood's father, William Maxwell Wood, used his influence to procure from President Grant an appointment-at-large to the United States Military Academy for Erskine. Any ambition Wood might have had to be a professional soldier he lost at West Point, where his academic performance was generally undistinguished and his military record bordered on disgrace. In his own words it was

> work, work, work, from reveille to taps. Sunday had a brief relaxation period but was really a study day. Saturday afternoon was a holiday for the orderly and well-behaved but I walked about every Saturday afternoon with a rifle on my shoulder ... for punishment.

More than once Erskine accumulated demerits just short of the number that would bring dismissal, and it is not surprising that in four years he never held a cadet rank.

Despite the demands of the academy regimen, Erskine found time to read the novels of William Gilmore Simms, Bulwer-Lytton, and Scott, as well as parts of Spenser, Chaucer, and Shakespeare, and to carry on a romance (with the girl he later married) so intense as to cause her guardian to forbid the sweethearts to correspond. Doubtless such beyond-the-border-of-duty activities contributed to Wood's indifferent showing at the academy. Nevertheless, in the tightly prescribed curriculum heavily weighted on the side of mathematics, engineering, and the physical sciences, there was little to inspire interest or effort on the part of a young man with creative inclinations, and although Wood stood well in ethics and law, only in military drawing did he excel.

Generally, however, for C. E. Scott Wood, as he was invariably listed on military rolls, the cadet years were unnaturally formal, gallingly restrictive, and depressingly drab—a time to be resented and endured, and little more. Years later in New York, Wood wrote inn his journal: "I never pass West Point without thinking of my cadet days.... I *hate* the memory of it even now."

Erskine's poor record in discipline, his harsh criticism of the West Point system, his threats to resign and offer his services to the Mexican or the Egyptian army or to go to Florida and grow oranges or, most persistently, to embark on a writing career worried his mother and brought long, measured, elegantly phrased letters of censure and advice from his father. In a typical letter written in Wood's fourth year, the father spelled out his son's shortcomings:

> It is this unreasonable desire to escape from the present to an unknown and uncertain future, which has been from the beginning ... one of the causes of your demerits. Again, I am pained to see the disrespectful manner in which you refer to your Commander in Chief, the President. You may not think of it, but such expressions are a violation of your oath, and if your language corresponds to your writing, upon a report, you would be justly disciplined.... My earnest and final advice to you is to abandon all feverish and restless desire after change ... and address yourself with honest and unceasing vigilance to the labor, the claims and obligations of the present around you—and of the place and position to which you are called.

His father's counsel prevailed, for when the class of 1874 was graduated, reduced from an entering strength of sixty-seven to forty-four, the rebellious Erskine stood academically almost precisely in the middle.

In clear contrast to Wood's four-year confinement in what seemed to him an educational straitjacket stands John Reed's experience thirty-six years later at Harvard in an academic atmosphere that Reed labeled approvingly as anarchistic. Allowed to select freely from a rich curriculum, Reed avoided the physical and social sciences, specializing heavily in writing and literature with a smattering of philosophy and the fine arts, in a course of study perhaps more narrow in this direction than was the West Point curriculum in the other. The difference, of course, was that Reed could choose.

At Harvard, John Reed continued to write—poetry, stories, plays, editorials, jokes, lyrics—whatever came to mind and hand. He showed facility and promise rather than genius, but writing was important to him, for it gave him the same assurance in the intellectual sphere that his unquestioned skill in swimming and water polo gave him in the physical sphere, and it helped him to social status as well.

By far the most profound personal influence on John Reed at Harvard was exerted by Charles Townshend Copeland, who was convinced of Reed's promise and gave him unstintingly of all that a dedicated teacher can impart to an eager disciple—criticism, encouragement, technique, inspiration, friendship. John Reed's deep gratitude to "Copey" was gracefully expressed in the dedication to *Insurgent Mexico*, the book that made Reed nationally known.

Three thousand miles west of the Charles on the Willamette was another man who had an interest in John Reed's writing career. In 1910 C. E. S. Wood wrote the Harvard senior a rambling, friendly letter about poetry, urging that Reed avoid the easy road of imitation and strive to achieve a new poetry that:

must not be a moral essay nor an economic tract but it positively must have the pulsing thought of the modern man. If it be full of the surge of the ocean and the wet south wind of an ever-recurring Spring it must also be full of the surge of human life-blood and wet with the tears of humanity. . . . I am looking for the young poet who will . . . breathe the thought of his time and the gospel of the masses of men—in a form eternal.

A large order, and one that Reed failed to fulfill.

With the outstanding exception of his intellectual debt to Charles Copeland, Reed was critical, almost contemptuous, of the university's academic aspects. For him the heart of Harvard lay outside the formal curriculum, and he classified himself as an activity man rather than an athlete or scholar. As an outlander, Reed hungered for the social acceptance he had easily won in prep school. To gain it he spread his energies in a sweeping arc. He was editor of the *Lampoon*, captain of the water polo team, frenetic song leader, president of the Cosmopolitan Club, vice-president of the Dramatic Club, elected to Hasty Pudding to write the lyrics for its annual musical comedy, leading spirit in the Western Club, member of Oracle, Round Table, and Symposium. Unquestionably he made his influence felt, but socially he never reached Harvard's top tier.

In the light of the rebel he later became, John Reed's position at Harvard was equivocal. Although in sympathy with its aims, he did not join the Socialist Club led by Walter Lippman; and in the democratic revolt of the Yard (the outsiders) against the Street (the insiders), Reed, although he lived on the Street, remained aloof until his senior year when he joined the aristocrats just in time to share in their defeat in the contest for class honors. At Harvard, John Reed was torn by a genuine ambivalence; a rebellious impulse against snobbery and injustice was countered by a strong urge toward the rewards that went with social distinction.

When Jack Reed left the university, he carried away a resentment against the Harvard patriciate that later hardened into hatred. He carried away, too, a firm conviction that he wanted to write but without knowing just how to begin. Following Copey's advice, Reed set out for Europe in the summer of 1910 in search of something to write about.

A Harvard man might pause for a time on the end of a career; a West Point graduate had orders. Second Lieutenant C. E. Scott Wood was assigned to frontier duty with the 21st Infantry, reporting in 1875 to Fort Bidwell in the northeast corner of California about 14 miles from the Oregon border. On the march from there to Fort Vancouver, his permanent post in the Pacific Northwest, Wood had his first contact with the Harney Desert, which he was later to evoke so powerfully in his poetry.

On the frontier Erskine got some of the adventure his restless and romantic temperament craved. He escorted a member of the United States Coast Survey on an early exploration of Alaska, returning in time to serve as aide to General Oliver O. Howard in the difficult and frustrating pursuit of the Nez Perces in their flight toward Canada and freedom that ended at Bear Paw Mountain, Montana Territory, 30 miles south of the international border. Lieutenant Wood's eloquent summary of Chief Joseph's sentiments when he surrendered can be found in most textbooks of United States history. Detached service in Washington, D.C., permitted the young Indian fighter, now a first lieutenant, to return to the national capital to marry his sweetheart of cadet days, Nanny Moale Smith, in November 1878.

Lieutenant Wood's far western experience gave him a taste at first hand of the power of the state in using its military arm to crush the rebellion of a desperate and dignified people whose major crime was simply that they were in the way. Further, his frontier service provided him with literary material. *Century Magazine* published pieces by Wood on his probing of Alaska and on Chief Joseph.

With the Pacific Northwest secure, General Howard was transferred from Fort Vancouver to West Point to head the United States Military Academy, and Wood returned with him to the scene of his unhappy cadet days, this time as adjutant. Not only was West Point duty dull, but Wood had had enough of a career not of his own choosing, and he was eyeing the law as a way out of the army. Under justification of improving his military efficiency, he was granted leave of absence to enroll in Columbia for courses in political science and law.

Shortly after Columbia granted Wood a bachelor of laws degree, in 1883, he resigned his commission and joined his wife and two children in Portland. There he began his career as attorney, a career he maintained for thirty-four years. His rise in the legal profession was not spectacular, but it was sound. In 1887 when George H. Williams, attorney general under Grant, joined Wood as a partner, the firm took on considerable prestige. By the turn of the century, Wood's family had grown to five children, his law practice was large, he represented an international banking firm as land agent for a vast wagon road grant, and he was a member of Portland's exclusive Arlington Club. Moreover, as a specialist in maritime and corporation law, he had become legal adviser and friend to some of the wealthiest and most influential people in the city, and he and his gracious wife moved on terms of easy intimacy with the Charles Ladds, the Henry Corbetts, the W. B. Ayers, and other members of Portland's social elite.

But there was another side to the Portland lawyer and man of distinction, a bohemian and rebellious side. "Colonel" Wood had not lost his creative impulse. He continued to write and sketch and paint wherever and whenever he was able. His journals are full of sonnets, ballads, ideas for stories, character sketches, snatches of dialogue, vignettes, philosophical and nature essays. Much of the work was facile or fragmentary. A good deal was personal, written to his wife to mark an anniversary or to his children and friends to remember a birthday. Despite his writing for the *Century*, Wood seems not to have been in a fever to publish.

Apparently Wood wrote and painted largely spontaneously and because this brought him satisfaction in a way that the practice of law did not. Much of his writing gives the impression of great vitality and considerable talent with but little discipline or direction. In costume and appearance Colonel Wood suggested the poet or artist rather than the professional man. When he dressed for the evening, he affected spotless, ruffled shirts of silk, which set off to full advantage the heavy, handsome beard he had worn since his army days. With his mass of curly hair, his wide-spaced, heavy-lidded eyes, a soft broad-brimmed stetson, and a dramatic black military cape to turn the Oregon weather, he made an elegant and romantic figure.

Inseparable from C. E. S. Wood's literary and artistic development was a gradual growth into radicalism. From the outset he had rebelled against authority, but these were abortive revolts. As he came into maturity and found himself secure in his surroundings, he began to release his resentment through his writing and to seek some theory or ideal through which he might express his belief in freedom and his contempt for any institution, code, or influence that inhibited the unfolding of the individual or suppressed the free exchange of ideas. Reading in Thoreau, Herbert Spencer, Henry George, Proudhon, and Kropotkin helped him to arrive at what he called philosophical or enlightened anarchism.

Other factors in his experience propelled him in the same direction. He disapproved of federal policy toward the Indians, and he was an outspoken anti-imperialist. He decried what he termed the feudal system of land tenure whereby property was distributed and held by virtue of the deed in fee simple. He was drawn to the cause of the underdog, and the unequal struggle against things as they are intrigued him.

In his associations with conservative colleagues and businessmen of wealth and power, he found them in the main uncomplex, narrow, ordinary. He preferred Bill Haywood to Harvey Scott. He found the steerage passengers of a coastal steamer more genuine, more alive, more colorful, than his first-class traveling companions. He could be counted on to bail Portland's radical labor agitator Tom Burns out of jail. When Emma Goldman was scheduled to appear in Portland on her more or less regular tours to the Pacific Coast, it was C. E. S. Wood who paved the way, arranging for halls in which "Red Emma" could be heard, lending the drawing power of his name to swell the crowds, and giving her legal counsel and defense when she was arrested. Restrictions on free speech aroused him to anger and scorn of a society that feared the airing of ideas such as single tax, birth control, free love, and anarchism.

Meanwhile, Colonel Wood had been provided with an outlet for his creative writing as well as a vehicle for his views. When the *Pacific Monthly*, a promotional and literary magazine, was launched in Portland in 1898, Wood was asked to become a contributor, and for more than a decade he obliged in a profusion made possible by manuscript reserves that had been accumulating for years. To disguise the degree of the monthly's dependence on him, Wood frequently wrote under such exotic pseudonyms as Felix Benguiat or Francis du Bosque, providing poetry, short stories, book reviews, and art criticism. 'Impressions," a monthly feature, appeared under his own name, and here he expressed his unorthodox ideas with vigor and candor. Between 1898 and 1911, when it merged with *Sunset*, the *Pacific Monthly*, with a peak circulation of over 100,000, was the primary vehicle of cultural expression in the Pacific Northwest, and Wood was its most versatile contributor and the only one to appear throughout the life of the magazine.

Colonel Wood was quite aware that the voluntary organization of society advocated by anarchists was not likely to be achieved, at least not for generations; but he used the anarchist position as a kind of touchstone against which to measure issues that confronted society, and this helps to explain his consistent support of liberal causes. Thus, although he was not a dominant figure in state or national politics, Wood entered the arena from time to time: he joined William S. U'Ren in the forging of direct legislation; he helped manage the Democrat Harry Lane's successful senatorial campaign in 1912; hoping to stay out of the war, he took the public platform in support of Wilson in 1916. To an uncompromising anarchist like Emma Goldman, this was opportunism, and she said so. Wood merely replied serenely, "I will take any wagon going my way."

Although Wood loved the natural beauty of the Pacific Northwest, he felt the cultural isolation that life in this far corner imposed. He could find no one equipped or inclined to share the creative and rebellious aspects of his life. Mrs. Wood's energies were absorbed by the family and by the limited but intense activities of their social set. She did not reproach her husband for his preoccupation with poetry and painting or for his radical views, but she was not sympathetic, and of course she could not join him. Wood maintained a secret office in the chamber of commerce building to facilitate his creative work, where, perhaps, it pleased him to turn out pointed social criticism from a stronghold of the status quo, just as later, all through the prohibition period, he delighted in fermenting wine from the grapes in his Los Gatos, California, vineyards. Salvaging hours at night and on weekends from his busy life, Wood withdrew to this office retreat to write or sketch or paint.

Early in 1911, C. E. S. Wood met a young woman, thirty years his junior, who exerted a marked influence on his writing and who ultimately changed his life. Sara Bard Field, wife of a Baptist minister, had come to Portland with her husband from Cleveland, where she had played a small role in the reform administration of Mayor Tom Johnson. She and Colonel Wood met at a dinner given by Clarence Darrow. "This girl," Darrow told Wood, "is an ardent Socialist. She has seen poverty at first hand in a poor parish in Cleveland." "Socialist?" Wood repeated seriously, but with friendly humor in his eyes. "That's all right for the immediate but she'll become an Anarchist in time. Socialism is just a halfway station toward that goal."

Similar interests in poetry and social reform quickly cemented a friendship between the two, and one day Erskine asked Sara to look through his writing that had piled up in a chest in a corner of his private office. She found the chest full of manuscripts, some prose, more verse, many fragments. She turned over one after another with mounting disappointment. There were too many trifles, too much occasional verse, too many threadbare themes unrelieved by original treatment, too much imitative style, and all of it evidence that Wood was wasting a portion of his power in riotous writing. Then, near the bottom, she uncovered a yellow-sheeted, paper-covered notebook containing free-verse sketches of the desert, which made the search worthwhile.

From the time of his military service on the desert's edge, Wood had returned again and again to this "lean and stricken land." To him the desert meant youth and freedom and peace. For him there was no fragrance to match the spicy scent of sagebrush after a rain. The desert's blinding light, its jutting rimrock, its crags and pillars of basalt or obsidian—bare monuments in a barren waste—its wide-arching skies were beautiful to his eyes, intoxicating beyond green mountain or restless sea. With Sara's help, expanded and chiseled as much as Erskine's free-moving hand would allow, these sketches and verse fragments became *Poet in the Desert*, in Wood's mind his major achievement.

The poem opens with a prologue describing the signs of the desert and comparing it romantically to a beautiful and imperious woman, infinite in the variety of her moods. Then the image of truth is evoked, and through a long series of poetic passages, some of them resembling psalms, some dialogues, some sermons, the poet seeks to weigh the world man has made out of bondage against the world nature makes in freedom.

The performance is uneven. There are passages of serene beauty simply and cleanly wrought. There is passionate denunciation of war with morbidly realistic descriptions of the destruction it brings. There are melodramatic vignettes of sweatshop and mine, and an ostentatious paean to bastardy. There is a gentle hymn to nature, rich in imagery and restrained in statement. The fifty-second segment, which brings the poem to a close, is a sharp cry for revolution. One reviewer described the work as a series of alternate "rhapsodies and recriminations." To another it was "a terrifying cosmic outcry against things as they are." William Allen White wrote: "In another day when democracy has served its place . . . some man delving in volumes of forgotten lore will find these songs . . . and will cry, 'Here is yesterday singing for today.' "

Poet in the Desert appeared first in 1915 and then went into three subsequent editions in English. The various versions reveal the continuous struggle within Wood between poet and propagandist. In a cheap 1918 edition, the special pleading was muted at Sara's insistence, and Wood worked for smoother articulation of the poem's parts. Bearing out her judgment, there is general consensus that Wood is most effective in the descriptive passages free from radical sentiment.

In the same year that *Poet in the Desert* appeared, C. E. S. Wood wrote a brief dialogue poking fun at Anthony Comstock, that "roundsman of the Lord," and his efforts to suppress Margaret Sanger's birth control movement. He sent the piece to the *Masses*, and the editors Max Eastman and Floyd Dell asked for more. Erskine struck off a number of dialogues, one after the other, and when the *Masses* was suppressed in October 1917, many of these satirical conversations, most of them unpublished, were returned to the author. Ten years later they were collected and brought out by Vanguard Press under the title *Heavenly Discourse*.

Little is sacred in these conversations in heaven among such personages as God (Wood in thin disguise), Jesus, Rabelais, Voltaire, Saint Peter, Teddy Roosevelt, Mark Twain, and Bob Ingersoll. The satirist had a good time with his subjects. There was Teddy Roosevelt storming heaven like a Cuban hill and threatening to marshal the angels in military order; Rabelais constantly lamenting having to leave his gullet on earth; and Anthony Comstock crying in high heaven for just one fig leaf. Frederic C. Howe, then commissioner of immigration, considered the dialogues one of the best things the *Masses* had printed. On the other hand, in the words of Vida D. Scudder, professor of literature at Wellesley, "the smart and cheap vulgarity of that thing was too much for me."

In one sense, of course, *Heavenly Discourse* is definitely dated, but some of the tendencies it attacked—war and censorship and discrimination—still threaten. Whether because this is true or because of its wit and humor, *Heavenly Discourse* has had a surprisingly tenacious hold on part of the public, having gone through more than twenty-five printings. Nothing else Wood wrote remotely approached in it popularity, and until recently the book was available in a Penguin paperback edition.

C. E. S. Wood spent more than a third of a century in the Pacific Northwest. During these years when his physical and mental powers were at full strength, he saw the region develop from frontier to settled community. Living in one of the hubs of the area and traveling from it in all directions, Colonel Wood could claim a hand in the transition. As a successful attorney, he maintained a varied practice and cared for a large family. Although his poetry and stories and editorials reached but a relative handful, through *Heavenly Discourse* his satire ultimately commanded a healthy following. His work with U'Ren, his fight for free speech, and his support of Lane and Wilson permitted him a measure of influence on the level of political action despite views that were considered quixotic, if not downright dangerous. As a self-proclaimed anarchist, he tried mightily to ruffle Portland placidity.

The question arises: Why did generally conservative Portlanders suffer such a man to live and work and thunder in their midst? Wood was tolerated, perhaps, in part, because his views were regarded as too chimerical to pose a genuine threat to society. More important probably, Wood was a compelling and polished personality, as much at ease in a banker's drawing room or at a full-dress dinner as he was on Bill Hanley's ranch or at a mass meeting protesting social injustice. Prominent Oregonians who detested and decried his radical doctrines liked his company, admired his style, and respected his judgment.

In the winter of 1910–11, the same winter that C. E. S. Wood and Sara Bard Field met, John Reed returned from Europe to learn that family finances were such that he would have to earn his own living. Certain that Portland was no place for a writer to make his start, Reed left for New York, where Lincoln Steffens, his father's friend, promised that the boy should have his chance. Jack Reed took a suite of rooms, with three other Harvard graduates, at 42 Washington Square and, thanks to Steffens, a job with *American Magazine*. He then set out to make himself a writer.

For some months after graduation, in fact all through his European tour, the undergraduate years at Harvard had loomed as the most significant experience in Jack Reed's life. Now, in New York, Harvard was quickly reduced to size, as Reed's postgraduate education began. He virtually devoured the city, wandering wide-eyed and restless from side to side and end to end, probing corners, learning the brilliant, sophisticated facets of New York life as well as its somber, wretched, sinister ones. His writing and conversation were full of the city expressed in extravagantly romantic terms. New York ratified his imagination and then transcended it. Much of his enchantment was poured into the ears of the tolerant and sympathetic Steffens who, after the death of his first wife, had come to live on Washington Square. Finally, Steffens, in order to reserve part of his nights for sleeping, urged Jack to "write it down."

This was 1911, and Greenwich Village was on the edge of its first great period of intellectual upheaval. Emma Goldman's *Mother Earth* office was a gathering place for anarchists and assorted rebels. Alfred Stieglitz was operating an unconventional American center for post-impressionist artists where the password was "experimental." Mabel Dodge was back from Italy, busy mixing people, ideas, and good food and drink in a salon where only bankers and "bourgeois pigs" were barred. Into this eruptive milieu, a tangle of unruly hair topping his moon-round Boy Scout face, burst John Reed.

While rejoicing in the rebellious and uninhibited side of the Village, Reed also yearned after conventional writing success. The Harvard ambivalence was with him yet, and he longed to see his name in the slick magazines along with the names of Julian Street, Owen Johnson, and Robert Chambers. For three years Reed courted the national magazines with moderate success, publishing in *Century, Smart Set, Saturday Evening Post*, and *American*, but he did not feel that these sketches and stories and poetry genuinely said what he wanted to say.

Reed was taken into the Dutch Treat Club, a weekly luncheon gathering of successful New York writers, illustrators, and editors, and he was flattered that he was selected to write the lyrics for their annual supper show at Delmonico's in 1912. With Bill Daly as composer, Reed produced a deceptively gentle satire called *Everymagazine, an Immorality Play*. In facile, clever verse Reed lampooned the popular monthlies. Representing the family magazine, a club member, swathed in bombazine and wearing sawdust curls, knitted primly as he sang:

> I'm a literary virgin—
> All the warmness of a salmon.
>   All the passion of a sturgeon.
> I'm aristocratic, very.
>
> I'm a live obituary
> Of the giants literary
>   Who have given up the ghost.
> In illuminating snatches
>   Since the spring of Sixty-one
> I've been publishing dispatches
>   From the battle of Bull Run.
>
> Of refinement I'm a symbol
>   On your literary table;
> All of culture in a thimble
>   By the new Atlantic cable.
> And though Congress does not heed me,
> And the public does not read me,
> I'm convinced the people need me
>   From the Hudson to the Coast.
> O when Trollope kicked the bucket
>   And when Dickens was no more
> I had half a mind to chuck it
>   Till I found the Civil War.

>   Aristocratic rather,
>   Exclusiveness my boast
> In fact I am the Father
>   The Son, and Holy Ghost.

In eight lines Reed nailed the *Cosmopolitan* to the wall:

> Every month I'm full of spice
> And naughty Robert Chambers makes it nice.
> Some lingerie, a glimpse of stocking.
> Lips unlocking, nothing shocking.
> And Gibson hints at hidden beauty,
> Lovers' booty, tutti frutti.
> Read me once and I'll bet I can
> Refresh the tired business man.

At the time none of the show was taken as serious satire, but there were enough barbs lying in the lyrics to cause uneasiness among a number of the Dutch Treaters. Something about the whole production was just a shade improper and unfair. One member, some years later, put into a pungent phrase the feeling of the more conventional segment of the club: "The trouble with Jack Reed was that he wasn't housebroken."

The defiance that lay beneath the surface in the Dutch Treat show broke out sharply when John Reed deserted "Everymagazine" for the *Masses*. This was a revolutionary magazine, revolutionary not merely in the disciplined Marxian pattern (although that was part of it), but in the broad, indiscriminate sense of striking out against complacency, convention, and compromise. Its contributors were a strange assortment—Gelett Burgess, Amy Lowell, Lincoln Steffens, Sherwood Anderson, Charles Edward Russell, William Rose Benét, John Sloan, Art Young, Floyd Dell, Louis Untermeyer, Carl Sandburg, Max Eastman—but they were united in rebellion and agreed with Floyd Dell that the *Masses* stood for "fun, truth, beauty, realism, freedom, peace, feminism, and revolution." The January 1913 *Masses* carried a story by Reed that had repeatedly been rejected by the national magazines because its theme was deemed unfit for family reading. Two months later Reed was listed as a contributing editor, and with Max Eastman he drafted a spirited statement of purpose, emphasizing the magazine's defiance.

Meanwhile, John Reed's social education proceeded apace. Lincoln Steffens introduced him to radicals of all sorts—single taxers, socialists, anarchists, labor leaders, atheists, and feminists. At Mabel Dodge's he heard Bill Haywood describe the class struggle as exemplified in the Paterson silk workers' strike and was so impressed that he went to see what was going on, was arrested, and spent four days in jail with Carlo Tresca, Bill Haywood, and the strikers. Out of this experience came the idea for the pageant staged by Reed and others under the auspices of the Industrial Workers of the World in Madison Square Garden, which massed the workers and their wives before a huge New York audience. Reed was becoming increasingly implicated in the radical movement, and although he left after the pageant's one-night stand to spend a romantic interlude with Mabel Dodge in Italy, he had taken a stride along the path that ended under stone beside the Kremlin wall.

Back in New York in October 1913, as managing editor of the *Masses*, Reed found himself drawn in two directions: pulled by the possessiveness of Mabel Dodge, on one hand, and moved toward Marxism and the class struggle, on the other. Moreover, he had not yet found his "lay" or "line," as Lincoln Steffens pointed out. The dilemma was shortly resolved when *Metropolitan*

Magazine hired Reed, on Steffen's recommendation, to cover Francisco Villa's exploits against the federalists in northern Mexico.

Characteristically, Reed lost himself in the local struggle. He met the Mexican leader and became an ardent Villa partisan. He was ignorant of Mexican history and only superficially aware of the issues, but he loved the simple, lusty peons and quoted approvingly one compañero's definition of freedom as "the right to do what I want to." Reed rode, slept, ate, and fought with the ragged troops, risking his life and learning that he could tolerate being under fire. As he ran headlong across a chaparral-studded plain, a federalist in hot pursuit, he kept repeating to himself: "Well, this is certainly an experience. I'm going to have something to write about." This was not the expression of a reporter exultant over a prospective scoop, but rather the delight of an artist and poet living through an experience that was providing him with something to say.

That John Reed had truly found his "line" was apparent in the enthusiastic reception of the dispatches he sent back to the *Metropolitan* and the New York *World*, and which formed the substance of his book *Insurgent Mexico*. Reed's undisputed ability to use his eyes and to record in rich, relevant detail and with a kind of impassioned precision all that they took in made of *Insurgent Mexico*, despite its lack of perspective and unity, a memorable book. For the moment, John Reed was the most popular correspondent in the country.

Between his Mexican adventures and the outbreak of war in Europe, Reed had one notable assignment. He was sent to Ludlow, Colorado, to investigate the violence in the coal mines. His report on the Ludlow strike was much less impressionistic than were his stories from Mexico, but there was little question where his sympathies lay, and the experience recalled him forcibly to the clash between the classes.

In Europe in 1914, the *Metropolitan* reporter could not identify himself with the struggle as he had in Mexico. To Reed this was strictly a war for profits; furthermore, it was dull, mechanistic, impersonal. News of one ill-advised and irresponsible attempt made by Reed and a companion to get the feel of the fighting by firing from the German trenches in the general direction of the French lines leaked and followed Reed the rest of his life. His work was a disappointment to the editors of *Metropolitan* as well as to himself. He returned to the United States with the laconic but emphatic message, "This is not our War." A month later John Reed and an artist from the *Masses* were back in Europe covering the eastern sectors and proceeding recklessly into Russia without proper passes. After a series of arrests and narrow escapes from imprisonment, expulsion, even execution, they were at last permitted to leave by way of Rumania. This trip was more exciting than the first, but Reed's conviction that it was a capitalist's war remained firm.

Once again in the United States, John Reed went home to Portland, where he met Louise Bryant Trullinger. They fell in love, and shortly Louise Bryant left her husband to join Jack Reed in New York, where he was busy with the *Masses*, writing up interviews for the *Metropolitan*, and, in the summer, helping to organize the Provincetown Players.

Reed's energies, however, were mainly enlisted in fighting the nation's drift toward involvement in the war. When pacifists and liberals and radicals of various shades and descriptions reversed their positions after Wilson's war message, Reed remained adamant against what he continued to call a trader's war. Disillusioned with the patriotism of the European socialists and discouraged by the docility of the American worker, John Reed, by this time a Marxist, left for Russia in August 1917 to report for the *Masses* and the Socialist *Call* the progress of the revolution then in the provisional government stage under Kerensky.

In Petrograd Reed sought to follow the mercurial scene with the same avidity that had characterized his observation of the Mexican insurrection, but this time with an intellectual as well as an emotional commitment. Reed roamed the streets and haunted the meeting halls, searching out the substance as well as the color of events. He got as close to the revolution as possible, shuttling from one faction to another to see how things were going and ripping posters from walls to help document the story that was taking shape in his notes and in his mind. By November 13 the Bolsheviks controlled Petrograd, the revolution was spreading through Russia, and Reed hailed the Red victory as the beginning of "a kingdom more bright than any heaven had to offer, and for which it was a glory to die."

After six months in revolutionary Russia, John Reed came home in the spring of 1918, having promised to carry the story of the struggle to the American proletariat. Reed's last sixteen months in the United States were troubled and strenuous. Along with other editors of the *Masses*, he faced charges of conspiracy to obstruct recruiting and enlistment, and when he spoke in eastern and midwestern cities in support of the revolution, he picked up other criminal indictments. Although he resigned from the staff of the *Liberator*, which had succeeded the repressed *Masses*, because he would not share editorial responsibility for a magazine which existed upon the sufferance of Postmaster General Burleson, he continued to contribute to the magazine as well as to the Socialist *Call*. The national journals that had once welcomed his work were, of course, closed to him. At the time of Reed's resignation from the *Liberator*, C. E. S. Wood wrote to him approving his action and offering financial aid.

With the armistice, left-wing radicals tried to organize bolshevism in the United States, and Reed was in the vanguard of the movement. The Socialist party splintered, and the left wing split into two factions, the Communist party and the Communist Labor party, each claiming to be revolutionary. Reed was a leader in the latter. His program called for the immediate training of the working class for the seizure of power. It was to gain recognition in Moscow for the Communist Labor party that Reed sailed for Russia late in September 1919.

Meanwhile, in March, his *Ten Days That Shook the World* had appeared, selling 9,000 copies in the first three months. This was the best writing of Reed's career. It had cohesion and a controlled vigor that *Insurgent Mexico* lacked. Although frankly pro-Bolshevik and sometimes in error, it was a full and faithful account of what Jack Reed had seen, backed up by substantial documentation. No other firsthand account of the Bolshevik rise to power is in its class.

In Russia Reed lived in a working-class quarter; he talked with Lenin from time to time, wrote about the revolutionary situation in America for the official Communist organ, and wandered about tirelessly, ranging as far as the Volga. When the executive committee of the Communist International produced a plan to secure the fusion of the two American Communist parties, it was time for Reed to return to the United States. He made two abortive attempts to do so, on the second try spending three months in a Finnish prison awaiting release through either the United States State Department or Moscow. The Russians acted first, exchanging two captive Finnish professors for Reed.

As a member of the executive committee planning for the second congress of the Communist International, Reed moved into full participation in the construction of the new social order. In the excitement of the congress's closing day, Reed, another American, and an Australian delegate, at Reed's signal, hoisted Lenin on their shoulders to receive the tribute of the people in the proper American grandstand manner. As the uncomprehending crowd gaped, Lenin kicked vigorously until the three set him down. There was still a streak of playfulness left in Jack Reed, and it had betrayed him into a breach of revolutionary decorum.

At the end of August 1920, Reed was sent to a congress of Oriental nations at Baku. When he returned to Moscow, his wife, Louise Bryant, was there to greet him, having made her way from the

United States. They spent a handful of days together in happy reunion, and then John Reed, his health already shattered by scurvy, fatigue, and strain, was stricken with typhus. By Sunday, October 17, 1920, three days before his thirty-third birthday, John Reed was dead.

When Reed was fighting indictments, writing up the Bolshevik revolution, and working to organize a properly activist American Communist party, C. E. S. Wood was immersed in final negotiations for the sale of the wagon road land grant running from Albany on the Willamette across the Cascades to Ontario on the Snake. It was Wood's million-dollar commission from this transaction that freed him from his law practice and permitted him in 1919 to break with his family, after providing for them financially through a series of trust instruments that are among the most lucid and thoughtful and moving things he ever wrote. He left Portland for northern California, where he spent the quarter century that remained to him in writing and sharing a rich and intellectually fruitful companionship with Sara Bard Field.

Most of the California years were spent on a Los Gatos hill in an unusual home of stone and steel and glass built under the colonel's supervision. A steep and narrow road twisted down from the house to the highway below, where two huge stone felines—one awake, the other dozing—guarded the entrance and gave the estate its name, "The Cats." Above the currents of reaction that characterized the 1920s, C. E. S. Wood continued to criticize society, and because he and Sara Bard Field were people of sympathy and warmth, The Cats was a kind of clearinghouse for causes and a place of appeal for victims of various forms of injustice and discrimination. On one occasion Wood, at seventy-eight, came through a heavy California storm to galvanize a Tom Mooney protest meeting from listlessness into shouting enthusiasm. Both poets spent hours of their time in writing letters on behalf of such lesser-known figures as Ella Young, an Irish poet who sought to avoid deportation; or Max Hayek, translator of Whitman and Tagore and of Wood's *Poet in the Desert* into German, who needed sponsors if he was to escape the anti-Jewish terror of the Nazis; and there were many more. Erskine and Sara, despite the possibilities of withdrawal at The Cats, were very much of this world.

Even in swiftly summarizing these California years, it is impossible to treat Wood apart from his companion, Sara. It is true that the creative work of the two progressed independently, but in a deep sense there was constant collaboration and consultation between them. Out of devotion to one another and from the beauty and grace of their surroundings they shaped a way of life that was as impressive as anything they wrote.

The last years of Wood's life were marred by illness. In 1937 he sustained a coronary thrombosis from which he made remarkable recovery, considering that he was eighty-four, but failing eyesight and ebbing vitality prevented his completing a number of projects. Charles Erskine Scott Wood died January 20, 1944, just one month short of his ninety-second birthday. His body was cremated and his ashes strewn through the live oak grove at The Cats, as he wished.

The quality of C. E. S. Wood's revolt is difficult to define. It is not surprising that a man who, until his late sixties, felt repressed by one kind of authority or another—father, the army, the legal profession, middle-class convention—should rebel in the direction of anarchism, a theory that provides the utmost leeway for the individual. However, he was not the same kind of rebel in 1918 or in 1935 that he was in the first decade of the century. In the early period his anarchism was clearly egoistic. It sprang largely from having to subdue artistic, romantic, and literary urges in the face of more demanding responsibilities imposed by family and law practice, both of them growing. There is a strident, vainglorious note in this passage from Wood's 1905 journal:

I rebel against the suppression of the individual, the lack of freedom and the falsity—the hypocrisy of the smooth successful life. . . . I am sick of worthy men who force others to their own ideas of worthiness. . . . Let each be free and the worthiest will come to the top. . . . I would have more hope from a society where men gambled freely if they wanted to, than from a society made to be good by force of law and by the thunders of the pulpit. . . . I have more hope that the uplift of the physical and mental man will be resumed when society permits free love than I have from a society which forces the passing glance of young nature to be one dead, eternal gaze. . . . I deify Rebellion, I glory in being a rebel—and a fanatic. These are only other names for mind—progress—earnestness.

Albert Camus describes a type of romantic rebel that he calls the "Dandy." Camus's Dandy delights in shocking people with extreme pronouncements. In Baudelaire's phrase, he achieves coherence in the ambition to live and die before a mirror, and he finds his mirror in the eyes of others. He can exist only through defiance. If he neither commits suicide nor goes mad, he sets out to amass wealth and become a success. There is a suggestion of the Dandy in the Wood of 1905—handsome, a bit vain, dramatically dressed, vociferous in his anarchism, and demanding for himself in Portland something of the freedom that John Reed, Floyd Dell, Mabel Dodge, and others were soon seeking and finding in Greenwich Village.

By 1918 Wood's anarchism is much broader, less self-centered, more humanitarian, less shrill. In *Poet in the Desert*, condemnation of the state and authority is explicit and hard hitting, but Wood does not renounce law; rather, he proclaims the impersonal law of nature as supreme. If man can only learn to understand and to submit to nature, then she will evolve his soul as she has his body. In this poem Wood is often closer to transcendentalism than to anarchism.

In the late 1920s and through most of the thirties, Colonel Wood turned to direct attack on some of what were to him currently remediable abuses of authority—prohibition, censorship, the Ku Klux Klan, the concentration of corporate power, judicial review. He watched the Russian revolution and the Soviet experiment with interest and approval as a heartening attempt at realizing much of what he had been advocating for more than twenty years. But he was suspicious of the Stalinist purges, and in a letter to the *Daily Worker* he penned a sharp remonstrance to American party-line Communists for being unable or unwilling to think independently of Moscow.

Young radicals who began with admiration for the colonel often became disillusioned, writing him off as a wily old hypocrite, living in comfort and mouthing rebellion. Reed may have been among these. In time, however, some came to believe that Wood was a shrewd and reasonable man with a keen knowledge of what was possible in human affairs, a man whose compromises were more a result of this worldly understanding than of ambivalence, weakness, or hypocrisy. Long life, broad employment of diverse talents, flexibility in point of view—these help explain why C. E. S. Wood cannot be confined to a label or captured in a phrase.

The road that John Reed took to radical rebellion, although circuitous, is reasonably well marked. There were first the Harvard years, when Reed discovered the conflict within him that he strove the rest of his life to resolve. Then came the heady experience of Greenwich Village, balanced by exposure to the poverty and depravity of New York's East Side pointing to the gulf between the privileged and the poor, with Lincoln Steffens standing by all the while as guide and father-confessor. There was the dramatization of the class struggle at Paterson and Ludlow; the romance of four months with the simple, beautiful Mexicans in their struggle for liberty and land; and finally, the workers, soldiers, and peasants of Russia showing timid American workers the way to a proletarian heaven.

Perhaps the quality that best explains why John Reed construed his experiences as he did is his proclivity for total, if temporary, commitment. He was forever throwing himself into some project or toward some person and in the process sacrificing perspective and balance for deep involvement in the immediate. Thus he sank himself in the cause of the Paterson strikers and worked to the point of exhaustion in planning a pageant that, however, impressive, could be staged but one night and shrank rather than swelled the strikers' fund. Reed fled from that scene into the arms of Mabel Dodge and an interlude of unalloyed bohemianism. He carried identification with Villa's mestizos to the point of jeopardizing his life in a cause which he accepted but scarcely understood.

The sympathetic interpretation is that, after fighting through various stages of indecision, Reed finally found himself in Marxism and the Bolshevik revolution. Fortunately perhaps, for this school of thought, Reed died in the early stages of the Soviet experiment. Even so, there is some testimony, albeit of questionable reliability, that disillusionment had set in before typhus struck him down. Still, it is more likely that after October 1917 the revolution was almost Reed's entire life. He spoke for it, wrote for it, hurt his mother and lost friends for it, wasted in prison and finally died for it. Marxists accepted this as a fitting climax to a life of persistent, if deviant, growth toward truth. On the other hand, Lincoln Steffens lamented the loss of a free and laughing spirit.

One of Reed's biographers implies without undue regret that a great poetic talent, perhaps genius, was lost in the making of a revolutionary. Reed himself once remarked to Max Eastman, "This class struggle plays hell with your poetry." Is it not possible, however, to argue that Reed may have embraced communism because he feared to face his failure as a poet? In a conversation with Sherwood Anderson, Reed confessed to doubts about his ability to write poetry, and certainly there is little in his published verse to suggest anything beyond competence.

Malcolm Cowley believed that Reed became a revolutionist for fundamentally literary reasons. Reed, he felt, could write superlatively on only one subject—"on men revolting against the institutions that prevented them from leading *human* lives." Reed discovered this first in Mexico and then again in Petrograd; and each time the romantic poet and journalist was transformed into a writer who had something close to genius. If Cowley's insight is valid and had John Reed lived to mature with the revolution, Boris Pasternak might have had an American-born counterpart.

There is not apt to be agreement on the meaning or the permanence of John Reed's rebellion. As George Kennan insists, after pointing out Reed's manifest weaknesses, "John Reed's was *one* American way of reacting to the Revolution. It deserves to be neither forgotten nor ridiculed."

Amid the festivities and ceremonies of this centennial year, when platoons of prominent and proper Oregonians are being called from quiet, honored graves and required to pass in historical review, it is perhaps also appropriate to have surveyed these two from out of the state's past who refused to stay in step, each counting a cadence peculiarly his own.

Bibliographical Note

Aside from John Reed's own works and his autobiographical essay "Almost Thirty," reprinted in the *New Republic*, Vol. 131 (Nov. 22, 1954), this article leans heavily on *John Reed: The Making of a Revolutionary* (New York, 1936), a persuasive biography by Granville Hicks with the assistance of John Stuart. A more recent life of Reed, published a number of years after this essay, is Robert A. Rosenstone, *Romantic Revolutionary: A Biography of John Reed* (New York, 1975). The entry in the *Dictionary of American Biography* is by Ernest Sutherland Bates.

There is no full-scale biography of Charles Erskine Scott Wood. The best and most convenient treatment is Sara Bard Field's introduction to *Collected Poems of Charles Erskine Scott Wood* (New York, 1949). C. E. S. Wood's son, Erskine, has written a life of his father published in a privately printed limited edition in 1978. The entry in the *Dictionary of American Biography* is by Thurman Wilkins. The largest body of Wood papers is in the Henry E. Huntington Library, San Marino, California. This collection was the gift of Sara Bard Field and has been used in the preparation of this paper with the kind permission of the donor. Other important Wood materials are housed in the Oregon Historical Society Library, Portland, and in the Hubert Howe Bancroft Library, Berkeley, California.

6
What Pragmatism Means
William James

It would be almost impossible to exaggerate the significance of William James to the intellectual and cultural history of America. The son of Henry James, Sr. and the older brother of Henry James the author, William James's contributions to American psychology and philosophy are enormous. A major force in the advancement of psychology in America, he is best known to us today for his development of the philosophy of pragmatism and humanism. James argued that it was important to test one's ideas and beliefs by their individual and social consequences. Unfortunately, many students misconstrue this idea to mean that ideas and values should be accepted merely by a test of expediency. Instead, James's philosophy was designed to restore the moral and individual dimension to a way of thinking marked by abstraction, alienation and de-humanization.

Some years ago, being with a camping party in the mountains, I returned from a solitary ramble to find every one engaged in a ferocious metaphysical dispute. The *corpus* of the dispute was a squirrel—a live squirrel supposed to be clinging to one side of a tree-trunk; while over against the tree's opposite side a human being was imagined to stand. This human witness tries to get sight of the squirrel by moving rapidly round the tree, but no matter how fast he goes, the squirrel moves as fast in the opposite direction, and always keeps the tree between himself and the man, so that never a glimpse of him is caught. The resultant metaphysical problem now is this: *Does the man go round the squirrel or not?* He goes round the tree, sure enough, and the squirrel is on the tree; but does he go round the squirrel? In the unlimited leisure of the wilderness, discussion had been worn threadbare. Every one had taken sides, and was obstinate; and the numbers on both sides were even. Each side, when I appeared therefore appealed to me to make it a majority. Mindful of the scholastic adage that whenever you meet a contradiction you must make a distinction, I immediately sought and found one, as follows: "Which party is right," I said, "depends on what you *practically mean* by 'going round' the squirrel. If you mean passing from the north of him to the east, then to the south, then to the west, and then to the north of him again, obviously the man does go round him, for he occupies these successive positions. But if on the contrary you mean being first in front of him, then on the right of him, then behind him, then on his left, and finally in front again, it is quite as obvious that the man fails to go round him, for by the compensating movements the squirrel makes, he keeps his belly turned towards the man all the time, and his back turned away. Make the distinction, and there is no occasion for any farther dispute. You are both right and both wrong according as you conceive the verb 'to go round' in one practical fashion or the other."

Although one or two of the hotter disputants called my speech a shuffling evasion, saying they wanted no quibbling or scholastic hair-splitting, but meant just plain honest English 'round,' the majority seemed to think that the distinction had assuaged the dispute.

I tell this trivial anecdote because it is a peculiarly simple example of what I wish now to speak of *as the pragmatic method.* The pragmatic method is primarily a method of settling metaphysical disputes that otherwise might be interminable. Is the world one or many?—fated or free?—material or spiritual?—here are notions either of which may or may not hold good of the world; and disputes over such notions are unending. The pragmatic method in such cases is to try to interpret each notion by tracing its respective practical consequences. What difference would it practically make to any one if this notion rather than that notion were true? If no practical difference whatever can be traced, then the alternatives mean practically the same thing, and all dispute is idle. Whenever a dispute is serious, we ought to be able to show some practical difference that must follow from one side or the other's being right.

A glance at the history of the idea will show you still better what pragmatism means. The term is derived from the same Greek word πρᾶγμα, meaning action, from which our words 'practice' and 'practical' come. It was first introduced into philosophy by Mr. Charles Peirce in 1878. In an article entitled 'How to Make Our Ideas Clear,' in the *Popular Science Monthly* for January of that year Mr. Peirce, after pointing out that our beliefs are really rules for action, said that, to develop a thought's meaning, we need only determine what conduct it is fitted to produce: that conduct is for us its sole significance. And the tangible fact at the root of all our thought-distinctions, however subtle, is that there is no one of them so fine as to consist in anything but a possible difference of practice. To attain perfect clearness in our thoughts of an object, then, we need only consider what conceivable effects of a practical kind the object may involve—what sensations we are to expect from it, and what reactions we must prepare. Our conception of these effects, whether immediate or remote, is then for us the whole of our conception of the object, so far as that conception has positive significance at all.

This is the principle of Peirce, the principle of pragmatism. It lay entirely unnoticed by any one for twenty years, until I, in an address before Professor Howison's philosophical union at the university of California, brought it forward again and made a special application of it to religion. By that date (1898) the times seemed ripe for its reception. The word 'pragmatism' spread, and at present it fairly spots the pages of the philosophic journals. On all hands we find the 'pragmatic movement' spoken of, sometimes with respect, sometimes with contumely, seldom with clear understanding. It is evident that the term applies itself conveniently to a number of tendencies that hitherto have lacked a collective name, and that it has 'come to stay.'

To take in the importance of Peirce's principle, one must get accustomed to applying it to concrete cases. I found a few years ago that Ostwald, the illustrious Leipzig chemist, had been making perfectly distinct use of the principle of pragmatism in his lectures on the philosophy of science, though he had not called it by that name.

"All realities influence our practice," he wrote me, "and that influence is their meaning for us. I am accustomed to put questions to my classes in this way: In what respects would the world be different if this alternative or that were true? If I can find nothing that would become different, then the alternative has no sense."

That is, the rival views mean practically the same thing, and meaning, other than practical, there is for us none. Ostwald in a published lecture gives this example of what he means. Chemists have long wrangled over the inner constitution of certain bodies called 'tautomerous.' Their properties seemed equally consistent with the notion that an instable hydrogen atom oscillates inside of them, or that they are instable mixtures of two bodies. Controversy raged, but never was decided. "It would never have begun," says Ostwald, "if the combatants had asked themselves what particular experimental fact could have been made different by one or the other view being correct. For it would then have appeared that no difference of fact could possibly ensue; and the quarrel was as unreal as if, theorizing in primitive times about the raising of dough by yeast, one party should have invoked a 'brownie,' while another insisted on an 'elf' as the true cause of the phenomenon."

It is astonishing to see how many philosophical disputes collapse into insignificance the moment you subject them to this simple test of tracing a concrete consequence. There can *be* no difference anywhere that doesn't *make* a difference elsewhere—no difference in abstract truth that doesn't express itself in a difference in concrete fact and in conduct consequent upon that fact, imposed on somebody, somehow, somewhere, and somewhen. The whole function of philosophy ought to be to find out what definite difference it will make to you and me, at definite instants of our life, if this world-formula or that world-formula be the true one.

There is absolutely nothing new in the pragmatic method. Socrates was an adept at it. Aristotle used it methodically. Locke, Berkeley, and Hume made momentous contributions to truth by its means. Shadworth Hodgson keeps insisting that realities are only what they are 'known as.' But these forerunners of pragmatism used it in fragments: they were preluders only. Not until in our time has it generalized itself, become conscious of a universal mission, pretended to a conquering destiny. I believe in that destiny, and I hope I may end by inspiring you with my belief.

Pragmatism represents a perfectly familiar attitude in philosophy, the empiricist attitude, but it represents it, as it seems to me, both in a more radical and in a less objectionable form than it has ever yet assumed. A pragmatist turns his back resolutely and once for all upon a lot of inveterate habits dear to professional philosophers. He turns away from abstraction and insufficiency, from verbal solutions, from bad *a priori* reasons, from fixed principles, closed systems, and pretended absolutes and origins. He turns towards concreteness and adequacy, towards facts, towards action and towards power. That means the empiricist temper regnant and the rationalist temper sincerely given up. It means the open air and possibilities of nature, as against dogma, artificiality, and the pretence of finality in truth.

At the same time it does not stand for any special results. It is a method only. But the general triumph of that method would mean an enormous change in what I called in my last lecture the 'temperament' of philosophy. Teachers of the ultrarationalistic type would be frozen out, much as the courtier type is frozen out in republics, as the ultra-montane type of priest is frozen out in Protestant lands. Science and metaphysics would come much nearer together, would in fact work absolutely hand in hand.

Metaphysics has usually followed a very primitive kind of quest. You know how men have always hankered after unlawful magic, and you know what a great part in magic *words* have always played. If you have his name, or the formula of incantation that binds him, you can control the spirit, genie, afrite, or whatever the power may be. Solomon knew the names of all the spirits, and having their names, he held them subject to his will. So the universe has always appeared to the natural mind as a kind of enigma, of which the key must be sought in the shape of some illuminating or power-bringing word or name. That word names the universe's *principle*, and to possess it is after a fashion to possess the universe itself. 'God,' 'Matter,' 'Reason,' 'the Absolute,' 'Energy,' are so many solving names. You can rest when you have them. You are at the end of your metaphysical quest.

But if you follow the pragmatic method, you cannot look on any such word as closing your quest. You must bring out of each word its practical cash-value, set it at work within the stream of your experience. It appears less as a solution, then, than as a program for more work, and more particularly as an indication of the ways in which existing realities may be *changed*.

Theories thus become instruments, not answers to enigmas, in which we can rest. We don't lie back upon them, we move forward, and, on occasion, make nature over again by their aid. Pragmatism unstiffens all our theories, limbers them up and sets each one at work. Being nothing essentially new, it harmonizes with many ancient philosophic tendencies. It agrees with nominalism for instance, in always appealing to particulars; with utilitarianism in emphasizing practical aspects; with positivism in its disdain for verbal solutions, useless questions and metaphysical abstractions.

All these, you see, are *anti-intellectualist* tendencies. Against rationalism as a pretension and a method pragmatism is fully armed and militant. But, at the outset, at least, it stands for no particular results. It has no dogmas, and no doctrines save its method. As the young Italian pragmatist Papini has well said, it lies in the midst of our theories, like a corridor in a hotel. Innumerable chambers open out of it. In one you may find a man writing an atheistic volume; in the next some one on his knees praying for faith and strength; in a third a chemist investigating a body's properties. In a fourth a system of idealistic metaphysics is being excogitated; in a fifth the impossibility of metaphysics is being shown. But they all own the corridor, and all must pass through it if they want a practicable way of getting into or out of their respective rooms.

No particular results then, so far, but only an attitude of orientation, is what the pragmatic method means. *The attitude of looking away from first things, principles, 'categories,' supposed necessities; and of looking towards last things, fruits, consequences, facts.*

So much for the pragmatic method! You may say that I have been praising it rather than explaining it to you, but I shall presently explain it abundantly enough by showing how it works on some familiar problems. Meanwhile the word pragmatism has come to be used in a still wider sense, as meaning also a certain *theory of truth*. . . .

One of the most successfully cultivated branches of philosophy in our time is what is called inductive logic, the study of the conditions under which our sciences have evolved. Writers on this subject have begun to show a singular unanimity as to what the laws of nature and elements of fact mean, when formulated by mathematicians, physicists and chemists. When the first mathematical, logical, and natural uniformities, the first *laws*, were discovered, men were so carried away by the clearness, beauty and simplification that resulted, that they believed themselves to have deciphered authentically the eternal thoughts of the Almighty. His mind also thundered and reverberated in syllogisms. He also thought in conic sections, squares and roots and ratios, and geometrized like Euclid. He made Kepler's laws for the planets to follow; he made velocity increase proportionately to the time in falling bodies; he made the law of the sines for light to obey when refracted; he established the classes, orders, families and genera of plants and animals, and fixed the distances between them. He thought the archetypes of all things and devised their variations; and when we rediscover any one of these his wondrous institutions, we seize his mind in its very literal intention.

But as the sciences have developed farther, the notion has gained ground that most, perhaps all, of our laws are only approximations. The laws themselves, moreover, have grown so numerous that there is no counting them; and so many rival formulations are proposed in all the branches of science that investigators have become accustomed to the notion that no theory is absolutely a transcript of reality, but that any one of them may from some point of view be useful. Their great use is to summarize old facts and to lead to new ones. They are only a man-made language, a conceptual shorthand, as some one calls them, in which we write our reports of nature; and languages, as is well known, tolerate much choice of expression and many dialects.

Thus human arbitrariness has driven divine necessity from scientific logic. If I mention the names of Sigwart, Mach, Ostwald, Pearson, Milhaud, Poincaré, Duhem, Ruyssen, those of you who are students will easily identify the tendency I speak of, and will think of additional names.

Riding now on the front of this wave of scientific logic Messrs. Schiller and Dewey appear with their pragmatistic account of what truth everywhere signifies. Everywhere, these teachers say, 'truth' in our ideas and beliefs means the same thing that it means in science. It means, they say, nothing but this, *that ideas (which themselves are but parts of our experience) become true just in so far as they help us to get into satisfactory relation with other parts of our experience,* to summarize them and get about among them by conceptual short-cuts instead of following the interminable succession of particular phenomena. Any idea upon which we can ride, so to speak; any idea that will carry us prosperously from any one part of our experience to any other part, linking things satisfactorily, working securely, simplifying, saving labor; is true for just so much, true in so far forth, true *instrumentally*. This is the 'instrumental' view of truth taught so successfully at Chicago, the view that truth in our ideas means their power to 'work,' promulgated so brilliantly at Oxford.

Messrs. Dewey, Schiller and their allies, in reaching this general conception of all truth, have only followed the example of geologists, biologists and philologists. In the establishment of these other sciences, the successful stroke was always to take some simple process actually observable in operation—as denudation by weather, say, or variation from parental type, or change of dialect by incorporation of new words and pronunciations—and then to generalize it, making it apply to all times, and produce great results by summating its effects through the ages.

The observable process which Schiller and Dewey particularly singled out for generalization is the familiar one by which any individual settles into *new opinions*. The process here is always the same. The individual has a stock of old opinions already, but he meets a new experience that puts them to a strain. Somebody contradicts them; or in a reflective moment he discovers that they contradict each other; or he hears of facts with which they are incompatible; or desires arise in him which they cease to satisfy. The result is an inward trouble to which his mind till then had been a stranger, and from which he seeks to escape by modifying his previous mass of opinions. He saves as much of it as he can, for in this matter of belief we are all extreme conservatives. So he tries to change first this opinion, and then that (for they resist change very variously), until at last some new idea comes up which he can graft upon the ancient stock with a minimum of disturbance of the latter, some idea that mediates between the stock and the new experience and runs them into one another most felicitously and expediently.

This new idea is then adopted as the true one. It preserves the older stock of truths with a minimum of modification, stretching them just enough to make them admit the novelty, but conceiving that in ways as familiar as the case leaves possible. An *outrée* explanation, violating all our preconceptions, would never pass for a true account of a novelty. We should scratch round industriously till we found something less excentric. The most violent revolutions in an individual's beliefs leave most of his old order standing. Time and space, cause and effect, nature and history, and one's own biography remain untouched. New truth is always a go-between, a smoother-over of transitions. It marries old opinion to new fact so as ever to show a minimum of jolt, a maximum of continuity. We hold a theory true just in proportion to its success in solving this 'problem of maxima and minima.' But success in solving this problem is eminently a matter of approximation. We say this theory solves it on the whole more satisfactorily than that theory; but that means more satisfactorily to ourselves, and individuals will emphasize their points of satisfaction differently. To a certain degree, therefore, everything here is plastic.

The point I now urge you to observe particularly is the part played by the older truths. Failure to take account of it is the source of much of the unjust criticism levelled against pragmatism. Their influence is absolutely controlling. Loyalty to them is the first principle—in most cases it is the only principle; for by far the most usual way of handling phenomena so novel that they would make for a serious rearrangement of our preconception is to ignore them altogether, or to abuse those who bear witness for them.

You doubtless wish examples of this process of truth's growth, and the only trouble is their superabundance. The simplest cast of new truth is of course the mere numerical addition of new kinds of facts, or of new single facts of old kinds, to our experience—an addition that involves no alteration in the old beliefs. Day follows day, and its contents are simply added. The new contents themselves are not true, they simply *come* and *are*. Truth is *what we say about* them, and when we say that they have come, truth is satisfied by the plain additive formula.

But often the day's contents oblige a rearrangement. If I should now utter piercing shrieks and act like a maniac on this platform, it would make many of you revise your ideas as to the probable worth of my philosophy. 'Radium' came the other day as part of the day's content, and seemed for a moment to contradict our ideas of the whole order of nature, that order having come to be identified with what is called the conservation of energy. The mere sight of radium paying heat away indefinitely out of its own pocket seemed to violate that conservation. What to think? If the radiations from it were nothing but an escape of unsuspected 'potential' energy, pre-existent inside of the atoms, the principle of conservation would be saved. The discovery of 'helium' as the radiation's outcome, opened a way to this belief. So Ramsay's view is generally held to be true, because, although it extends our old ideas of energy, it causes a minimum of alteration in their nature.

I need not multiply instances. A new opinion counts as 'true' just in proportion as it gratifies the individual's desire to assimilate the novel in his experience to his beliefs in stock. It must both lean on old truth and grasp new fact; and its success (as I said a moment ago) in doing this, is a matter for the individual's appreciation. When old truth grows, then, by new truth's addition, it is for subjective reasons. We are in the process and obey the reasons. That new idea is truest which performs most felicitously its function of satisfying our double urgency. It makes itself true, gets itself classed as true, by the way it works; grafting itself then upon the ancient body of truth, which thus grows much as a tree grows by the activity of a new layer of cambium.

Now Dewey and Schiller proceed to generalize this observation and to apply it to the most ancient parts of truth. They also once were plastic. They also were called true for human reasons. They also mediated between still earlier truths and what in those days were novel observations. Purely objective truth, truth in whose establishment the function of giving human satisfaction in marrying previous parts of experience with newer parts played no role whatever, is nowhere to be found. The reasons why we call things true is the reason why they *are* true, for 'to be true' *means* only to perform this marriage-function.

The trail of the human serpent is thus over everything. Truth independent; truth that we *find* merely; truth no longer malleable to human need; truth incorrigible, in a word; such truth exists indeed superabundantly—or is supposed to exist by rationalistically minded thinkers; but then it means only the dead heart of the living tree, and its being there means only that truth also has its paleontology, and its 'prescription,' and may grow stiff with years of veteran service and petrified in men's regard by sheer antiquity. But how plastic even the oldest truths nevertheless really are has been vividly shown in our day by the transformation of logical and mathematical ideas, a transformation which seems even to be invading physics. The ancient formulas are reinterpreted as special expressions of much wider principles, principles that our ancestors never got a glimpse of in their present shape and formulation.

Mr. Schiller still gives to all this view of truth the name of 'Humanism,' but, for this doctrine too, the name of pragmatism seems fairly to be in the ascendant, so I will treat it under the name of pragmatism in these lectures.

Such then would be the scope of pragmatism—first, a method, and second, a genetic theory of what is meant by truth. And these two things must be our future topics.

What I have said of the theory of truth will, I am sure, have appeared obscure and unsatisfactory to most of you by reason of its brevity. I shall make amends for that hereafter. In a lecture on 'common sense' I shall try to show what I mean by truths grown petrified by antiquity. In another lecture I shall expatiate on the idea that our thoughts become true in proportion as they successfully exert their go-between function. In a third I shall show how hard it is to discriminate subjective from objective factors in Truth's development. You may not follow me wholly in these lectures; and if you do, you may not wholly agree with me. But you will, I know, regard me at least as serious, and treat my effort with respectful consideration.

You will probably be surprised to learn, then, that Messrs. Schiller's and Dewey's theories have suffered a hailstorm of contempt and ridicule. All rationalism has risen against them. In influential quarters Mr. Schiller, in particular, has been treated like an impudent schoolboy who deserves a spanking. I should not mention this, but for the fact that it throws so much sidelight upon that rationalistic temper to which I have opposed the temper of pragmatism. Pragmatism is uncomfortable away from facts. Rationalism is comfortable only in the presence of abstractions. This pragmatist talk about truths in the plural, about their utility and satisfactoriness, about the success with which they 'work,' etc., suggests to the typical intellectualist mind a sort of coarse lame second-rate makeshift article of truth. Such truths are not real truth. Such tests are merely subjective. As against this, objective truth must be something non-utilitarian, haughty, refined, remote, august, exalted. It must be an absolute correspondence of our thoughts with an equally absolute reality. It must be what we *ought* to think unconditionally. The conditioned ways in which we *do* think are so much irrelevance and matter for psychology. Down with psychology, up with logic, in all this question!

See the exquisite contrast of the types of mind! The pragmatist clings to facts and concreteness, observes truth at its work in particular cases, and generalizes. Truth, for him, becomes a class-name for all sorts of definite working-values in experience. For the rationalist it remains a pure abstraction, to the bare name of which we must defer. When the pragmatist undertakes to show in detail just *why* we must defer, the rationalist is unable to recognize the concretes from which his own abstraction is taken. He accuses us of *denying* truth; whereas we have only sought to trace exactly why people follow it and always ought to follow it. Your typical ultra-abstractionist fairly shudders at concreteness: other things equal, he positively prefers the pale and spectral. If the two universes were offered, he would always choose the skinny outline rather than the rich thicket of reality. It is so much purer, clearer, nobler.

I hope that as these lectures go on, the concreteness and closeness to facts of the pragmatism which they advocate may be what approves itself to you as its most satisfactory peculiarity. It only follows here the example of the sister-sciences, interpreting the unobserved by the observed. It brings old and new harmoniously together. It converts the absolutely empty notion of a static relation of 'correspondence' . . . between our minds and reality, into that of a rich and active commerce (that any one may follow in detail and understand) between particular thoughts of ours, and the great universe of other experiences in which they play their parts and have their uses.

But enough of this at present! The justification of what I say must be postponed. I wish now to add a word in further explanation of the claim I made at our last meeting, that pragmatism may be a happy harmonizer of empiricist ways of thinking with the more religious demands of human beings.

Men who are strongly of the fact-loving temperament, you may remember me to have said, are liable to be kept at a distance by the small sympathy with facts which that philosophy from the present-day fashion of idealism offers them. It is far too intellectualistic. Old fashioned theism was bad enough, with its notion of God as an exalted monarch, made up of a lot of unintelligible or preposterous 'attributes'; but, so long as it held strongly by the argument from design, it kept some touch with concrete realities. Since, however, Darwinism has once for all displaced design from the minds of the 'scientific,' theism has lost that foothold; and some kind of an immanent or pantheistic deity working *in* things rather than above them is, if any, the kind recommended to our contemporary imagination. Aspirants to a philosophic religion turn, as a rule, more hopefully nowadays towards idealistic pantheism than towards the older dualistic theism, in spite of the fact that the latter still counts able defenders.

But . . . the brand of pantheism offered is hard for them to assimilate if they are lovers of facts, or empirically minded. It is the absolutistic brand, spurning the dust and reared upon pure logic. It keeps no connexion whatever with concreteness. Affirming the Absolute Mind, which is its substitute for God, to be the rational presupposition of all particulars of fact, whatever they may be, it remains supremely indifferent to what the particular facts in our world actually are. Be they what they may, the Absolute will father them. Like the sick lion in Esop's fable, all footprints lead into his den, but *nulla vestigia retrorsum*. You cannot redescend into the world of particulars by the Absolute's aid, or deduce any necessary consequences of detail important for your life from your idea of his nature. He gives you indeed the assurance that all is well with *Him*, and for his eternal way of thinking; but thereupon he leaves you to be finitely saved by your own temporal devices.

Far be it from me to deny the majesty of this conception, or its capacity to yield religious comfort to a most respectable class of minds. But from the human point of view, no one can pretend that it doesn't suffer from the faults of remoteness and abstractness. It is eminently a product of what I have ventured to call the rationalistic temper. It disdains empiricism's needs. It substitutes a pallid outline for the real world's richness. It is dapper, it is noble in the bad sense, in the sense in which to be noble is to be inapt for humble service. In this real world of sweat and dirt, it seems to me that when a view of things is 'noble,' that ought to count as a presumption against its truth, and as a philosophic disqualification. The prince of darkness may be a gentleman, as we are told he is, but whatever the God of earth and heaven is, he can surely be no gentleman. His menial services are needed in the dust of our human trials, even more than his dignity is needed in the empyrean.

Now pragmatism, devoted though she be to facts, has no such materialistic bias as ordinary empiricism labors under. Moreover, she has no objection whatever to the realizing of abstractions, so long as you get about among particulars with their aid and they actually carry you somewhere. Interested in no conclusions but those which our minds and our experiences work out together, she has no *a priori* prejudices against theology. *If theological ideas prove to have a value for concrete life, they will be true, for pragmatism, in the sense of being good for so much. For how much more they are true, will depend entirely on their relations to the other truths that also have to be acknowledged.*

What I said just now about the Absolute of transcendental idealism, is a case in point. First, I called it majestic and said it yielded religious comfort to a class of minds, and then I accused it of remoteness and sterility. But so far as it affords such comfort, it surely is not sterile; it has that amount of value; it performs a concrete function. As a good pragmatist, I myself ought to call the Absolute true 'in so far forth,' then; and I unhesitatingly now do so.

But what does *true in so far forth* mean in this case? To answer, we need only apply the pragmatic method. What do believers in the Absolute mean by saying that their belief affords them comfort? They mean that since, in the Absolute finite evil is 'overruled' already, we may, therefore, whenever we wish, treat the temporal as if it were potentially the eternal, be sure that we can trust its outcome, and, without sin, dismiss our fear and drop the worry of our finite responsibility. In short, they mean that we have a right ever and anon to take a moral holiday, to let the world wag in its own way, feeling that its issues are in better hands than ours and are none of our business.

The universe is a system of which the individual members may relax their anxieties occasionally, in which the don't-care mood is also right for men, and moral holidays in order,—that, if I mistake not, is part, at least, of what the Absolute is 'known-as,' that is the great difference in our particular experiences which his being true makes, for us, that is his cash-value when he is pragmatically interpreted. Farther than that the ordinary lay-reader in philosophy who thinks favorably of absolute idealism does not venture to sharpen his conceptions. He can use the Absolute for so much, and so much is very precious. He is pained at hearing you speak incredulously of the Absolute, therefore, and disregards your criticisms because they deal with aspects of the conception that he fails to follow.

If the Absolute means this, and means no more than this, who can possibly deny the truth of it? To deny it would be to insist that men should never relax, and that holidays are never in order.

I am well aware how odd it must seem to some of you to hear me say that an idea is 'true' so long as to believe it is profitable to our lives. That it is *good*, for as much as it profits, you will gladly admit. If what we do by its aid is good, you will allow the idea itself to be good in so far forth, for we are the better for possessing it. But is it not a strange misuse of the word 'truth,' you will say, to call ideas also 'true' for this reason?

To answer this difficulty fully is impossible at this stage of my account. . . . Let me now say only this, that truth is *one species of good*, and not, as is usually supposed, a category distinct from good, and coordinate with it. *The true is the name of whatever proves itself to be good in the way of belief, and good, too, for definite, assignable reasons.* Surely you must admit this, that if there were *no* good for life in true ideas, or if the knowledge of them were positively disadvantageous and false ideas the only useful ones, then the current notion that truth is divine and precious, and its pursuit a duty, could never have grown up or become a dogma. In a world like that, our duty would be to *shun* truth, rather. But in this world, just as certain foods are not only agreeable to our taste, but good for our teeth, our stomach, and our tissues; so certain ideas are not only agreeable to think about, or agreeable as supporting other ideas that we are fond of, but they are also helpful in life's practical struggles. If there be any life that it is really better we should lead, and if there be any idea which, if believed in, would help us to lead that life, then it would be really *better for us* to believe in that idea, *unless, indeed, belief in it incidentally clashed with other greater vital benefits*.

'What would be better for us to believe'! This sounds very like a definition of truth. It comes very near to saying 'what we *ought* to believe': and in *that* definition none of you would find any oddity. Ought we ever not to believe what it is *better for us* to believe? And can we then keep the notion of what is better for us, and what is true for us, permanently apart?

Pragmatism says no, and I fully agree with her. Probably you also agree, so far as the abstract statement goes, but with a suspicion that if we practically did believe everything that made for good in our own personal lives, we should be found indulging all kinds of fancies about this world's affairs, and all kinds of sentimental superstitions about a world hereafter. Your suspicion here is undoubtedly well founded, and it is evident that something happens when you pass from the abstract to the concrete that complicates the situation.

I said just now that what is better for us to believe is true *unless the belief incidentally clashes with some other vital benefit.* Now in real life what vital benefits is any particular belief of ours most liable to clash with? What indeed except the vital benefits yielded by *other beliefs* when these prove incompatible with the first ones? In other words, the greatest enemy of any one of our truths may be the rest of our truths. Truths have once for all this desperate instinct of self-preservation and of desire to extinguish whatever contradicts them. My belief in the Absolute, based on the good it does me, must run the gauntlet of all my other beliefs. Grant that it may be true in giving me a moral holiday. Nevertheless, as I conceive it,—and let me speak now confidentially, as it were, and merely in my own private person,—it clashes with other truths of mine whose benefits I hate to give up on its account. It happens to be associated with a kind of logic of which I am the enemy, I find that it entangles me in metaphysical paradoxes that are inacceptable, etc., etc. But as I have enough trouble in life already without adding the trouble of carrying these intellectual inconsistencies, I personally just give up the Absolute. I just *take* my moral holidays; or else as a professional philosopher, I try to justify them by some other principle.

If I could restrict my notion of the Absolute to its bare holiday-giving value, it wouldn't clash with my other truths. But we can not easily thus restrict our hypotheses. They carry supernumerary features, and these it is that clash so. My disbelief in the Absolute means then disbelief in those other supernumerary features, for I fully believe in the legitimacy of taking moral holidays.

You see by this what I meant when I called pragmatism a mediator and reconciler and said, borrowing the word from Papini, that she 'unstiffens' our theories. She has in fact no prejudices whatever, no obstructive dogmas, no rigid canons of what shall count as proof. She is completely genial. She will entertain any hypothesis, she will consider any evidence. It follows that in the religious field she is at a great disadvantage both over positivistic empiricism, with its anti-theological bias, and over religious rationalism, with its exclusive interest in the remote, the noble, the simple, and the abstract in the way of conception.

In short, she widens the field of search for God. Rationalism sticks to logic and the empyrean. Empiricism sticks to the external senses. Pragmatism is willing to take anything, to follow either logic or the senses and to count the humblest and most personal experiences. She will count mystical experiences if they have practical consequences. She will take a God who lives in the very dirt of private fact—if that should seem a likely place to find him.

Her only test of probable truth is what works best in the way of leading us, what fits every part of life best and combines with the collectivity of experience's demands, nothing being omitted. If theological ideas should do this, if the notion of God, in particular, should prove to do it, how could pragmatism possibly deny God's existence? She could see no meaning in treating as 'not true' a notion that was pragmatically so successful. What other kind of truth could there be, for her, than all this agreement with concrete reality?

. . . But you see already how democratic she [pragmatism] is. Her manners are as various and flexible, her resources as rich and endless, and her conclusions as friendly as those of mother nature.

—1907

7
The Will to Believe
William James

One of James's most famous and important essays, "The Will to Believe" represents his attempt to articulate the crisis of religious belief for a modern popular audience. In the essay, he attempts to explain and justify a belief in God for an age that was increasingly characterized by radical disbelief and cynicism. However, the essay really engages the whole question of why and how any individual should espouse and act upon moral and humanistic beliefs. James squarely faced the isolation and terror and loneliness at the core of human existence and came away believing that the individual moral imagination could meet the challenge of such existential guilt.

In the recently published Life by Leslie Stephen of his brother, Fitz-James, there is an account of a school to which the latter went when he was a boy. The teacher, a certain Mr. Guest, used to converse with his pupils in this wise: "Gurney, what is the difference between justification and sanctification?—Stephen, prove the omnipotence of God!" etc. In the midst of our Harvard freethinking and indifference we are prone to imagine that here at your good old orthodox College conversation continues to be somewhat upon this order; and to show you that we at Harvard have not lost all interest in these vital subjects, I have brought with me to-night, something like a sermon on justification by faith to read to you,—I mean an essay in justification *of* faith, a defence of our right to adopt a believing attitude in religious matters, in spite of the fact that our merely logical intellect may not have been coerced. "The Will to Believe," accordingly, is the title of my paper.

I have long defended to my own students the lawfulness of voluntarily adopted faith; but as soon as they have got well imbued with the logical spirit, they have as a rule refused to admit my contention to be lawful philosophically, even though in point of fact they were personally all the time chock-full of some faith or other themselves. I am all the while, however, so profoundly convinced that my own position is correct, that your invitation has seemed to me a good occasion to make my statements more clear. Perhaps your minds will be more open than those with which I have hitherto had to deal. I will be as little technical as I can, though I must begin by setting up some technical distinctions that will help us in the end.

I

Let us give the name of *hypothesis* to anything that may be proposed to our belief; and just as the electricians speak of live and dead wires, let us speak of any hypothesis as either *live* or *dead*. A live hypothesis is one which appeals as a real possibility to him to whom it is proposed. If I ask you to believe in the Mahdi, the notion makes no electric connection with your nature,—it refuses to scintillate with any credibility at all. As an hypothesis it is completely dead. To an Arab, however (even if he be not one of the Mahdi's followers), the hypothesis is among the mind's possibilities; it is alive. This shows that deadness and liveness in an hypothesis are not intrinsic properties, but relations to the individual thinker. They are measured by his willingness to act. The maximum of liveness in an hypothesis means willingness to get irrevocably. Practically that means belief; but there is some believing tendency wherever there is willingness to act at all.

Next, let us call the decision between two hypotheses an *option*. Options may be of several kinds. They may be—1, *living or dead;* 2, *forced or avoidable;* 3, *momentous or trivial;* and for our purposes we may call an option a *genuine* option when it is of the forced, living , and momentous kind.

1. A living option is one in which both hypotheses are live ones. If I say to you: "Be a theosophist or be a Mohammedan," it is probably a dead option, because for you neither hypothesis is likely to be alive. But if I say: "Be an agnostic or be a Christian," it is otherwise: trained as you are, each hypothesis makes some appeal, however small, to your belief.

2. Next, if I say to you: "Choose between going out with your umbrella or without it," I do not offer you a genuine option, for it is not forced. You can easily avoid it by not going out at all. Similarly, if I say, "Either love me or hate me," "Either call my theory true or call it false," your option is avoidable. You may remain indifferent to me, neither loving nor hating, and you may decline to offer any judgment as to my theory. But if I say, "Either accept this truth or go without it," I put on you a forced option, for there is no standing place outside of the alternative. Every dilemma based on a complete logical disjunction, with no possibility of not choosing, is an option of this forced kind.

3. Finally, if I were Dr. Nansen and proposed to you to join my North Pole expedition, your option would be momentous; for this would probably be your only similar opportunity, and your choice now would either exclude you from the North Pole sort of immortality altogether or put at least the chance of it into your hands. He who refuses to embrace a unique opportunity loses the prize as surely as if he tried and failed, *Per contra,* the option is trivial when the opportunity is not unique, when the stake is insignificant, or when the decision is reversible if it later prove unwise. Such trivial options abound in the scientific life. A chemist finds an hypothesis live enough to spend a year in its verification: he believes in it to that extent. But if his experiments prove inconclusive either way, he is quit for his loss of time, no vital harm being done.

It will facilitate our discussion if we keep all these distinctions well in mind.

II

The next matter to consider is the actual psychology of human opinion. When we look at certain facts, it seems as if our passional and volitional nature lay at the root of all our convictions. When we look at others, it seems as if they could do nothing when the intellect had once said its say. Let us take the latter facts up first.

Does it not seem preposterous on the very face of it to talk of our opinions being modifiable at will? Can our will either help or hinder our intellect in its perceptions of truth? Can, we, by just willing it, believe that Abraham Lincoln's existence is a myth, and that the portraits of him in McClure's Magazine are all of some one else? Can we, by any effort of our will, or by an strength of wish that it were true, believe ourselves well and about when we are roaring with rheumatism in bed, or feel certain that the sum of the two one-dollar bills in our pocket must be a hundred dollars?

We can *say* any of these things, but we are absolutely impotent to believe them; and of just such things is the whole fabric of the truths that we do believe in made up,—matters of fact, immediate or remote, as Hume said, and relations between ideas, which are either there or not there for us if we see them so, and which if not there cannot be put there by any action of our own.

In Pascal's *Thoughts* there is a celebrated passage known in literature as Pascal's wager. In it he tries to force us into Christianity by reasoning as if our concern with truth resembled our concern with the stakes in a game of chance. Translated freely his words are these: You must either believe or not believe that God is—which will you do? Your human reason cannot say. A game is going on between you and the nature of things which at the day of judgment will bring out either heads or tails. Weigh what your gains and your losses would be if you should stake all you have on heads, or God's existence: if you win in such case, you gain eternal beatitude; if you lose, you lose nothing at all. If there were an infinity of chances, and only one for God in this wager, still you ought to stake your all on God; for though you surely risk a finite loss by this procedure, any finite loss is reasonable, even a certain one is reasonable, if there is but the possibility of infinite gain. Go, then, and take holy water, and have masses said; belief will come and stupefy your scruples,—*Cela vous fera croire et vous abêtira.* Why should you not? At bottom, what have you to lose?

You probably feel that when religious faith expresses itself thus, in the language of the gaming-table, it is put to its last trumps. Surely Pascal's own personal belief in masses and holy water had far other springs; and this celebrated page of his is but an argument for others, a last desperate snatch at a weapon against the hardness of the unbelieving heart. We feel that a faith in masses and holy water adopted wilfully after such a mechanical calculation would lack the inner soul of faith's reality; and if we were ourselves in the place of the Deity, we should probably take particular pleasure in cutting off believers of this pattern from their infinite reward. It is evident that unless there be some pre-existing tendency to believe in masses and holy water, the option offered to the will by Pascal is not a living option. Certainly no Turk ever took to masses and holy water on its account; and even to us Protestants these means of salvation seem such foregone impossibilities that Pascal's logic, invoked for them specifically, leaves us unmoved. As well might the Mahdi write to us, saying, "I am the Expected One whom God has created in his effulgence. You shall be infinitely happy if you confess me; otherwise you shall be cut off from the light of the sun. Weigh, then, your infinite gain if I am genuine against your finite sacrifice if I am not!" His logic would be that of Pascal; but he would vainly use it on us, for the hypothesis he offers us is dead. No tendency to act on it exists in us to any degree.

The talk of believing by our volition seems, then, from one point of view, simply silly. From another point of view it is worse than silly, it is vile. When one turns to the magnificent edifice of the physical sciences, and sees how it was reared; what thousands of disinterested moral lives of men lie buried in its mere foundations; what patience and postponement, what choking down of preference, what submission to the icy laws of outer fact are wrought into its very stones and mortar; how absolutely impersonal it stands in its vast augustness,—then how besotted and contemptible seems every little sentimentalist who comes blowing his voluntary smoke-wreaths, and pretending to decide things from out of his private dream! Can we wonder if those bred in the rugged and manly school of science should feel like spewing such subjectivism out of their mouths? The whole system of loyalties which grow up in the schools of science go dead against its toleration; so that it is only natural that those who have caught the scientific fever should pass over to the opposite extreme, and write sometimes as if the incorruptibly truthful intellect ought positively to prefer bitterness and unacceptableness to the heart in its cup.

> It fortifies my soul to know
> That, though I perish, Truth is so—

sings Clough, while Huxley exclaims: "My only consolation lies in the reflection that, however bad our posterity may become, so far as they hold by the plain rule of not pretending to believe what they have no reason to believe, because it may be to their advantage so to pretend [the word 'pretend' is surely here redundant], they will not have reached the lowest depth of immortality." And that delicious *enfant terrible* Clifford writes: "Belief is desecrated when given to unproved and unquestioned statements for the solace and private pleasure of the believer.... Whoso would deserve well of his fellows in this matter will guard the purity of his belief with a very fanaticism of jealous care, lest at any time it should rest on an unworthy object, and catch a stain which can never be wiped away.... If [a] belief has been accepted on insufficient evidence [even though the belief be true, as Clifford on the same page explains] the pleasure is a stolen one.... It is sinful because it is stolen in defiance of our duty to mankind. That duty is to guard ourselves from such beliefs as from a pestilence which may shortly muster our own body and then spread to the rest of the town.... It is wrong always, everywhere, and for every one, to believe anything upon insufficient evidence."

III

All of this strikes one as healthy, even when expressed, as by Clifford, with somewhat too much of robustious pathos in the voice. Free-will and simple wishing do seem, in the matter of our credences, to be only fifth wheels to the coach. Yet if any one should thereupon assume that intellectual insight is what remains after wish and will and sentimental preferences have taken wing, or that pure reason is what then settles our opinions, he would fly quite as directly in the teeth of the facts.

It is only our already dead hypothesis that our willing nature is unable to bring to life again. But what has made them dead for us is for the most part a previous action of our willing nature of an antagonistic kind. When I say "willing nature," I do not mean only such deliberate volitions as may have set up habits of belief that we cannot now escape from,—I mean all such factors of belief as fear and hope, prejudice and passion, imitation and partisanship, the circumpressure of our caste and set. As a matter of fact we find ourselves believing, we hardly know how or why. Mr. Balfour gives the name of "authority" to all those influences, born of the intellectual climate, that make hypotheses possible or impossible for us, alive or dead. Here in this room, we all of us believe in molecules and the conservation of energy, in democracy and necessary progress, in Protestant Christianity and the duty of fighting for "the doctrine of the immortal Monroe," all for no reasons worthy of the name. We see into these matters with no more inner clearness, and probably with much less, than any disbeliever in them might possess. His unconventionality would probably have some grounds to show for its conclusions; but for us, not insight, but the *prestige* of the opinions, is what makes the spark shoot from them and light up our sleeping magazines of faith. Our reason is quite satisfied, in nine hundred and ninety-nine cases out of every thousand of us, if it can find a few arguments that will do to recite in case our credulity is criticized by some one else. Our faith is faith in some one else's faith, and in the greatest matters this is most the case. Our belief in truth itself, for instance, that there is a truth, and that our minds and it are made for each other,—what is it but a passionate affirmation of desire, in which our social system backs us up? We want to have a truth; we want to believe that our experiments and studies and discussions must put us in a continually better and better position towards it; and on this line we agree to fight out our thinking lives. But if a pyrrhonistic sceptic asks us *how we know* all this, can our logic find a reply? No! certainly it cannot. It is just one volition against another,—we willing to go in for life upon a trust or assumption which he, for his part, does not care to make.

As a rule we disbelieve all facts and theories for which we have no use. Clifford's cosmic emotions find no use for Christian feelings. Huxley belabors the bishops because there is no use for sacerdotalism in his scheme of life. Newman, on the contrary, goes over to Romanism, and finds all sorts of reasons good for staying there, because a priestly system is for him an organic need and delight. Why do so few "scientists" even look at the evidence for telepathy, so called? Because they think, as a leading biologist, now dead, once said to me, that even if such a thing were true, scientists ought to band together to keep it suppressed and concealed. It would undo the uniformity of Nature and all sorts of other things without which scientists cannot carry on their pursuits. But if this very man had been shown something which as a scientist he might *do* with telepathy, he might not only have examined the evidence, but even have found it good enough. This very law which the logicians would impose upon us—if I may give the name of logicians to those who would rule out our willing nature here—is based on nothing but their own natural wish to exclude all elements for which they, in their professional quality of logicians, can find no use.

Evidently, then, our non-intellectual nature does influence our convictions. There are passional tendencies and volitions which run before and others which come after belief, and it is only the latter that are too late for the fair; and they are not too late when the previous passional work has been already in their own direction. Pascal's argument, instead of being powerless, then seems a regular clincher, and is the last stroke needed to make our faith in masses and holy water complete. The state of things is evidently far from simple; and pure insight and logic, whatever they might do ideally are not the only things that really do produce our creeds.

IV

Our next duty, having recognized this mixed-up state of affairs, is to ask whether it be simply reprehensible and pathological, or whether, on the contrary, we must treat it as a normal element in making up our minds. The thesis I defend is, briefly stated, this: *Our passional nature not only lawfully may, but must, decide an option between propositions, whenever it is a genuine option that cannot by its nature be decided on intellectual grounds; for to say, under such circumstances, "Do not decide, but leave the question open," is itself a passional decision,—just like deciding yes or no,—and is attended with the same risk of losing the truth.* The thesis thus abstractly expressed will, I trust, soon become quite clear. But I must first indulge in a bit more of preliminary work.

V

It will be observed that for the purposes of this discussion we are on "dogmatic" ground,—ground, I mean, which leaves systematic philosophical scepticism altogether out of account. The postulate that there is truth, and that it is the destiny of our minds to attain it, we are deliberately resolving to make, though the sceptic will not make it. We part company with him, therefore, absolutely, at this point. But the faith that truth exists, and that our minds can find it may be held in two ways. We may talk of the *empiricist* way and of the *absolutist* way of believing in truth. The absolutists in this matter say that we not only can attain to knowing truth, but we can *know when* we have attained to knowing it; while the empiricists think that although we may attain it, we cannot infallibly know when. To *know* is one thing, and to know for certain *that* we know is another. One may hold to the first being possible without the second; hence the empiricists and the absolutists, although neither of them is a sceptic in the usual philosophic sense of the term, show very different degrees of dogmatism in their lives.

If we look at the history of opinions, we see that the empiricist tendency has largely prevailed in science, while in philosophy the absolutist tendency has had everything its own way. The characteristic sort of happiness, indeed, which philosophies yield has mainly consisted in the conviction felt by each successive school or system that by it bottom-certitude has been attained. "Other philosophies are collections of opinions, mostly false; *my* philosophy gives standing-ground forever,"—who does not recognize in this the key-note of every system worthy of the name? A system, to be a system at all, must come as a *closed* system, reversible in this or that detail, perchance, but in its essential features never!

Scholastic orthodoxy, to which one must always go when one wishes to find perfectly clear statement, has beautifully elaborated this absolutist conviction in a doctrine which it calls that of "objective evidence." If, for example, I am unable to doubt that I now exist before you, that two is less than three, or that if all men are mortal then I am mortal too, it is because these things illumine my intellect irresistibly. The final ground of this objective evidence possessed by certain propositions is the *adæquatio intellectûs nostri cum rê*. The certitude it brings involves an *aptitudimem ad extorquendum certum assensum* on the part of the truth envisaged, and on the side of the subject a *quietum in cognitione,* when once the object is mentally received, that leaves no possibility of doubt behind; and in the whole transaction nothing operates but the *entitas ipsa* of the object and the *entitas ipsa* of the mind. We slouchy modern thinkers dislike to talk in Latin,—indeed, we dislike to talk in set terms at all; but at bottom our own state of mind is very much like this whenever we uncritically abandon ourselves: You believe in objective evidence, and I do. Of some things we feel that we are certain: we know, and we know that we do know. There is something that gives a click inside of us, a bell that strikes twelve, when the hands of our mental clock have swept the dial and meet over the meridian hour. The greatest empiricists among us are only empiricists on reflection: when left to their instincts, they dogmatize like infallible popes. When the Cliffords tell us how sinful it is to be Christians on such "insufficient evidence," insufficiency is really the last thing they have in mind. For them the evidence is absolutely sufficient, only it makes the other way. They believe so completely in an anti-christian order of the universe that there is no living option: Christianity is a dead hypothesis from the start.

VI

But now, since we are all such absolutists by instinct, what in our quality of students of philosophy ought we do about the fact? Shall we espouse and indorse it? Or shall we treat it as a weakness of our nature from which we must free ourselves, if we can?

I sincerely believe that the latter course is the only one we can follow as reflective men. Objective evidence and certitude are doubtless very fine ideals to play with, but where on this moonlit and dream-visited planet are they found? I am, therefore, myself a complete empiricist so far as my theory of human knowledge goes. I live, to be sure, by the practical faith that we must go on experiencing and thinking over our experience, for only thus can our opinions grow more true; but to hold any one of them—I absolutely do not care which—as if it never could be reinterpretable or corrigible, I believe to be a tremendously mistaken attitude, and I think that the whole history of philosophy will bear me out. There is but one indefectibly certain truth, and that is the truth that pyrrhonistic scepticism itself leaves standing,—the truth that the present phenomenon of consciousness exists. That, however, is the bare starting-point of knowledge, the mere admission of a stuff to be philosophical about. The various philosophies are but so many attempts at expressing what this stuff really is. And if we repair to our libraries what disagreement do we discover! Where is a certainly true answer found? Apart from abstract propositions of comparison (such as two and two are the same as four), propositions which tell us nothing by themselves about concrete reality, we find no proposition ever regarded by any one as evidently certain that has not either been called a falsehood, or at least had its truth sincerely questioned by some one else. The transcending of the axioms of geometry, not in play but in earnest, by certain of our contemporaries (as Zöllner and Charles H. Hinton), and the rejection of the whole Aristotelian logic by the Hegelians, are striking instances in point.

No concrete test of what is really true has ever been agreed upon. Some make the criterion external to the moment of perception, putting it either in revelation, the *consensus gentium,* the instincts of the heart, or the systematized experience of the race. Others make the perceptive moment its own test,—Descartes, for instance, with his clear and distinct ideas guaranteed by the veracity of God; Reid with his "common-sense"; and Kant with his forms of synthetic judgment *a priori.* The inconceivability of the opposite; the capacity to be verified by sense; the possession of complete organic unity or self-relation, realized when a thing is its own other,—are standards which, in turn, have been used. The much lauded objective evidence is never triumphantly there; it is a mere aspiration or *Grenzbegriff,* marking the infinitely remote ideal of our thinking life. To claim that certain truths now possess it, is simply to say that when you think them true and they *are* true, then their evidence is objective, otherwise it is not. But practically one's conviction that the evidence one goes by is of the real objective brand, is only one more subjective opinion added to the lot. For what a contradictory array of opinions have objective evidence and absolute certitude been claimed! The world is rational through and through,—its existence is an ultimate brute fact; there is a personal God,—a personal God is inconceivable; there is an extra-mental physical world immediately known,—the mind can only know its own ideas; a moral imperative exists,—obligation is only the resultant of desires; a permanent spiritual principle is in every one,—there are only shifting states of mind; there is an endless chain of causes,—there is an absolute first cause; an eternal necessity;—a freedom; a purpose,—no purpose; a primal One,—a primal —any; a universal continuity,—an essential discontinuity in things; an infinity,—no infinity. There is this,—there is indeed nothing which some one has not thought absolutely true, while his neighbor deemed it absolutely false; and not an absolutist among them seems ever to have considered that the trouble may all the time be essential, and that the intellect, even with truth directly in its grasp, may have no infallible signal for knowing whether it be truth or no. When, indeed, one remembers that the most striking practical application to life of the doctrine of objective certitude has been the conscientious labors of the Holy Office of the Inquisition, one feels less tempted than ever to lend the doctrine a respectful ear.

But please observe, now, that when as empiricists we give up the doctrine of objective certitude, we do not thereby give up the quest or hope of truth itself. We still pin our faith on its existence, and still believe that we gain an ever better position towards it by systematically continuing to roll up experiences and think. Our great difference from the scholastic lies in the way we face. The strength of his system lies in the principles, the origin, the *terminus a quo* of his thought; for us the strength is in the outcome, the upshot, the *terminus ad quem.* Not where it comes from but what it leads to is to decide. It matters not to an empiricist from what quarter an hypothesis may come to him: he may have acquired it by fair means or by foul; passion may have whispered or accident suggested it; but if the total drift of thinking continues to confirm it, that is what he means by its being true.

VII

One more point, small but important, and our preliminaries are done. There are two ways of looking at our duty in the matter of opinion,—ways entirely different, and yet ways about whose difference the theory of knowledge seems hitherto to have shown very little concern. *We must know the truth;* and *we must avoid error,*—these are our first and great commandments as would-be knowers; but they are not two ways of stating an identical commandment, they are two separable laws. Although it may indeed happen that when we believe the truth A, we escape as an incidental consequence from believing the falsehood B, it hardly ever happens that by merely disbelieving B we necessarily believe A. We may in escaping B fall into believing other falsehoods, C or D, just as bad as B; or we may escape B by not believing anything at all, not even A.

Believe truth! Shun error!—these, we see, are two materially different laws; and by choosing between them we may end by coloring differently our whole intellectual life. We may regard the chase for truth as paramount, and the avoidance of error as secondary; or we may, on the other hand, treat the avoidance of error as more imperative, and let truth take its chance. Clifford, in the instructive passage which I have quoted, exhorts us to the latter course. Believe nothing, he tells us, keep your mind in suspense forever, rather than by closing it on insufficient evidence incur the awful risk of believing lies. You, on the other hand, may think that the risk of being in error is a very small matter when compared with the blessings of real knowledge, and be ready to be duped many times in your investigation rather than postpone indefinitely the chance of guessing true. I myself find it impossible to go with Clifford. We must remember that these feelings of our duty about either truth or error are in any case only expressions of our passional life. Biologically considered, our minds are as ready to grind out falsehood as veracity, and he who says, "Better go without belief forever than believe a lie!" merely shows his own preponderant private horror of becoming a dupe. He may be critical of many of his desires and fears, but this fear he slavishly obeys. He cannot imagine any one questioning its binding force. For my own part, I have also a horror of being duped; but I can believe that worse things than being duped may happen to a man in this world: so Clifford's exhortation has to my ears a thoroughly fantastic sound. It is like a general informing his soldiers that it is better to keep out of battle forever than to risk a single wound. Not so are victories either over enemies or over nature gained. Our errors are surely not such awfully solemn things. In a world where we are so certain to incur them in spite of all our caution, a certain lightness of heart seems healthier than this excessive nervousness on their behalf. At any rate, it seems the fittest thing for the empiricist philosopher.

VIII

And now, after all this introduction, let us go straight at our question. I have said, and now repeat it, that not only as a matter of fact do we find our passional nature influencing us in our opinions, but that there are some options between opinions in which this influence must be regarded both as an inevitable and as a lawful determinant of our choice.

I fear here that some of you my hearers will begin to scent danger, and lend an inhospitable ear. Two first steps of passion you have indeed had to admit as necessary,—we must think so as to avoid dupery, and we must think so as to gain truth; but the surest path to those ideal consummations, you will probably consider, is from now onwards to take no further passional step.

Well, of course, I agree as far as the facts will allow. Wherever the option between losing truth and gaining it is not momentous, we can throw the chance of *gaining truth* away, and at any rate save ourselves from any chance of *believing falsehood,* by not making up our minds at all till objective evidence has come. In scientific questions, this is almost always the case; and even in human affairs in general, the need of acting is seldom so urgent that a false belief to act on is better than no belief at all. Law courts, indeed, have to decide on the best evidence attainable for the moment, because a judge's duty is to make law as well as to ascertain it, and (as a learned judge once said to me) few cases are worth spending much time over: the great thing is to have them decided on *any* acceptable principle, and got out of the way. But in our dealings with objective nature we obviously are recorders, not makers, of the truth; and decisions for the mere sake of deciding promptly and getting on to the next business would be wholly out of place. Throughout the breadth of physical nature facts are what they are quite independently of us, and seldom is there any such hurry about them that the risks of being duped by believing a premature theory need be faced. The questions here are always trivial options, the hypotheses are hardly living (at any rate not living for us spectators), the choice between believing truth or falsehood is seldom forced. The attitude of sceptical balance is therefore the absolutely wise one if we would escape mistakes. What difference, indeed, does it make to most of us whether we have or have not a theory of the Röntgen rays, whether we believe or not in mind-stuff, or have a conviction about the causality of conscious states? It makes no difference. Such options are not forced on us. On every account it is better not to make them, but still keep weighing reasons *pro et contra* with an indifferent hand.

I speak, of course, here of the purely judging mind. For purposes of discovery such indifference is to be less highly recommended, and science would be far less advanced than she is if the passionate desires of individuals to get their own faiths confirmed had been kept out of the game. See for example the sagacity which Spencer and Weismann now display. On the other hand, if you want an absolute duffer in an investigation, you must, after all, take the man who has no interest whatever in its results: he is the warranted incapable the positive fool. The most useful investigator, because the most sensitive observer, is always he whose eager interest in one side of the question is balanced by an equally keen nervousness lest he become deceived. Science has organized this nervousness into a regular *technique,* her so-called method of verification; and she has fallen so deeply in love with the method that one may even say she has ceased to care for truth by itself at all. It is only truth as technically verified that interests her. The truth of truths might come in merely affirmative form, and she would decline to touch it. Such truth as that, she might repeat with Clifford, would be stolen in defiance of her duty to mankind. Human passions, however, are stronger than technical rules. "Le cœur a ses raisons," as Pascal says, "que la raison ne connaît pas"; and however indifferent to all but the bare rules of the game the umpire, the abstract intellect, may be, the concrete players who furnish him the materials to judge of are usually, each one of them, in love with some pet "live hypothesis" of his own. Let us agree, however, that wherever there is no forced option, the dispassionately judicial intellect with no pet hypothesis, saving us, as it does, from dupery at any rate, ought to be our ideal.

The question next arises: Are there not somewhere forced options in our speculative questions, and can we (as men who may be interested at least as much in positively gaining truth as in merely escaping dupery) always wait with impunity till the coercive evidence shall have arrived? It seems *a priori* improbable that the truth should be so nicely adjusted to our needs and powers as that. In the great boarding-house of nature, the cakes and the butter and the syrup seldom come out so even and leave the plates so clean. Indeed, we should view them with scientific suspicion if they did.

IX

Moral questions immediately present themselves as questions whose solution cannot wait for sensible proof. A moral question is a question not of what sensibly exists, but of what is good, or would be good if it did exist. Science can tell us what exists; but to compare the *worths*, both of what exists and of what does not exist, we must consult not science, but what Pascal calls our heart. Science herself consults her heart when she lays it down that the infinite ascertainment of fact and correction of false belief are the supreme goods for man. Challenge the statement, and science can only repeat it oracularly, or else prove it by showing that such ascertainment and correction bring man all sorts of other goods which man's heart in turn declares. The question of having moral beliefs at all or not having them is decided by our will. Are our moral preferences true of false, or are they only odd biological phenomena, making things good or bad for *us,* but in themselves indifferent? How can your pure intellect decide? If your heart does not *want* a world of moral reality, your head will assuredly never make you believe in one. Mephistophelian scepticism, indeed, will satisfy the head's play-instincts much better than any rigorous idealism can. Some men (even at the student age) are so naturally cool-hearted that the moralistic hypothesis never has for them any pungent life, and in their supercilious presence the hot young moralist always feels strangely ill at ease. The appearance of knowingness is on their side, of *naïveté* and gullibility on his. Yet, in the inarticulate heart of him, he clings to it that he is not a dupe, and that there is a realm in which (as Emerson says) all their wit and intellectual superiority is not better than the cunning of a fox. Moral scepticism can no more be refuted or proved by logic than intellectual scepticism can. When we stick to it that there *is* truth (be it of either kind), we do so with our whole nature, and resolve to stand or fall by the results. The sceptic with his whole nature adopts the doubting attitude; but which of us is the wiser, Omniscience only knows.

Turn now from these wide questions of good to a certain class of questions of fact, questions concerning personal relations, states of mind between one man and another. *Do you like me or not?*—for example. Whether you do or not depends, in countless instances, on whether I meet you half-way, am willing to assume that you must like me, and show you trust and expectation. The previous faith on my part in your liking's existence is in such cases what makes your liking come. But if I stand aloof, and refuse to budge an inch until I have objective evidence, until you shall have done something apt, as the absolutists say, *ad extorquendum assensum meum,* ten to one your liking never comes. How many women's hearts are vanquished by the mere sanguine insistence of some man that they *must* love him! he will not consent to the hypothesis that they cannot. The desire for a certain kind of truth here brings about that special truth's existence; and so it is in innumerable cases of other sorts. Who gains promotions, boons, appointments, but the man in whose life they are seen to play the part of live hypotheses, who discounts them, sacrifices other things for their sake before they have come, and takes risks for them in advance? His faith acts on the powers above him as a claim, and creates its own verification.

A social organism of any sort whatever, large or small, is what it is because each member proceeds to his own duty with a trust that the other members will simultaneously do theirs. Wherever a desired result is achieved by the co-operation of many independent persons, its existence as a fact is a pure consequence of the precursive faith in one another of those immediately concerned. A government, an army, a commercial system, a ship, a college, an athletic team, all exist on this condition, without which not only is nothing achieved, but nothing is even attempted. A whole train of passengers (individually brave enough) will be looted by a few highwaymen, simply because the latter can count on one another, while each passenger fears that if he makes a movement of resistance, he will be shot before any one else backs him up. If we believed that the whole carfull would rise at once with us, we should each severally rise, and train-robbing would never even be attempted. There are, then, cases where a fact cannot come at all unless a preliminary faith exists in its coming. *And where faith in a fact can help create the fact,* that would be an insane logic which should say that faith running ahead of scientific evidence is the ''lowest kind of immorality'' into which a thinking being can fall. Yet such is the logic by which our scientific absolutists pretend to regulate our lives!

X

In truths dependent on our personal action, then, faith based on desire is certainly a lawful and possibly an indispensable thing.

But now, it will be said, these are all childish human cases, and have nothing to do with great cosmical matters, like the question of religious faith. Let us then pass on to that. Religions differ so much in their accidents that in discussing the religious question we must make it very generic and broad. What then do we mean by the religious hypothesis? Science says things are; morality says some things are better than other things; and religion says essentially two things.

First, she says that the best things are the more eternal things, the overlapping things, the things in the universe that throw the last stone, so to speak, and say the final word. ''Perfection is eternal,''—this phrase of Charles Secrétan seems a good way of putting this first affirmation of religion, an affirmation which obviously cannot yet be verified scientifically at all.

The second affirmation of religion is that we are better off even now if we believe her first affirmation to be true.

Now, let us consider what the logical elements of this situation are *in case the religious hypothesis in both its branches be really true.* (Of course, we must admit that possibility at the outset. If we are to discuss the question at all, it must involve a living option. If for any of you religion be a hypothesis that cannot, by any living possibility be true, then you need go no farther. I speak to the ''saving remnant'' alone.) So proceeding, we see, first that religion offers itself as a *momentous* option. We are supposed to gain, even now, by our belief, and to lose by our non-belief, a certain vital good. Secondly, religion is a *forced* option, so far as that good goes. We cannot escape the issue by remaining sceptical and waiting for more light, because, although we do avoid error in that way *if religion be untrue,* we lose the good, *if it be true,* just as certainly as if we positively chose to disbelieve. It is as if a man should hesitate indefinitely to ask a certain woman to marry him because he was not perfectly sure that she would prove an angel after he brought her home. Would he not cut himself off from that particular angel-possibility as decisively as if he went and married some one else? Scepticism, then, is not avoidance of option; it is option of a certain particular kind of risk. *Better risk loss of truth than chance of error,*—that is your faith-vetoer's exact position. He is actively playing his stake as much as the believer is; he is backing the field against the religious hypothesis, just as the believer is backing the religious hypothesis against the field. To preach scepticism to us as a duty until ''sufficient evidence'' for religion be found, is tantamount therefore to telling us, when in presence of the religious hypothesis, that to yield to our fear of its being error is wiser and better than to yield to our hope that it may be true. It is not intellect against all passions, then; it is only intellect with one passion laying down its law. And by what, forsooth, is the supreme wisdom of this passion warranted? Dupery for dupery, what proof is there that dupery through hope is so much worse than dupery through fear? I, for one, can see no proof; and I simply refuse obedience to the scientist's command to imitate his kind of option, in a case where my own stake is important enough to give me the right to choose my own form of risk. If religion be true and the evidence for it be still insufficient, I do not wish, by putting your extinguisher upon my nature (which feels to me as if it had after all some business in this matter), to forfeit my sole chance in life of getting upon the winning side,—that chance depending, of course, on my willingness to run the risk of acting as if my passional need of taking the world religiously might be prophetic and right.

All this is on the supposition that it really may be prophetic and right, and that even to us who are discussing the matter, religion is a live hypothesis which may be true. Now, to most of us religion comes in a still further way that makes a veto on our active faith even more illogical. The more perfect and more eternal aspect of the universe is represented in our religions as having personal form. The universe is no longer a mere *It* to us, but a *Thou,* if we are religious; and any relation that may be possible from person to person might be possible here. For instance, although in one sense we are passive portions of the universe, in another we show a curious autonomy, as if we were small active centers on our own account. We feel, too, as if the appeal of religion to us were made to our own active good-will, as if evidence might be forever withheld from us unless we met the hypothesis half-way. To take a trivial illustration: just as a man who in a company of gentlemen made no advances, asked a warrant for every concession, and believed no one's word without proof, would cut himself off by such churlishness from all the social rewards that a more trusting spirit would earn,—so here, one who should shut himself up in snarling logicality and try to make the gods extort his recognition willy-nilly, or not get it at all, might cut himself off forever from his only opportunity of making the gods' acquaintance. This feeling, forced on us we know not whence, that by obstinately believing that there are gods (although not to do so would be so easy both for our logic and our life) we are doing the universe the deepest service we can, seems part of the living essence of the religious hypothesis. If the hypothesis *were* true in all its parts, including this one, then pure intellectualism, with its veto on our making willing advances, would be an absurdity: and some participation of our sympathetic nature would be logically required. I, therefore, for one, cannot see my way to accepting the agnostic rules for truth-seeking, or willfully agree to keep my willing nature out of the game. I cannot do so for this plain reason, that *a rule of thinking which would absolutely prevent me from acknowledging certain kinds of truth if those kinds of truth were really there, would be an irrational rule.* That for me is the long and short of the formal logic of the situation, no matter what the kinds of truth might materially be.

I confess I do not see how this logic can be escaped. But sad experience makes me fear that some of you may still shrink from radically saying with me, *in abstracto,* that we have the right to believe at our own risk any hypothesis that is live enough to tempt our will. I suspect, however, that if this is so, it is because you have got away from the abstract logical point of view altogether, and are thinking (perhaps without realizing it) of some particular religious hypothesis which for you is dead. The freedom to "believe what we will" you apply to the case of some patent superstition; and the faith you think of is the faith defined by the schoolboy when he said, "Faith is when you believe something that you know ain't true." I can only repeat that this is misapprehension. *In concreto,* the freedom to believe can only cover living options which the intellect of the individual cannot by itself resolve; and living options never seem absurdities to him who has them to consider. When I look at the religious question as it really puts itself to concrete men, and when I think of all the possibilities which both practically and theoretically it involves, then this command that we shall put a stopper on our heart, instincts, and courage, and *wait*—acting of course meanwhile more or less as if religion were *not* true—till doomsday, or till such time as our intellect and senses working together may have raked in evidence enough,—this command, I say, seems to me the queerest idol ever manufactured in the philosophic cave. Were we scholastic absolutists, there might be more excuse. If we had an infallible intellect with its objective certitudes, we might feel ourselves disloyal to such a perfect organ of knowledge in not trusting to it exclusively, in not waiting for its releasing word. But if we are empiricists, if we believe that no bell in us tolls to let us know for certain when truth is in our grasp, then it seems a piece of idle fantasticality to preach so solemnly our duty of waiting for the bell. Indeed we *may* wait if we will,—I hope you do not think that I am denying that,—but if we do so, we do so at our peril as much as if we believed. In either case we *act,* taking our life in our hands. No one of us ought to issue vetoes to the other, nor should we bandy words of abuse. We ought, on the contrary, delicately and profoundly to respect one another's mental freedom: then only shall we bring about the intellectual republic; then only shall we have that spirit of inner tolerance without which all our outer tolerance is soulless, and which is empiricism's glory; then only shall we live and let live, in speculative as well as in practical things.

I began by a reference to Fitz-James Stephen; let me end by a quotation from him. "What do you think of yourself? What do you think of the world? . . . These are questions with which all must deal as it seems good to them. They are riddles of the Sphinx, and in some way or other we must deal with them. . . . In all important transactions of life we have to take a leap in the dark. . . . If we decide to leave the riddles unanswered, that is a choice; if we waver in our answer, that, too, is a choice: but whatever choice we make, we make it at our peril. If a man chooses to turn his back altogether on God and the future, no one can prevent him; no one can show beyond reasonable doubt that he is mistaken. If a man thinks otherwise and acts as he thinks, I do not see that any one can prove that *he* is mistaken. Each must act as he thinks best; and if he is wrong, so much the worse for him. We stand on a mountain pass in the midst of whirling snow and blinding mist, through which we get glimpses now and then of paths which may be deceptive. If we stand still we shall be frozen to death. If we take the wrong road we shall be dashed to pieces. We do not certainly know whether there is any right one. What must we do? 'Be strong and of a good courage.' Act for the best, hope for the best, and take what comes. . . . If death ends all, we cannot meet death better."

—1897

8
The Radical Individualism of William James
A Theory of Experience and the Self for Today
Sam B. Girgus

The following essay argues that James' philosophy of radical empiricism provides an important modern foundation for democracy and individualism while also countering the tendency toward abstraction and alienation in other schools of thought. The essay comes from *The Law of the Heart: Individualism and the Modern Self in American Literature* by Sam B. Girgus (Austin and London: University of Texas Press, 1979).

The work of William James play a crucial role in the history of American individualism, especially during the past century. On this subject Frederick J. Hoffmann writes, "I think the major turning point in this history is William James' superbly detailed, yet suspiciously naive, analysis of consciousness in his *Principles of Psychology* (1890). Searching for a definition of 'self,' James there had to conclude that the self is not substantively tenable but is only a *process* of experiencing. He therefore anticipated, in his own special, indigenously well-intentioned American way, the melodrama of Jean-Paul Sartre's description of choice, freedom and responsibility.[1] However, rather than exploring this anticipation of Sartre and existentialism, Hoffmann argues that James dealt with this dilemma of a nonsubstantial self in the manner of an "antecedent of the twentieth-century romantic" who becomes forced by his refusal to surrender the idea of the self to rely upon "Victorian reassurances" of its existence and also upon "a Victorian-democratic definition of the will."[2] With his disdain for the modernist understanding of the self, Hoffman naturally reads James' ideas as something of a disaster that furthered the existential idea of the self and influenced "the imagistic-oriented literature of the 1920s."[3] For Hoffmann James' attempt to see "the ultimate character of reality" as a "willed thing" amounts to an argument for the self in terms of transcendence.[4]

Another scholar and critic, Quentin Anderson, sees James as furthering a tradition of the self whose "wide authority over reality" in American culture and literature "has a religious origin."

From Sam B. Girgus: *The Law of the Heart: Individualism and the Modern Self in American Literature*. Copyright © 1979 by the University of Texas Press, Austin, Texas, Reprinted with permission.

Anderson argues that this religious impulse toward the self resulted in the deification of such "visionary" thinkers as Emerson, Thoreau, and Whitman to the denigration of more "practical" thinkers.[5] Believing that for such visionaries "action in the world is a threat to our sense of ourselves," Anderson goes on to include both John Dewey and James as "examples of this visionary distortion of the national scene."[6] Thus, to Hoffman and Anderson the concept of self in James epitomizes the crisis of individualism and freedom in the modern age. For them James' relevance is derogatory because of their understanding of his work as the continued presentation of an isolated and diminished self. For them the themes of modernism as used by James inherently insist on the ultimate impoverishment of the self.

However, what Hoffman and Anderson see as negative aspects of James' philosophy of experience and the self, others interpret as a major breakthrough in the attempt of contradictory thought to develop a theory of democratic individualism both relevant to modern consciousness and "radical" in its faith in the capacity of the individual to deal with modern experience. To such advocates, James' work represents one of the clearest statements of individual freedom of the modern period. Thus James, to the philosopher William Barrett, "belongs to our time, he is our contemporary in the 20th century." "He speaks," Barrett continues, "to us now, I believe, more forcefully than at any time since his death in 1910."[7] For diverse others as well—Gay Wilson Allen, his biographer; John Wild, the philosopher; Rollo May, the existential psychologist—this sense of his presence is derived to a considerable extent from the originality of his direct confrontation with the very issues, themes, and language of modernism, including his refusal to rule out the possibility in "the modern tradition" of freedom and individualism.[8]

What I consider to be James' commitment to radical individualism is derived from his understanding of the empirical and individual nature of human experience. In James the basis for individuality rests, as Hoffman says, upon the process involved in the individual's way of experiencing reality in the world. James was pragmatic when it came to naming this process. He varied between calling his philosophy a wider pragmatism, radical empiricism, radical pluralism, and humanism. Each term places a different emphasis on a particular aspect of James' understanding of the process involved in the individual's relationship to experience and reality. But each term in its own way also emphasizes the individual and the concrete in experience as opposed to the abstract and the "viciously intellectual." Noting in "Monistic Idealism" that "neither abstract oneness nor abstract independence *exists,* only concrete real things exist," James contrasts his philosophy with that of rationalistic systems that attempt to find truths based on abstractions.[9] In another essay, "A World of Pure Experience," he writes: "I give the name of "radical empiricism" to my Weltanschuung. Empiricism is known as the opposite of rationalism. Rationalism tends to emphasize universals and to make wholes prior to parts in the order of logic as well as in that of being. Empiricism, on the contrary, lays the explanatory stress upon the part, the element, the individual, and treats the whole as a collection and the universal as an abstraction." To be radical, an empiricism must neither admit into its construction any element that is not directly experienced, nor exclude from them any element that is directly experienced," he writes (*ERE,* pp. 24–25).

With its concentration on real, radical, and pure experience, James' radical empiricism moves toward an open, pluralistic philosophy of the universe that makes individuals self-supporting but condemns them to insecurity and freedom within a continuing creative flux of change and experience. In "Humanism and Truth" James says, "Must not something end by supporting itself? Humanism is willing to let finite experience be self-supporting."[10] He realized, of course, that such a view runs counter not only to the desire of many for permanence but to important systems of philosophy as well. In his brilliant essay on Hegel's method, James notes that Hegel "considers that the immediate finite data of experience are 'untrue' because they are not their own others. They are negated by what is external to them. The absolute is true because it and it only has no external environment, and has attained to being its own other'' (*PU,* p. 173). James goes on to state that, if one grants Hegel's argument that "to be true a thing must in some sort be its own other, everything hinges on whether he is right in holding that the several pieces of finite experience themselves cannot be said to be in any wise *their* own others." Following Hegel's intellectualist method, James could never prove the truth of self-dependent "pieces" of "the immediate finite data of experience." He says, "When conceptually or intellectualistically treated, they of course cannot be their own others. Every abstract concept as such excludes what it doesn't include, and if such concepts are adequate substitutes for reality's concrete pulses, the latter must square themselves with intellectualistic logic, and no one of them in any sense can claim to be its own other'' (*PU,* pp. 173–174).

In his subsequent essay on Henri Bergson, however, James makes this argument about the possibility for experience to be its "own other" by changing the terms of the discussion so that the stream of experience is proffered over abstractions as a means for discovering truth. Using Bergson's work, James impugns traditional logic and conceptualization as ultimate forms of truth. "The whole process of life is due to life's violation of our logical axioms," he writes (*PU,* p. 245). He maintains that the "faculty of abstracting and fixing concepts" is a process of convenience that gives us only one kind of practical truth. "What we do in fact is to *harness up* reality in our conceptual systems in order to drive it the better," he says (*PU,* p. 238). Stating that "when we conceptualize, we cut out and fix, and exclude everything but what we have fixed," he argues that in the flow of "the real concrete sensible flux of life experiences compenetrate each other so that it is not easy to know just what is excluded and what not" (*PU,* pp. 243,244). In this flux of "direct" or "immediate" or "sensible" experience, it becomes perfectly possible then for aspects of experience to be self-supporting or, in Hegel's terms, its "own other." James writes:

> The absolute is said to perform its feats by taking up its other into itself. But that is exactly what is done when every individual morsel of the sensational stream takes up the adjacent morsels by coalescing with them. This is just what we mean by the stream's sensible continuity. No element *there* cuts itself off from any other element, as concepts cut themselves from concepts. No part *there* is so small as not to be a place of conflux. No part there is not really *next* its neighbors; which means that there is literally nothing between; which means again that no part goes exactly so far and no farther; that no part absolutely excludes another, but that they compenetrate and are cohesive; that if you tear out one, its roots bring out more with them; that whatever is real is telescoped and diffused into other reals; that, in short, every minutest thing is already its hegelian 'own other,'' in the fullest sense of the term. (*PU,* p. 252)

James' description of experience as self-sustaining within a continuous stream of experience has important implications for the idea of radical individualism. This view of experience places the individual in the middle of the action. It enables the individual to develop a creative relationship with reality through the use of what James terms the "living understanding" of the process of continuous creation within experience. "Philosophy," he says, "should seek this kind of living understanding of the movement of reality, not follow science in vainly patching together fragments of its dead results" (*PU,* p. 248). Through the process of living understanding individuals do more than respond to and reflect their environment. They become central to the process of creation itself. "What really *exists* is not things made but things in the making," he says. "Once made, they are dead, and an infinite number of alternative conceptual decompositions can be used in defining them.

But put yourself *in the making* by a stroke of intuitive sympathy with the thing and, the whole range of possible decompositions coming at once into your possession, you are no longer troubled with the question which of them is the more absolutely true" (*PU,* p. 248).

James' view of experience provides an important life-enhancing contrast with philosophies of abstraction and death. It invests new power in the individual and moves the focus of philosophy from dead objects and ideas to growth and process. At the same time, by emphasizing the individual's freedom within a wider flux of experience, it also engages the reality of finitude and death. "Somewhere," says James, "being must immediately breast nonentity."[11] Concentrating on individual freedom, finitude, and independence from external standards, the self faces its own death and limitations as part of the process of growth. Anticipating modern existentialism, as Hoffman and others say, in a way that makes him startlingly relevant to contemporary thought, James understood that many people prefer a kind of death in life in a world with absolute answers to life's problems and moral dilemmas. People often choose illusions rather than painful realities, realities requiring faith in action and themselves.

Thus, James brilliantly discerned the powerful relationship between the fear of death and the unknown and the things in which we believe. The desire to overcome death helps maintain the resilience of the hold that absolute systems of truth have on many people. Just as the perverse self, in the stories of Poe and in the existentialism of Kierkegaard and Tillich, attempts to kill death though suicide, thus escaping the threat of death, the absolutist perverts the search for truth and the nature of experience by adopting absolute systems that incorporate disagreement, negation, and the unknown. In his essay on Hegel's method, James suggests that the dialectic involves such an attempt to find a death-killing absolute. He writes:

> Formally, this scheme of an organism of truth that has already fed as it were on its own liability to death, so that, death once dead for it, there's no more dying then, is the very fulfillment of the rationalistic aspiration. That one and only whole, with all its parts involved in it, negating and making one another impossible if abstracted and taken singly, but necessitating and holding one another in place if the whole of them be taken integrally, is the literal ideal sought after; it is the very diagram and picture of that notion of *the* truth with no outlying alternative, to which nothing can be added, nor from it anything withdrawn, and all variations from which are absurd, which so dominates the human imagination (*PU,* p. 171)

Hegel's presentation of a determined and complete universe that incorporates death also eliminates for James the individual and freedom. A system that so neatly arrogates truth through abstraction also dissembles the basic process through which the individual operates "in the making" of experience and truth. For James, in the intellectual life of the mind as in the psychological domain of the self, the attempt to kill death produces sterility. From Hegel's model of the law of the heart—the perverted self in isolation from others because of the sense of moral superiority—we get to what James calls "this dumb region of the heart in which we dwell alone with our willingnesses and unwillingnesses, our faith and fears."[12] From the highly verbalistic and intellectualistic world of Hegel, we move to James' idea of an inner self of experience beyond words.

For James the humanistic understanding of experience invites a concomitant religious interpretation of experience. Instead of coming from an external absolute with divine powers, religion emerges from the experience of the self in the flow of life. Understanding aspects of experience as religious in turn feeds and strengthens the self as it contributes to the death and power of the totality of human experience. Thus, in James the religious drive remains, as Quentin Anderson says, "confided to a new temple, the self." However, instead of immobilizing us, as Anderson also claims, for James the religious impulse sustains and even makes action possible in the practical world.

In fact, this impulse serves the most practical purpose of all in providing a positive answer to the question, "Is Life Worth Living?" In the essay by that name James confesses that only a belief in his own ability to provide life with meaning and to have an impact upon life makes the pain of life bearable. He writes: "Once more it is a case of *maybe;* and once more *maybes* are the essence of the situation. I confess that I do not see why the very existence of an invisible world may not in part depend on the personal response which any one of us may make to the religious appeal. God himself, in short, may draw vital strength and increase of very being from our fidelity."[13] Thus, James argues that only faith in an invisible world of higher meaning can make such a world happen and that only through making it happen can life seem worthwhile. He calls such beliefs faiths that verify themselves. "Now, in this description of faiths that verify themselves I have assumed that our faith in an invisible order is what inspires those efforts and that patience which make this visible order good for moral men." The alternative to faith in the invisible world is the "surrender to the nightmare view" that invites pessimism and suicide. But James' own understanding of experience makes the individual responsible for such nihilism. "This life," he writes, "*is* worth living, we can say, *since it is what we make it, from the moral point of view;* and we are determined to make it from that point of view, so far as we have anything to do with it, a success."[14]

In arguing that life divorced from ethical and moral considerations becomes worthless, James further argues that religious belief enables the individual to convert a sense of isolation and desperation into a source of spiritual energy for access to a higher world of ethical meaning. For James religious humanism preserves those very qualities of personal strength and action that comprise meaningful individualism. "You see now why I have been so individualistic throughout these lectures and why I have seemed so bent on rehabilitating the element of feeling in religion and subordinating its intellectual part," he writes in *The Varieties of Religious Experience*. "Individuality is founded in feeling; and the recesses of feeling, the darker, blinder strata of character, are the only places in the world in which we catch real fact in the making, and directly perceive how events happen, and how work is actually done. Compared with this world of living individualized feelings, the world of generalized objects which the intellect contemplates is without solidity or life."[15]

James maintains that the "ideal impulses" originate in "an altogether other dimension of existence from the sensible and merely 'understandable world.'" He feels that we "belong" to this "other dimension" of experience "in a more intimate sense than that in which we belong to the visible world, for we belong in the most intimate sense wherever our ideals belong" (*VRE,* p. 506). Thus James, to use Quentin Anderson's terms, believes that the "visionary" dimension of life operates directly and immediately upon the "practical." In fact, he feels that the measure of the value of that higher life is derived from its consequences upon the individual and the way individuals act with each other. "Yet," he writes, "the unseen region in question is not merely ideal, for it produces effects in this world. When we commune with it, work is actually done upon our finite personality, for we are turned into new men, and consequences in the way of conduct follow in the natural world upon or regenerative change. But that which produces effects within another reality must be termed a reality itself, so I feel as if we had no philosophic excuse for calling the unseen or mystical world unreal" (*VRE,* pp. 506–507).

In accordance with this "thoroughly 'pragmatic' view of religion," James also argues that "God is real since he produces real effects" (*VRE,* pp. 508, 507). For James, of course, this is not the traditional monistic God but a more personal and individual "sort of polytheism" in which each person's God affects that person's life. People assume, says James, God "as a matter of course to be 'one and only' and to be 'infinite'; and the notion of many finite gods is one which hardly any one thinks it worthwhile to consider, and still less to uphold. Nevertheless, in the interests of intellectual clearness, I feel bound to say that religious experience, as we have studied it, cannot be cited as unequivocally supporting the infinitest belief. The only thing that it unequivocally testifies to is that we can experience union with *something* larger than ourselves and in that union find our greatest peace'' (*VRE,* pp. 514–515). In order to have the power to change lives God, says James, ''might conceivably even be only a larger and more godlike self, of which the present self would then be but the mutilated expression, and the universe might conceivably be a collection of such selves, of different degrees of inclusiveness, with no absolute unity realized in it at all'' (*VRE,* p. 515). Based on the highly personal nature of religious experience, James suggests in his essay on Hegel that the real ''enemy'' of the God in which most people actually believe is the absolute picture of him that religions generally proffer. He writes, ''Only thoroughgoing monists or pantheists believe in the absolute. The God of our popular Christianity is but one member of a pluralistic system. He and we stand outside of each other, just as the devil, the saints, and the angels stand outside of both of us. I can hardly conceive of anything more different from the absolute than the God, say, of David or of Isaiah'' (*PU,* p. 174).

Ironically, such seemingly unconventional views about God in fact put James within a basic tradition in America which relates the innermost feelings and fears of individuals to their religious beliefs and practices. For example, in his study of the origins of American culture and character, Richard Slotkin compares the captivity myths of the Puritans to the terror sermons of Jonathan Edwards. Slotkin writes that ''Jonathan Edward's 'Sinners in the Hands of an Angry God'' (1749)—the archetypal revival sermon by the most subtle student of the psychology of personal conversion—suggests the relevance of the captivity to the psychology of conversion.''[16] Slotkin maintains that the precariousness of the individual in the captivity myth provides a model for the precariousness of the soul in the terror sermon. Accepting this interesting connection, one can see James' discussion of the self and religion as a modern version of the same story of the precariousness of the self. Soul and self, saintliness and sanity, intermingle in his ethical and religious writings. In the opening lines of ''The Will to Believe,'' James says to his audience, ''I have brought with me tonight something like a sermon on justification by faith to read to you—I mean an essay in justification *of* faith, a defence of our right to adopt a believing attitude in religious matters, in spite of the fact that our merely logical intellect may not have been coerced.''[17]

Using a form and a terminology appropriate to his own time, James in effect rendered a message about psychological and spiritual survival. He lived through the last stages of what some critics and historians call the country's age of innocence. Thus, his personal experience with darkness and despair still fell outside the basic national consciousness and experience. Although the world had changed, few were aware of the full significance of these changes. Today everyone knows. Therefore, James' words may have a special compelling quality to us. His justification of belief amounts to a major response to the issues that such a contemporary sociologist and thinker as Daniel Bell sees as most crucial to our time. Bell writes: ''The real problem of *modernity* is the problem of belief. To use an unfashionable term, it is a spiritual crisis, since the new anchorages have proved illusory and the old ones have become submerged. In a situation which brings us back to nihilism; lacking a past or a future, there is only a void.'' He goes on to say, ''What religion can restore is the continuity of generations, returning us to the existential predicaments which are the ground of humility and care for others. Yet such a continuity cannot be manufactured, nor a cultural revolution engineered. That thread is woven out of those experiences which give one a tragic sense of life, a life that is lived on the knife-edge of finitude and freedom.''[18]

Of course, others besides James understood the complex relationship in modern culture among the paralysis of belief, the dissipation of the religious impulse, and the vitiation of the values of individualism. James, however, felt a special concern over the power of absolutes as palliatives for those who were most insecure over the crisis of belief. He felt that philosophies that create false absolutes to ease the pain of living, in Bell's phrase, "on the knife-edge of finitude and freedom" often influence in important ways the quality of life for people without ever facing serious pragmatic examination. Thus, for James such philosophies relate to neither humanism nor culture in any meaningful sense and also help put the realm of moral experience and ethics on an uncertain foundation. James clearly was frustrating for many in his own day and is for many in ours because he expressed without apology his belief in the importance of issues involving freedom, life, and moral action for which there are no final solutions. Yet his insistence on writing about these very issues when he could have concentrated on the search for new technologies of human behavior and social organization made him appear to some like an eccentric who belonged in another age.

More recently, James has been faulted for lacking enough sensitivity to the social and political needs of minorities and women, for espousing elitism along with educational reform, and for holding to his individualism when collective action was needed to create pressure for liberal and reform cases.[19] Such criticism certainly helps to balance our understanding of James' place in our history and to correct possible misconceptions that have arisen about him concerning his role as a crusader and reformer. We need to understand him in his entirety, not in terms of a romanticized ideal. However, measuring him against some sort of preconceived checklist of causes of and positions on current events can also lead to a superficial treatment of both James and those issues. While he was concerned about these social and political issues, his attention focused mostly on different problems and questions that were less fashionable and explosive. He was deeply concerned about finding a way to relate the domain of the inner self and its sense of spiritual value to the world of action. He felt that without that connection life could not be meaningful. He therefore searched for, in Tolstoy's words, "the faith that gave the possibility of living" (*VRE,* p. 181). With this basic concern, he predicted that systems that ask for the surrender of individual freedom and selfhood would ultimately fail. Whatever their intention, their destruction of the inner life and the moral sphere would make their contributions impersonal, dehumanizing, and meaningless. Such understanding on his part leads me to believe that in his own day James spoke not only to the present but to the future and that the age in which he belongs is our own.

Notes

1. Hoffman, "Dogmatic Innocence," pp. 114–115.
2. Ibid., p. 115.
3. Hoffman further maintains that James' arguments are "an act of desperation; the major concern is to restore to the self the possibilities that it may guarantee its continuity in time, that such a continuance of conscious being is a supreme responsibility (a 'dreadful freedom,' as the existentialists put it) of a conative being" (ibid., pp. 118, 115).
4. Hoffman, "William James and the Modern Literary Consciousness," further states, "The Results of his analysis of the self pushed James further and further away from science itself and toward a transcendent affirmation of the self that seems a mixture of exasperation and nostalgia."
5. See Quentin Anderson, "Practical and Visionary Americans," *The American Scholar* 45 (Summer 1976): 406, 408.
6. Ibid., pp. 408, 406, 417.
7. William Barrett, "Our Contemporary, William James," *Commentary,* December 1975, p. 55.
8. See Gay Wilson Allen, *William James: A Biography* (New York: Viking, 1967); John Wild, *The Radical Empiricism of William James* (New York: Doubleday Anchor, 1970); Rollo May, "William James' Humanism and the Problem of Will," in *William James: Unfinished Business,* ed. Robert MacLeod (Washington, D.C.: American Psychological Association, 1969); and Rollo May, *Love and Will* (New York: Norton, 1969).
9. William James, "Monistic Idealism," *A Pluralistic Universe,* in *Essays in Radical Empiricism and A Pluralistic Universe,* ed. Ralph Barton Perry, introduction by Richard J. Bernstein (New York: Dutton, 1971), p. 150. All future

references to essays included in *Essays in Radical Empiricism* (1912) or *A Pluralistic Universe* (1909) will be to this edition of both works and will be included parenthetically in the text and cited as *ERE* and *PU*.

10. William James, "Humanism and Truth," in his *The Meaning of Truth: A Sequel to Pragmatism,* introduction by Ralph Ross (1909; rpt. Ann Arbor: University of Michigan Press, 1970), p. 92.
11. Ibid.
12. William James, "Is Life Worth Living?" in *Essays on Faith and Morals,* p. 31.
13. Ibid., p. 30.
14. Ibid., pp. 30, 29,20.
15. William James, *The Varieties of Religious Experience: A Study in Human Nature* (New York: Modern Library, 1902), p. 492. All subsequent references to this book will be to this edition and will be included parenthetically in the text and cited as *VRE*.
16. Slotkin, *Regeneration through Violence,* p. 103.
17. James, "The Will to Believe," in *Essays on Faith and Morals,* pp. 32–33.
18. Daniel Bell, *The Cultural Contradictions of Capitalism* (New York: Basic Books, 1976), pp. 28–29, 30.
19. See George R. Garrison and Edward H. Madden, "William James—Warts and All," *American Quarterly* 29 (Summer 1977): 207–221.

9
The American Quest for Religious Certainty 1880–1915
Ferenc Szasz

The following essay discusses some aspects of the social, intellectual and cultural background of the period during which James wrote. Ferenc Szasz is a professor of social and intellectual history at the University of New Mexico. The essay is from *The American Self: Myth, Ideology and Popular Culture,* edited by Sam B. Girgus (Albuquerque: University of New Mexico Press, 1980).

In 1907, Charles E. Jefferson, popular pastor of New York City's Broadway Tabernacle, gave a series of sermons on what he termed the "Fundamentals," proclaiming the "undoubted fact" that "we are living in an age that is full of confusion."[1] Jefferson placed his finger squarely on one of the obvious realities of his day: most aspects of turn-of-the-century American life teemed with uncertainty.

At the heart of this "age of confusion," however, lay the ferment that characterized the world of American religious thought. *Fine de siécle* citizens watched in bewilderment as a new variety of religious expressions emerged. These included self-proclaimed Christs, new prophets, new sects, communal experiments, heresies, and the introduction of Eastern faiths. For many, whirl had become king, having displaced Zeus.

A number of contemporary accounts attest to this religious turmoil.[2] Journalist Ray Stannard Baker, for example, recalled the era of Jacob Coxey's march to Washington in 1893–94, which he covered, as filled with the marvels of faith healing, hypnotism, mind cure, and spiritualism. He entitled his later study of American religious life *The Spiritual Unrest* (1910).[3] In 1913, George T. Bushnell of Pacific Grove University charted the number of movements as follows: "organized philanthropy, social service, laymen's missionary movements, Sunday school reform, psychical research, spiritualism, Christian Science, New Thought, theosophy, gifts of tongues, psychical therapeutics—their number is without end."[4] Some observers saw this as a sign of irreligion, but Charles M. Stuart, president of Garret Biblical Institute in Evanston, disagreed. "The immense number of religions and quasi-religious cults is indicative not of an irreligious but of a religious age," he said, "bewildered and vagrant if you will, but seriously and positively religious."[5] This

From *The American Self: Myth, Ideology and Popular Culture,* Sam B. Girgus, ed. Copyright © 1981 by University of New Mexico Press, Albuquerque, New Mexico. Reprinted with permission.

confusion became so much a part of everyday life that in 1910 the Equitable Life Insurance Company could run an advertisement stating, "Old-life insurance—like old-fashioned religion—is what is needed today in this age of isms' in theology and fads and schemes in life insurance."[6]

Contemporary scholars were fascinated by this phenomenon. Philosopher William James noted that it was obvious that a wave of religious activity, analogous in some respects to the spread of early Christianity, Buddhism, and Islam, was passing over American life. He could not have improved on the title of his classic work, *The Varieties of Religious Experience* (1902). Religious statistician H. C. Carroll could find no other nation in the world to match the variety of faiths available in *fin de siecle* America.[7] Writing in 1932, Gaius Glenn Atkins suggested that one would have to return to the first three hundred years of Christendom to find a similar creative period in religion such as America had undergone since 1880.[8] The English jibe that America was a "vast commonwealth of sects," and the French sneer that America had "thirty-six religions but only two sauces" was never so true as in the years flanking the end of the nineteenth century.[9] One would have to return to antebellum Boston, where, as Emerson said, every man carried the plan for a new community in his waistcoat pocket, or to college campuses in the late 1960s to find a comparable period of popular religious ferment.

Why such activity at this time is a question easier posed than answered. Psychohistory to the contrary, the world of the prophet and his intimate contact with God has proven a difficult region for historians to enter. In general, however, one can say that new prophets and new sects tend to rise and/or succeed whenever the existing religious frameworks do not provide sufficient flexibility to transmit their message. Certainly this was true for the rise of Quakers, Baptists, and Methodists in colonial times; it was also true at the turn of the nineteenth century.

Although contemporaries were never certain that one of the new movements (Christian Scientists being the most likely) might not sweep over the nation, eventually these fears proved groundless. None of the sects matched the triumph of the nineteenth-century Baptists or Methodists.

In fact, the successes of these movements were as varied as the movements themselves. Many have completely disappeared. The utopian communities have vanished and one looks in vain today for the followers of Francis Schlatter, devotees of the Oahspe Bible, or adherents of the Church Triumphant. Others, such as the experiments begun at Shadyside, Washington, or Zion, Illinois, have changed beyond recognition. Today Shadyside is just another small town in the Yakima Valley and Zion is just another suburb of Chicago. Still others, such as the Spiritualists, both branches of the Bahais, and the Theosophists, are secure from collapse; but they have given up hopes of ever having a mass following. The fortunate few—Christian Scientists, Seventh-Day Adventists, the Salvation Army, Unity Church, Jehovah's Witnesses, and the Church of the Nazarene have all traveled the familiar road from sect to denomination.[10]

In general one may say that the Protestant denominations were the ones most affected by this turmoil. Papal Encyclicals halted the spread of Modernism in the Catholic Church and Reform Judaism still remained small in numbers. As far as can be determined, most of the newer sects directed their appeal primarily to dissatisfied Protestants. Perhaps one way to examine the rise and success of the new groups is to classify them as (1) those which moved beyond the traditional Christian framework regarding reason, and (2) those which moved beyond the traditional Christian framework regarding faith.

American Protestantism has always been strongest when it held faith and reason in a creative tension. The various denominations—say, Congregationalists, Unitarians, and Episcopalians on one hand as opposed to Baptists, Methodists, and Adventists on the other—have offered considerable latitude in their emphasis on faith and/or reason. Still, the merging of the two was deemed essential for proper perspective. In the period under discussion, however, the balance between faith and reason began to become unsettled.

The late nineteenth century had great confidence in the power of reason. Given this outlook, one might have expected considerable expansion from those Protestant denominations which already had strong tendencies in that direction. Yet for the Congregationalists and Unitarians, the most likely candidates, no such expansion seems to have occurred.[11]

Instead, people who placed increased stress on the rational faculties of the mind often moved beyond traditional Congregationalism and Unitarianism. One early split came in 1867 when a group of dissatisfied Unitarians set up the Free Religious Association. This organization was based in the large eastern cities, but in spite of able leadership from Francis E. Abbott, O. B. Frothingham, and Felix Adler, its influence never extended very far.

Felix Adler's Society for Ethical Culture proved a more lasting testimony to the power of reason. Brilliant son of the rabbi of New York's Temple Emanu-El, Adler was only twenty-five when he began his new society in 1876. Frankly admitting that a wave of skepticism was passing over the country, the Ethical Culturists tried to build up the moral life of those whom the churches had ceased to influence. Revising the dominant opinion that morality was a corollary of religion, Ethical Culturists argued that when people became morally regenerate, they were then more open to spiritual truths. The organization boasted of having no creed, prayers, or music. It laid its stress directly on ethics and social righteousness. In 1894 Felix Adler defined their message: "that the good life is possible to all without the previous acceptance of any creed, irrespective of religious opinion or philosophic theory; that the way of righteousness is open and can be entered directly without a previous detour through the land of faith or philosophy."[12]

Similar rationalist organizations arose simultaneously, but they tended to be smaller, more ephemeral, and, oftentimes, more militant in their outlook. In 1883 a "gentleman" advertised in the New York *Herald* for others "who, while they do not recognize the existence of the Deity, desire to make some organized effort for the establishment of a rational system of worship." Interested parties were to write "Reformation." In Waco, Texas, J. D. Shaws began a short-lived Religious and Benevolent Association which held "Sunday discussions" instead of sermons. A Miss Bartlett headed a "People's Church" in Kalamazoo, Michigan. With no creed or regulations, its stated object was to make people happy in this world. Freethinker Robert G. Ingersoll attended one of Bartlett's services and spoke well of it.[13]

Rather loud support for the rationalist outlook came from two iconoclastic editors with national circulation: William Cowper Brann and Elbert Hubbard. In February 1895, Brann began his paper, *The Iconoclast*, in Waco, Texas. It soon achieved such notoriety that circulation soared to 100,000 a year. Born the son of a midwestern Presbyterian minister, Brann escaped formal schooling but gained his considerable knowledge through prodigious reading. All this he turned into shotgun attacks on pretense, intolerance, hypocrisy, and religious sentimentality in general, and Baylor University and the Southern Baptists in particular.

While Brann insisted that he was not against Christianity or the churches, the burden of his message spoke otherwise. He seldom missed an opportunity to denounce the Salvation Army, foreign missionaries, or clergymen. He loudly defended Robert. G. Ingersoll and free thought and delighted in having *The Iconoclast* labeled an atheist sheet. Here are some examples of his rhetoric: "The Baptists of today would crush liberty of conscience and freedom of speech." "The average pulpiteer is a party who persistently stinks for attention. Like the skunk, he compels even the nobility to notice him."[14] Not surprisingly he was shot and killed in 1898. But, and this is surprising, he had support from several liberal clergymen in his area, and he was given an Episcopal funeral.

Brann's northern counterpart, who turned out to be much more important in the long run, was Elbert Hubbard. He is remembered now, if at all, for his little pamphlet *A Message to Garcia*. Cut from the same piece of cloth, Hubbard was also raised in a deeply religious middlewestern atmosphere. His education, too, came entirely through reading. In June 1895, four months after Brann began his *The Iconoclast,* Hubbard founded *The Philistine* in East Aurora, New York, subtitling it "a periodical of protest." His long and successful career gave *The Philistine* and his numerous other publications wide circulation. They spread doubt about conventional religion wherever they landed.

A man of many facets, Hubbard should not, perhaps, be seen solely as a spreader of popular doubt. But for much of his career—until 1910 or so—he played the role of national lay philosopher, asking (and answering) the big questions of existence. Where religion was concerned, the answers he gave were resoundingly gray. He wrote a rationalist commentary on the *Song of Songs* and the book of *Job,* and he borrowed heavily from Ernest Renan for his rationalist biography of Jesus entitled *The Man of Sorrows*. Removing all supernatural references from Scripture, he published *An American Bible,* which was described as "a book without mystery, myth, miracle or metaphysics—a common sense book for redblooded people who do their own thinking."[15]

Although Hubbard is frequently dismissed by historians as appealing chiefly to the sentimental, his influence can hardly be overestimated. Being the nation's foremost popular philosopher is not an easy task, yet he remained in the public eye steadily for over twenty years until he and his wife went down with the Lusitania on 7 May 1915.[16]

Neither Brann nor Hubbard was exactly a freethinker, for both believed in an amorphous spiritual power greater than humanity. But they were much against the prevailing Christian orthodoxy, and their attacks often hit the churches at their weakest points. Even farther to the left in their use of reason were the American freethinkers, who also began to appear prominently in the magazines and newspapers of the late Gilded Age. While freethinkers had played a part in American life ever since the Revolution—for some reason they were usually blacksmiths or doctors—they seldom had lasting influence. Dwight D. Eisenhower once recalled that during his boyhood in Kansas, every little town had its freethinker and its village Democrat. In the late nineteenth century, however, they began to organize. In 1873 the periodical *The Freethinker* first appeared and in 1873, 1874, and 1875, Englishman Charles Bradlaugh, infamous president of the National Society of Secularists, came over for popular lecture tours. In 1876 the American Secular Union was formed. National conventions were held periodically, and by 1915 there were few large cities without some type of organized freethinkers' society.[17]

Most of the national publicity that free thought received, however, came from the activities of Robert G. Ingersoll. From the middle 1870s until his death, "Royal Bob," with his trinity of "reason, observation, and science," played the role of national infidel with style and verve. Through his Chautauqua appearances—one of his managers called him the "best card in America"—and his collected speeches (*What Is Religion? Why I Am An Agnostic, About the Holy Bible, The Mistakes of Moses,* and others) he served as America's ideal enemy. Humorist Josh Billings once remarked that he wouldn't give five cents to hear Bob Ingersoll on the mistakes of Moses, but that he would give $500 to hear Moses on the mistakes of Bob Ingersoll. Historian Martin Marty has suggested that had Ingersoll not existed as the ideal enemy of conventional society, America would have had to invent him.[18]

The social impact of Gilded Age free thought is hard to assess. Few people actually joined freethinking societies, for joining them meant, in effect, a binding commitment to attack religion. In spite of claims to the contrary, they never numbered over a few thousand. Instead, the writings of Ingersoll and others helped break down the hold which conventional religion had on ordinary people. This, in turn, sent people on different searches in different directions.

The angst of ordinary churchgoers, the public hand-wringing of the clergy, the jibes of Brann and Hubbard, and the thrusts and defiance of Ingersoll all fed into a mood of disbelief that characterized much of the late nineteenth and early twentieth century. All the nation's religious leaders noticed it. Rabbi Gustave Gottheil of New York's Temple Emanu-El declared his generation was living in "a material, skeptical age."[19] The Bishop's Address to the General Conference of the Methodist Episcopal Church in 1888 called attention to the "subtle and ever-varying forms of skepticism rife in our times." Henry Van Dyke entitled his popular Yale lectures on preaching *The Gospel for an Age of Doubt* (1896). This phrase remained current in religious circles for over twenty years.[20]

Usually this mood of doubt was labeled simply "agnosticism." By the 1890s this term had assumed a life of its own. From recent college graduates to fearful ministers, it was glibly bandied about on all sides. "Agnosticism" was often associated with the English writers Thomas Huxley and Herbert Spencer, for they were among the first to popularize it. They and other adherents insisted that agnosticism was not denial—the thundering "No"—but simply doubt: the gray "I do not know."[21]

Regardless of definition, however, the idea was very much in the news during these years. The *New York Times* termed agnosticism "a temper of mind."[22] Contemporary citizens, it noted, moved between the world they lived in and the living God they half believed in.[23] Few religious leaders could be convinced that agnosticism was not atheism in a new disguise. Many saw it as the chief opposition to late-nineteenth-century Christianity. The traditional foes of Christianity—atheism, Deism, Gnosticism, and so forth—were often subsumed under this new phrase.[24] "The agnostic fever is even now far more prevalent than the typhoid," warned W. P. Marwick in 1886, "and much more fatal in its results."[25]

While many pushed reason beyond the bounds of traditional Christianity, so, too, did many search in other directions for faith. A surprising number of prophets, communal sects, Asiatic faiths, and splits from existing denominations appeared during the turn-of-the-century years.

In late 1890, the *New York Times* marveled at the number of false Christs who had recently emerged. The number was, indeed, amazing. In 1888, a man named Patterson, who resided in Soddy, a town in eastern Tennessee, claimed that his assistant, A. J. Brown, was the second coming of Christ. They attracted large crowds as Brown went around forgiving sins and healing diseases. The sheriff of Chattanooga eventually drove both of them out of the area. Similar excitement developed in 1889–90 among the black community along the Savannah River in Georgia and South Carolina. There a whole series of men emerged, each proclaiming himself the Christ. The most prominent of these was a man named Bell who traversed the area urging all who would be saved to follow him. Hundreds of blacks heeded his advice. They left their sawmills and cotton fields to set up a "temple" where they assumed the name "Wilderness Worshipers." Bell was soon arrested, but on his release he spoke to even larger crowds. According to his prediction, the world was to end on 16 August 1890. At that time, all white men would turn black and all black men white. Any who wished to purchase wings for the occasion could do so from him alone. Eventually, Bell was committed to an asylum but his successors, who also claimed to be divine, prolonged the excitement for over a year afterward.[26]

About the same time, the Reverend George T. Schweinfurth of Rockford, Illinois, proclaimed himself divine. He alleged that he was the spiritual heir of the late Dora Beekamn, who, in 1874, had declared herself the immortal reincarnation of Jesus. Other local evangelists in Indiana, Missouri, and Illinois initiated similar extravagances with wild prophecies, visions, and trances. In western Missouri in 1888, a man named Silas Wilcox formed a band of "Samaritans." These people preached that drinking blood was a major means of curing diseases. This led to the bleeding of children. A woman in Oak Ridge Park, Illinois, proclaimed that she could change water into wine. A Mrs. Woodworth attracted many followers by predicting that a tidal wave would crush Oakland, California. In 1895 Benjamin Purnell announced that he was the Seventh Messenger appointed to fulfill the prophecy of old. Later he proclaimed himself "the younger brother of Christ." After 1903 he and his followers retired to Benton Harbor, Michigan, where he founded a religious colony, the House of David, later famed for its baseball teams.[27]

Perhaps the most fascinating of these *fin de siécle* prophets was Francis Schlatter, the "Western Messiah," who astounded New Mexico and Colorado with his divine healing during 1895. Schlatter's memoirs—only four copies of which are still extant—offer a fascinating key to his thought, which was extremely radical. Conversant with the New Thought writings, not only did he provide personal healing (if people would only have faith), he also predicted the imminent destruction of America because of the injustices he saw all about him. Remembering his own days as a workingman, he bitterly attacked the "Plutocracy" as "the blood-sucking parasites on the common people." When the time came, he predicted, all would be avenged. There was little hope for Americans unless they established the Kingdom of God immediately.[28]

The antebellum period is usually seen as the high tide for experiments in communal living arrangements, but the *fin de siécle* years were almost as prolific. Numerous leaders were able to gather their followers into communes. Historian Robert Fogarty had counted thirty-six communal experiments which began in the 1890s and twenty-two others originating between 1910 and 1919.[29] In 1910, H. C. Carroll discovered thirty-seven with a membership of over 4,000 people. Over fourteen states hosted such experiments, with several in Georgia, Alabama, Washington, New Mexico, and California.[30] The Faithist Community outside of present-day Las Cruces, New Mexico (based on the Oahspe Bible) and the healing community of Zion, Illinois (founded by John Alexander Dowie), were probably the two most famous of these experiments.[31]

Such activities were so common that the editor of *The Chautauquan* said he had begun to expect a number of "freak" movements of salvation each year. When 1901 arrived, he was pleasantly surprised when none occurred.[32]

Some of the other movements of faith, however, proved more lasting—the Seventh-Day Adventists, Jehovah's Witnesses, New Thought, and Christian Science. Here the prophets were able to institutionalize their messages and to offer major contributions to the American religious tradition.

In the late 1830s New York farmer William Miller began preaching that the world would end in 1843–44. The Seventh-Day Adventists, officially formed in 1860, were the largest group to base their ideas on Miller's teachings. They remained small during their early years—perhaps only 20,000 or so. But from the 1880s on, they began to increase in numbers and their teachings began to spread across the country.

This expansion was due to the writings of Ellen G. White, especially her *The Great Controversy* (originally published in 1888) and to the numerous food reforms which emerged from their world-famous Battle Creek Health Sanitarium in Michigan. Wheat flakes, corn flakes, grape nuts, coffee substitutes, and peanut butter are only a few of the health foods introduced there.

Although Ellen G. White was never as widely known as Mary Baker Eddy, when White died in 1915, at the age of eighty-seven, she had firmly established herself as one of the founders of a major religious sect. The Loma Linda College in California, begun in 1910, soon made the mission worldwide.[33]

The name Jehovah's Witnesses was not assumed until 1931, but the organization was founded in the early 1870s by "Pastor" Charles Taze Russell, ex-haberdasher, of Allegheny, Pennsylvania. Initially, his followers were termed the International Bible Students Association, Russellites, or Millennial Dawnists; from the beginning they were the most militant of the Adventist sects. Russell claimed himself the Seventh Messenger of the Church, declared that the Parousia had already occurred, and announced that the world was now in the millennium. Christ returned to the "upper aire" in 1874, and in 1875 all apostles and "the little flock" who had died were raised to meet him. They also were floating about in the air. Russell predicted that the consummation of all things would occur in 1914, and the outbreak of World War I that year lent his prophecies special credence. Before long, the Witnesses were distributing their *Watchtower* tracts in every state of the Union. As Jehovah's sole witnesses, they were most eager to spread their message.[34]

While some have traced the origins of spiritualism back to Immanuel Swedenborg and the seventeenth century, modern spiritualism really dates from the "demonstrations" of Margaretta and Catherine Fox of Hydesville, New York (near Rochester) in 1847–48. From there it spread to the East Coast and, aided by the writings of Andrew Jackson Davis, achieved considerable influence during the Civil War years. Spiritualism influenced such diverse people as Robert Owen, Robert Dale Owen, Abraham Lincoln (who allowed seances to be held in the White House to humor his wife), William Cullen Bryant, George Ripley, George Bancroft, and Mark Hanna. In 1870 Lester Frank Ward predicted that spiritualism would eventually become America's prevailing faith.[35]

Attractive to all types of quacks and to a large number of ex-actors, spiritualism grew steadily in the post-Civil War years. Then, on 21 October 1888, perhaps the most dramatic incident occurred—in a movement filled with drama—when Margaretta Fox Kane, with sister Kate sitting nearby, confessed to a packed crowd that she and her sister had only been cracking their toe joints to simulate contact with the spirit world. Oddly enough, this confession only stunned spiritualism; it did not kill it. In fact, the "confession" gave the movement even more publicity. When Margaretta retracted her words the following year, she was reaccepted into medium circles. Kate, too, continued to hold occasional seances for years afterward.

By the 1890s, spiritualism had become a familiar, albeit still somewhat peripheral, part of American life. It had found its way into the pages of B. O. Flower's *Arena,* and the literature of William Dean Howells, Henry James, and Mark Twain, though not always favorably.[36] It found more positive support from novelist Sir Arthur Conan Doyle and scientist Alfred R. Wallace, one of the early theorists of evolution. Alfred R. Wallace broke from Darwin's naturalistic view of the evolutionary process largely because he felt that spiritualism could be scientifically proven.[37]

Spiritualism grew steadily—in the late 1890s it claimed several million followers—but the seance proved a difficult item on which to base an organized religion. "Spiritualism, in short," said the Chicago *Chronicle* in 1899, "is an unorganized body of people who agree upon one proposition and disagree concerning pretty nearly everything else in theology, ethics, and revelation."[38] This is still true today.

Few contemporary observers could divorce themselves from an emotional reaction of either support or contempt for the movement to see it for what it was: an unorthodox response to the problem of increasing religious doubt. Spiritualism was a search for tangible proof of a faith beyond faith itself. For many people it took the place of organized religion or fused with the old beliefs.

Spiritualism purported to harmonize religion and science. It claimed that a person could believe in an afterlife without fear; the seance showed that the afterlife could be proven "scientifically." Few other churches could promise so much.

Of more lasting impact than the spiritualists were the numerous sects grouped under what we now call New Thought, although contemporaries often termed it Mind Cure. Rejecting ideas of sin and guilt, New Thought grew largely out of the American experience and drew heavily on such varied sources as Ralph Waldo Emerson, the Transcendentalists, Andrew Jackson Davis, P. P. Quimby, and Warren F. Evans. Basically, New Thought stressed the Quaker idea of the "Christ consciousness," or the still small voice within. Since it, too, considered itself scientific, New Thought also tried to bridge the gap between science and religion. Many of its adherents also became involved in healing. In the East, the movement emerged as Christian Science; in the West as Divine Science or the Unity Church of Practical Christianity.

At first, adherents of New Thought ideas had no plans to found separate denominations; only gradually did they emerge as distinct entities. The Divine Science Church, which had its beginnings in the middle 1880s, claimed several founders. Malinda E. Cramer, who supplied the name "Divine Science," was one of the more important. After years of suffering, Cramer had moved to California where she suddenly found herself miraculously cured. This occurred when she intuitively realized that she could be healed only by and through the Omnipresent Spirit. In 1885 she began to teach the results of her thinking and soon made this her life's mission.

In the early 1880s, the three Brooks sisters of Pueblo, Colorado—Althea Brooks Small, Fannie Brooks James, and Nona Lovel Brooks—began to study similar metaphysical subjects. Malinda Cramer moved to Denver in 1887 and soon began working with them. In 1898, Nona Brooks was ordained by Mrs. Cramer, and the next year the Divine Science Church was formally organized. Nona Brooks became Denver's first woman minister, serving her church for thirty years. When Mrs Cramer died in 1907, Denver became the center of the western branch of the New Thought movement.[39] The last major New Thought group to emerge in the West was the Church of Religious Science, founded in the second decade of the new century by Ernest Holmes. All of these groups stressed the realization or consciousness of God's presence as the main healing force. Healing came from an awareness that God works through each person. "God is everywhere," the Brooks sisters told their pupils, "therefore God is here. God is health. Health is everywhere. Therefore health is here."[40]

In addition to Divine Science, New Thought groups came in many other forms. Some tended toward a non-Christian eclecticism, recognizing a divine inspiration in all religions. Others tried to interpret the Bible both metaphysically and metaphorically, and still considered themselves Christian. Eventually many of the sects joined to form a loose union in the National New Thought Alliance.

The largest offshoot of the New Thought movement, and one of the few groups to consider itself definitely Christian, was the Unity Church of Practical Christianity. It was founded in Kansas City, Missouri, in 1889 by Myrtle and Charles Fillmore, after Mrs. Fillmore's miraculous recovery from illness. Thoroughly conversant with Buddhism, Brahminism, Theosophy, Rosicrucianism, as well as all sects of Christianity—they confessed to having taken over forty courses in metaphysical subjects—the Fillmores moved gradually from the middle 1880s to what would eventually become Unity.

Except, perhaps, for their belief in reincarnation, Ralph Waldo Emerson and the early Quakers would have felt comfortable with most of the Fillmores' ideas. In his nine books and countless articles and speeches, Charles Fillmore endeavored to show that science and religion were but two approaches to the same truth. Modern scientists were only using a different set of terms to describe the same truths proclaimed by Jesus when He spoke of the Kingdom of Heaven and the power of faith and prayer. Once Charles Fillmore said that Unity could be defined simply as "Christian mysticism practically applied to everyday living."[41]

Probably the most important of the New Thought movements—although they denied the connection—were the Christian Scientists. The origins of the faith are still shrouded in mystery. While most historians feel that P. P. Quimby, eccentric New England healer, provided many of the formative ideas, Christian Scientists trace their founding solely to the thoughts of Mary Baker Eddy, one of the most remarkable women of the nineteenth century.

Long troubled by anguish and ill health, Mrs. Eddy published the first edition of her *Science and Health* (later frequently revised) in 1875 and four years later founded the Church of Christ, Scientist. She taught that evil in general and physical illness in particular could be overcome through prayer and a deeper understanding of God. In the 1880s, the movement grew slowly, for there were many similar forms of competition. In fact, wrote a California follower in 1886, "Institutes of Metaphysical Science have been started [here] which include the teaching of mind-cure, animal magnetism, spiritualism, clairvoyance, and mediumship; while we, as Christian Scientists, are denounced for having our jacket on too straight."[42]

Gradually, however, Mary Baker Eddy distinguished Christian Science from its rivals, and while many of them begin to fade, the Scientists continued to grow. By the early 1890s, they claimed about nine thousand adherents. The Mother Church in Boston was founded in 1892, and the *Christian Science Monitor* dates from 1908. By the middle 1890s, moreover, Christian Scientists had clearly entered the American religious mainstream. In 1901, the *Altantic Monthly* named Mrs. Eddy as the most popular author of the day. When *Outlook* reporter Ernest H. Abbott made his religious tour of the nation that same year, he was astounded to find Christian Science reading rooms in every city he visited. At her death nine years later, Mary Baker Eddy's faith had become a secure part of American life.[43]

The variety of sects reflected the diversity of the New Thought prophets. While most of the sects remained small, as a whole the movement was very important. William James was most impressed with it and considered the rise of New Thought as significant for American life as the Reformation had been for its day. In 1950, Sidney E. Mead estimated that between fifteen and twenty million Americans had been influenced by its teachings. One need only pick up the works of Reverend Norman Vincent Peale, Bishop Fulton J. Sheen, or Rabbi Joshua L. Liebman to see the extent (largely unnoticed) to which it has influenced modern Christianity and Judaism.[44] By the first decade of the twentieth century, then, New Thought had assumed a distinct place among the American faiths. It touched numerous denominations and formed a specific body of thought, related to, yet separate and distinct from, orthodox Christianity.[45]

From 1887 through 1889, the *North American Review* ran a series of articles on the theme of religious pluralism, entitled "Why I Am a (Quaker, Heathen, Moslem, Spiritualist, Free Religionist, and so on)." A few years later the Parliament of Religions, held in conjunction with the Chicago World's Fair of 1893, gave a major impetus to this idea of the diversity of faiths. Here Americans first became acquainted with Theosophy, the Baha'i Movement, Hinduism, and Islam.

The darling of the fair, by all accounts, was Theosophy, founded by another of the nineteenth century's store of remarkable women, Madam Helena P. Blavatsky. The first Theosophical Society in America emerged in New York in 1875. Bearing resemblances to the ideas of Emerson, Transcendentalism, and Spiritualism, the movement grew slowly until 1890 when it claimed thirty-eight chartered branches and several publications, *The Path,* edited by W. Q. Judge, being the most important. Yet it was not until 1893 that the nation really became aware of Blavatsky's ideas. Events surrounding the World's Fair gave them wide publicity.

Madam Blavatsky taught the existence of spiritual beings, the Mahatmas, who lived in the Himalayas, and who sent psychic messages to those who believed. She also felt that she had been entrusted by them to reveal "The Path" to the world. Although Theosophists did engage in some social activities, such as setting up a labor exchange and safe, cheap lodging houses for women, their main goal was more ethereal: "to form a nucleus of a Universal Brotherhood of Humanity without distinction of race, creed, and color"; to promote the study of Eastern literature, religion, and science, and to "investigate unexplained laws of nature and the physical powers latent in man."[46]

Although the movement was heaped with obloquy, even its enemies regarded Madame Blavatsky with awe. Journalist W. T. Stead praised her for restoring mystery and spiritual values to a generation obsessed with the material and mechanical.[47] She died in 1891, but her ideas continued to grow under her successor, Annie Besant. In 1916 the organization claimed several thousand adherents in the United States alone and boasted a thriving Theosophist commune in Point Loma, California.[48]

Most Americans knew virtually nothing about the Baha'i faith until the 1893 Parliament. Founded in 1844 by a rich Persian, Baha'u'llah, Bahais advocated the oneness of mankind and the union of all religions into one universal religion. With the publicity provided by the parliament, however, interest in the movement began to widen considerably.

Numerous Oriental faiths also gained popularity from the World's Fair. After it was over, several Hindu priests remained in the United States to tour the country giving lectures on their religion. Their reception was often disappointing, however, for the Christian clergy warned their flocks not to attend. Swami Vivekeanda, perhaps the most famous of these itinerants, remained in the United States for several years afterward. In 1894 he founded the Vedanta Society in New York. Another branch of the society emerged in California shortly after 1900.[49] "As a result," groaned Upton Sinclair, "we have here in America a plague of Eastern cults, with 'swamis' using soft yellow robes and soft brown eyes to win the souls of idle society ladies."[50]

In 1899 the Japanese Buddhists began missionary work in America, and it was not long before the first Buddhist temple was erected in San Francisco. Another appeared shortly afterward in Sacramento and a third in Chicago.

The doctrines of Mohammed were first introduced to the American public by Alexander Russell Webb, a New Englander who had converted to Islam while heading the United States consolate at Manila. In the fall of 1893, Webb helped establish small branches of the Moslem Brotherhood in Brooklyn, Manhattan, Philadelphia, and Washington. In the fall of the previous year he had visited India, where he advocated the conversion of America to Islam. Able to convince several wealthy Indians to help finance this operation, Webb returned to the states to set up headquarters on the Hudson River. Although he published a monthly paper, *The Moslem World and the Voice of Islam,* his successes were nil. The Nawab of Basoda, a ruling prince of India, left America in disgust when he could find no concrete results from his extensive financial contributions. In spite of claims to the contrary, there is no evidence that Webb convinced any Americans to accept the Islamic faith. The rise of mosques in America had to await later Arab immigration.[51]

In addition to the introduction of Eastern faiths, the existing Protestant denominations were themselves not immune to change. Not all of the new sects were imported from abroad, for several were formed by splits from the existing churches. These splinterings were often created by differences which were sometimes theological, sometimes social, but most often a combination of the two.

Social class distinctions were very clear at the turn of the century, and by 1900 the major Protestant denominations had become largely institutions of the middle class.[52] Consequently, between 1890 and 1910 over fifty splinter groups emerged in protest against this situation. The most important of these were probably the numerous holiness groups (several of which combined in 1907-8 to form the Church of the Nazarene) and the Pentecostals. The British Salvation Army—a familiar sight on most American city streets by 1895—was one of the few groups that addressed itself primarily to the social question of the Gilded Age.

Churchgoers of the time were amazed by this panorama. Methodists and Baptists looked with envy on the 200-300 percent membership gains claimed by Spiritualists and Christian Scientists, remembering fondly their earlier, more halcyon years. Moreover, as far as can be determined (the Salvation Army excepted), the new sects drew their followers not so much from the unchurched as from members of existing churches. Spiritualists initially drew from the Presbyterians. Christian Scientists drew chiefly from Spiritualists in their early days, but it was not long before they were raiding other denominations for members, chiefly Congregationalists and Methodists. The dean of the Moody Bible Institute claimed that the departure of so many church members to the Christian Scientists was a major tragedy of the time. John Dowie's converts for Zion, Illinois, seem to have been largely Baptists, Presbyterians, and Methodists.[53] As a result, these sects soon came under severe condemnation from the established denominations.

Contemporaries found themselves bewildered by this religious ferment but from a later perspective the picture becomes a little clearer. With new immigrants, new knowledge, new technology, and new social class divisions, it was obvious that the established churches were not meeting the religious needs of the American people. Where they failed, the sects moved in to fill the gaps. This occurred primarily in the following: the expanding areas of knowledge and reason (all rationalist groups) in those of deep, personal communion with God (New Thought, Christian Science, Holiness, Pentecostals), social action (Salvation Army, Holiness, Communes, Volunteers of America), healing (Francis Schlatter, Christian Science, New Thought, Unity, John A. Dowie), the awareness of comparative religion and the messages of other faiths (Bahais, Theosophy), and the blending of science and religion (Spiritualism, Theosophy, New Thought).

The "long search" for religious certainty was in full force during the tumultuous years 1880-1915. It introduced a variety of new faiths, many of which were very different from the familiar Judaism or Christianity, in any of their varied forms. During these years the spectrum of the American religious experience widened steadily; a genuine religious pluralism was in the making.

Notes

1. Charles Edward Jefferson, *Fundamentals* (New York, 1907), pp. 11-12.
2. John R. Commons, *Myself* (New York, 1934), p. 53; Edward Roundthaler, *The Memorabilia of Fifty Years, 1977-1927* (Raleigh, 1928), p. 291; Lordy Bryce as cited by William Prall in "Socialism," *Papers and Speeches of the Church Congress* [Washington, 1891] (New York, 1892), p. 61.
3. Ray S. Baker, *The Spiritual Unrest* (New York, 1910);*American Chronicle* (New York, 1945) is his autobiography.
4. George T. Bushnell, "The Place of Religion in Modern Life," *American Journal of Theology* 17 (October 1913):530.
5. Charles M. Stuart, "Foreword," in Paul Little, ed., *The Pacific Northwest Pulpit* (New York, 1915), p.10.
6. Quoted in Daniel Pope, "The Development of National Advertising. 1865-1920" Ph.D. diss., Columbia University, 1973), p. 167.
7. William James,*The Varieties of Religious Experience* (New York, 1902); H. C. Carroll, *The Religious Forces of the United States* (New York, 1912), pp. xiv-xvi.
8. Gaius G. Atkins, *Religion in Our Times* (New York, 1932), p. 63.
9. Paul A. Carter, *The Spiritual Crisis of the Gilded Age* (Dekalb, Ill., 1971) is an excellent study of this period. It stops around 1895.
10. For a superb survey of America's religious life see Sydney E. Ahlstrom, *A Religious History of the American People* (New Haven, 1972).

11. David B. Parke, *The Epic of Unitarianism* (Boston, 1957), p. xi; Earl M. Wilbur, *The First Century of the Liberal Movement in American Religion* (Boston, 1916), pamphlet in the archives of Andover-Newton Theological Seminary, Newton Centre, Mass.
12. Felix Adler *What Do We Stand For?* (Philadelphia, 1894), p. 3, pamphlet Andover-Newton. Howard B. Badest, *Toward Common Ground: The Story of the Ethical Societies in the United States* (New York, 1969).
13. Robert G. Ingersoll, *New York Times,* 24 January 1883; Charles Carver, *Brann and the Iconoclast* (Austin, 1957), pp. 38–39; The Rochester *Herald,* 25 February 1896, in *Sixty-Five Press Interviews with Robert Ingersoll* (Girard, Kans, n.d.(p. 141).
14. W. C. Brann, "The Iconoclast and the Clergy," and "If Our Country Were Catholic," in *The Complete Works of Brann the Iconoclast,* (New York, 1919), 5:119, 279.
15. Elbert Hubbard II, ed., *The Philosophy of Elbert Hubbard* (New York, 1930); Elbert Hubbard, *A Thousand and One Epigrams* (New York, 1973), p. 184; Freeman Champney, *Art and Glory: The Story of Elbert Hubbard* (New York, 1968), p. 113.
16. Charles F. Hamilton, *As Bees in Honey Drown: Elbert Hubbard and the Roycrofters* (London, 1973), is a good biography.
17. Stow Persons, *Free Religion: An American Faith* (New Haven, 1947) and Sidney Warren, *American Freethought, 1860–1914* (New York, 1943) are two excellent studies.
18. Eva Ingersoll Wakefield, ed., *The Life and Letters of Robert Green Ingersoll* (London, 1952), pp. 72–76; Cf. J. M. Peebles, "Ingersollism or Christianity: Which?" (Hammonton, N. J., 1882), pamphlet at the Stowe-Day Library, Hartford, Conn.; Martin Marty, *The Infidel* (Cleveland, 1967); C. H. Cramer, *Royal Bob: The Life of Robert G. Ingersoll* (Indianapolis, 1952), is the best biography.
19. Gustave Gottheil, *New York Times,* 23 January 1887.
20. *Journal of the General Conference,* 1888, p. 40, cited in Emory S. Bucke, ed., *The Century of American Methodism,* (Nashville, 1964), 2:595; Henry Van Dyke, *The Gospel for the Age of Doubt* (New York, 1896); Herbert Swan Wilkinson, "The Gospel for an Age of Doubt," in Paul Little, ed., *The Pacific Northwest Pulpit* (New York, 1915).
21. *New York Times,* 25 March 1889; Lyman Abbott, "A Word with Professor Huxley," *North AmericanReview* 149(July 1889); 157; Robert G. Ingersoll, "Professor Huxley and Agnosticism," *North American Review* 148(April 1889):403–5.
22. *New York Times,* 24 February 1889.
23. Even though the *Times* was not the national newspaper it is today, it did provide a thorough coverage of the world of the churches and the changes in religion.
24. Edwin Mims, "The Religious Tone of Victorian Literature," *Methodist Quarterly Review* 61(July 1912):456.
25. W. P. Marwick, "Overcoming: A Sermon," February 7, 1886, pamphlet in the Methodist Archives, Lake Junaluska, N. C.
26. *New York Times,* 30 November 1890.
27. Vance Randolph, *Americans Who Thought They Were God* (Girard, Kans., 1943), pp. 11–13.
28. *The Life of the Harp in the Hand of the Harper* (Denver, 1897), pp. 147, 153, 154, 167, 176. I have treated him more fully in "Francis Schlatter: The Healer of the Southwest," *New Mexico Historical Review* 54(1979):89–104.
29. Robert S. Fogarty, "American Communes, 1885–1914," *Journal of American Studies* 9(August 1975):145–62.
30. Charles Pierce LeWarne, *Utopias on Puget Sound, 1885–1915* (Seattle, 1975); Robert V. Vine, *California's Utopian Colonies* (New York, 1975).
31. Daniel Nathan Simundson, "John Ballou Newbrough and the Oahspe Bible" (Ph.D. diss., University of New Mexico, 1972) is the best study of Shalam. "God raised up John Alexander Dowie for a specific work," noted a biographer, "which was to reintroduce Divine healing to the church." Gordon Lindsay, *The Life of John Alexander Dowie* (n.p., 1951), p. ix; John A. Dowie, "Do You Know God's Way of Healing" and "He is Just the Same Today," *A Voice from Zion* 4(January 1900):12–13.
32. *The Chautauquan* 32(January 1901):362.
33. The essays in Edwin S. Gaustand, ed., *The Rise of Adventism: Religion and Society in Mid-Nineteenth-Century America* (New York, 1974) are informative as is P. Gerard Damsteegt, *Foundations of the Seventh-Day Adventist Message and Mission* (Grand Rapids, Mich., 1977), especially Chapter 5; Ronald L. Numbers, *Prophetess of Health: A Story of Ellen G. White* (New York, 1976), pp. ix, 199. See also Hardee B. Powell, *The Original Has This Signature—W. K. Kellogg* (Englewood Cliffs, N. J., 1956), pp. 85–113.
34. Elmer T. Clark, *The Small Sects in America* (Rev. ed. Nashville, 1949), pp. 45–47; cf. Royston Pike, *Jehovah's Witnesses* (New York, 1954); Morley Cole, *Jehovah's Witnesses* (New York, 1955).
35. R. Laurence Moore, "Spiritualism," in Gausted, ed., *The Rise of Adventism,* pp. 79–103; Robert W. Delp, "Andrew Jackson Davis: Prophet of American Spiritualism," *Journal of American History* 54(June 1967):43–56; cf. Emma Hardinge, *Modern American Spiritualism* (New York, 1870).
36. Howard Kerr, *Mediums, and Spirit-Rappers, and Roaring Radicals: Spiritualism in American Literature, 1850–1900* (Urbana, Ill., 1972), pp. 173, 188.
37. Malcolm Jay Kottler, "Alfred Russell Wallace, The Origin of Man and Spiritualism," *Isis* 65(June 1974):145–92.
38. *Chicago Chronicle* as reported in *Public Opinion* 26(March 1899):275.

39. Virginia Culver, "Divine Science Origins Traced," *Denver Post*, 19 August 1972: cf. A Whitney Griswold, "New Thought: A Cult of Success," *American Journal of Sociology* 40(November 1934):309–18.
40. Culver, "Divine Science Origins Traced."
41. James Millet Freeman, *The Household of Faith: The Story of Unity* (Lee's Summit, Mo., 1951), p. 188.
42. Quoted in Stephen Gottschalk, *The Emergence of Christian Science in American Religious Life* (Berkeley, 1973), p. 115. Cf. J. Stillson Judah, *The History and Philosophy of the Metaphysical Movements in America* (Philadelphia, 1967), pp. 242–243.
43. Eugene Wood, "What the Public Wants to Read," *Atlantic Monthly*. October 1901, p. 569. The foremost historian of Christian Science is Robert Peel. See his *Mary Baker Eddy: The Years of Discovery, 1821–1875* (New York, 1966); *Mary Baker Eddy: The Years of Trial, 1876–1891* (New York, 1971); *Mary Baker Eddy: The Years of Authority* (New York, 1977).
44. Cf. Sidney Mead's review of Charles S. Braden, *These Also Believe* and Elmber Clark, *The Small Sects in America*, *Journal of Religion* 30 (April 1950):142–44; Joshua L. Liebman, *Peace of Mind* (New York, 1946); Fulton J. Sheen, *Peace of Soul* (New York, 1949); Norman V. Peale, *The Power of Positive Thinking* (New York, 1952).
45. Judah, *Metaphysical Movements in America*, p. 273.
46. Carroll, *Religious Forces*, pp. 353–54; E. T. Hargrove, "The Progress of Theosophy in the United States, *North American Review* 162(January–June 1896):698–704.
47. William T. Stead, "Two Views of Madame Blavatsky," *American Review of Reviews* 3(January–July 1891):613–14.
48. *Christian Century* 27(March 1911):297; Madame Blavatsky, "Recent Progress in Theosophy," *North American Review* 151(July–December 1890):177–78. Exposés were in New York *Sun*, 1 June 1890 and 20 July 1890; *New York Times*, 8 June 1893.
49. *Current Literature* 32(March 1902):291.
50. Upton Sinclair, *The Profits of Religion* (Pasadena, 1918), p. 255.
51. *New York Times*, 1 December 1895; 6 August 1893.
52. Gregory H. Singleton, " 'Mere Middle-Class Insitutions': Urban Protestantism in Nineteenth-Century America," *Journal of Social History* 6(Summer 1973):489–504.
53. Gottachalk, *Emergence of Christian Science*, pp. xv, xxi, 143, 199; John A. Dowie, "The Life of the Ram's Horn." *A Voice from Zion* 4(March 1900):8–9.

II
The American Way of Alienation The Example of Huck

10
Huck's Sound Heart and Deformed Conscience

Henry Nash Smith

The late Henry Nash Smith's studies of the American West and American consciousness have become classics of American literary and cultural scholarship. The following essay is one of his most highly regarded pieces. It was originally published as a "A Sound Heart and Deformed Conscience" and was a key chapter in Smith's *Mark Twain: The Development of a Writer.*

I

In writing *Huckleberry Finn* Mark Twain found a way to organize into a larger structure the insights that earlier humorists had recorded in their brief anecdotes.[1] This technical accomplishment was of course inseparable from the process of discovering new meanings in his material. His development as a writer was a dialectic interplay in which the reach of his imagination imposed a constant strain on his technical resources, and innovations of method in turn opened up new vistas before his imagination.

The dialectic process is particularly striking in the gestation of *Huckleberry Finn.* The use of Huck as a narrative persona, with the consequent elimination of the author as an intruding presence in the story, resolved the difficulties about point of view and style that had been so conspicuous in the earlier books. But turning the story over to Huck brought into view previously unsuspected literary potentialities in the vernacular perspective, particularly the possibility of using vernacular speech for serious purposes and of transforming the vernacular narrator from a mere persona into a character with human depth. Mark Twain's response to the challenge made *Huckleberry Finn* the greatest of his books and one of the two or three acknowledged masterpieces of American literature. Yet this triumph created a new technical problem to which there was no solution; for what had

Reprinted by permission of the publishers from *Mark Twain: The Development of a Writer* by Henry Nash Smith, Cambridge, Mass.: The Belknap Press of Harvard University Press, Copyright © 1962 by The President and Fellows of Harvard College.

begun as a comic story developed incipiently tragic implications contradicting the premises of comedy.

Huckleberry Finn thus contains three main elements. The most conspicuous is the story of Huck's and Jim's adventures in their flight toward freedom. Jim is running away from actual slavery, Huck from the cruelty of his father, from the well-intentioned "sivilizing" efforts of Miss Watson and the Widow Douglas, from respectability and routine in general. The second element in the novel is social satire of the towns along the river. The satire is often transcendently funny, especially in episodes involving the rascally Duke and King, but it can also deal in appalling violence, as in the Grangerford-Shepherdson feud or Colonel Sherburn's murder of the helpless Boggs. The third major element in the book is the developing characterization of Huck.

All three elements must have been present to Mark Twain's mind in some sense from the beginning, for much of the book's greatness lies in its basic coherence, the complex interrelation of its parts. Nevertheless, the intensive study devoted to it in recent years, particularly Walter Blair's establishment of the chronology of its composition[2], has demonstrated that Mark Twain's search for a structure capable of doing justice to his conceptions of theme and character passed through several stages. He did not see clearly where he was going when he began to write, and we can observe him in the act of making discoveries both in meaning and in method as he goes along.

The narrative tends to increase in depth as it moves from the adventure story of the early chapters into the social satire of the long middle section, and thence to the ultimate psychological penetration of Huck's character in the moral crisis of Chapter 31. Since the crisis is brought on by the shock of the definitive failure of Huck's effort to help Jim, it marks the real end of the quest for freedom. The perplexing final sequence on the Phelps plantation is best regarded as a maneuver by which Mark Twain beats his way back from incipient tragedy to the comic resolution called for by the original conception of the story.

II

Huck's and Jim's flight from St. Petersburg obviously translates into action the theme of vernacular protest. The fact that they have no means of fighting back against the forces that threaten them but can only run away is accounted for in part by the conventions of backwoods humor, in which the inferior social status of the vernacular character placed him in an ostensibly weak position. But it also reflects Mark Twain's awareness of his own lack of firm ground to stand on in challenging the established system of values.

Huck's and Jim's defenselessness foreshadows the outcome of their efforts to escape. They cannot finally succeed. To be sure, in a superficial sense they do succeed; at the end of the book Jim is technically free and Huck still has the power to light out for the Territory. But Jim's freedom has been brought about by such an implausible device that we do not believe in it. Who can imagine the scene in which Miss Watson decides to liberate him? What were her motives? Mark Twain finesses the problem by placing this crucial event far offstage and telling us nothing about it beyond the bare fact he needs to resolve his plot. And the notion that a fourteen-year-old boy could make good his escape beyond the frontier is equally unconvincing. The writer himself did not take it seriously. In an unpublished sequel to *Huckleberry Finn* called "Huck Finn and Tom Sawyer among the Indians," which he began soon after he finished the novel, Aunt Sally takes the boys and Jim back to Hannibal and then to western Missouri for a visit "with some of her relations on a hemp farm out there." Here Tom revives the plan mentioned near the end of *Huckleberry Finn:* he "was dead set on having us run off, some night, and cut for the Injun country and go for adventures." Huck says, however, that he and Jim "kind of hung fire. Plenty to eat and nothing to do. We was very well satisfied." Only after an extended debate can Tom persuade them to set out with him. Their expedition falls into the stereotyped pattern of Wild West stories of travel out the Oregon Trail, makes a few gibes at Cooper's romanticized Indians, and breaks off.[3]

The difficulty of imagining a successful outcome for Huck's and Jim's quest had troubled Mark Twain almost from the beginning of his work on the book. After writing the first section in 1876 he laid aside his manuscript near the end of Chapter 16.[4] The narrative plan with which he had impulsively begun had run into difficulties. When Huck and Jim shove off from Jackson's Island on their section of a lumber raft (at the end of Chapter 11) they do so in haste, to escape the immediate danger of the slave hunters Huck has learned about from Mrs. Loftus. No long-range plan is mentioned until the beginning of Chapter 15, when Huck says that at Cairo they intended to "sell the raft and get on a steamboat and go way up the Ohio amongst the free states, and then be out of trouble."[5] But they drift past Cairo in the fog, and a substitute plan of making their way back up to the mouth of the Ohio in their canoe is frustrated when the canoe disappears while they are sleeping: "we talked about what we better do, and found there warn't no way but just to go along down with the raft till we got a chance to buy a canoe to go back in."[6] Drifting downstream with the current, however, could not be reconciled with the plan to free Jim by transporting him up the Ohio, hence the temporary abandonment of the story.

III

When Mark Twain took up his manuscript again in 1879, after an interval of three years, he had decided upon a different plan for the narrative. Instead of concentrating on the story of Huck's and Jim's escape, he now launched into a satiric description of the society of the prewar South. Huck was essential to this purpose, for Mark Twain meant to view his subject ironically through Huck's eyes. But Jim was more or less superfluous. During Chapters 17 and 18, devoted to the Grangerford household and the feud, Jim has disappeared from the story. Mark Twain had apparently not yet found a way to combine social satire with the narrative scheme of Huck's and Jim's journey on the raft.

While he was writing his chapter about the feud, however, he thought of a plausible device to keep Huck and Jim floating southward while he continued his panoramic survey of the towns along the river. The device was the introduction of the Duke and the King. In Chapter 19 they come aboard the raft, take charge at once, and hold Huck and Jim in virtual captivity. In this fashion the narrative can preserve the over-all form of a journey down the river while providing ample opportunity for satire when Huck accompanies the two rascals on their forays ashore. But only the outward form of the journey is retained. Its meaning has changed, for Huck's and Jim's quest for freedom has in effect come to an end. Jim is physically present but he assumes an entirely passive role, and is hidden with the raft for considerable periods. Huck is also essentially passive; his function now is that of an observer. Mark Twain postpones acknowledging that the quest for freedom has failed, but the issue will have to be faced eventually.

The satire of the towns along the banks insists again and again that the dominant culture is decadent and perverted. Traditional values have gone to seed. The inhabitants can hardly be said to live a conscious life of their own; their actions, their thoughts, even their emotions are controlled by an outworn and debased Calvinism, and by a residue of the eighteenth century cult of sensibility. With few exceptions they are mere bundles of tropisms, at the mercy of scoundrels like the Duke and the King who know how to exploit their prejudices and delusions.

The falseness of the prevalent values finds expression in an almost universal tendency of the townspeople to make spurious claims to status through self-dramatization. Mark Twain has been concerned with this topic from the beginning of the book. Chapter 1 deals with Tom Sawyer's plan to start a band of robbers which Huck will be allowed to join only if he will "go back to the widow and be respectable";[7] and we also hear about Miss Watson's mercenary conception of prayer. In Chapter 2 Jim interprets Tom's prank of hanging his hat on the limb of a tree while he is asleep as evidence that he has been bewitched. He "was most ruined for a servant, because he got stuck up on account of having seen the devil and been rode by witches."[8] Presently we witness the ritual by which Pap Finn is to be redeemed from drunkenness. When his benefactor gives him a lecture on temperance,

> the old man cried, and said he'd been a fool, and fooled away his life; but now he was a going to turn over a new leaf and be a man nobody wouldn't be ashamed of, and he hoped the judge would help him and not look down on him. The judge said he could hug him for them words; so *he* cried, and his wife she cried again; pap said he'd been a man that had always been misunderstood before, and the judge said he believed it. The old man said that what a man wanted that was down was sympathy, and the judge said it was so; so they cried again.[9]

As comic relief for the feud that provides a way of life for the male Grangerfords Mark Twain dwells lovingly on Emmeline Grangerford's pretensions to culture—her paintings with the fetching titles and the ambitious "Ode to Stephen Dowling Bots, Dec'd.," its pathos hopelessly flawed by the crudities showing through like the chalk beneath the enameled surface of the artificial fruit in the parlor: "His spirit was gone for to sport aloft/In the realms of the good and great."[10]

The Duke and the King personify the theme of fraudulent role-taking. These rogues are not even given names apart from the wildly improbable identities they assume in order to dominate Huck and Jim. The Duke's poses have a literary cast, perhaps because of the scraps of bombast he remembers from his experience as an actor. The illiterate King has "done considerable in the doctoring way," but when we see him at work it is mainly at preaching, "workin' camp-meetin's, and missionaryin' around."[11] Pretended or misguided piety and other perversions of Christianity obviously head the list of counts in Mark Twain's indictment of the prewar South. And properly: for it is of course religion that stands at the center of the system of values in the society of this fictive world and by implication in all societies. His revulsion, expressed through Huck, reaches its highest pitch in the scene where the King delivers his masterpiece of "soul-butter and hogwash" for the benefit of the late Peter Wilks's fellow townsmen:

> By and by the king he gets up and comes forward a little, and works himself up and slobbers out a speech, all full of tears and flapdoodle, about its being a sore trial for him and his poor brother to lose the diseased, and to miss seeing diseased alive after the long journey of four thousand mile, but it's a trial that's sweetened and sanctified to us by this dear sympathy and these holy tears, and so he thanks them out of his heart and out of his brother's heart, because out of their mouths they can't, words being too weak and cold, and all that kind of rot and slush, till it was just sickening; and then he blubbers out a pious goody-goody Amen, and turns himself loose and goes to crying fit to bust.[12]

IV

Huck is revolted by the King's hypocrisy: "I never see anything so disgusting." He has had a similar reaction to the brutality of the feud: "It made me so sick I most fell out of the tree."[13] In describing such scenes he speaks as moral man viewing an immoral society, an observer who is himself free of the vices and even the weaknesses he describes. Mark Twain's satiric method requires that Huck be a mask for the writer, not a fully developed character. The method has great ironic force, and is in itself a technical landmark in the history of American fiction, but it prevents Mark Twain from doing full justice to Huck as a person in his own right, capable of mistakes in perception and judgment, troubled by doubts and conflicting impulses.

Even in the chapters written during the original burst of composition in 1876 the character of Huck is shown to have depths and complexities not relevant to the immediate context. Huck's and Jim's journey down the river begins simply as a flight from physical danger; and the first episodes of the voyage have little bearing on the novelistic possibilities in the strange comradeship between outcast boy and escaped slave. But in Chapter 15, when Huck plays a prank on Jim by persuading him that the separation in the fog was only a dream, Jim's dignified and moving rebuke suddenly opens up a new dimension in the relation. Huck's humble apology is striking evidence of growth in moral insight. It leads naturally to the next chapter in which Mark Twain causes Huck to face up for the first time to the fact that he is helping a slave to escape. It is as if the writer himself were discovering unsuspected meanings in what he had thought of as a story of picaresque adventure. The incipient contradiction between narrative plan and increasing depth in Huck's character must have been as disconcerting to Mark Twain as the difficulty of finding a way to account for Huck's and Jim's continuing southward past the mouth of the Ohio. It was doubtless the convergence of the two problems that led him to put aside the manuscript near the end of Chapter 16.[14]

The introduction of the Duke and the King not only took care of the awkwardness in the plot but also allowed Mark Twain to postpone the exploration of Huck's moral dilemma. If he is not a free agent he is not responsible for what happens and is spared the agonies of choice. Throughout the long middle section, while he is primarily an observer, he is free of inner conflict because he is endowed by implication with Mark Twain's own unambiguous attitude toward the fraud and folly he witnesses.

In Chapter 31, however, Huck escapes from his captors and faces once again the responsibility for deciding on a course of action. His situation is much more desperate than it had been at the time of his first struggle with his conscience. The raft has borne Jim hundreds of miles downstream from the pathway of escape and the King has turned him over to Silas Phelps as a runaway slave.[15] The quest for freedom has "all come to nothing, everything all busted up and ruined." Huck thinks of notifying Miss Watson where Jim is, since if he must be a slave he would be better off "at home where his family was." But then Huck realizes that Miss Watson would probably sell Jim down the river as a punishment for running away. Furthermore, Huck himself would be denounced by everyone for his part in the affair. In this fashion his mind comes back once again to the unparalleled wickedness of acting as accomplice in a slave's escape.

The account of Huck's mental struggle in the next two or three pages is the emotional climax of the story. It draws together the theme of flight from bondage and the social satire of the middle section, for Huck is trying to work himself clear of the perverted value system of St. Petersburg. Both adventure story and satire, however, are now subordinate to an exploration of Huck's psyche which is the ultimate achievement of the book. The issue is identical with that of the first moral crisis, but the later passage is much more intense and richer in implication. The differences appear clearly if the two crises are compared in detail.

In Chapter 16 Huck is startled into a realization of his predicament when he hears Jim, on the lookout for Cairo at the mouth of the Ohio, declare that "he'd be a free man the minute he seen it, but if he missed it he'd be in a slave country again and no more show for freedom." Huck says: "I begun to get it through my head that he *was* most free—and who was to blame for it? Why, *me*. I couldn't get that out of my conscience, no how nor no way." He dramatizes his inner debate by quoting the words in which his conscience denounces him: "What had poor Miss Watson done to you that you could see her nigger go off right under your eyes and never say one single word? What did that poor old woman do to you that you could treat her so mean? Why, she tried to learn you your book, she tried to learn you your manners, she tried to be good to you every way she knowed how. *That's* what she done." The counter argument is provided by Jim, who seems to guess what is passing through Huck's mind and does what he can to invoke the force of friendship and gratitude: "Pooty soon I'll be a-shout'n' for joy, en I'll say, it's all on accounts o' Huck; I's a free man, en I couldn't ever ben free ef it hadn' ben for Huck: Huck done it. Jim won't ever forgit you, Huck; you's de bes' fren' Jim's ever had; en you's de *only* fren' ole Jim's got now." Huck nevertheless sets out for the shore in the canoe "all in a sweat to tell on" Jim, but when he is intercepted by the two slave hunters in a skiff he suddenly contrives a cunning device to ward them off. We are given no details about how his inner conflict was resolved.[16]

In the later crisis Huck provides a much more circumstantial account of what passes through his mind. He is now quite alone; the outcome of the debate is not affected by any stimulus from the outside. It is the memory of Jim's kindness and goodness rather than Jim's actual voice that impels Huck to defy his conscience: "I see Jim before me all the time: in the day and in the night-time, sometimes moonlight, sometimes storms, and we a-floating along, talking and singing and laughing."[17] The most striking feature of this later crisis is the fact that Huck's conscience, which formerly had employed only secular arguments, now deals heavily in religious cant:

> At last, when it hit me all of a sudden that here was the plain hand of Providence slapping me in the face and letting me know my wickedness was being watched all the time from up there in heaven, whilst I was stealing a poor old woman's nigger that hadn't ever done me no harm, and now was showing me there's One that's always on the lookout, and ain't a-going to allow no such miserable doings to go only just so fur and no further, I most dropped in my tracks I was so scared.[18]

In the earlier debate the voice of Huck's conscience is quoted directly, but the bulk of the later exhortation is reported in indirect discourse. This apparently simple change in method has remarkable consequences. According to the conventions of first-person narrative, the narrator functions as a neutral medium in reporting dialogue. He remembers the speeches of other characters but they pass through his mind without affecting him. When Huck's conscience speaks within quotation marks it is in effect a character in the story, and he is not responsible for what it says. But when he paraphrases the admonitions of his conscience they are incorporated into his own discourse. Thus although Huck is obviously remembering the bits of theological jargon from sermons justifying slavery, they have become a part of his vocabulary.

The device of having Huck paraphrase rather than quote the voice of conscience may have been suggested to Mark Twain by a discovery he made in revising Huck's report of the King's address to the mourners in the Wilks parlor (Chapter 25).[19] The manuscript version of the passage shows that the King's remarks were composed as a direct quotation, but in the published text they have been put, with a minimum of verbal change, into indirect discourse. The removal of the barrier of quotation marks brings Huck into much more intimate contact with the King's "rot and slush" despite the fact that the paraphrase quivers with disapproval. The voice of conscience speaks in the precise accents of the King but Huck is now completely uncritical. He does not question its moral authority; it is morality personified. The greater subtlety of the later passage illustrates the difference between the necessarily shallow characterization of Huck while he was being used merely as a narrative persona, and the profound insight which Mark Twain eventually brought to bear on his protagonist.

The recognition of complexity in Huck's character enabled Mark Twain to do full justice to the conflict between vernacular values and the dominant culture. By situating in a single consciousness both the perverted moral code of a society built on slavery and the vernacular commitment to freedom and spontaneity, he was able to represent the opposed perspectives as alternative modes of experience for the same character. In this way he gets rid of the confusions surrounding the pronoun "I" in the earlier books, where it sometimes designates the author speaking in his own person, sometimes an entirely distinct fictional character. Furthermore, the insight that enabled him to recognize the conflict between accepted values and vernacular protest as a struggle within a single mind does justice to its moral depth, whereas the device he had used earlier—in *The Innocents Abroad,* for example—of identifying the two perspectives with separate characters had flattened the issue out into melodrama. The satire of a decadent slaveholding society gains immensely in force when Mark Twain demonstrates that even the outcast Huck has been in part perverted by it. Huck's conscience is simply the attitudes he has taken over from his environment. What is still sound in him is an impulse from the deepest level of his personality that struggles against the overlay of prejudice and false valuation imposed on all members of the society in the name of religion, morality, law, and refinement.

Finally, it should be pointed out that the conflict in Huck between generous impulse and false belief is depicted by means of a contrast between colloquial and exalted styles. In moments of crisis his conscience addresses him in the language of the dominant culture, a tawdry and faded effort at a high style that is the rhetorical equivalent of the ornaments in the Grangerford parlor. Yet speaking in dialect does not in itself imply moral authority. By every external criterion the King is as much a vernacular character as Huck. The conflict in which Huck is involved is not that of a lower against an upper class or of an alienated fringe of outcasts against a cultivated elite. It is not the issue of frontier West versus genteel East, or of backwoods versus metropolis, but of fidelity to the uncoerced self versus the blurring of attitudes caused by social conformity, by the effort to achieve status or power through exhibiting the approved forms of sensibility.

The exploration of Huck's personality carried Mark Twain beyond satire and even beyond his statement of a vernacular protest against the dominant culture into essentially novelistic modes of writing. Some of the passages he composed when he got out beyond his polemic framework challenge comparison with the greatest achievements in the world's fiction.

The most obvious of Mark Twain's discoveries on the deeper levels of Huck's psyche is the boy's capacity for love. The quality of the emotion is defined in action by his decision to sacrifice himself for Jim, just as Jim attains an impressive dignity when he refuses to escape at the cost of deserting the wounded Tom. Projected into the natural setting, the love of the protagonists for each other becomes the unforgettable beauty of the river when they are allowed to be alone together. It is always summer, and the forces of nature cherish them. From the refuge of the cave on Jackson's Island the thunderstorm is an exhilarating spectacle; Huck's description of it is only less poetic than his description of the dawn which he and Jim witness as they sit half-submerged on the sandy bottom.[20]

Yet if Mark Twain had allowed these passages to stand without qualification as a symbolic account of Huck's emotions he would have undercut the complexity of characterization implied in his recognition of Huck's inner conflict of loyalties. Instead, he uses the natural setting to render a wide range of feelings and motives. The fog that separates the boy from Jim for a time is an externalization of his impulse to deceive Jim by a Tom Sawyerish practical joke. Similarly Jim's snake bite, the only injury suffered by either of the companions from a natural source, is the result of another prank played by Huck before he has learned what friends owe one another.[21]

Still darker aspects of Huck's inner life are projected into the natural setting in the form of ghosts, omens, portents of disaster—the body of superstition that is so conspicuous in Huck's and Jim's world. At the end of Chapter 1 Huck is sitting alone at night by his open window in the Widow Douglas' house:

> I felt so lonesome I most wished I was dead. The stars were shining, and the leaves rustled in the woods ever so mournful; and I heard an owl, away off, who-whooing about somebody that was dead, and a whippowill and a dog crying about somebody that was going to die; and the wind was trying to whisper something to me, and I couldn't make out what it was, and so it made the cold shivers run over me. Then away out in the woods I heard that kind of a sound that a ghost makes when it wants to tell about something that's on its mind and can't make itself understood, and so can't rest easy in its grave, and has to go about that way every night grieving. I got so downhearted and scared I did wish I had some company.[22]

The whimpering ghost with something incommunicable on its mind and Huck's cold shivers suggest a burden of guilt and anxiety that is perhaps the punishment he inflicts on himself for defying the mores of St. Petersburg. Whatever the source of these sinister images, they develop the characterization of Huck beyond the needs of the plot. The narrator whose stream of consciousness is recorded here is much more than the innocent protagonist of the pastoral idyl of the raft, more than an ignorant boy who resists being civilized. The vernacular persona is an essentially comic figure; the character we glimpse in Huck's meditation is potentially tragic. Mark Twain's discoveries in the buried strata of Huck's mind point in the same direction as does his intuitive recognition that Huck's and Jim's quest for freedom must end in failure.

A melancholy if not exactly tragic strain in Huck is revealed also by the fictitious autobiographies with which he so often gets himself out of tight places. Like the protocols of a thematic apperception test, they are improvisations on the basis of minimal clues. Huck's inventions are necessary to account for his anomalous situation as a fourteen-year-old boy alone on the river with a Negro man, but they are often carried beyond the demands of utility for sheer love of fable-making. Their luxuriant detail, and the fact that Huck's hearers are usually (although not always) taken in, lend a comic coloring to these inventions, which are authentically in the tradition of the tall tale. But their total effect is somber. When Huck plans his escape from Pap in Chapter 7, he does so by imagining his own death and planting clues which convince everyone in St. Petersburg, including Tom Sawyer, that he has been murdered. In the crisis of Chapter 16 his heightened emotion leads him to produce for the benefit of the slave hunters a harrowing tale to the effect that his father and mother and sister are suffering from smallpox on a raft adrift in mid-river, and he is unable to tow the raft ashore. The slave hunters are so touched by the story that they give him forty dollars and careful instructions about how to seek help—farther downstream. Huck tells the

Grangerfords "how pap and me and all the family was living on a little farm down at the bottom of Arkansaw, and my sister Mary Ann run off and got married and never was heard of no more, and Bill went to hunt them and he warn't heard of no more, and Tom and Mort died, and then there warn't nobody but just me and pap left, and he was just trimmed down to nothing, on account of his troubles; so when he died I took what there was left, because the farm didn't belong to us, and started up the river, deck passage, and fell overboard."[23]

V

It has become a commonplace of criticism that the drastic shift in tone in the last section of *Huckleberry Finn,* from Chapter 31 to the end, poses a problem of interpretation. The drifting raft has reached Arkansas, and the King and the Duke have delivered Jim back into captivity. They make their exit early in the sequence, tarred and feathered as punishment for one more effort to work the "Royal Nonesuch" trick. . . .

At this point in the story Mark Twain was obliged to admit finally to himself that Huck's and Jim's journey down the river could not be imagined as leading to freedom for either of them. Because of the symbolic meaning the journey had taken on for him, the recognition was more than a perception of difficulty in contriving a plausible ending for the book. He had found a solution to the technical problem that satisfied him, if one is to judge from his evident zest in the complicated pranks of Tom Sawyer that occupy the last ten chapters. But in order to write these chapters he had to abandon the compelling image of the happiness of Huck and Jim on the raft and thus to acknowledge that the vernacular values embodied in his story were mere figments of the imagination, not capable of being reconciled with social reality. To be sure, he had been half-aware from the beginning that the quest of his protagonists was doomed. Huck had repeatedly appeared in the role of a Teiresias powerless to prevent the deceptions and brutalities he was compelled to witness. Yet Providence had always put the right words in his mouth when the time came, and by innocent guile he had extricated himself and Jim from danger after danger. Now the drifting had come to an end.

At an earlier impasse in the plot Mark Twain had shattered the raft under the paddle wheel of a steamboat.[24] He now destroys it again, symbolically, by revealing that Huck's and Jim's journey, with all its anxieties, has been pointless. Tom Sawyer is bearer of the news that Jim has been freed in Miss Watson's will. Tom withholds the information, however, in order to trick Huck and Jim into the meaningless game of an Evasion that makes the word (borrowed from Dumas) into a devastating pun. Tom takes control and Huck becomes once again a subordinate carrying out orders. As if to signal the change of perspective and the shift in his own identification, Mark Twain gives Huck Tom's name through an improbable mistake on the part of Aunt Sally Phelps. We can hardly fail to perceive the weight of the author's feeling in Huck's statement on this occasion: "it was like being born again, I was so glad to find out who I was."[25] Mark Twain has found out who he must be in order to end his book: he must be Tom.

In more abstract terms, he must withdraw from his imaginative participation in Huck's and Jim's quest for freedom. If the story was to be stripped of its tragic implications, Tom's perspective was the logical one to adopt because his intensely conventional sense of values made him impervious to the moral significance of the journey on the raft. Huck can hardly believe that Tom would collaborate in the crime of helping a runaway slave, and Huck is right. Tom merely devises charades involving a man who is already in a technical sense free. The consequences of the shift in point of view are strikingly evident in the treatment of Jim, who is subjected to farcical indignities. This is disturbing to the reader who has seen Jim take on moral and emotional stature, but it is necessary if everything is to be forced back into the framework of comedy. Mark Twain's portrayal of Huck and Jim as complex characters has carried him beyond the limits of his original plan: we must not forget that the literary ancestry of the book is to be found in backwoods humor. As Huck approaches the Phelps plantation the writer has on his hands a hybrid—a comic story in which the protagonists have acquired something like tragic depth.

In deciding to end the book with the description of Tom's unnecessary contrivances for rescuing Jim, Mark Twain was certain to produce an anticlimax. But he was a great comic writer, able to score local triumphs in the most unlikely circumstances. The last chapters have a number of brilliant touches—the slave who carries the witch pie to Jim, Aunt Sally's trouble in counting her spoons, Uncle Silas and the ratholes, the unforgettable Sister Hotchkiss.[26] Even Tom's horseplay would be amusing if it were not spun out to such length and if we were not asked to accept it as the conclusion of *Huckleberry Finn*. Although Jim is reduced to the level of farce, Tom is a comic figure in the classical sense of being a victim of delusion. He is not aware of being cruel to Jim because he does not perceive him as a human being. For Tom, Jim is the hero of a historical romance, a peer of the Man in the Iron Mask or the Count of Monte Cristo. Mark Twain is consciously imitating *Don Quixote*, and there are moments not unworthy of the model, as when Tom admits that "we got to dig him out with the picks, and *let on* it's case-knives."[27]

But Tom has no tragic dimension whatever. There is not even any force of common sense in him to struggle against his perverted imagination as Huck's innate loyalty and generosity struggle against his deformed conscience. Mark Twain maintains a satiric distance from Tom, even adding him to the list of characters who employ the soul-butter style of false pathos. The inscriptions Tom composes for Jim to "scrabble onto the wall" of the cabin might have been composed by the Duke:

1. Here a captive heart busted.
2. Here a poor prisoner, forsook by the world and friends, fretted his sorrowful life.
3. Here a lonely heart broke, and a worn spirit went to its rest, after thirty-seven years of solitary captivity.
4. Here, homeless and friendless, after thirty-seven years of bitter captivity, perished a noble stranger, natural son of Louis XIV.

While he was reading these noble sentiments aloud, "Tom's voice trembled . . . and he most broke down."[28]

VI

Mark Twain's partial shift of identification from Huck to Tom in the final sequence was one response to his recognition that Huck's and Jim's quest for freedom was only a dream: he attempted to cover with a veil of parody and farce the harsh facts that condemned it to failure. The brief episode involving Colonel Sherburn embodies yet another response to his disillusionment. The extraordinary vividness of the scenes in which Sherburn figures—only a half-dozen pages all told—is emphasized by their air of being an intrusion into the story.[29] Of course, in the episodic structure of *Huckleberry Finn* many characters appear for a moment and disappear. Even so, the Sherburn episode seems unusually isolated. None of the principal characters is involved in or affected by it: Jim, the Duke, and the King are offstage, and Huck is a spectator whom even the author hardly notices. We are told nothing about his reaction except that he did not want to stay around. He goes abruptly off to the circus and does not refer to Sherburn again.

Like Huck's depression as he nears the Phelps plantation, the Sherburn episode is linked with Mark Twain's own experience. The shooting of Boggs follows closely the murder of "Uncle Sam" Smarr by a merchant named Owsley in Hannibal in 1845, when Sam Clemens was nine years old.[30] Although it is not clear that he actually witnessed it, he mentioned the incident at least four times at intervals during his later life, including one retelling as late as 1898, when he said he had often dreamed about it.[31] Mark Twain prepares for the shooting in *Huckleberry Finn* by careful attention to the brutality of the loafers in front of the stores in Bricksville. "There couldn't anything wake them up all over, and make them happy all over, like a dog-fight—unless it might be putting turpentine on a stray dog and setting fire to him, or tying a tin pan to his tail and see him run himself to death."[32] The prurient curiosity of the townspeople who shove and pull to catch a glimpse of Boggs as he lies dying in the drugstore with a heavy Bible on his chest, and their pleasure in the reenactment of the shooting by the man in the big white fur stovepipe hat, also help to make Bricksville an appropriate setting for Sherburn's crime.

The shooting is in Chapter 21, and the scene in which Sherburn scatters the mob by his contemptuous speech is in the following chapter. There is evidence that Mark Twain put aside the manuscript for a time near the end of Chapter 21.[33] If there was such an interruption in his work on the novel, it might account for a marked change in tone. In Chapter 21 Sherburn is an unsympathetic character. His killing of Boggs is motivated solely by arrogance, and the introduction of Boggs's daughter is an invitation to the reader to consider Sherburn an inhuman monster. In Chapter 22, on the other hand, the Colonel appears in an oddly favorable light. The townspeople have now become a mob; there are several touches that suggest Mark Twain was recalling the descriptions of mobs in Carlyle's *French Revolution* and other works of history and fiction.[34] He considered mobs to be subhuman aggregates generating psychological pressures that destroyed individual freedom of choice. In a passage written for *Life on the Mississippi* but omitted from the book Mark Twain makes scathing generalizations about the cowardice of mobs, especially in the South but also in other regions, that closely parallel Sherburn's speech.[35]

In other words, however hostile may be the depiction of Sherburn in Chapter 21, in Chapter 22 we have yet another instance of Mark Twain's identifying himself, at least partially, with a character in the novel other than Huck. The image of Sherburn standing on the roof of the porch in front of his house with the shotgun that is the only weapon in sight has an emblematic quality. He is a solitary figure, not identified with the townspeople, and because they are violently hostile to him, an outcast. But he is not weaker than they, he is stronger. He stands above the mob, looking down on it. He is "a heap the best dressed man in that town," and he is more intelligent than his neighbors. The scornful courage with which he defies the mob redeems him from the taint of cowardice implied in his shooting of an unarmed man who was trying to escape. Many members of the mob he faces are presumably armed; the shotgun he holds is not the source of his power but merely a symbol of the personal force with which he dominates the community.

The Colonel's repeated references to one Buck Harkness, the leader of the mob, whom he acknowledges to be "half-a-man," suggest that the scene represents a contest between two potential leaders in Bricksville. Harkness is the strongest man with whom the townspeople can identify themselves. In his pride Sherburn chooses isolation, but he demonstrates that he is stronger than Harkness, for the mob, including Harkness, obeys his command to "*leave*—and take your half-a-man with you."

Sherburn belongs to the series of characters in Mark Twain's later work that have been called "transcendent figures."[36] Other examples are Hank Morgan in *A Connecticut Yankee;* Pudd'nhead Wilson; and Satan in *The Mysterious Stranger.* They exhibit certain common traits, more fully developed with the passage of time. They are isolated by their intellectual superiority to the community; they are contemptuous of mankind in general; and they have more than ordinary power. Satan, the culmination of the series, is omnipotent. Significantly, he is without a moral sense—that is, a conscience, a sense of guilt. He is not torn by the kind of inner struggle that Huck experiences. But he is also without Huck's sound heart. The price of power is the surrender of all human warmth.

Colonel Sherburn's cold-blooded murder of Boggs, his failure to experience remorse after the act, and his withering scorn of the townspeople are disquieting portents for the future. Mark Twain, like Huck, was sickened by the brutality he had witnessed in the society along the river. But he had an adult aggressiveness foreign to Huck's character. At a certain point he could no longer endure the anguish of being a passive observer. His imagination sought refuge in the image of an alternative persona who was protected against suffering by being devoid of pity or guilt, yet could denounce the human race for its cowardice and cruelty, and perhaps even take action against it. The appearance of Sherburn in *Huckleberry Finn* is ominous because a writer who shares his attitude toward human beings is in danger of abandoning imaginative insight for moralistic invective. The slogan of "the damned human race" that later became Mark Twain's proverb spelled the sacrifice of art to ideology. Colonel Sherburn would prove to be Mark Twain's dark angel. His part in the novel, and that of Tom Sawyer, are flaws in a work that otherwise approaches perfection as an embodiment of American experience in a radically new and appropriate literary mode.

Notes

1. This essay makes constant use of Walter Blair's impressive *Mark Twain & Huck Finn* (Berkeley, 1960). But my reading of *Huckleberry Finn* has of course been influenced also by other books and articles. I should mention particularly chapter 15 in Daniel G. Hoffman's *Form and Fable in American Fiction* (New York, 1961), which deals expertly with the folklore in the novel.
2. "When Was *Huckleberry Finn* Written?" *American Literature* 30:1-25 (March 1959)
3. The story is preserved in the form of galley proof of type set by the Paige machine, DV 303, Mark Twain Papers.
4. *Mark Twain & Huck Finn*, p. 151.
5. *Writings* (Definitive Edition, New York, 1922-25), XIII, 112.
6. *Writings*, XIII, 130.
7. *Writings*, XIII.
8. *Writings*, XIII.
9. *Writings*, XIII, 30.
10. *Writings*, XIII, 143.
11. *Writings*, XIII, 169.
12. *Writings*, XIII, 227–228.
13. *Writings*, XIII, 160.
14. In *Mark Twain and Southwestern Humor* (Boston, 1959, pp. 216-219) Kenneth Lynn points out that Mark Twain's dawning recognition of moral depth in Huck's character created a difficulty for him at this point. Mr. Lynn's analysis has led me to modify my earlier view of the problem of plot construction in the novel.
15. *Writings*, XIII, 294.
16. *Writings*, XIII, 122–124.
17. *Writings*, XIII, 296.
18. *Writings*, XIII, 294–295.
19. The revision of this passage was called to my attention by Walter Blair.
20. The thunderstorm: *Writings*, XIII, 67-68; dawn on the river: XIII, 163–165.
21. The fog: *Writings*, XIII, 112–116; the snake bite: XIII, 73–74.
22. *Writings*, XIII, 4.
23. Huck's planting of false clues: *Writings*, XIII, 45–47; deception of the slave hunters: XIII, 125–126; deception of the Grangerfords: XIII, 137–138.
24. *Mark Twain & Huck Finn*, p. 151.
25. *Writings*, XIII, 310.
26. Nat, the Phelps's slave: *Writings*, XIII, 346–347; counting the spoons: XIII, 353–354; the ratholes: XIII, 352–353; Sister Hotchkiss: XIII, 386–389.
27. Case-knives: *Writings*, XIII, 341.

28. *Writings,* XIII, 359.
29. The Sherburn episode: *Writings,* XIII, 195–204.
30. The shooting of Smarr is described by Dixon Wecter in *Sam Clemens of Hannibal* (Boston, 1952), pp. 106–109.
31. In addition to the version of the shooting and attempted lynching in *Huckleberry Finn,* Mark Twain described the episode in his *Autobiography* in 1898 (I, 131) and in the unpublished manuscript "Villagers of 1840-3" (DV 47, Mark Twain Papers). In "The United States of Lyncherdom" (1901), he mentions seeing "a brave gentleman deride and insult a mob and drive away" (*Writings,* XXIX, 245). Walter Blair suggests that the description of a shooting in a footnote to Chapter 40 of *Life on the Mississippi* also draws on Mark Twain's memory of the shooting of Smarr (*Mark Twain & Huck Finn,* p. 306).
32. *Writings,* XIII, 195.
33. Walter Blair fixes the date of composition of Chapter 21 as "probably . . . before March 19, 1883," and says that the rest of the novel was written after June 15, 1883 (*American Literature,* XXX, 20). Except for a sequence corresponding to part of Chapter 12 and all of Chapters 13 and 14, the manuscript preserved in the Buffalo Public Library begins with Chapter 22. The manuscript of Chapters 15-16 has not survived.
34. *Mark Twain & Huck Finn,* pp. 310–311.
35. *Mark Twain & Huck Finn,* pp. 292–294.
36. Paul Baender, "Mark Twain's Transcendent Figure," unpublished dissertation, University of California (Berkeley), 1956.

11
Huck Finn's Humor Today
Hamlin Hill

Hamlin Hill, Distinguished Professor at Texas A & M University and chairman of the Department of English, is widely regarded as one of the world's leading Mark Twain scholars. He is co-author with Walter Blair of *America's Humor*.

No one ever reads the same book twice: as our lives change and our perspectives alter, the same sentence, chapter, or book alters with us, like a patina on the surface of silver. We bring ourselves to literature, in spite of all that critics say about the purity of the text itself, this truism is perhaps more true of *Huckleberry Finn* than any other familiar work of fiction: We are saturated with the book through school and university, we are familiar with the movie versions, television adaptations, even comic-strip transmutations of the plot and characters. And as we change, the book changes along with us.

That same truth applies to generations of readers as well as to individuals. Books like *Walden* and *A Connecticut Yankee in King Arthur's Court* seem prophetic, now that we have a hindsight their contemporary readers lacked. Millennial texts from the past now seem naive; apocalyptic ones seem especially trenchant. And the same formula that changes *Huck* for the individual also operates for generations of readers.

When *Huck* first appeared, it was labeled a children's book—and a dangerous one at that. *Life* magazine condemned it; the Concord Public Library banned it, because, as the *Boston Transcript* reported, it was "rough, coarse and inelegant, dealing with a series of experiences not elevating, the whole book being more suited to the slums than to intelligent, respectable people."[1] Louisa May Alcott, who had emitted *Little Women* a decade and half earlier, announced, *"If Mr. Clemens cannot think of something better to tell our pure-minded lads and lasses, he had best stop writing for them."*[2] *Huck* became something of an "underground" book, partly because of its subscription marketing, which kept it out of bookstores as dramatically as it is now kept out of high-school libraries. Joel Chandler Harris praised it—privately—and Andrew Long labeled it a historical novel "more valuable than *Uncle Tom's Cabin*."

At the end of the nineteenth century, even though the novel had gone through seven American and five English editions,[3] critical commentators praised in safely impressionistic terms its "epic"

Reprinted from *One Hundred Years of Huckleberry Finn: The Boy, His Book, and American Culture* edited by Robert Sattelmeyer and J. Donald Crowley, by permission of the University of Missouri Press. Copyright © 1985 by the Curators of the University of Missouri.

panorama, its characterization, its "Americanness," all the while neglecting those aspects of complexity, moral paradox, and ironic subtlety that more recent serious criticism has found in the book. Discussions of The Great American Novel included it as a possible dark horse. At the time of Mark Twain's death in 1910, two eulogists declared that *Huck* was "of quite inferior quality" as a work of art and that it would "remain [in print] for perhaps two decades."[4]

During this century *Huck* climbed his way to social acceptance.[5] As early as 1901, Barrett Wendell proposed in *A Literary History of America* that *Huckleberry Finn* was "a book which in certain moods one is disposed for all its eccentricity to call the most admirable work of literary art as yet produced on this continent."[6] By 1950, Lionel Trilling had called Huck and Jim "a community of saints"; Hemingway had announced, "All American literature begins with *Huckleberry Finn*"; and even T. S. Eliot had managed to restrain his fastidiousness long enough to call it "a masterpiece." Reassured, scholars and critics began to consider the book fair game and during the next decade built up a body of secondary material about its structure, its irony, its unreliable narrator, which they claimed to be unrivaled by any other American book.

Almost without exception, this segment of critical commentary was ecstatic. Because he achieved a freedom that transcended his society and his own training, Huck himself was labeled a "Liberator." His decision, "All right, then, I'll go to hell," was called the finest moment in all American literature. And his enlightenment as a result of his journey on the raft was hailed, repeatedly, as the victory of instinctive "right" over cultural suppression and coercion. He became by midcentury, at least in high-school classes and on college campuses, the literary symbol for the democratic spirit: the triumphant common American who reached heroic dimensions by following the egalitarian instincts of his own heart.

Since the 1960s, Huck has slowly changed again, not as quickly as Lon Chaney turning into the Wolfman, but just as dramatically. The book we now discuss is not the one that was published by subscription in the mid-1880s, peddled door-to-door like an Avon lipstick and barred from sale in metropolitan bookstores. Nor is it the book the first two-thirds of this century thought it was. We continue to laugh, but for reasons that would have shocked and puzzled readers during its first seventy-five years of existence. I would like to explore how and why *Huckleberry Finn* has been transformed by its audience to accommodate modern (and possibly postmodern) notions of what literature should be.[7]

II

James E. Miller has attempted to define the basic ingredients of our contemporary novels. He proposed,

> For the first time in our literature, after World War II, the world that dominated our fiction was sick, hostile, or treacherous, and . . . the recurring stance of the modern fictional hero reflected some mixture of horror, bewilderment, and sardonic humor—or, to use the popular term, alienation. The common pattern of action which recurred was the pattern of the quest, the quest absurd in a world gone insane or turned opaque and inexplicable, or become meaningless. . . . The nightmare world, alienation and nausea, the quest for identity, and the comic doomsday vision—these are the four elements that characterize recent American fiction.[8]

They are, I would like argue, also the qualities in *Huck Finn* that make it popular in the late twentieth century, subject it to continuing debate and re-evaluation, and keep it alive while the works of almost all of Mark Twain's contemporaries seem like curious museum-piece anachronisms.

First, Huck himself lives in a nightmare world. He learns to settle in to Miss Watson's "sivilized" routine in the early chapters, but that world makes no sense to him. Its rules are not his, and he cannot understand why "when you got to the table you couldn't go right to eating, but you had to wait for the widow to tuck down her head and grumble a little over the victuals, though there warn't really anything the matter with them" (p.18). He states his suspicion of the widow's altruistic theology:

> I says to myself, if a body can get anything they pray for, why don't Deacon Winn get back the money he lost on pork? Why can't the widow get back her silver snuff-box that was stole? Why can't Miss Watson fat up? No, says I to myself, there ain't nothing in it. I went and told the widow about it, and she said the thing a body could get by praying for it was "spiritual gifts." This was too many for me, but she told me what she meant—I must help other people, and do everything I could for other people, and look out for them all the time, and never think about myself. This was including Miss Watson, as I took it. I went out in the woods and turned it over in my mind a long time, but I couldn't see no advantage about it—except for other people. (pp. 29–30)

None of Huck's other touchstones to reality—Tom's elaborate subterfuges, depending on a debased version of Romanticism; or Jim's superstitiousness, in which most omens portend unavoidable evil; or Pap's bigoted pragmatism—finally serves Huck as a method for dealing with his world.

He must surrender passively as the river determines his course to freedom; but, ironically, as the King and the Duke commandeer the raft, and as Tom reappears to manipulate the terms of Jim's escape in the following chapters, he is carried in a direction diametrically opposite to the one he and Jim desire. Huck's plans are constantly frustrated or reversed by unexpected circumstance.

History and language, too, assume an unreliable and nightmarish quality. Huck attempts to catalog English history from Henry VIII to the American Revolution for Jim:

> My, you ought to seen old Henry the Eight when he was in bloom. He *was* a blossom. He used to marry a new wife every day, and chop off her head next morning. And he would do it just as indifferent as if he was ordering up eggs. "Fetch up Nell Gwynn," he says. They fetch her up. Next morning, "Chop off her head!" And they chop it off. "Fetch up Jane Shore," he says; and up she comes. Next morning "Chop off her head"—and they chop it off. "Ring up Fair Rosamun." Fair Rosamun answers the bell. Next morning, "Chop off her head." And he made every one of them tell him a tale every night; and he kept that up till he had hogged a thousand and one tales that way, and then he put them all in a book, and called it Doomsday Book—which was a good name and stated the case. . . . Well, Henry he takes a notion he wants to get up some trouble with this country. How does he go at it—give notice?—give the country a show? No. All of a sudden he heaves all the tea in Boston harbor overboard, and whacks out a declaration of independence, and dares them to come on. . . . He had suspicions of his father, the Duke of Wellington. Well, what did he do?—ask him to show up? No—drownded him in a butt of mamsey, like a cat. (Pp. 199–200)

The past, indeed, is unreliable and as unpredictable as the future in Huck's world.

Huck has five opportunities to deny history and reality and to invent a universe more to his own preference. When Mrs. Judith Loftus asks Huck his story in Chapter 11, he responds, "I told her my father and mother was dead, and the law had bound me out to a mean old farmer in the country thirty mile back from the river, and he treated me so bad I couldn't stand it no longer; he went away to be gone a couple of days, and so I took my chance and stole some of his daughter's old clothes, and cleared out'' (p. 89). Next in Chapter 13, Huck tells the ferryboat keeper that "pap, and mam, and sis" and Miss Hooker are all stranded on the sinking *Walter Scott*, while three others have drowned. In Chapter 16, a fictional pap and mam and sister Mary Ann are stricken with smallpox and unable to get help from anyone onshore. When Huck is stranded at the Grangerfords, the invention becomes even more catastrophic: "I told them how pap and me and all the family was living on a little farm down at the bottom of Arkansaw, and my sister Mary Ann run off and got married and never was heard of no more, and Bill went to hunt them and he warn't heard of no more, and Tom and Mort died, and then there warn't nobody but just me and pap left, and he was just trimmed down to nothing, on account of his troubles; so when he died I took what there was left, because the farm didn't belong to us, and started up the river" (pp. 135-36). Finally, when it is necessary for Huck to invent a background for the Duke and the Dauphin, in Chapter 20, he recites what is by now a familiar ritual:

> My folks was living in Pike County, in Missouri, where I was born, and they all died off but me and pa and my brother Ike. Pa, he 'lowed he'd break up and go down and live with Uncle Ben, who's got a little one-horse place on the river, forty-four mile below Orleans. Pa was pretty poor, and had some debts; so when he'd squared up there warn't nothing left but sixteen dollars and our nigger, Jim. That warn't enough to take us fourteen hundred mile, deck passage nor no other way. Well, when the river rose, pa had a streak of luck one day; he ketched this piece of a raft; so we reckoned we'd go down to Orleans on it. Pa's luck didn't hold out; a steamboat run over the forrard corner of the raft, one night, and we all went overboard and dove under the wheel; Jim and me come up, all right, but pa was drunk, and Ike was only four years old, so they never come up no more. (pp. 167–68)

The total: four dead fathers and one with smallpox; three dead mothers and one marooned on a steamboat sinking in the Mississippi; three dead brothers and one disappeared; ubiquitous sister Mary Ann "married and never . . . heard of no more," depoxed, and very possibly also on the *Walter Scott;* other family members, too numerous to mention, simply died off. Huck's imagination is fertile but lethal. It allows him no escape from the carnage, the misery, and the unpredictability of the world in which he actually lives. It provides no escape, offers no possibility of waking up in better circumstances. Huck is, to use his own word, too "ornery" to believe in an idealistic universe.

Nor does language provide a reliable means of communication. Huck's attempt to explain in a warped syllogism why Frenchmen do not speak English founders before Jim's common sense:

> "Spose a man was to come to you and say *Polly-voo-franzy*—what would you think?"
>
> "I wouldn' think nuff'n; I'd take and bust him over de head. Dat is, if he warn't white. I wouldn't 'low no nigger to call me dat."
>
> "Shucks, it ain't calling you anything. It's only saying do you know how to talk French."
>
> "Well, den, why couldn't he *say* it?"
>
> "Why, he *is* a-saying it. That's a Frenchman's *way* of saying it."
>
> "Well, it's a blame' ridicklous way, and I doan' want to hear no mo' 'bout it. Dey ain' no sense in it."
>
> "Looky here, Jim; does a cat talk like we do?"
>
> "No, a cat don't."

>"Well, does a cow?"
>"No, a cow don't, nuther."
>"Does a cat talk like a cow, or a cow talk like a cat?"
>"No, dey don't."
>"It's natural and right for 'em to talk different from each other, ain't it?"
>"'Course."
>"And ain't it natural and right for a cat and a cow to talk different from *us*?"
>"Why, mos' sholy it is."
>"Well, then, why ain't it natural and right for a *Frenchman* to talk different from us? You answer me that."
>"Is a cat a man, Huck?"
>"No."
>"Well, den, dey ain't no sense in a cat talkin' like a man. Is a cow a man?—er is a cow a cat?"
>"No, she ain't either of them."
>"Well, den, she ain' got no business to talk like either one or the yuther of 'em. Is a Frenchman a man?"
>"Yes."
>"*Well*, den? Dad blame it, why doan' he *talk* like a man? You answer me *dat*!"

As Huck points out, meaning more than he realizes, "I see it warn't no use wasting words" (pp. 113-14).

Later, the King does some fancy footwork with etymology when he mistakenly uses the word *orgy* for *obsequies:*

>"I say orgies, not because it's the common term, because it ain't—obsequies bein' the common term—but because orgies is the right term. Obsequies ain't used in England no more, now—it's gone out. We say orgies now, in England. Orgies is better because it means the thing you're after, more exact. It's a word that's made up out'n the Greek *orgo*, outside, open, abroad; and the Hebrew *jeesum*, to plant, cover up; hence in*ter*. So, you see, funeral orgies is an open or public funeral." (p. 217)

In the same episode at the Wilkses' town, the Duke protects his disguise by pretending to be a mute.

It would be wrong to impute more to these comic techniques than they deserve. Mark Twain constantly exploited the humorous values of the incongruity of mixed historical references and, even more often, of speakers who cannot communicate to one another (as he had done, say, in "Buck Fanshaw's Funeral" in *Roughing It*). But if we are not in the world of Barthelme's *dreck* and many modern novelists' private languages, we are not far from it in *Huckleberry Finn*.

III

To discuss Huck's sense of alienation in the world he did not create, cannot control or command, and attempts to outgrow and reject would simply be to summarize the last several decades of criticism of the novel. We are aware that Huck cannot live comfortably in any of the worlds he inhabits. He searches for a father he cannot find, having killed, at least symbolically, the legal one. He cannot find a home, at Widow Douglas's, in Pap's cabin, on Jackson's Island, at the Grangerfords, on the raft, or at the Phelps plantation, either because none of his worlds is insulated from outside interference or because he loses them to circumstance or expediency. The entire structure of the novel is one of frustrated attempt to escape from restrictions only to find the refuge susceptible to invasion and destruction. Judith Loftus's husband is "after us"; the slave-hunters and the Duke and Dauphin violate the pastoral immunity of the raft; Tom Sawyer appears at the Phelpses to orchestrate an attempt at freedom.

What has not been noticed sufficiently, however, is that Huck's response to the events he chronicles is frequently one of sickness—the nausea of Miller's catalog. When he attempts to turn Jim in to the slave-hunters in Chapter 16, "I just felt sick." When Buck Grangerford is murdered, "It made me so sick I most fell out of the tree. I ain't agoing to tell *all* that happened—it would make me sick again if I was to do that" (p. 154). When the Duke and the Dauphin pretend to be the English Wilks heirs, "It was enough to make a body ashamed of the human race" (p. 210); and when the King feigns bereavement, "I never see anything so disgusting" (p. 212). At the end of Chapter 29, when the King and Duke manage to escape the Wilks mob and reach the raft, "I wilted right down onto the planks, then, and give up; and it was all I could do to keep from crying" (p. 260). But when the King and Duke are tarred and feathered (in Chapter 33), "Well, it made me sick to see it.... It was a dreadful thing to see" (p. 291). Huck's reaction to the events of the novel tends toward exactly the sickness that takes physical form in Miller's definition.

Huck's quest for identity, or his success in finding it, is the subject of major controversy among critics. But, more and more, the tendency is to view that quest as abortive and absurd. Huck attempts to outgrow his society—its slaveholding mentality, its morality, its theological beliefs. Ultimately, in order to achieve the transcendence for which we all hope as readers, he must outgrow his own conscience as well. As we watch, Huck appears to make a move for geographical freedom (ironic because of the direction in which he is propelled), from his society's economic sanctions, and finally in Chapter 31 from the underlying religious code. We cheer, and if we are optimistic ourselves we believe Huck has succeeded. But his "identities" throughout the novel are constantly devious strategies that invent dead parents and tragic circumstances; and finally, after the triumph of Chapter 31, he becomes Tom Sawyer—the nemesis of his attempt to free himself from external control.

The concluding chapters of *Huck Finn* have probably produced more alibis, explanations, and defenses than any other passage of similar length in American literature. In spite of them, we cannot help feeling that the tone of the novel has lowered to burlesque, that the stature Jim had achieved earlier has been sacrificed to make him a minstrel-show straight man, and that Huck—if, indeed, he has surmounted all his background and training—has acquiesced too willingly and complacently to the real Tom's grandiose foolishness. But the serious absurdity of Huck's attempt to find his identity should not blind us to the hilarity of the final chapters themselves. It is *only* because we have hoped for so much from Huck that we react with depression to the Evasion. The last chapters present the reader with a cosmic custard-pie response to Huck's quest for his identity probably unmatched until *Miss Lonelyhearts* or Vonnegut.

Tom's schemes foreshadow the zaniness of the Marx Brothers at their best. His suggestion that Jim play music on the jew's-harp to the rats and snakes illustrates the quality:

"You want to set on your bed, nights, before you go to sleep, and early in the mornings, and play your jews-harp; play The last Link is Broken—that's the thing that'll scoop a rat, quicker'n anything else: and when you've played about two minutes, you'll see all the rats, and the snakes, and spiders, and things begin to feel worried about you, and come. And they'll just fairly swarm over you, and have a noble good time."

"Yes, *dey* will, I reck'n, Mars Tom, but what kine er time is *Jim* havin'?" (p. 330)

Consider, too, Huck trapped with a stick of butter under his hat in a warm room until "a streak of butter come a trickling down my forehead, and Aunt Sally she see it, and turns white as a sheet, and says: 'For the land's sake what *is* the matter with the child!—he's got the brain fever as shore as you're born, and they're oozing out'" (p. 342). This is the result of Tom and Huck's storing two dozen garter snakes in the attic:

> We didn't half tie the sack, and they worked out, somehow, and left. But it didn't matter much, because they was still on the premises somewheres. So we judged we could get some of them again. No, there warn't no real scarcity of snakes about the house for a considerable spell. You'd see them dripping from the rafters and places, every now and then; and they generally landed in your plate, or down the back of your neck, and most of the time where you didn't want them. Well, they was handsome, and striped, and there warn't no harm in a million of them; but that never made no difference to Aunt Sally, she despised snakes, be the breed what they might, and she couldn't stand them no way you could fix it; and every time one of them flopped down on her, it didn't make no difference what she was doing, she would just lay that work down and light out. I never see such a woman. And you could hear her whoop to Jerico. (p. 334)

Similarly surreal is Huck's explanation to the doctor about Tom's leg wound: "He had a dream and it shot him." Finally, Sister Hotchkiss's monologue in Chapter 41 is a cameo vignette of empty-headed inanity.

In fact, then, even if Huck's search for independence and freedom is doomed to failure, the failure itself is rendered in a context that cannot help provoking laughter.

IV

In 1941, V. S. Pritchett shrewdly observed, "Everything really American, really non-English, comes out of that pair of spiritual derelicts, those two scarecrow figures with their half-lynched minds," Mark Twain and Edgar Allan Poe. "The peculiar power of American nostalgia," Pritchett went on, referring specifically to *Huckleberry Finn*, "is that it is not only harking back to something lost in the past, but suggests also the tragedy of a lost future."[9] And in Huck's "future" we sense apocalypse, Miller's "comic doomsday vision" as drastically as at the end of the movie *Dr. Strangelove* or the conclusion of *Cat's-Cradle*.

Whatever else the circularity of the novel does for its form, it returns us to the opening—Tom in charge, Huck as a servile sidekick, society settled back into its normal ruts, and the game of "Let's Pretend" the model for behavior. Huck has traveled eleven hundred miles only to find that he has gone nowhere. If his trip has moved him southward in linear progression, it has also been a treadmill with only the illusion of movement.

Huck's "Providence" is synonymous with Luck, not with a benevolent deity; and putting his trust in it suggests the chanciness of his future. The Territory to which he plans to light out is no less vicious and anarchistic than the society along the Mississippi. It's morality, as Mark Twain himself had accurately presented it in *Roughing It*, is even more brutal than the one that guides the shore folk in *Huck*. Depravity is universal: as Huck says, "human beings *can* be awful cruel to one another." Even after presumably freeing himself from the constrictions of "conscience" in Chapter 31, when he decides to go to hell, Huck admits (in Chapter 33), "it don't make no difference whether you do right or wrong, a person's conscience ain't got no sense, and just goes for him *anyway.*" We have no reason to believe that Huck is still not chained to his own conscience as firmly as he was at the beginning of the novel.

All this is to ask how, with so bleak a vision, can the apocalyptic forecast of *Huckleberry Finn* be called "comic." The answer lies in a series of sardonic ironies that permeate the novel and to which we have become accustomed in recent fiction in ways that the nineteenth-century reader was not. For instance, when Tom learns at the conclusion that Jim has been reincarcerated, he melodramatically rises from his bed and announces, "Turn him loose! He ain't no slave; he's as free as any cretur that walks this earth!" (p. 360). But, given the movement of the entire novel, that is a mordantly ironic statement. None of the creatures who populate the novel is free. Each one is bound to convention, to self-interest, to some external pressure that controls his actions and behavior. Even in the act of speaking the line, Tom Sawyer strikes his typically authoritative and sensational pose, "his eye hot, and his nostrils opening and shutting like gills."

In the same way, Huck's decision in Chapter 31 to go to hell as a consequence of helping Jim escape has been comically foreshadowed early in the novel, when Miss Watson "told me all about the bad place, and I said I wished I was there. . . . She said it was wicked to say what I said; said she wouldn't say it for the whole world; *she* was going to live so as to go to the good place. Well, I couldn't see no advantage in going where she was going, so I made up my mind I wouldn't try for it" (p. 19). His heroic desire to avoid being "sivilized" at the conclusion is comically deflated when compared with his definition of that word in the early part of the book: in context, what he wishes to escape is, as he summarizes it, saying blessings at meals, wearing shoes, not smoking, being "dismal regular and decent."

The words upon which a heroic interpretation of *Huckleberry Finn* depends—hell, Providence, "sivilization," and freedom—are in fact comic words in the book, ones whose value to Huck is much more trivial than their value to the postmodern reader. We are, in fact, according to one interpretation of the novel, strung along on a grand hoax, willing ourselves to believe in a nobility unjustified by the action of the story or the personalities of the characters. Huck sees himself more clearly in the final chapters than readers anticipate; his unmasking reveals the same character who began the action—"brung up to wickedness" himself but aware that Tom Sawyer could never "help a body set a nigger free, with his bringing-up."

As a result, Huck's unreliability as a narrator extends only to the surface. His admiration of the Grangerfords' home furnishings is sincere:

> Well, there was a big outlandish parrot on each side of the clock, made out of something like chalk, and painted up gaudy. By one of the parrots was a cat made of crockery, and a crockery dog by the other; and when you pressed down on them they squeaked, but didn't open their mouths nor look different nor interested. They squeaked through underneath. There was a couple of big wild-turkey-wing fans spread out behind those things. On a table in the middle of the room was a kind of a lovely crockery basket that had apples and oranges and peaches and grapes piled up in it which was much redder and yellower and prettier than real ones is, but they warn't real because you could see where pieces had got chipped off and showed the white chalk or whatever it was, underneath. (p. 137)

For Huck's adjective *gaudy*, we would substitute *shabby*, but there is no justification for questioning the validity of his aesthetic judgment. When Huck philosophizes, "If you notice, most folks don't go to church only when they've got to; but a hog is different," we see the ironic implication, but Huck plays it sincerely straight. He records his personal opinion and comprehension of the events he witnesses, and readers are left to read more into those comments and circumstances than Huck possibly can. In that light, the famous passage in Chapter 32 becomes especially significant.

> "We blowed out a cylinder-head."
> "Good gracious! anybody hurt?"
> "No'm. Killed a nigger."
> "Well, it's lucky; because sometimes people do get hurt." (P. 280)

Clearly, Aunt Sally does not view a black as a person; but does Huck, even after his debate with his conscience a chapter earlier, provide any evidence that he views racial matters differently? Is he devious, is he even capable of such instant duplicity?

What exists in the novel, then, are its audience's high hopes, which Mark Twain consistently undercuts, thwarts, and batters in a complex strategy that he was to lose in his old age. As with so many modern novelists, so with Mark Twain: the reader is the writer's prey. The text itself becomes a battleground between author and audience, the goal of the former being to strip away the latter's idealistic delusions and replace them with a soberer notion of Huck's and the reader's own imperfectability. That Twain does so in the context of a range of humor from broad slapstick to razor-honed irony fulfills the very modern requirement of "comic doomsday vision."

And so *Huckleberry Finn* evolved over nearly a century of reading and interpretation. Huck is no longer the inexcusably unsatisfactory teenager in a world of exaggerated brutality and violence, as the Brahmin reviewers saw him. Nor is he the outcast hero, whose decision to go to hell represents moral victory over injustice and slaveries of any kind, as the first half of the twentieth century saw him. Because the world has changed radically in the past hundred years, we are not shocked at lynchings or duels or tarrings and featherings. The world we see reflected in *Huckleberry Finn* is our own—and ours, incidentally, is one that would not surprise Mark Twain. It is the one he predicted incessantly in the last third of his life and one he believed represented the true characteristics of the damned human race. It would not disturb him to know that, for us, Huck represents the typically helpless victim of a world in which nightmare, absurd quests for identity, alienation, and apocalypse are the facts of daily life.

Notes

1. *Boston Transcript*, 17 March 1885, reprinted in Thomas Asa Tenney, *Mark Twain: A Reference Guide* (Boston: G. K. Hall, 1977), p. 14.
2. Quoted in Thomas Beer, *The Mauve Decade* (New York: Vintage Books, 1961), p. 9.
3. Walter Blair, *Mark Twain and Huck Finn* (Berkeley: University of California Press, 1960), pp. 373, 376.
4. Arnold Bennett and Harry Thurston Peck, both in Frederick Anderson, ed., *Mark Twain: The Critical Heritage* (London: Routledge & Kegan Paul, 1971), pp. 285, 292.
5. See Jay B. Hubbell, *Who Are the Major American Writers?* (Durham: Duke University Press, 1972), pp. 135-44, for a detailed account of the shifts in Mark Twain's reputation.
6. Quoted in Tenney, *Mark Twain*, p. 36.
7. The debate that began the slow change in Huck's reputation focused originally upon disagreement over the ending of the novel, most auspiciously with Leo Marx's "Mr. Eliot, Mr. Trilling, and *Huckleberry Finn*," *ASch* 22 (1953): 423–40. That debate has continued for thirty years; in addition, it has stimulated an increasingly large segment of "negative" commentary on the novel.
8. *Quests Surd and Absurd* (Chicago: University of Chicago Press, 1967), pp. 3–30, elaborates the malaise in the works of modern novelists.
9. "Books in General," *New Statesman and Nation* (London) 22 (3 August 1941): 113.

III
Age of Alienation and Dissent The 1920s
12
Introduction to Dewey
John J. Stuhr

John Dewey's social and cultural philosophy constitutes a uniquely American response to the conditions of alienation during the 1920s. The following essay by John J. Stuhr, Professor of Philosophy and Director of the Humanities Center at the University of Oregon, puts Dewey's work in an important social and cultural perspective.

John Dewey (1859–1952) is America's greatest philosopher, and "The Lost Individual" is one of his most brilliant and radical essays of cultural analysis and criticism. Reading it today is like winning an intellectual lottery: you're suddenly overwhelmed with a new wealth of insights, and at the same time immediately challenged to redirect your life so as to put these new riches to good use.

Dewey lived a remarkably long life during a period of sweeping change in America and the world. His ninety-two years spanned the American Civil War, the Russian Revolution, World War I, the Great Depression, and World War II, and thus he witnessed the publication of Darwin's *Origin of Species,* the development of relativity theory and quantum mechanics, and the creation of the electric light, telephone, television, automobile, airplane, computer, and atom bomb.

Throughout his life, Dewey was remarkably active. He founded an important laboratory school in Chicago, worked in the public schools there, and contributed to programs aimed at helping immigrants deal with urban problems. After moving to New York City, he founded the American Association of University Professors, and played a central role in the teacher union movement nationally. He chaired the International Commission of Inquiry into the Charges Made Against Leon Trotsky in the Moscow Trials. And, his extensive lectures and travels spurred educational changes in many foreign countries, including Japan, China, Turkey, Mexico, and the U.S.S.R.

At the same time, he consistently produced an astonishing amount of both scholarly and popular writing. His collected works total more than 35 volumes, and cover a vast array of topics—art, ethics, education, sociology, religion, logic, war, economics, psychology, the history of philosophy, and many important events of the time. His pragmatic political philosophy is most explicitly developed and set forth in several superb books: Democracy and Education (1916), The Public and Its Problems (1927), Individualism: Old and New (1930), Philosophy and Civilization (1931), Liberalism and Social Action (1935), Freedom and Culture (1939), and Problems of Men (1946).

Remarkably, these books continue to have immediate relevance and deep value. They speak directly and imaginatively to our pressing cultural problems and our efforts to ameliorate them.

Basically, Dewey argues that in America, traditional liberal philosophy—and its understanding of intelligence, freedom, and individuality—now is dangerously obsolete. Although this philosophy has not been "disproven," recent sweeping changes (brought on in large part by rapid scientific and technological developments) in the actual conditions of social life make this philosophy outdated.

However, Dewey points out that we still hold on to this outdated view, clinging from habit to outmoded theories that are counterproductive in practice. We fail to see that these earlier views are not immutable, eternal truths, but instead are historically conditioned and historically relative. Our beliefs and values, Dewey shows, have not kept pace with recent, rapid changes and so no longer fit the actual conditions of our lives. As a result, our lives often feel meaningless, bewildered, isolated, busy but lacking significant accomplishment.

What is needed? Dewey argues that we must reconstruct our political ideals and philosophy in order to address effectively our contemporary situation. And, guided by this reconstructed theory, we also must reconstruct our practice. That is, we must struggle to make fundamental changes in our actions and institutions—in our economy, our government, our schools, our families, and our personal lives. To put it briefly, Dewey claims that we must begin to think differently and act differently.

"The Lost Individual" allows us to begin to do this. Given that individualism is a fundamental American value, Dewey asks: what does individualism mean today in our increasingly outwardly corporate, organized society? Dewey calls our commonplace view "rugged individualism"—and sometimes, in criticism, "ragged individualism." We understand individuality as something each person somehow possesses, as what makes each person different from and independent of others. We picture John Wayne or the Marlboro man, living on the frontier, as individuals—self-sufficient, free of entanglements, and non-conformist.

But, according to Dewey, this view of individuality is almost wholly wrong in theory and almost wholly paralyzing in practice. It misses the fact that individuals emerge from and are products of society. The fact of socialization renders the frontier image of personal self-sufficiency a myth. And it renders ironic all attempts to be an individual by simply being different or non-conformist—since this kind of reactive non-conformity is simply another kind of conformity.

Fortunately, individuality does not require the absence of social relations. Instead, social relations and conditions that support and sustain the development of individuality are required: "Assured and integrated individuality is the product of definite social relationships and publicly acknowledged functions." This means that individuality is not something innate or given; rather it is something that must be developed or accomplished. This means, unfortunately, that a person—you or me, for instance—can fail to be a genuine individual.

Dewey calls such persons "lost." They lack the conditions necessary for their own self-creation and self-realization. They lack the loyalties and social relationships necessary to develop and give meaning to their own lives. Why? Because recent changes in social life have destroyed older values, institutions, and allegiances, but new loyalties have not taken their place: "Individuals vibrate between a past that is intellectually too empty to give stability and a present that is too diversely crowded and chaotic to afford balance or direction to ideas and emotion." The evidence of this, Dewey thinks, is everywhere: economic insecurity, busy but empty lives, political apathy, religious separations and disputes, superficial personal relations, and failing efforts to achieve individual well-being and social harmony through outward laws alone.

So, how can the lost individual be re-found? We must develop a "new individualism"—a new account of the nature of individuality given contemporary social realities. On such an account, individuality must be understood as self-development, as the ongoing growth or realization of a person's highest capacities.

This requires social change and the invention of new social institutions to serve this new individualism. This means, for instance, that schools must educate rather than merely train. They must develop students' abilities of imagination, criticism, and social action. They must not simply produce immature but efficient "industrial fodder." It means, further, that government leaders must act as public educators. Social problems, like problems in the natural sciences, must be resolved not by custom or bias but by intelligent inquiry. The results of this inquiry must be communicated to the public to ensure public participation in and direction of the decision-making that affects the lives of all. Without this, America will be a democracy in form alone. And, it means that fundamental economic change is needed. We must create a truly free economy. This would not be an economy directed by government to serve private pecuniary ends, but rather an economy directed so as to create and provide the public with the conditions and means needed for individuality. Freedom, as Dewey makes clear, is not simply the absence of restraints, but also the presence of those conditions necessary for individual self-creation and self-development. What we need is not "The United States, Incorporated" but the United States, a genuine community of free individuals.

"Choice is implicated in observation," Dewey concludes. To agree with Dewey's pragmatism is not simply to say that you agree with him—perhaps in a class or on a test. His philosophy is not that easy or safe. To agree with Dewey, ultimately, is to act with him. A new individualism requires difficult social action, and this social action begins with the action of individual selves. Dewey has articulated the challenge to act. You can ignore it. But you cannot avoid it.

13
The Lost Individual
John Dewey

The development of a civilization that is outwardly corporate—or rapidly becoming so—has been accompanied by a submergence of the individual. Just how far this is true of the individual's opportunities in action, how far initiative and choice in what an individual does are restricted by the economic forces that make for consolidation, I shall not attempt to say. It is arguable that there has been a diminution of the range of decision and activity for the many along with exaggeration of opportunity of personal expression for the few. It may be contended that no one class in the past has the power now possessed by an industrial oligarchy. On the other hand, it may be held that this power of the few is, with respect to genuine individuality, specious; that those outwardly in control are in reality as much carried by forces external to themselves as are the many; that in fact these forces impel them into a common mold to such an extent that individuality is suppressed.

What is here meant by "the lost individual" is, however, so irrelevant to this question that it is not necessary to decide between the two views. For by it is meant a moral and intellectual fact which is independent of any manifestation of power in action. The significant thing is that the loyalties which once held individuals, which gave them support, direction, and unity of outlook on life, have well-nigh disappeared. In consequence, individuals are confused and bewildered. It would be difficult to find in history an epoch as lacking in solid and assured objects of belief and approved ends of action as is the present. Stability of individuality is dependent upon stable objects to which allegiance firmly attaches itself. There are, of course, those who are still militantly fundamentalist in religious and social creed. But their very clamor is evidence that the tide is set against them. For the others, traditional objects of loyalty have become hollow or are openly repudiated, and they drift without sure anchorage. Individuals vibrate between a past that is intellectually too empty to give stability and a present that is too diversely crowded and chaotic to afford balance or direction to ideas and emotion.

Assured and integrated individuality is the product of definite social relationships and publicly acknowledged functions. Judged by this standard, even those who seem to be in control, and to carry the expression of their special individual abilities to a high pitch, are submerged. They may be captains of finance and industry, but until there is some consensus of belief as to the meaning of finance and industry in civilization as a whole, they cannot be captains of their own souls—their beliefs and aims. They exercise leadership surreptitiously and, as it were, absentmindedly. They lead, but it is under cover of impersonal and socially undirected economic forces. Their reward is

Reprinted by permission of The Putnam Publishing Group from INDIVIDUALISM OLD AND NEW by John Dewey. Copyright © 1929, 1930, by John Dewey.

found not in what they do, in their social office and function, but in a deflection of social consequences to private gain. They receive the acclaim and command the envy and admiration of the crowd, but the crowd is also composed of private individuals who are equally lost to a sense of social bearings and uses.

The explanation is found in the fact that while the actions promote corporate and collective results, these results are outside their intent and irrelevant to that reward of satisfaction which comes from a sense of social fulfillment. To themselves and to others, their business is private and its outcome is private profit. No complete satisfaction is possible where such a split exists. Hence the absence of a sense of social value is made up for by an exacerbated acceleration of the activities that increase private advantage and power. One cannot look into the inner consciousness of his fellows; but if there is any general degree of inner contentment on the part of those who form our pecuniary oligarchy, the evidence is sadly lacking. As for the many, they are impelled hither and yon by forces beyond their control.

The most marked trait of present life, economically speaking, is insecurity. It is tragic that millions of men desirous of working should be recurrently out of employment; aside from cyclical depressions there is a standing army at all times who have no regular work. We have not any adequate information as to the number of these persons. But the ignorance even as to numbers is slight compared with our inability to grasp the psychological and moral consequences of the precarious condition in which vast multitudes live. Insecurity cuts deeper and extends more widely than bare unemployment. Fear of loss of work, dread of the oncoming of old age, create anxiety and eat into self-respect in a way that impairs personal dignity. Where fears abound, courageous and robust individuality is undermined. The vast development of technological resources that might bring security in its train has actually brought a new mode of insecurity, as mechanization displaces labor. The mergers and consolidations that mark a corporate age are beginning to bring uncertainty into the economic lives of the higher salaried class, and that tendency is only just in its early stage. Realization that honest and industrious pursuit of a calling or business will not guarantee any stable level of life lessens respect for work and stirs large numbers to take a chance of some adventitious way of getting the wealth that will make security possible: witness the orgies of the stock-market in recent days.

The unrest, impatience, irritation and hurry that are so marked in American life are inevitable accompaniments of a situation in which individuals do not find support and contentment in the fact that they are sustaining and sustained members of a social whole. They are evidence, psychologically, of abnormality, and it is as idle to seek for their explanation within the deliberate intent of individuals as it is futile to think that they can be got rid of by hortatory moral appeal. Only an acute maladjustment between individuals and the social conditions under which they live can account for such widespread pathological phenomena. Feverish love of anything as long as it is a change which is distracting, impatience, unsettlement, nervous discontentment, and desire for excitement, are not native to human nature. They are so abnormal as to demand explanation in some deep-seated cause.

I should explain a seeming hypocrisy on the same ground. We are not consciously insincere in our professions of devotion to ideals of "service"; they mean something. Neither the Rotarian nor the big business enterprise uses the term merely as a cloak for "putting something over" which makes for pecuniary gain. But the lady doth protest too much. The wide currency of such professions testifies to a sense of a social function of business which is expressed in words because it is so lacking in fact, and yet which is felt to be rightfully there. If our external combinations in industrial activity were reflected in organic integrations of the desires, purposes and satisfactions of individuals, the verbal protestations would disappear, because social utility would be a matter of course.

Some persons hold that a genuine mental counterpart of the outward social scheme is actually forming. Our prevailing mentality, our "ideology," is said to be that of the "business mind" which has become so deplorably pervasive. Are not the prevailing standards of value those derived from pecuniary success and economic prosperity? Were the answer unqualifiedly in the affirmative, we should have to admit that our outer civilization is attaining an inner culture which corresponds to it, however much we might disesteem the quality of that culture. The objection that such a condition is impossible, since man cannot live by bread, by material prosperity, alone, is tempting, but it may be said to beg the question. The conclusive answer is that the business mind is not itself unified. It is divided within itself and must remain so as long as the results of industry as the determining force in life are corporate and collective while its animating motives and compensations are so unmitigatedly private. A unified mind, even of the business type, can come into being only when conscious intent and consummation are in harmony with consequences actually effected. This statement expresses conditions so psychologically assured that it may be termed a law of mental integrity. Proof of the existence of the split is found in the fact that while there is much planning of future development with a view to dividends within large business corporations, there is no corresponding coördinated planning of social development.

The growth of corporateness is arbitrarily restricted. Hence it operates to limit individuality, to put burdens on it, to confuse and submerge it. It crowds more out than it incorporates in an ordered and secure life. It has made rural districts stagnant while bringing excess and restless movement to the city. The restriction of corporateness lies in the fact that it remains on the cash level. Men are brought together on the one side by investment in the same joint stock company, and on the other hand by the fact that the machine compels mass production in order that investors may get their profits. The results affect all society in all its phases. But they are as inorganic as the ultimate human motives that operate are private and egoistic. An economic individualism of motives and aims underlies our present corporate mechanisms, and undoes the individual.

The loss of individuality is conspicuous in the economic region because our civilization is so predominantly a business civilization. But the fact is even more obvious when we turn to the political scene. It would be a waste of words to expatiate on the meaninglessness of present political platforms, parties and issues. The old-time slogans are still reiterated, and to a few these words still seem to have a real meaning. But it is too evident to need argument that on the whole our politics, as far as they are not covertly manipulated in behalf of the pecuniary advantage of groups, are in a state of confusion; issues are improvised from week to week with a constant shift of allegiance. It is impossible for individuals to find themselves politically with surety and efficiency under such conditions. Political apathy broken by recurrent sensations and spasms is the natural outcome.

The lack of secure objects of allegiance, without which individuals are lost, is especially striking in the case of the liberal. The liberalism of the past was characterized by the possession of a definite intellectual creed and program; that was its distinction from conservative parties which needed no formulated outlook beyond defense of things as they were. In contrast, liberals operated on the basis of a thought-out social philosophy, a theory of politics sufficiently definite and coherent to be easily translated into a program of policies to be pursued. Liberalism to-day is hardly more than a temper of mind, vaguely called forward-looking, but quite uncertain as to where to look and what to look forward to. For many individuals, as well as in its social results, this fact is hardly less than a tragedy. The tragedy may be unconscious for the mass, but they show its reality in their aimless drift, while the more thoughtful are consciously disturbed. For human nature is self-possessed only as it has objects to which it can attach itself.

I do not think it is fantastic to connect our excited and rapacious nationalism with the situation in which corporateness has gone so far as to detach individuals from their old local ties and allegiances but not far enough to give them a new center and order of life. The most militaristic of nations secures the loyalty of its subjects not by physical force but through the power of ideas and emotions. It cultivates ideals of loyalty, of solidarity, and common devotion to a common cause. Modern industry, technology and commerce have created modern nations in their external form. Armies and navies exist to protect commerce, to make secure the control of raw materials, and to command markets. Men would not sacrifice their lives for the purpose of securing economic gain for a few if the conditions presented themselves to their minds in this bald fashion. But the balked demand for genuine coöperativeness and reciprocal solidarity in daily life finds an outlet in nationalistic sentiment. Men have a pathetic instinct toward the adventure of living and struggling together; if the daily community does not feed this impulse, the romantic imagination pictures a grandiose nation in which all are one. If the simple duties of peace do not establish a common life, the emotions are mobilized in the service of a war that will supply its temporary simulation.

I have thus far made no reference to what many persons would consider the most serious and the most overtly evident of all the modes of loss of secure objects of loyalty—religion. It is probably easy to exaggerate the extent of the decadence of religion in an outward sense, church membership, church-going and so on. But it is hardly possible to overstate its decline as a vitally integrative and directive force in men's thought and sentiments. Whether even in the ages of the past that are called religious, religion was itself the actively central force that it is sometimes said to have been may be doubted. But it cannot be doubted that it was the symbol of the existence of conditions and forces that gave unity and a center to men's views of life. It at least gathered together in weighty and shared symbols a sense of the objects to which men were so attached as to have support and stay in their outlook on life.

Religion does not now effect this result. The divorce of church and state has been followed by that of religion and society. Wherever religion has not become a merely private indulgence, it has become at best a matter of sects and denominations divided from one another by doctrinal differences, and united internally by tenets that have a merely historical origin, and a purely metaphysical or else ritualistic meaning. There is no such bond of social unity as once united Greeks, Romans, Hebrews, and Catholic medieval Europe. There are those who realize what is portended by the loss of religion as an integrating bond. Many of them despair of its recovery through the development of social values to which the imagination and sentiments of individuals can attach themselves with intensity. They wish to reverse the operation and to form the social bond of unity and of allegiance by regeneration of the isolated individual soul.

Aside from the fact that there is no consensus as to what a new religious attitude is to center itself about, the injunction puts the cart before the horse. Religion is not so much a root of unity as it is its flower or fruit. The very attempt to secure integration for the individual, and through him for society, by means of a deliberate and conscious cultivation of religion, is itself proof of how far the individual has become lost through detachment from acknowledged social values. It is no wonder that when the appeal does not take the form of dogmatic fundamentalism, it tends to terminate in either some form of esoteric occultism or private estheticism. The sense of wholeness which is urged as the essence of religion can be built up and sustained only through membership in a society which has attained a degree of unity. The attempt to cultivate it first in individuals and then extend it to form an organically unified society is fantasy. Indulgence in this fantasy infects such interpretations of American life as are found, to take one signal example, in Waldo Frank's* "The Rediscovery of America." It marks a manner of yearning and not a principle of construction.

For the idea that the outward scene is chaotic because of the machine, which is a principle of chaos, and that it will remain so until individuals reinstitute wholeness within themselves, simply reverses the true state of things. The outward scene, if not fully organized, is relatively so in the corporateness which the machine and its technology have produced; the inner man is the jungle which can be subdued to order only as the forces of organization at work in externals are reflected in corresponding patterns of thought, imagination and emotion. The sick cannot heal themselves by means of their disease, and disintegrated individuals can achieve unity only as the dominant energies of community life are incorporated to form their minds. If these energies were, in reality, mere strivings for private pecuniary gain, the case would indeed be hopeless. But they are constituted by a collective art of technology, which individuals merely deflect to their private ends. There are the beginnings of an objective order through which individuals may get their bearings.

Conspicuous signs of the disintegration of individuality due to failure to reconstruct the self so as to meet the realities of present social life have not been mentioned. In a census that was taken among leaders of opinion concerning the urgency of present social problems, the state of law, the courts, lawlessness and criminality stood at the head of the list, and by a considerable distance. We are even more emphatically than when Kipling wrote the words, the people that make "the laws they flout, and flout the laws they make." We combine an ardor unparalleled in history for "passing" laws with a casual and deliberate disregard for them when they are on the statute books. We believe—to judge by our legislative actions—that we can create morals by law (witness the prohibition amendment for an instance on a large scale) and neglect the fact that all laws except those which regulate technical procedures are registrations of existing social customs and their attendant moral habits and purposes. I can, however, only think of this phenomenon as a symptom, not as a cause. It is a natural expression of a period in which changes in the structure of society have dissolved old bonds and allegiances. We attempt to make good this social relaxation and dissolution by legal enactments, while the actual disintegration discloses itself in the lawlessness which reveals the artificial character of this method of securing social integrity.

Volumes could be formed by collecting articles and editorials written about relaxation of traditional moral codes. A movement has caught public attention, which, having for some obscure reason assumed the name "humanism," proposes restraint and moderation, exercised in and by the higher volition of individuals, as the solution of our ills. It finds that naturalism as practiced by artists and mechanism as taught by philosophers who take their clew from natural science, have broken down the inner laws and imperatives which can alone bring order and loyalty. I should be glad to be able to believe that artists and intellectuals have any such power in their hands; if they had, after using it to bring evil to society, they might change face and bring healing to it. But a sense of fact, together with a sense of humor, forbids the acceptance of any such belief. Literary persons and academic thinkers are now, more than ever, effects, not causes. They reflect and voice the disintegration which new modes of living, produced by new forms of industry and commerce, have introduced. They give witness to the unreality that has overtaken traditional codes in the face of the impact of new forces; indirectly, they proclaim the need of some new synthesis. But this synthesis can

---

*After a brilliant exposition of the dissolution of the European synthesis, he goes on to say "man's need of order and his making of order are his science, his art, his religion; and these are all to be referred to the initial sense of order called the self," quite oblivious of the fact that this doctrine of the primacy of the self is precisely a reaction of the romantic and subjective age to the dissolution he has depicted, having its meaning only in that dissolution.

be humanistic only as the new conditions are themselves taken into account and are converted into the instrumentalities of a free and humane life. I see no way to "restrain" or turn back the industrial revolution and its consequences. In the absence of such a restraint (which would be efficacious if only it could occur), the urging of some inner restraint through the exercise of the higher personal will, whatever that may be, is itself only a futile echo of just the old individualism that has so completely broken down.

There are many phases of life which illustrate to anyone who chooses to think in terms of realities instead of words the utter irrelevance of the proposed remedy to actual conditions. One might take the present estate of amusements, of the movies, the radio, and organized vicarious sport, and ask just how this powerful eruption in which the resources of technology are employed for economic profit is to be met by the application of the inner *frein* or brake. Perhaps the most striking instance is found in the disintegration due to changes in family life and sex morale. It was not deliberate human intention that undermined the traditional household as the center of industry and education and as the focus of moral training; that sapped the older institution of enduring marriage. To ask the individuals who suffer the consequences of the general undermining and sapping to put an end to the consequences by acts of personal volition is merely to profess faith in moral magic. Recovery of individuals capable of stable and effective self-control can be had only as there is first a humbler exercise of will to observe existing social realities and to direct them according to their own potentialities.

Instances of the flux in which individuals are loosened from the ties that once gave order and support to their lives are glaring. They are indeed so glaring that they blind our eyes to the causes which produce them. Individuals are groping their way through situations which they do not direct and which do not give them direction. The beliefs and ideals that are uppermost in their consciousness are not relevant to the society in which they outwardly act and which constantly reacts upon them. Their conscious ideas and standards are inherited from an age that has passed away; their minds, as far as consciously entertained principles and methods of interpretation are concerned, are at odds with actual conditions. This profound split is the cause of distraction and bewilderment.

Individuals will refind themselves only as their ideas and ideals are brought into harmony with the realities of the age in which they act. The task of attaining this harmony is not an easy one. But it is more negative than it seems. If we could inhibit the principles and standards that are merely traditional, if we could slough off the opinions that have no living relationship to the situations in which we live, the unavowed forces that now work upon us unconsciously but unremittingly would have a chance to build minds after their own pattern, and individuals might, in consequence, find themselves in possession of objects to which imagination and emotion would stably attach themselves.

I do not mean, however, that the process of rebuilding can go on automatically. Discrimination is required in order to detect the beliefs and institutions that dominate merely because of custom and inertia, and in order to discover the moving realities of the present. Intelligence must distinguish, for example, the tendencies of the technology which produce the new corporateness from those inheritances proceeding out of the individualism of an earlier epoch which arrest and divide the operation of the new dynamics. It is difficult for us to conceive of individualism except in terms of stereotypes derived from former centuries. Individualism has been identified with ideas of initiative and invention that are bound up with private and exclusive economic gain. As long as this conception possesses our minds, the ideal of harmonizing our thought and desire with the realities of present social conditions will be interpreted to mean accommodation and surrender. It will even be understood to signify rationalization of the evils of existing society. A stable recovery of individuality waits upon an elimination of the older economic and political individualism, an elimination which will liberate imagination and endeavor for the task of making corporate society contribute to the free culture of its members. Only by economic revision can the sound element in the older individualism—equality of opportunity—be made a reality.

It is the part of wisdom to note the double meaning of such ideas as "acceptance." There is an acceptance that is of the intellect; it signifies facing facts for what they are. There is another acceptance that is of the emotions and will; that involves commitment of desire and effort. So far are the two from being identical that acceptance in the first sense is the precondition of all intelligent refusal of acceptance in the second sense. There is a prophetic aspect to all observation; we can perceive the meaning of what exists only as we forecast the consequences it entails. When a situation is as confused and divided within itself as is the present social estate, choice is implicated in observation. As one perceives different tendencies and different possible consequences, preference inevitably goes out to one or the other. Because acknowledgment in thought brings with it intelligent discrimination and choice, it is the first step out of confusion, the first step in forming those objects of significant allegiance out of which stable and efficacious individuality may grow. It might even perform the miracle of rendering conservatism relevant and thoughtful. It certainly is the prerequisite of an anchored liberalism.

14
Why Paris
George Wickes

While Dewey and others focused on the social and philosophical roots of American alienation, many of America's greatest talents expressed their sense of estrangement and change by joining the cultural, artistic and intellectual avant-garde of Europe. Of course, the center for this modernistic movement was Paris. Beginning with a discussion of Paris from the perspective of Gertrude Stein, George Wickes, Professor of English at the University of Oregon, introduces us to the people who helped make that city and that era so exciting and important. The following essay is from George Wickes, *Americans in Paris* (New York: Da Capo Paperback, 1980).

In the doubtful autumn of 1939 when Frenchmen were being mobilized and demobilized and no one knew whether this time there was going to be a war or not, Gertrude Stein had retired to the mountain village of Bilignin where for many years she had spent her summers. It was a good place to be at that uncertain time, removed from the highroad of armies and political turmoil, close to the soil, where one could be sure of finding enough to eat if the worst happened. Gertrude Stein hoped that the worst would not happen, but she thought it prudent to be prepared. She took a detached view of political events, a characteristic French view that daily life went on anyhow through wars and turmoil. After all, she had been through one war already.

So in 1939, when another war threatened, she stayed on in Bilignin after the summer was over, she and her inseparable companion of thirty-odd years, Alice Toklas. They were to weather the war in that part of France and to come through it quite well, considering that they were both Jewish and American. For even in occupied France they enjoyed a privileged status that protected them from the Germans.

It was in Bilignin some seven years before that Gertrude Stein had written her memoirs, *The Autobiography of Alice B. Toklas.* Now once again the place gave her the leisure, and the times put her in a reflective mood. By now she had spent more than half of her life in Paris, and she had childhood memories of Paris going back to the age of four. Looking back over sixty years' experience, she wrote *Paris France,* a loving tribute to the city, the country, and the people. In its unpretentious way this little book explains why a wise old American woman had made France her home for most of her life and would stay there till the end. It also explains better than anything else that has been written what Paris and France meant to American writers and artists during the first four decades of this century.

Reprinted by permission of The Plenum Publishing Corporation from AMERICANS IN PARIS by George Wickes.

"Paris, France is exciting and peaceful," the book begins, suggesting both the stimulus of the great metropolis and the well-ordered calm of its everyday life that made Paris a good place to live. Like most Americans who stayed for any length of time, Gertrude Stein lived *bourgeoisement* in a quiet neighborhood where she did her marketing, walked her dog, and knew all sorts of ordinary citizens. This side of Paris was as important to her as any, and she found the daily life congenial, democratic, easy, and comfortable. At the same time people respected her privacy and let her live as she chose, free from the pressures for conformity that she would have felt in America. Such qualities, she felt, made the French the most civilized people on earth. For the Americans who found Paris a good environment to live and work in, French civilization did not necessarily mean the sort of thing taught in courses for foreigners at the Sorbonne—the Gothic cathedrals, the court of Louis XIV, Racine and Corneille. Gertrude Stein pays no attention to the official glories in *Paris France*. Instead she tells little anecdotes which demonstrate how civilized the ordinary Frenchman is in his daily life—how sensitive, unsentimental, polite, frank, reserved, logical, and sensible. The French, she finds, have a down-to-earth understanding of the basic facts of life and death, the family and the soil.

"But really what they do do is to respect art and letters, if you are a writer you have privileges, if you are a painter you have privileges and it is pleasant having those privileges." Underlying French civilization is a traditional respect for certain values, which Gertrude Stein illustrates through an anecdote about having her car parked in an already overcrowded garage, a homely instance of the rule that in France a woman of letters takes precedence over a millionaire or a politician. As many Americans have discovered to their surprise, the police and other authorities tend to treat artists and writers deferentially, regarding them as useful members of the commonwealth, not as oddities or parasites. The French take it for granted that the arts have a place in the national well-being. This does not mean that every Frenchman aspires to be an artist or would substitute art for plumbing, but simply that he recognizes its function and respects its practitioner. To an artist coming from a land where altogether different values exerted pressure on the arts, the French attitude was a reassuring source of self-respect.

More specifically, Gertrude Stein theorizes about the impact of Paris on the modern arts. Much of the book is devoted to the thesis that "Paris was where the twentieth century was." Civilization and the arts are governed by mysterious laws. For some undiscovered reason certain ages and certain countries are more creative than others. After speculating about the alternatives, Gertrude Stein concludes that Paris was the right place to be from 1900 to 1939. England refused to leave the nineteenth century, America was overwhelmed by the technology of the twentieth century, but France remained relatively unaffected. In an age when the new science made the world a disturbing place, Paris still gave the impression that the world was round. She was both modern and traditional, she accepted change but did not let it change her, and thus she provided a background of cultural stability conducive to the arts. "So Paris was the place that suited those of us that were to create the twentieth century art and literature, naturally enough."

Certainly Paris was where the avant-garde was, the great international center for creative experiment in all the arts. Most of the creating, according to Gertrude Stein, was done by foreign artists and writers. Paris had always been hospitable to foreign artists, and in the twentieth century the three great geniuses of Paris—Picasso in painting, Stravinsky in music, Joyce in literature—were all foreigners. There was plenty of native genius too, providing a rich humus for the cultivation of new talent.

Experiment was the keynote of the arts of Paris. All kinds of new movements and styles proliferated there, in a constant evolution from the turn of the century on—fauvism, cubism, dada, surrealism, to mention only the major developments. And all the arts worked together in Paris in a total synthesis that enriched them all. To an American working in relative isolation or at best in a Greenwich Village, such an atmosphere opened up new worlds and enlarged his sensitivity to all the arts.

Inevitably the question of expatriation arises. Why couldn't the artist stay home and be just as creative? Why must he go whoring after foreign fashions? There are several answers, the best of them provided by Gertrude Stein: "American is my country but Paris is my home town." She always remained thoroughly American and found that living in France made here more aware of her native country. She had a theory that a writer must live abroad to be fully alive to his inner feelings and able to express himself. "That is why writers have to have two countries, the one where they belong and the one in which they live really." She was not an expatriate in the sense of being an exile; she never felt alienated from her native land. She had gone to Europe in response to a deep-seated cultural instinct. The distinction is an important one, for the expatriates discussed in this book went abroad for positive rather than negative reasons. Some of them may have been at odds with their society, but the important thing is that they settled in Paris to work seriously.

This book is not about that overworked subject, the rootless expatriates of the lost generation. It is about the American writers, artists, and composers who lived and worked in Paris during the first four decades of this century. A certain amount of anecdote is part of the story, but the point is not that the protagonists were odd characters who did funny things but that they were artists who did highly original things. Bohemia is part of the setting, not because *la vie de bohème* is picturesque but because Bohemia is where the avant-garde was.

So many Americans went to Paris that it is impossible to do them all justice. This book does not even mention Alexander Calder, Glenway Wescott, Stuart Davis, Katherine Anne Porter, Peggy Guggenheim, Janet Flanner, Abraham Rattner, and a hundred others. Since the subject is inexhaustible, it seemed best to focus on a few exemplary figures who would then stand for all the others. These artists, writers, or composers all lived in Paris for an appreciable length of time—several years, a decade, half a lifetime—and produced some of their most significant work there—in most cases their best work. Individually and collectively, they present an impressive record of the impact of Paris on the American imagination.

Paris meant something different to each of them, a pleasant ambience, a sense of freedom, a foreign temperament that challenged and complemented their own, or a way of life conducive to creation. All of them found it a good place to work. Naturally they learned about their art and craft from the artists they encountered. What they produced cannot be called French, though one or two adopted a Parisian style, and none was unaffected. Chiefly they felt the all-pervasive classical spirit of France, even in an iconoclastic age. Under this influence they became more conscious of form, style, language, or medium than any previous generation of Americans.

Each of them responded differently to the opportunities Paris offered. Before the war Gertrude Stein and her circle collected the modern art of Paris, with far-reaching consequences for American art—and perhaps literature. In her experimental writing Gertrude Stein seemed to be imitating the cubist painters. Daniel-Henry Kahnweiler, the great apostle of cubism, sees close similarities between her writing, Schoenberg's music, and the painting of Picasso and Gris. But perhaps the analogy can be pushed too far. One of the so-called cubist poets, Pierre Reverdy, rejected the whole notion: "*La poésie cubiste? Terme ridicule!*" Picasso himself, when Gertrude Stein's brother Leo asked his opinion, did not see how words could be used abstractly, apart from their meanings. In any case Gertrude Stein evolved as a writer during a period which she spent mostly in the company of painters, surrounded by French-speaking people. These circumstances may account for her idiosyncratic style. Then too, living abroad left her free from the restraints of convention, free to develop the eccentricity that was an essential part of her talent.

E. E. Cummings and John Dos Passos represent the war experience of their generation that brought them to Paris in the first place and induced them to return afterward. This is the story told by Malcolm Cowley in *Exile's Return,* the best chronicle of his generation's collective experience. The "gentlemen volunteers" he writes about were more privileged than the doughboys and their experience less typical, but they happened to be more literate, so their war record remains. Cowley lists the writers who drove ambulances and camions during the last two years of the war: Cummings, Dos Passos, Hemingway, Slater Brown, Robert Hillyer, John Howard Lawson, Julian Green, William Seabrook, Harry Crosby, Sidney Howard, Louis Bromfield, and Dashiell Hammett. Almost all of them returned to Paris during the early twenties. Cowley feels that the war uprooted his contemporaries by transporting them to a foreign land where they became mere spectators with no share in what was going on, that the armistice left them both disengaged from society and restless for further adventures. But there were plenty of good positive reasons for going to Paris after the war, beginning with the fact that many Americans had fallen in love with its charms while in uniform.

After the war American poets flocked to the city of Villon and Baudelaire. Besides Cummings, Robert Hillyer, Ezra Pound, William Carlos Williams, Archibald MacLeish, Stephen Vincent Benét, Allen Tate, and Hart Crane all gravitated to Paris, some staying four or five years. Before the war T. S. Eliot had studied philosophy at the Sorbonne for a year and even contemplated becoming a French poet like the two American-born symbolists, Stuart Merrill and Francis Vielé-Griffin. After the war Pound spent four years in Paris, where his Montparnasse studio was the scene of his multifarious activities as sculptor, composer, editor, literary dictator, and occasionally poet. Through their poetry and criticism Eliot and Pound made American writers more susceptible to French literature than ever before. Laforgue, Eliot said toward the end of his life, "was the first to teach me how to speak," and the symbolists, he added, "are now as much in our bones as Shakespeare or Donne."

Ernest Hemingway, more than any other American, epitomizes Montparnasse in its heyday, a glamorous, legendary Arcadia for postwar disillusionment. Actually Hemingway was critical of its wastrels and poseurs, as were most serious writers. Still, Montparnasse was the headquarters of the American literary avant-garde in the twenties, and scornful or not, the writers congregated in its cafés. Quite a few of them were first published there in little magazines or in subsidized volumes produced by amateur publishers. Hemingway himself owed much to both and even played his part in editing Ford Madox Ford's *Transatlantic Review.* Hemingway spent his apprentice years in Paris, produced much of his best work there, and later looked back upon those years as his best.

Man Ray also lived in Montparnasse, but his orbit was less exclusively American. In fact he knew no Americans at first and was surrounded by French poets and artists from the moment of his arrival. In New York during the war he had belonged to a circle that included several Parisian refugees and with two of them had formed the nucleus that was later known as New York dada. Thus when he went to Paris a few years later, he was welcomed by the local dadaists. Of the many American artists who worked in Paris, two in particular were accepted as members of French movements, Mary Cassatt in the nineteenth century and Man Ray in the twentieth. Just as she had settled down among the impressionists, so he became identified with the dadaists and surrealists successively. During the period between the wars he played a conspicuous part on the Paris art scene as a master technician who experimented in all the visual arts.

Virgil Thomson represents the generation of composers that chose Paris as the best place to study music. Like most of his contemporaries he felt the need for a cosmopolitan setting to develop his gifts and instinctively rejected the Germanic musical tradition which prevailed in America. During the teens of this century Paris suddenly emerged as an international center of music and ballet. During the twenties many young American composers studied with Nadia Boulanger, acquiring from that great teacher a liberal education as well as a classical discipline. To American audiences French music still meant Debussy, but composers in Paris like Thomson and George Antheil felt the more modern influence of Erik Satie and the neoclassicism of Stravinsky. Antheil had a brief, precocious career in Paris in the mid-twenties. Thomson, who had to wait until the thirties for recognition, introduced America to a new concept of musical theater with *Four Saints in Three Acts,* a work that achieved a synthesis of the arts in the Parisian manner.

Henry Miller went to Paris when most of the Americans were coming home. In New York he had long felt the influence of Paris through such manifestations as the Armory Show and little magazines like *Transition.* He had been writing for years but had been completely frustrated in his efforts to express himself. Paris was the catalyst he needed. The city satisfied his emotional, intellectual, and creative needs as New York had never done. There he was able to find himself as a writer and do his best work in the dadaist and surrealist vein. There he found the material for his first published novel and the only conceivable place where it could be published. In one of the earliest reviews of *Tropic of Cancer* Edmund Wilson called the book "the epitaph for the whole generation of American writers and artists that migrated to Paris after the war." The book can also be read as a satire on that generation, exposing all the comic and sordid reality behind the romantic expatriate myth. In his cancerous view Miller best represents the period of the depression and the foreshadowing of a second world war that was to bring the era to a close.

IV
Woman as Outsider

15
Freedom and Desire: Charlotte Perkins Gilman and Kate Chopin

Sam B. Girgus

Two books appeared in the last two years of the nineteenth century, Kate Chopin's *The Awakening* (1899) and Charlotte Perkins Gilman's *Women and Economics* (1898), that were destined to become classics of modern feminist thought and sensibility. Both books, one an exquisitely written novel about a woman's sexual and psychological "awakening" and the other, an important economic and sociological treatise on the status of women, are major intellectual sources of modern feminism. Landmarks in the drive toward the liberation of women, the books describe the exclusion of women from the rhetoric and ideology of consensus. However, while Chopin and Gilman are revolutionary in their examinations of women, they are also interesting for their differences. They evince radically contrasting perspectives on how women can achieve freedom in the modern era. For Gilman women's liberation can be gained only through major reform of the social and economic structures that influence behavior. Even in her classic psychological story, "The Yellow Wallpaper," she maintains that individual psychology and internal emotional states are reflections of the external social environment and of oppressive ideological systems of belief. Basically she sees desire as an enemy of women on the road to freedom. In contrast, Kate Chopin, while equally radical in her insistence on the independence of women, saw freedom as a process of relationships involving the psychology of desire and social ideologies. For Chopin sexuality serves as a vital and inexorable source of identity and strength, whereas for Gilman sexuality and sexual differences have been a major source for the oppression of women. Probably Gilman's ideological emphasis on reform and social reorganization has dominated the feminist drive toward equality; it, therefore, provides an interesting contrast with Chopin's position. At the same time, Gilman proffers an important delineation of the social and economic forces which barred women from full participation in the American consensus and stifled their creativity. I, therefore, would like to briefly examine Gilman's major book as a social and economic context for Kate Chopin's works and as a contrast with Chopin's vision of the relationship between desire and consensus.

I

As Gary Scharnhorst says, Gilman's *Women and Economics* "was the culmination of the feminist and socialist critique she had formulated over the previous decade."[1] Written as a tract and polemic for change, the book argues that all aspects of women's condition, including sexuality, the home, family, personal identity and freedom, evolve around their situation of dependence upon

From a Forthcoming book, *Desire and Consensus Ideology and the Unconscious in American Literature* by Sam B. Girgus to be published in 1989.

men. It sets forth a coherent analysis of women's situation based on Gilman's vision of women as enslaved to domestic and sexual functions. Thus, her theory centers on her idea of an inseparable link for women between the sexual function and the economic function. Women perform their sexual function to achieve a living while men work to have sex on a regular basis. "She gets her living by getting a husband. He gets his wife by getting a living. It is to her individual economic advantage to secure a mate. It is to his individual sex-advantage to secure economic gain. The sex-functions to her have become economic functions. Economic functions to him have become sex-functions."[2] Such explosive ideas expressed in an immediate and powerful prose style help account for Gilman's international recognition. As Carl N. Deglar writes, "The book attracted wide attention; ultimately seven editions appeared in the United States and Great Britain and it was translated into seven languages, including Japanese, Russian and Hungarian. As a result of this book, the ideas of which she endlessly expounded in other books, articles and lectures, Charlotte Gilman became the leading intellectual in the women's movement in the United States during the first two decades of the twentieth century" (p. xiii).

Gilman maintained that the combination of sexual power and economics, "when the mate becomes also the master, when economic necessity is added to sex-attraction" (p. 38), perverts the relationship between men and women. It turns men and women into grotesques. The woman's reliance on her sexuality for survival turns all women into "over-sexed" versions of prostitutes. "Because of the economic dependence on the human female on her mate, she is modified to sex to an excessive degree" (pp. 38–39). There is, she emphasizes, a "morbid tendency" to be "over-sexed" (pp. 39, 40) in our culture. Whether seen as a "milch cow," "non-productive consumer," a "cupid in the kitchen" or "the priestess of the temple of consumption" (pp. 43, 116, 236, 120), the woman becomes a monstrosity. Accordingly, *Women and Economics* urges an end to the bond connecting sexuality and economic dependence. Many years after writing the book, she recalled what motivated her to write "my first book, in prose, named by the publishers, *Women and Economics*." She says, "Full of the passion for world improvement, and seeing the position of women as responsible for much, very much, of our evil condition, I had been studying it for years as a problem of instant importance. The political equality demanded by the suffragists was not enough to give real freedom. Women whose industrial position is that of a house-servant, or who do no work at all, who are fed, clothed, and given pocket-money by men, do not reach freedom and equality by the use of the ballot."[3] Thus, seeing economic independence as the only viable basis from which women could build their freedom and individuality, she put forth a program for a society free from over-sexualization. To do this required a major attack against the conventional family and household and its replacement by new forces for the professionalization and socialization of women's traditional roles. As Scharnhorst says, "Gilman built her case against the home on the pillars of economics and sociology."[4]

In arguing for the assumption of traditional domestic roles by a new cadre of professionals and social scientists, Gilman was developing an idea whose roots went back to the Jacksonian era. However, the movement made major advances at the end of the last century as part of a new ideology of the social sciences that demanded the rationalization and organization of society. Placing Gilman in this ever more powerful school of thought, William Leach writes, "The discovery of scientific social laws made possible the realization of the positivist goal: the unified and centralized organization of the new social order. This organization would be obtained by reliance on a new class of scientific experts and by the moral regeneration of the people. Scientific experts were supposed to discover the law of society in an apolitical, nonpartisan way, while it was the government's purpose to implement these laws. Other intellectuals prepared the people for the moral acceptance of this organized society. For positivists, moral reform had to precede other material changes. Before the introduction of other reforms, people had to learn to sacrifice their individual, private interests to the interests of the community."[5] Believing the family to be a kind of prison for women, Gilman argued that the new scientific professionalism that Leach describes would enable women to escape the confines of the home and to discover their true creative potential. A new "trained professional service" would satisfy "the growing social need . . . for the specializing of the industries practiced in the home and for the proper mechanical provision for them" (pp. 241, 243). Therefore, in combination with her ideas for new communal planning, including the construction of apartment dwellings "for professional women with families" (p. 242), the professional social scientists would not only save beleaguered housewives from the confinement of domestic duties, but also would make society itself better and more efficient. Instead of simply focusing their abilities upon one small household unit, women could apply their talents to the whole society. As Scharnhorst says, "The cult of domesticity and the idealization of motherhood hinder women from discharging their larger social duties. Gilman refused to genuflect at the alter of household gods and dismissed the matriolatry implicit in celebrations of the maternal instinct."[6]

Gilman's attack on the family extended to conventional views of motherhood. She believed that for most women the idealization of motherhood was a result of over-sexualization. It was a product of the segregation of women in the family. Thus, she argued for the professionalism of mothering as part of the specialization of all domestic functions. Individuals who are especially talented or interested in nurturing should be encouraged to do so for the benefit of the whole society. "Some women there are, and some men, whose highest service to humanity is the care of children. Such should not concentrate their powers upon their own children alone—a most questionable advantage—but should be so placed that their talent and skill, their knowledge and experience, would benefit the largest number of children. Many women there are, and many men, who though able to bring forth fine children, are unable to educate them properly. Simply to bear children is a personal matter—an animal function. Education is collective, human, a social function" (p. 283). Many of her stories, especially those published in her magazine, *The Forerunner,* dramatize these views on the family and motherhood. The stories often illustrate that the intrusion of a social expert into a terrible domestic situation could save a family. In "The Unnatural Mother," a title that reflected her recollection of the condemnation of her decision to surrender custody of her own daughter, a dead women is vilified by society for her actions, while in "Mr. Peeble's Heart," the interference of a modern, independent sister-in-law in a conventional and boring marriage creates fresh opportunities for happiness and self-fulfillment.

Even by today's standards, Gilman's program seems radical. It amounted to nothing less than a major de-sexualization of society designed to encourage equality and to transfer power and authority from individuals and the family to new and larger social structures and forces. Society itself would become a family. "What we need is not less home, but more; not a lessening of the love of human beings for a home, but its extension through new and more effective expression" (p. 223). This view of society demonstrated Gilman's basic creed and faith in the power of the social and cultural environment to change human personality and character. As Degler says, "Convinced of the molding power of environment, she stressed the plasticity of human nature" (p. xxii). Thus, at the very beginning of her book she expresses her central tenet: "the general course of life shows the inexorable effect of conditions upon humanity" (pp. 1–2). Therefore, by manipulating and controlling the economic and cultural environment, social engineers and technicians will influence and alter human character and compensate for the injustices committed in earlier ignorance of the powers of social science.

While Gilman's view of the family may seem original, radical and extreme, she was not alone. She was, as Christopher Lasch maintains, part of a broad assault upon the modern family. "Historians of the family have paid too little attention to the way in which public policy, sometimes conceived quite deliberately not as a defense of the family at all but as an invasion of it, contributed to the deterioration of domestic life. The family did not simply evolve in response to social and economic influences; it was deliberately transformed by the intervention of planners and policymakers. Educators and social reformers saw that the family, especially the immigrant family, stood as an obstacle to what they conceived as social progress—in other words, to homogenization and 'Americanization.'" Unfortunately, Gilman's sometimes reactionary views about race and immigrants lend support to Lasch's theory of the motivation behind efforts at reform of the family. However, this program for the transformation of the family formed a major component of the overall goal of the progressive movement to, as Lasch says, "regulate anarchic business conditions, reduce social and economic inequality through educational reform and taxation, and promote 'cooperation' between workers and capitalists, government and industry. Convinced that 'interdependence' had emerged as the ruling principle of industrial society, American progressives hoped to eliminate selfish individualism by exposing children as early as possible to the influence of the school, the juvenile courts, and other agencies of socialized tuition."[7]

To make such radical changes occur, Gilman felt it would be necessary to redirect the energy of sexual relations toward society itself. "The time has come when we are open to deeper and wider impulses than the sex-instinct; the social instincts are strong enough to come into full use at last" (p. 138). Such a redirection of the sexual instinct would encourage "the increase of social consciousness" (p. 138) for the elevation of social life to a higher moral plane. "The intensification of sex-energy as a social force results in such limitless exaggeration of sex-instinct as finds expression sexually in the unnatural vices of advanced civilization, and socially, in the strained economic relations between producer and consumer which breaks society in two" (pp. 141–142).

Of course, from a psychoanalytic point of view, Gilman's ideas constitute a program for neurosis. Rather than redirect sexual energy and love toward socially useful purposes, it would frustrate and antagonize such force and drive it underground to fester and create the very corruption Gilman wishes to avoid. Furthermore, her hopes to desexualize society, to literally extirpate the drive from the psyche and replace it with a new social consciousness, ultimately would institute a sexual police force. It is interesting, therefore, that in her biography she indicates obvious personal discomfort with sexuality. "Perhaps the most salient change of the present period is the lowering of standards in sex relations, approaching some of the worst periods in ancient history. In my youth there was a fine, earnest movement toward an equal standard of chastity for men and women, and equalizing upward to the level of what women were then. But now the very word 'chastity' seems to have become ridiculous. Even if complete promiscuity is avoided, there is a preliminary promiscuity of approach which leaves little to be desired."[8] In Gilman's case such a relatively conventional and moralistic attack on promiscuity really masks an aversion to sexuality itself. As Ann J. Lane says, "The murky world of the unconscious must have frightened Charlotte Gilman. Conceding to these subterranean forces, the very ones that almost destroyed her, she saw as a denial of one's unique quality as a thinking creature. The psychiatric notions of her day, particularly when she was a young woman, certainly had proved themselves dangerous to her."[9] Similarly Degler notes, "The new-found interest in Freudian psychology and sex she thought excessive. . . . In several places she made it clear that she thought sex was intended by nature only for procreation, not for 'recreation,' as she scornfully summed up her view of the sexual revolution of the 1920's" (p. xv). About the "rush" to "Freudian psychology" and "the flock of 'psycho-analysts'" she wrote in her autobiography: "Always it has amazed me to see how apparently intelligent persons would permit these mind-meddlers, having no claim to fitness except that of having read certain utterly unproven books, to paddle among their thoughts and feelings, and extract confessions of the last intimacy. Men and women with no warrant in professional education, setting up offices and giving treatment—for handsome fees—became plentiful." She reacted with great anger upon discovering an unsolicited "long psychoanalysis of my case" by an individual who reputedly resented her resistance to being " 'psyched.' " She gave the report to her second husband, George Houghton Gilman. " 'I don't want to read this stuff,' I said. 'You look it over and tell me what it is about.' This he did, to my utter disgust. 'Burn it up, do,' I urged. 'I haven't the least curiosity to know what this person thinks is the matter with me.' "[10]

Some important facts about Gilman's biography should provide valuable background for understanding the circumstances that contributed to forming her opinions about sexuality, women and the family. She was born on 30 July 1860. Her father, Frederic Beecher Perkins, was the grandson of Lyman Beecher. This connection to the noted New England theologian meant that she also was related to Catherine Beecher, the reformer, Harriet Beecher Stowe and Henry Ward Beecher, the famous Congregational minister. A writer of note and a librarian, Perkins apparently was a distant and silent man who abandoned Charlotte's family soon after her birth. This resulted in a childhood and adolescence that were marked by poverty and a personal quest for independence and strength. However, it also touched her psychologically. Two comments in her autobiography seem especially important as indications of psychic damage done to her because of the absence in her early life of visible signs of love and emotion. "Looking back on my uncuddled childhood it seems to me a sad mistake of my heroic mother to withhold from me the petting I so craved, the sufficing comfort of maternal caresses."[11] She later recounts a visit with her father in California where she had gone in the hope of recuperating from a nervous breakdown. "My father was then at the head of the San Francisco Public Library. He met me on the Oakland side, and took me across to a room he had engaged for me for a day or two. Here he solemnly called on me, as would any acquaintance, and went with me across the ferry again when I started south." The use of the word "acquaintance" with all its cold distance accentuates the pain she associates with the encounter. The conversation she recounts confirms this impression of bitterness: " 'If you ever come to Providence again I hope you will come to see me,' said I politely, as we parted, to which he courteously replied, 'Thank you. I will bear your invitation in mind.' "[12]

In spite of her derogatory remarks about psychoanalysis, Gilman had considerable insight into the relationship between the loveless situation of her youth and her later breakdown and problems. "That part of the ruin was due to the conditions of childhood I do not doubt, and part to the rigid stoicism and constant effort in character-building of my youth; I was 'over-trained,' had wasted my substance in riotous—virtues." However, she considered her "mismarriage" to handsome and considerate Charles Walter Stetson, a young artist she met in Rhode Island, as the "immediate" cause of her breakdown.[13] Ultimately, she and Stetson divorced and she allowed him to raise their daughter, Katherine. Stetson later married one of her closest friends, Grace Channing, an event that seems to have cemented the friendship all three felt for each other. She then married Charles Houghton Gilman, a cousin, who also was related to Daniel Coit Gilman, the president of Johns Hopkins University. In any event, the subject of her breakdown became the basis for her most famous story, "The Yellow Wallpaper," which earned the praise of William Dean Howells and was included in his collection *Great American Short Stories* in 1920. In the story she describes the breakdown of a woman who is clearly victimized by her physician husband who treats her very much the way that Gilman was treated by Dr. S. Weir Mitchell of Philadelphia, "the greatest nerve specialist in the country," as Gilman herself described him.[14] Confined to rest in a room with hideous wallpaper, she imagines that the paper achieves a kind of organic life of its own and that the paper houses and imprisons a woman like herself. While depicting perfectly the woman's sense of victimization and persecution, the story never quite renders her internal state of being. The victim's psychic state is a reflection of her environment. Thus, the story is part of Gilman's attempt to demonstrate, as Lane says, "the social roots of mental illness."[15]

There is a certain irony in that someone as familiar as Gilman with the fragility of human experience should place so much faith in the power of social science and structure to control and determine character and events. Although aware—perhaps to a certain extent even obsessed—with the power of sexuality and the secrets of the mind, Gilman's philosophy of freedom insisted on the ability of state agencies to control and direct those forces of hidden rebellion. This view of the social sciences creates an illusion of security that diminishes the capacity of the individual to understand oppression and counter it. While she remains a true pioneer of social thought and feminism, her work ultimately reflects a stronger faith in social science than in freedom and autonomy. It puts in the hands of the state a power and authority that infringe upon any interior domain to resist control. As part of the larger movement and advancement of the social sciences, her body of work developed the idea of the inadequacy of individuals to deal with the complexity of the social and cultural environment. Gilman saw desire as the enemy within and expelled it, thereby strengthening the forces of social conditioning. While she argued that the absence of women from the ideology of consensus was oppressive, her denial of the importance of the dynamics of the interior self also could undermine her search for freedom. In contrast, Kate Chopin saw desire and consensus as involved in a constant process of interaction, separation and reconstruction. Thus, for Chopin freedom could not be imposed from without but involved a continuing dialog of internal and external forces. Liberation requires not only strong social organization and reenforcement, but internal strength and structure as well. The failure to achieve this balance as part of an ever changing relationship of internal and external forces creates its own version of oppression in the form of the narcissistic fear of engaging the self with the limitations of psychological and social realities. Kate Chopin's work introduces this theme of narcissism and internal strength into the relationship between freedom and desire.

II

After several decades of neglect, Kate Chopin now occupies an important place in our literary tradition. The recognition that *The Awakening* is an important and controversial feminist work helps to explain the revivification of Chopin's literary reputation during the past twenty years.[16] Chopin's heroine, Edna Pontellier, leaves her husband and children and attempts to create a new identity and style of life for herself. Victorian readers naturally found Chopin's story of adultery, sexual passion and pleasure, abandonment, liberation and suicide to be shocking. However, even radical changes in contemporary standards, life and institutions do not diminish the impact upon today's reader of this novel. In fact, our recent social and sexual history probably increases the relevance to our own age of Edna's emotional and instinctive probings into the labyrinth of moral and psychological issues that comprise sexual, marital and familial relationships. While Chopin's depiction of Edna's rebellion against conventional standards and mores firmly establishes *The Awakening* as a feminist classic, the novel also places Edna's quest for freedom within a broad context of psychological and philosophical issues. The book delineates Edna's search for freedom and identity as a woman in terms of questions about the nature of freedom itself. It asks how interior psychological development and maturity relate to the forces of the cultural and social environments in enabling the individual to achieve a degree of autonomy and freedom. Chopin's understanding of freedom as a dialectic involving internal and external forces in many ways dramatizes and parallels the insights and ideas of another thinker and writer who studied late Victorian values and morals—Sigmund Freud. On the verge of producing the great works of psychoanalysis that would revolutionize modern thought, Freud in 1899 would have been interested in Chopin's presentation of Edna Pontellier's character, life and death. Chopin's *The Awakening* seems especially open to psychoanalytical interpretation. The important themes of the novel—sexuality, domestic and family life, child rearing, love and survival—are subjects of fundamental importance to Freudian psychoanalysis, and therefore, make a psychoanalytical reading of the novel truly appropriate. Both Freud and Chopin in their own ways illuminate the interiorization in the unconscious of the ideologies of the Victorian era. Thus, in a seminal essay on *The Awakening,* Cynthia Griffin Wolff renders a compelling psychoanalytical interpretation of the novel that brilliantly analyzes Edna's character without forgetting the historical and cultural contexts of the book. Wolff's psychoanalytical study of the book serves to explain why, as she says, "reading it can be a devastating and unforgettable experience."[17]

However, recent interpretations of Freud can render a fresh understanding of the psychological, cultural and social complexity of the novel. Thus, Janine Chasseguet-Smirgel's studies of the ego ideal that we discussed earlier, can be used to expand upon Wolff's initial insight into Edna Pontellier's narcissistic character. Edna's narcissism, as elucidated by Chasseguet-Smirgel's theory of the body ego, psychic ego and the ego ideal, also manifests itself in Edna's use of language. The novel suggests a connection between Edna's narcissism and a form of speechlessness and thoughtlessness. It indicates a parallel between Edna's psycho-sexual development and her frequent failure to speak and think coherently. Edna embodies the unfulfilled desire at the center of human identity and psychology that fails, in her case, to structure and organize itself through the use of symbols and language. The role of language and desire in forming character and human relationships that *The Awakening* dramatizes has been the subject of study and research by two writers and feminists whom we also have discussed before, Juliet Mitchell and Jacqueline Rose. Their development of Jacques Lacan's theory of sexuality and symbolization helps to explain not only the power of *The Awakening* but also how it anticipates contemporary concerns about sex, language and desire.

The pattern of sex, language and desire in *The Awakening* also delineates an ideological position regarding freedom. Chopin's work proffers an ideology of love and desire that provides the foundation for the individual's relationship to external cultural and social environments. For Chopin the influence of these external forces upon the organization of internal impulses of love and desire is limited. Thus, she suggests the possibility of a realm recalcitrant to economic and cultural control. Freedom, in other words, cannot be reduced to being the end product of social and cultural change and reform. At the same time, if political and social action cannot in themselves guarantee Chopin's conception of individual liberation, freedom also cannot be secured by a retreat from external reality into a domain of self-love and isolation. Individual freedom for Chopin requires love to find the words and langauge to organize itself and develop beyond a perverted form of narcissism. In her quest for freedom, Chopin's heroine must steer between the silent death of narcissism and the repression of a patriarchal culture. By charting this journey for Edna, Chopin wrote a major American novel and contributed to the history of sexuality and women's freedom in America. Her work plays an unusual role in the tradition of modern feminism and liberation because of her emphasis on the uniqueness of each individual's interior life and development as a loving, sexual and needing being.

Chopin's work, including *The Awakening,* clearly demonstrates that an important element of her view of freedom and liberation involves a sensitive awareness of the need to assure equality between the sexes as well as women's rights. Such stories as "Wiser than a God," "A Point at Issue," "The Story of an Hour," and "A Respectable Woman" reveal Chopin's acutely innovative and unconventional attitude toward marriage, the family and sexuality. Nevertheless, social reform without regard for the internal, psychological basis for freedom was clearly anathema to her. Reformers could simply substitute one form of social oppression for another. Thus, her biographer Per Seyersted describes her as having "no desire to reform, but only to understand with the clear conscience of the rebel, yet unembittered by society's massive lack of understanding."[18] In fact, one of her most interesting stories constitutes a careful dissection of a reformer in the character of Miss Georgia McEnders, a member of the Women's Reform Club and author of "The Dignity of Labor." Chopin's acerbic portrait of her as a self-centered hypocrite sustains Seyersted's claim that she did not believe in "progress" nor "in idealism or reform."[19] Certainly, throughout her career, Chopin concentrated upon the sources of freedom and character in the unconscious and in the erotic nature of desire. Thus, in regard to her own work, she said, "I am completely at the mercy of unconscious selection" (*CW,* II, 722). Similarly, in a critical piece on Hamlin Garland she writes, "Human impulses do not change and cannot so long as men and women continue to stand in the relation to one another which they have occupied since our knowledge of their existence began. . . . The author of 'Crumbling Idols' would even lightly dismiss from the artist's consideration such primitive passions as love, hate, etc. He declares that in real life people do not talk love. How does he know? I feel very sorry for Mr. Garland" (*CW,* II, 693–694). Chopin's poetry and stories provide further evidence of her fascination for eros and freedom. The explicitly sexual nature of "If some day I, with casual, wanton glance/ Should for a moment's space thine eyes ensnare;/Or more, if I should dare/ To rest my finger tips upon thy sleeve,/Or, grown more bold, upon they swarthy cheek" (*CW,* II, 730) confirms the restlessness and energy of "The Vagabonds,"a story about a mysterious nighttime encounter.

Other stories describe in even greater depth Chopin's commitment to a vision of freedom as a balance between sexual or instinctive impulse and cultural or moral demand. "The Storm," one of her most famous stories, perhaps even notorious for Victorian tastes, deals with the consummation of a love that originated years before in an earlier story. Without condemning the freedom of extramarital love, the story's power derives from its dramatization of the tension between passion and control. In "Athenaise" an immature and spoiled bride requires additional time to learn to love her husband. Significantly, in this story Chopin seems to condemn Athenaise's spiteful behavior while insisting on her rights as a woman to respect, equality and freedom. Only with the awareness of her pregnancy does Athenaise realize her love for her husband, Cazeau. In this story pregnancy symbolizes the fulfillment of sexual difference, equality and identity. Finally, a somewhat neglected story, "A Vocation and A Voice," emphasizes the need to overcome the obstacles the self creates out of fear of love. Such stories show the significance Chopin placed in an open, loving and sexual relationship between a man and a woman, a significance apparently confirmed, according to Seyersted, in her own marriage that ended abruptly with her husband's early death, but not before she bore six children in their twelve years of married life. Chopin's interests in these matters of love, sex and freedom as evidenced in her poetry, stories and novel of divorce, *At Fault* (1890), all culminate in her masterpiece, *The Awakening.*

While critics today may debate over the nature of the feminism in *The Awakening,* most probably would agree that in the beginning of the novel Edna provides a perfect example of what Charlotte Perkins Gilman considered the "over-sexed" woman who is forced to survive by performing domestic functions. Certainly, the parrot imagery in the first line of the novel, as Jules Chametzky says, and the exchanges between Edna and her husband, Leonce, in the first section of the book, justify a view of her as a victim of her marriage. In this early scene, Leonce expresses annoyance because his wife has sunbathed in the midst of the day. " 'You are burnt beyond recognition,' he added, looking at his wife as one looks at a valuable piece of personal property which has suffered some damage."[20] Obviously, the word "property" signals the need for Edna to challenge her inferior status in the Pontellier home. In this and other scenes with similar tensions, pettiness and anger, the novel clearly asserts the rights of women for independence and equality in marriage. At one point Chopin so carefully constructs the psychological mood of a scene that the reader can almost feel Edna's feet hit the floor as Leonce exploits his children to rouse Edna from bed in order to get her attention. Unfortunately for Leonce, he soon discovers that his victories over Edna come at a great cost because the novel insists that just like Athenaise, Edna and any other woman should not be abused. By the middle of the novel, Leonce himself tells Dr. Mandelet, the family friend and physician. " 'She's got some sort of notion in her head concerning the eternal rights of women; and—you understand—we meet in the morning at the breakfast table' " (*TA*, p. 65).

While the novel establishes the importance of women's rights and equality, it also examines the meaning of freedom. It explores this question of freedom in terms and ways that are familiar to psychoanalysis. In fact, one chapter relatively early in the novel presents something of a psychoanalytical portrait of Edna that provides a basis for her character in the rest of the novel and for the elaboration of the book's dominant themes. The chapter is all the more remarkable in that it functions in a manner very much like the process of psychoanalysis as Edna gains some rudimentary insight into the operations of her mind by searching for the meaning of a string of memories and associations that are triggered by her recollection of a childhood event. The scene functions similarly to Cazeau's thoughts in "Athenaise" about the slave tree when he sees that his attitude toward his wife compares to a master's treatment of a slave. The significance of this process for Edna is indicated when she agrees to "retrace my thoughts" for her best friend, Madame Adele Ratignolle, and Madame Ratignolle confirms how difficult it is to "think about thinking" (*TA*, p. 17). The exchange about thinking suggests that both Edna an Adele sense that Edna's thoughts and mind are a key to her problems. Edna, indeed, will "think about thinking" in an attempt to "retrace" the origins of her growing restlessness. Never, however, will she be able to satisfactorily articulate and comprehend the situation.

The first paragraph of the chapter under discussion, chapter VII, immediately declares its psychological and philosophical intentions. Chopin writes, "Even as a child she had lived her own small life all within herself. At a very early period she had apprehended instinctively the dual life—that outward existence which conforms, the inward life which questions" (*TA*, p. 15). The split between inner and outer, true and false selves can be explained psychoanalytically, as Wolff and others do, by using R. D. Laing's existential study of schizophrenia. However, in light of Edna's narcissism, Chassaguet-Smirgel's discussion of the split between the body and psychic ego also is useful in understanding Edna. She argues that the conflict between the body ego, the experience of the self in terms of the physical exterior, and the psychic ego, a sense of self that precedes physical determination, is consistent with her overall theory of narcissism and the formation of the ego ideal. Following the lead of Freud, Victor Tausk and Bela Grunberger, she argues that the body ego impedes the desire of the psychic ego to achieve an illusion of fusion with all experience. She says "that on the road back to primary narcissistic fusion the subject experiences his body as a worthless garment to be cast off in order to go beyond the bounds imposed by embodiment."[21] Of course, Edna in *The Awakening* will do precisely such casting off by drowning herself in the ocean. Put in its most simple terms, for Chasseguet-Smirgel primary narcissism involves the desire of the child for permanent pre-Oedipal fusion with the mother. The failure to achieve such fusion creates the ego ideal, an approving psychic alternative to the mother that loves and supports the ego. Thus, as the "heir to primary narcissism," the ego ideal "is a substitute for primary narcissistic perfection, but a substitute from which the ego is separated by a gulf."[22]

The narcissism at the root of Edna's character helps to explain the pattern of her actions that ultimately leads to her self-destruction, including her unsatisfactory love affairs with Alcee Arobin and Robert Lebrun, her detachment from her children, her failed friendships, her frustrated fantasies of a creative life as an artist, her unhappy marriage to Leonce and even her infantile eating and sleeping habits. In all of these experiences and relationships, Edna substitutes illusions of totality and fusion for reality. The chapter in *The Awakening* that begins with the discussion of the split between Edna's mind and body also reveals one source of Edna's narcissism in her early relationship with her mother. It is of great importance that in the same scene Edna's thoughts are provoked by her proximity to and physical contact with Madame Ratignolle, who is the representative in the novel of motherhood and domesticity. Madame Ratignolle's loving, physical and emotional response to Edna's presence and words contrasts sharply with the austerity of emotion and affection in Edna's own youth. Furthermore, the scene takes place on the beach, within the sight and sound of the ocean, the ultimate narcissistic symbol that finally will take Edna's life. Chopin writes, "Madame Ratignolle laid her hand over that of Mrs. Pontellier, which was near her. Seeing that the hand was not withdrawn, she clasped it firmly and warmly. She even stroked it a little fondly, with the other hand, murmuring in an undertone, '*Pauvre cherie*' " (*TA*, p. 18). In the next paragraph, we learn of the elements in Edna's background that make such a motherly gesture so important to her. "The action was at first a little confusing to Edna, but she soon lent herself readily to the Creole's gentle caress. She was not accustomed to an outward and spoken expression of affection, either in herself or in others. She and her younger sister, Janet, had quarreled a good deal through force of unfortunate habit. Her older sister, Margaret, was matronly and dignified, probably from having assumed matronly and house-wifely responsibilities too early in life, their mother having died when they were quite young. Margaret was not effusive; she was practical" (*TA*, p. 18). Chopin goes on to explain how these bonds helped determine for Edna "the reserve of her own character" and the nature of her detached friendships with others. Originally entitled *A Solitary Soul*, the novel charts Edna's attempts to combat her feeling of alienation and solitude by searching within herself for the motherly love and security that childhood and youth denied her.

Given this pattern of narcissistic behavior, it also is important to recognize how Chopin uses the image of the sea to dramatize the complex psychological and philosophical implications of the false freedom involved in Edna's illusion of fusion. In a chapter of only seven brief paragraphs that really serves as a prolegomenon to the crucial chapter VII, Chopin envisions the sea as a symbol of the way Edna's quest for freedom will become lost in unsatisfied desire. She writes, "In short, Mrs. Pontellier was beginning to realize her position in the universe as a human being, and to recognize her relations as an individual to the world within and about her. This may seem like a ponderous weight of wisdom to descend upon the soul of a young woman of twenty-eight—perhaps more wisdom than the Holy Ghost is usually pleased to vouchsafe to any woman" (*TA*, pp. 14–15). Chopin then anticipates Edna's failure to complete the task before her. She writes, "But the beginning of things, of a world especially, is necessarily vague, tangled, chaotic, and exceedingly disturbing. How few of us ever emerge from such beginning! How many souls perish in its tumult! The voice of the sea is seductive; never ceasing, whispering, clamoring, murmuring, inviting the soul to wander for a spell in abysses of solitude; to lose itself in mazes of inward contemplation. The voice of the sea speaks to the soul. The touch of the sea is sensuous, enfolding the body in its soft, close embrace'' (*TA*, p. 15). Considering the mind/body split, the voice of the sea that spoke directly to Edna's soul really promises that her quest for fulfillment and freedom will lead to disaster. Confusion between inner and outer selves will continually confound Edna. Her misperception of inner wishes for union with the demands of external reality will leave her frustrated and finally helpless. The potential psychological consequences of this situation are explained by Chasseguet-Smirgel: "It can be seen that the failure to achieve this ideal, and the obstacles that are run up against in attempting to reach it (in particular the 'incest-barrier' in the oedipal phase), may cause a regression towards a more archaic form of 'narcissistic reinstatement', or even towards psychotic megalomania in which the original lack of differentiation between internal and external perceptions recurs."[23]

If the image of the sea connotes a compelling voice of freedom that draws Edna toward a mystical but impossible fusion with the mother, one must ask what happened in Edna's life to prolong this need for her mother. Of course, in Freudian theory, this requires discussion of the role of the father in establishing the superego or moral sense and in decreasing dependence upon the mother. As Chasseguet-Smirgel says, "The superego comes between the child and the mother, the ego ideal—as I have said—pushes him towards fusion. The setting up of the superego provides some relief from the limitless demands of the ego ideal by instituting the incest barrier and by transforming the child's intrinsic impotence into obedience to an interdict." Here Chasseguet-Smirgel participates in advancing Freudian theory by helping to define the relationship of the ego ideal to the superego. Accepting the superego as the last of the Freudian "agencies of the psychic apparatus to appear," she sees it as an "heir to the Oedipus complex" in that it emerges out of the prohibition against incest. She argues that the success of the superego in its mission becomes the developmental process's mature way of achieving narcissistic fulfillment. While recognizing the importance of arguments that view the superego as an agency for the reality principle, she "would agree with Grunberger in seeing the superego as still representing some attempt at a recouping of narcissism by holding an interdict responsible for that which actually stems from the child's sexual impotence, and which is the result of the discrepancy between oedipal wishes and the capacity to satisfy them. Seen in this light the superego is a compromise formation, doubtless relatively the most acceptable."[24] Thus, for Chasseguet-Smirgel and others, the development of the superego cannot be separated from the history of the ego ideal.

Accordingly, we must ask about the role of Edna's father in shaping her personality and helping her to mature. Significantly but not surprisingly, important information about this relationship also appears in chapter VII in the scene on the beach with Edna's substitute mother, Madame Ratignolle. The scene continues to function as a sort of dramatization of psychoanalysis as Edna tries to understand the memories that flood her consciousness. In this part of the scene, Edna's memories return to the very heart of her unconscious in touching upon her experiences with men as originating with her father. Considering the absence of a strong and loving maternal influence, Edna's associations regarding her father are especially moving. We get the image of a father who engenders fear and distance rather than love and moral authority. She tells Madame Ratignolle, " 'The hot wind beating in my face made me think—without any connection that I can trace—of a summer day in Kentucky, of a meadow that seemed as big as the ocean to the very little girl walking through the grass, which was higher than her waist. She threw out her arms as if swimming when she walked, beating the tall grass as one strikes in the water.' " Edna then seems to pause thoughtfully in her speech as she says, " 'Oh, I see the connection!' " (*TA*, p. 17) The reader never learns precisely what it is that Edna thinks she sees. This is important because it contributes to the ambiguity of

Edna's character, but also because it sustains the overall theme of Edna's incoherence and inarticulateness. What she sees tends to be additional images and associations; however, the reader must discern their ultimate meaning. She tells Madame Ratignolle that on that day in the grass in Kentucky she was hoping to escape from her father, just as she tries in later life to flee from her husband. She says, " 'Likely as not it was Sunday,' she laughed; 'and I was running away from prayers, from the Presbyterian service, read in a spirit of gloom by my father that chills me yet to think of' " (*TA*, p. 18). Madame Ratignolle suggests that Edna continues to run from prayers and Edna confesses that " 'Sometimes I feel this summer as if I were walking through the green meadows again; idly, aimlessly, unthinking and unguided' " (*TA*, p. 18).

Edna's words require comment. Obviously, Edna wishes to flee from masculine authority while the association of the grass and the sea and the presence of Madame Ratignolle suggest the continuing search for the security and protection of a mother figure. Equally important, however, is that such flight does not give her any sense of real direction or purpose. Instead, she is lost, adrift so to speak, on a sea of emotions she never fully understands or controls. While Edna intuits that this early memory has something to do with the nature of all her subsequent relationships to men, she can only touch the surface of their meaning and fails to see their source in her own unconscious and her early infantile relationships. The event she recalls requires an ability to interpret experience that is unavailable to her. Thus, Chopin writes, "Edna often wondered at one propensity which sometimes had inwardly disturbed her without causing any outward show or manifestation on her part. At a very early age—perhaps it was when she traversed the ocean of waving grass—she remembered that she had been passionately enamored of a dignified and sad-eyed cavalry officer who visited her father in Kentucky" (*TA*, p. 18). In addition to this cavalry officer, Edna in her youth had other infatuations, one for a visitor to a nearby plantation and the other for an actor, a "tragedian" whom she knew only through a picture on her desk. Her marriage to Leonce follows this pattern and is consistent with her character. Chopin describes this marriage as "purely an accident" (*TA*, p. 19). By "accident," I think Chopin means that it was done impetuously, without conscious thought on Edna's part. Such impulsiveness over a serious matter in itself reveals the potential for unconscious sources of motivation in Edna. Thus, Wolff describes the marriage as "a defensive maneuver designed to maintain the integrity of the two 'selves' that formed her character."[25]

In terms of the realities of her life, Edna's marriage indeed constitutes a "defensive" act because it enables her to escape from her father whose visit to her home on one occasion dramatizes his differences from Leonce and his cruel power over her. In comparison to her father's dominating power, Leonce seems relatively easy and trivial. " 'You are too lenient, too lenient by far, Leonce,' asserted the Colonel. 'Authority, coercion are what is needed. Put your foot down and hard; the only way to manage a wife. Take my word for it' " (*TA*, p. 71). Chopin follows the Colonel's advice with a comment to counter the father's harsh philosophy of life and marriage. She writes, "The Colonel was perhaps unaware that he had coerced his own wife into her grave. Mr. Pontellier had a vague suspicion of it which he thought it needless to mention at that late day" (*TA*, p. 71). Even for Leonce the father represents an extreme form of patriarchal power. Edna can escape from the Colonel's physical presence through her marriage, but she cannot escape his influence over her mind and character. From a psychoanalytical point of view, Edna's relationship with her father shows the impossibility for her of establishing what Freud considered to be a "positive Oedipus complex." She cannot find security in her sexual identity by forming a healthy and loving relationship with her father. There is no love for her with this embodiment of unqualified paternal domination. While she can feel this power over her, Edna's failure to understand it contributes to the fatalism of her subsequent relationships to men.

Freud, of course, argues that girls take "refuge" in their fathers only after realizing their incapacity to satisfy their mothers in the pre-Oedipal stage of development. He states that "the great dependence on the father in women merely takes over the heritage of an equally great attachment to the mother."[26] The implications of the Freudian model are that the emotional intensity of the girl's connection to the father receives its impetus from the force of the feelings originally felt toward the mother. Thus, it can be maintained that Edna's unsatisfactory pre-Oedipal connection to her mother or mother surrogate forms a foundation for her unhappy relationship with her father. Since Freud's time the relationship of the pre-Oedipal and Oedipal stages remains a subject of controversy. As Chasseguet-Smirgel indicates, psychological development seems to indicate a synthesis of both stages. Certainly, such a synthesis appears necessary for the creation of a new kind of symbolic order for women's liberation from patriarchy. In any case, for Edna the question of a meaningful synthesis and organization appears impossible because of the weakness of both stages. Denied the affection of her mother and brutalized, at least psychologically, by her father, she lacks clear foundations in either relationship. Unfortunately, when she begins to perceive her condition, it is too late for her to act meaningfully.

Furthermore, Edna's place in two radically different cultures and societies, one of her birth and the other of her marriage, exacerbates the paradoxes of her failed search for self and for freedom. Both her husband and father are emblematic of two markedly different ways of life. The father represents a strict and autocratic society that proves suffocating to her and arouses her flight. This background stifles her ability to love. Thus, in regard to Edna's American roots Larzer Ziff says that she "was an American woman, raised in the Protestant mistrust of the senses and in the detestation of sexual desire as the root of evil."[27] Unfortunately, the radical disjunction between this strict society of repression and the comparative freedom and exuberance of the Creole society of her marriage assures the absence of continuity and coherence to form a foundation for healthy growth for Edna. The extreme change in the standards of both societies, which Ziff notes, does not nurture stability, especially in a character like Edna, who survives by forcing the conformity of an external self upon an uncertain inner self. The story suggests that the openness and freedom of Creole society ultimately undermine Edna's search for freedom because she lacks the maturity and internal stolidity to deal with such an explosion of new experiences and opportunities.

Moreover, it also needs to be understood that this change between a strict Protestant society and the relaxed Creole society occurs within the context of a greater transition. The novel was written during a time of immense national transformation. The period was marked by great industrialization and urbanization. Women, in one sense, were left behind with continuing responsibilities for bearing children, maintaining the home, developing their strengths through social and public service. Thus, we see the emergence of a society of men, such as those in *The Awakening*, who are increasingly irrelevant to matters of affection and domesticity and of women who need alternative lifestyles to fulfill themselves.

The uncertainty of Edna's place and role in society is aggravated by her inability to use language to articulate her situation. In the terms of some contemporary psychoanalytical theorists, such as Juliet Mitchell and Jacqueline Rose, the novel asserts that language attempts to bridge the gap between the insatiable desire of the infantile ego and meaningful, creative freedom. In abandoning language, Edna avoids the frustration of learning of language's ultimate failure at finding absolute truth, but she also circumvents an important aspect of maturation. She obviously misses a flawed but crucial instrument for self-understanding. Accordingly, *The Awakening* demonstrates the extent of Edna's failure to reconstruct her past and identity by exposing her incapacity for articulation and language. As Mitchell writes, "The human animal is born into language and it is within the terms of language that the human subject is constructed."[28] The establishment of sexual differentiation under the auspices of the Oedipal and castration complexes constitutes a main component of the construction of the self through symbols and language. However, both language and sexuality are part of a process of inherent unsatisfaction or incompleteness, what Lacan and Chasseguet-Smirgel both call desire. Jacqueline Rose explains further, "Symbolisation starts, therefore, when the child gets its first sense that something could be missing; words stand for objects, because they only have to be spoken at the moment when the first object is lost. For Lacan, the subject can only operate within language by constantly repeating that moment of fundamental and irreducible division. The subject is therefore constituted in language as this division or splitting (Freud's *Ichspaltung* or splitting of the ego)."[29] The result of such division, including sexual differentiation, is the permanence of desire. As Mitchell says, "Desire persists as an effect of a primordial absence and it therefore indicates that, in this area, there is something fundamentally impossible about satisfaction itself."[30] The drama of desire and language pervades Chopin's story of Edna Pontellier.

Moreover, the association of sexuality, language, desire and freedom achieves its most powerful unity in the novel's development of Edna's attitude toward motherhood.[31] Edna's confusion about the meaning and implication of her feelings and responsibilities as a mother toward her children are intertwined with her problems with language and thought. Thus, Edna discusses children and freedom in an important comment to Madame Ratignolle about halfway through the novel. She says, " 'I would give my life for my children; but I wouldn't give myself. I can't make it more clear; it's only something which I am beginning to comprehend, which is revealing itself to me' " (*TA*, p. 48). Readers who cite this passage as an example of Edna's steady awakening and growing commitment to existential freedom and identity sometimes overlook Madame Ratignolle's response in the next line. Madame Ratignolle, whose life epitomizes commitment to family and children, answers Edna in a light-hearted but perceptive manner. Madame Ratignolle's tone resembles that of a mother talking to a child with poorly conceived notions. " 'I don't know what you would call the essential, or what you mean by the unessential,' said Madame Ratignolle cheerfully; 'but a woman who would give her life for her children could do no more than that' " (*TA*, p. 48). For Madame Ratignolle, Edna's comment really reflects continuing confusion. Her idea about the essential craves clarification. Edna, however, never can articulate what comprises the essential for her. She acts out of unconscious need and desires that finally reach their sad fulfillment in two scenes at the end of the novel: the birth scene and her suicide. The psychoanalytical implication of this juxtaposition seems obvious. Edna responds to the insistence of life and freedom with her own demand for total fusion and, therefore, the abolition of the self. There can be no middle ground for her of symbol or langauge in her engagement with desire.

In a version of what Freud considered to be the compulsion to repeat what one fears or cannot understand, Edna witnesses Madame Ratignolle's delivery of another child. Edna is overwhelmed by the scene. Chopin writes, "She began to wish she had not come; her presence was not necessary. She might have invented a pretext for staying away; she might even invent a pretext now for going. But Edna did not go. With an inward agony, with a flaming, outspoken revolt against the ways of Nature, she witnessed the scene [of] torture" (*TA*, p. 109). It is characteristic that while the event renders Edna speechless, Madame Ratignolle, the mother figure, articulates the significance of the birth scene to Edna. Chopin writes of Edna, "She was still stunned and speechless with emotion when later she leaned over her friend to kiss her and softly say goodbye. Adele, pressing her cheek, whispered in an exhausted voice: 'Think of the children, Edna. Oh think of the children! Remember them!' " (*TA*, p. 109) The admonition expresses not just concern for the children but also for Edna whom Adele regards, we remember, as a daughter. Adele appreciates Edna's penchant for the boundless freedom that can destroy her and those who love her. Like Athenaise in the short story, Adele sees birth as a biologically rooted source of identity that is unacceptable to Edna. As though to prove that Adele's fears for Edna are justified, in the chapter that separates the birth scene and Edna's death, Edna tells the doctor: " 'I'm not going to be forced into doing things' " (*TA*, p. 109). Indicating that her rebellion really is directed toward the meaning of the preceding birth scene, Edna immediately returns to the subject of children. Significantly, she cannot complete her thought. In the very expression of her desire for absolute freedom, the basic symbolic structures of freedom fail her: speech, coherence, articulation. She says, " 'Nobody has any right—except children, perhaps—and even then, it seems to me—or it did seem—' " (*TA*, p. 109). In the absence of the completed sentence, Chopin writes, "She felt her speech was voicing the incoherency of her thoughts, and stopped abruptly" (*TA*, p. 109). In that line, the artistry of the novel perfectly sustains its theme of silence and inarticulation.

The subject of speechlessness and silence follows Edna to her death in the sea. While she remains inarticulate, the thread of images in her mind confirms the continuing power upon her of the unconscious forces that danced through her mind while on the beach with Madame Ratignolle. When compared to her thoughts of her sons and her own youth, Edna's failure to find happiness through her lovers, most notably Robert Lebrun but Alcee Arobin as well, indicates the existence of deeper desires. Edna's infatuations and loves, like her passion for art under the influence of Mlle. Reisz, represent the attempt to go beyond the human limits and frustrations of desire to a totality of experience and feeling. Such unity she finds in the sea. In her thoughts first a lover, then her husband and her children are linked. " 'To-day it is Arobin; tomorrow it will be some one else. It makes no difference to me, it doesn't matter about Leonce Pontellier—but Raoul and Etienne!' " She then recalls her earlier comment to Adele "that she would give up the unessential, but she would never sacrifice herself for her children" (*TA*, p. 113). This idea of refusing to sacrifice one's self to children receives elaboration in the next paragraph. "The children appeared before her like antagonists who had overcome her; who had overpowered and sought to drag her into the soul's slavery for the rest of her days. But she knew a way to elude them" (*TA*, p. 113). Seen as "antagonists" and slave drivers, the children, as George Arms indicates, actually occupy very little of her time.[32] However, in the final scene of the novel the children become symbols of Edna's entire way of loving and being in the world. They symbolize her refusal to compromise with her wish for total freedom and with the exigencies of life. They epitomize her denial of limitations on her ego, freedom and needs. Ultimately, the children come to represent her refusal even to think, to move from unstructured emotion and image to symbols and langauge as a means for organizing the anarchy and chaos of recalcitrant human experience. Accordingly, Chopin writes, "She was not thinking of these things when she walked down to the beach" (*TA*, p. 113). The absence of words indicates the absence as well of conscience and culture. There is only the self merging with the sea.

In fulfillment of the novel's symbols and themes, Edna goes naked into the sea. Disrobing, she witnesses her own rebirth into a totally narcissistic state, no longer needing to worry about whom to love or who loves her. Chopin writes that "for the first time in her life she stood naked in the open air, at the mercy of the sun, the breeze that beat upon her, and the waves that invited her. How strange and awful it seemed to stand naked under the sky! how delicious! She felt like some new-born creature, opening its eyes in a familiar world that it had never known" (*TA*, p. 113). The sea of boundless love, desire and freedom takes Edna. "The touch of the sea is sensuous, enfolding the body in its soft, close embrace" (*TA*, p. 113). And her final thoughts as she merges with the sea return to her childhood, to her original nudity and birth, to her desire for love and security that are never fulfilled by her sister and father. Always seeking love but protecting herself against its failure, lacking the coherence to invest the symbols of life with her own love, she dies remembering those she first wanted but could never fully have. "She looked into the distance, and the old terror flamed up for an instant, then sank again, Edna heard her father's voice and her sister Margaret's. She heard the barking of an old dog that was chained to the sycamore tree. The spurs of the cavalry officer clanged as he walked across the porch. There was the hum of bees, and the musky odor of pinks filled the air" (*TA*, p. 114).

In a forceful and comprehensive article about *The Awakening*, Elizabeth Fox-Genovese notes how Chopin "weds" Edna's "personal pathology" to the social and sexual themes of the novel. She argues that Chopin's conservative proclivities turn "the indictment of the social system" into the personal issue of "the case history of an aberrant individual."[33] Thus, failing to find fulfillment according to the prescribed psycho-social pattern of her sex, Edna also lacks the power and direction to create a new system of symbols for herself. Moreover, Edna's search and defeat anticipate our own century of freedom. Chopin argues that such freedom requires more than reform, but love and depth of character as well. Without these qualities, we are all like Edna, internalizing chaos and disorder and demand rather than freedom and creativity. Edna indicates the importance of a balance between internal and external structures of freedom. Unlike either Calixta in "The Storm" or Athenaise, Edna does not have the internal resources to survive. She can only rebel. And rebellion for its own sake becomes another form of slavery and death.

Notes

1. Gary Scharnhorst, *Charlotte Perkins Gilman* (Boston: Twayne, 1985), p. 51. See also Scharnhorst, Charlotte Perkins Gilman: A Bibliography (Metuchen and London: Scarecrow, 1985).
2. Gilman, *Women and Economics*, ed. Carl N. Degler (New York: Harper Torchbook, 1966), p. 110. All subsequent references to this book will be to this edition and will be included parenthetically in the text.
3. Gilman, *The Living of Charlotte Perkins Gilman: An Autobiography* (1935; rpt. New York: Arno, 1972), p. 235.
4. Scharnhorst, *Charlotte Perkins Gilman*, p. 70.
5. William Leach, *True Love and Perfect Union: The Feminist Reform of Sex and Society* (New York: Basic Books, 1980), p. 155.
6. Scharnhorst, *Charlotte Perkins Gilman*, p. 67.
7. Christopher Lasch, *Haven in a Heartless World: The Family Besieged* (New York: Harper Colophon, 1977), pp. 13–14.
8. Gilman, *The Living of Charlotte Perkins Gilman*, p. 323.
9. Ann J. Lane, "The Fictional Worlds of Charlotte Perkins Gilman" in *The Charlotte Perkins Gilman Reader*, ed. Lane (New York: Pantheon, 1980), p. xxxv.
10. Gilman, *The Living of Charlotte Perkins Gilman*, p. 314.
11. Ibid., p. 78.
12. Ibid., p. 93.
13. Ibid., pp. 97–98.
14. Ibid., p. 95.
15. Lane, "The Fictional Worlds of Charlotte Perkins Gilman," p. xli.
16. Critics who tend to see this novel in terms of feminism are Elizabeth Fox-Genovese, "Kate Chopin's Awakening," *Southern Studies*, 18 (Fall 1979), 261–290; Judith Fryer, *The Faces of Eve* (Oxford: Oxford University Press, 1976); Jules Chametzky, "Our Decentralized Literature," *Jahrbuch for Amerikastudien* (1972), pp. 56–72 rpt. in Kate Chopin, *The Awakening*," ed. Margaret Culley (New York: Norton, 1976); Joyce Ruddel Ladenson, "Paths to Suicide: Rebellion Against Victorian Womanhood in Kate Chopin's *The Awakening*," *Intellect*, 104 (July–August 1975), 52–55; Emily Toth, "The Independent Woman and 'Free' Love," *Massachusetts Review*, 16 (Autumn 1975), 647–664; Otis B. Wheeler, "The Five Awakenings of Edna Pontellier," *Southern Review*, 11 (January 1975), 118–128. Critics who view the novel primarily in terms of individual character are George Arms, "Kate Chopin's *The Awakening* in the Perspective of Her Literary Career," *Essays on American Literature in Honor of Jay Hubbell*, ed. Clarence Gohdes (Durham: Duke University Press, 1967), pp. 215–228 and Cynthia Griffin Wolff, "Thanatos and Eros: Kate Chopin's *The Awakening*," ed. Culley; Nancy Walker, "Feminist or Naturalist: The Social Context of Kate Chopin's *The Awakening*," *Southern Quarterly*, 17 (Winter 1979), 95–103.
17. Wolff, "Eros and Thanatos," *American Quarterly*, p. 450.
18. Per Seyersted, *Kate Chopin: A Critical Biography* (Baton Rouge: Louisiana State University Press, 1969), p. 198.

19. *The Complete Works of Kate Chopin,* ed. Per Seyersted (Baton Rouge: Louisiana State University Press, 1969), I, 23. All future references to this edition will be cited parenthetically in the text as *CW*.
20. Kate Chopin, *The Awakening,* ed. Margaret Culley (New York: Norton, 1976), p. 4. All subsequent references to this novel will be to this text and will be quoted parenthetically as *TA*.
21. Janine Chasseguet-Smirgel, *The Ego Ideal: A Psychoanalytical Essay on the Malady of the Ideal,* intro. Christopher Lasch, trans. Paul Burrows (New York: Norton, 1985), p. 58.
22. Chasseguet-Smirgel, *The Ego Ideal,* pp. 76, 4–5.
23. Ibid., p. 28.
24. Ibid., pp. 76–77, 139.
25. Wolff, "Eros and Thanatos," p. 452.
26. Sigmund Freud, "Feminine Sexuality" in *Freud: Sexuality and the Psychology of Love,* ed. Phillip Rieff (1931: rpt. New York: Collier Books, 1963), pp. 195, 196.
27. See Larzer Ziff, *The American 1890's: Life and Times of a Lost Generation* (New York: Viking, 196), pp. 304, 297–198.
28. Juliet Mitchell, "Introduction-I," *Feminine Sexuality: Jacques Lacan and the ecole freudienne,* eds. Juliet Mitchell and Jacqueline Rose, trans. Jacqueline Rose (New York: Norton, 1982), p. 5.
29. Jacqueline Rose, "Introduction-II," *Feminine Sexuality,* p. 31.
30. Mitchell, "Introduction-I," *Feminine Sexuality,* p. 6.
31. Chasseguet-Smirgel's comments on the relationship between motherhood and narcissism are interesting, especially regarding the character of Edna Pontellier. Chasseguet-Smirgel, *The Ego Ideal,* p. 35, says, "Even if her eroticism runs counter to her wish to eliminate the gap between ego ideal and ego through a primary narcissistic fusion, it is nonetheless the case that for the girl motherhood is a solution that allows her to reconcile, in a sense, her erotic wishes which are directed towards her father with her wish to recapture the primitive state of fusion with her mother. The mother can reexperience with her child, admittedly on a much more evolved level, the sense of fusion which as a child she experienced with her own mother."
32. George Arms, "Kate Chopin's *The Awakening,*" *Essays on American Literature in Honor of Jay Hubbell,* p. 220.
33. Elizabeth Fox-Genovese, "Kate Chopin's Awakening," p. 289.

16
The Blight of Southern Womanhood
Louise Westling

The situation of Southern women in America has been unique. In the following essay, Louise Westling, Associate Professor of English at the University of Oregon, discusses their "distinctive burden." The following is from Louise Westling. *Sacred Groves and Ravaged Gardens: The Fiction of Eudora Welty, Carson McCullers, and Flannery O'Connor* (Athens: University of Georgia Press, 1985.

Although Southern belles enjoyed an enviable reputation from the middle of the nineteenth century through the early decades of our own, their traditional position has come under increasingly critical scrutiny in recent years. More and more we understand that Southern white women carried a distinctive burden as the darlings of their world. Their case is in many ways an especially long-lived version of the Victorian situation of women, with all its attendant ironics. Special difficulties arose, however, from the South's peculiar racial institution. The Southern lady was supposed to embody the ideals of her culture, but that culture was torn by profound contradictions and forced into a defensive position by wider national pressures. Thus the white female representative of Christian virtues was lauded in public to divert attention from problems of slavery and racism, but the scope of her activities was severely limited. "Enforcement of gender and family conventions was community business," as Bertram Wyatt-Brown explains in his book *Southern Honor*. "All ranks of men agreed that women, like other dependents upon male leadership and livelihood, should be subordinate, docile. As Dr. James Norcom of North Carolina put it, 'God in his inscrutable wisdom, has appointed a place & a duty for females, *out of which* they can neither accomplish their destiny nor secure their happiness!!' "[1] This proprietary restriction of women's lives is of course typical of patriarchies, but it gained special urgency in the traditional world of white supremacy. The Southern lady had to represent a racial purity which was required by her men for the maintenance of their caste but which many of them regularly transgressed in their own sexual behavior. Further increasing the weight of responsibility carried by the Southern woman in her ideal form was the traditional view of the land itself as feminine. Southern gentlemen loved their land and fought a disastrous war to preserve what they felt was their honor and their proper stewardship. Yet they knew they had abused its integrity with greedy and destructive methods of husbandry. Their attitude towards its

Reprinted from *Sacred Groves and Ravaged Gardens: The Fiction of Eudora Welty, Carson McCullers, and Flannery O'Connor* by Louise Westling, © 1985 the University of Georgia Press. Reprinted by permission of the University of Georgia Press.

fecundity was often as ambivalent as their attitude towards the females with whom it was associated.

Into this tangled feminine heritage Eudora Welty, Carson McCullers, and Flannery O'Connor were born. Any study of their imaginative lives must begin with an understanding of the traditional attitudes their culture imposed upon them.[2] Even if old-fashioned definitions of feminine virtue were losing their grip in the modern era, no section of the nation clung more fiercely to its past than the South. Popular national tastes seemed in fact to conspire with the Southern myth of the Lost Cause and the image of the enchanting ladies who epitomized the antebellum world, as evidenced by the remarkable success of Margaret Mitchell's novel *Gone with the Wind* and the even wilder triumph of the film version, which had its premiere in Atlanta in 1939. Welty, McCullers, and O'Connor were formed by the same world which produced Margaret Mitchell; they had to define themselves and their destinies against the same ideal of the Southern lady.

In 1915, when Eudora Welty was six years old, Professor Edwin Mims of Vanderbilt University made the following claim to the graduating class of Randolph-Macon Woman's College in Virginia before advising them how to conduct their lives as educated Southern women: "If there is one thing upon which Southern people have prided themselves, it is their reverence for womanhood. Long after Burke had pathetically lamented the passing of the age of chivalry in Europe, we maintained the outward form and the inward spirit of chivalry—in our ante-bellum social life and more especially our chivalric attitude towards the gentler sex."[3]

This chivalric attitude required the veneration of woman as a sacred being in traditionally hyperbolic Southern terms which W.J. Cash paraphrased when he exclaimed in *The Mind of the South*: "She was the South's Palladium, this Southern woman—the shield-bearing Athena gleaming whitely in the clouds, the standard for its rallying, the mystic symbol of its nationality in the face of the foe. She was the lily-pure maid of Astolat and the hunting goddess of the Boetian hill. And—she was the pitiful Mother of God. Merely to mention her name was to send strong men into tears—or shouts."

As evidence he quoted the following toast presented at the Georgia Centennial in the 1830s: "Woman!! The centre and circumference, diameter and periphery, sine, tangent and secant of all our affections!"[4] Although the geometrical dimensions of this conceit are perhaps unique, the same general sentiments are echoed in public declarations throughout the nineteenth century and survive into the twentieth in the fiction of Southern apologists such as Thomas Nelson Page and Thomas Dixon, Jr. A number of recent historical studies have even argued that the South made a literary conquest of the rest of the nation which reversed the effects of the Civil War and Reconstruction, just as "Carpetbagger" Judge Albion W. Tourgee predicted in 1867.[5] Among the propagandists for the South, Thomas Dixon was particularly successful in gaining Northern acceptance for his favorable view of Southern civilization and the women who were its crowning symbol, because his own considerable popularity as a novelist was paralleled by the overwhelming national success of D. W. Griffith's film epic *The Birth of a Nation*, based on Dixon's novel *The Clansman*.[6] The white gowns and fluttering graces of Giffith's Southern heroines effectively convey Dixon's assertion that "the young Southern woman was the divinity that claimed and received the chief worship of man." Indeed, the whole treatment of women in the film echoes the following sentiments from the novel's tribute to the Southern hero's mother: "Never had he seen his mother so beautiful—her face calm, intelligent and vital, crowned with a halo of gray. . . . Her whole being reflected the years of homage she had inspired in husband, children, and neighbours. What a woman! She had made war inevitable, fought it to the bitter end; and in the despair of a Negro reign of terror, still the prophetess and high priestess, of a people, serene, undismayed and defiant."[7]

Not only was this woman seen as prophetess and priestess, but she was also identified with the landscape itself by traditional habits of thought, many of them originating with the earliest European explorers. Although the concept of earth as mother is an ancient one, the European explorers and settlers of the New World emphasized another, equally old feminine dimension in their view of the land as a virginal garden, as commentators on American culture have pointed out for many years.[8] The expression of this tendency is especially marked in the South and ultimately influences the culture's view of women. From the beginning the land was seen as female, and the Southern white male's stewardship of this rich possession reflected similar paradoxes to those in his relations with consorts and daughters. Uneasiness and guilt about his surrender to female seductiveness led him to severely subdue his public ideology. But the guilt lingered in the white male imagination, as perhaps some deeper sense of the land's independent power to withhold her fruits did also.

Virginia, named for the queen who presided over her nation's emergence as a Renaissance European power, was regularly described as feminine in the early days of exploration and settlement. Arthur Barlowe reported in 1584 that his ship was "allured" toward her shore by "so strong a smell, as if we had been in the midst of some delicate garden abounding with all kinde of odoriferous flowers." Such imagery continued to be the basis for praises of the natural abundance of the new land, such as that of John Rolfe's *A True Relation of the State of Virginia*(1616). Rolfe stresses the temperateness of the climate, the fertility of the soil, and the hidden bounty in "the womb of the Land" which lies ready to be mined by man. His treatise was intended to refute gloomy stories about famine and pestilence among the Jamestown settlers which had found their way back to England, and he and other early Virginia colonists were ultimately successful in fixing the fruitful garden image in the imagination of the home country. This is a sharp contrast to William Bradford's account of the landscape which greeted his group of Puritans from Yorkshire upon their famous landing at Plymouth in 1620. Arriving in the cruel season of winter, "what could they see but a hideous and desolate wilderness, full of wild beasts & wild men?" The Northern landscape and climate could not sustain the hopeful Edenic visions of its first explorers once it was actually colonized, but the South continued to support sensuous feminine associations.[9]

These could be frankly erotic, as Annette Kolodny has shown, citing the mid-seventeenth-century protests of John Hammond, who felt obliged to defend his native Maryland from the kind of adverse rumors that John Rolfe had denied forty years earlier about Virginia. Hammond referred to Virginia and Maryland as Jacob's brides, entitling his tract "Leah and Rachel, Or, The Two Fruitful Sisters Virginia and Maryland" (1656). For Hammond, enough difficulties had arisen in the young colonies to lead to despair. He deplored "the general neglect and licensiousness" of Virginia, but saw more active vice in Maryland. "Twice hath [Maryland] been deflowred by her own Inhabitants, stript, shorne, and made deformed; yet such a natural fertility and comelinesse doth she retain that she cannot but be loved, but be pitied."[10] Robert Beverley sensed the debilitating qualities of such a generous landscape, as is evident in his *History and Present State of Virginia*(1705).[11] Beverley catalogued the bounties of the country, but warned that "the exceeding plenty of good things" led to shameful laziness among his fellow colonists. The language of the following passage wallows in the sensuality which the habit of feminine associations excites in his mind: "Here all [people's] Senses are entertain'd with an endless Succession of Native Pleasures. Their Eyes are *ravished with the Beauties of Naked Nature.* Their Ears and Seranaded with the perpetual murmur of the Brooks, and the thorow-base which the Wind plays, when it *wantons* through the Trees" (my emphasis)[12]

Because these implications are too dangerous to be long indulged, or because of general changes in taste, references to the Southern landscape focused increasingly upon maternal qualities as the eighteenth century progressed. Whatever the reason, the erotic abandon betrayed by Beverley was curbed and chastened. Throughout the next century, the South both as landscape and as culture would continue to evoke feminine images in the minds of her sons, but they would be pious rather than erotic, moving between the virginal and the maternal. In a defense of the Southern way of life during the troubled years before the Civil War, William Gilmore Simms protested to his audience in Buffalo, New York, "You would not, surely, have me speak coldly in the assertion of a Mother's honour." In 1867, after the South's defeat in the war, Virginia professor Robert L. Dabney sought to restore her honor by writing a defense of the South which he believed was personified in his native state. The purpose of his book, he wrote, was to "lay this pious and filial defense upon the tomb of my murdered mother, Virginia." Such poems as the following from an anthology published in 1872 established the conceit of the fallen South as a ravished maiden, in unconscious harmony with Hammond's view of Virginia and Maryland more than two hundred years before.

Trampled to Death

A fair young body trampled to death—
    This beautiful, glorious Lady of ours!
Bring spices and wine and all the spring's breath,
    And bathe her with kisses and shroud her with flowers.

O breasts whose twin lilies are purpled with blood!
    O face, whose twin roses with ashes are white!
O dead golden hair, at whose far splendor stood
    Millions of true souls entranced with delight!

Wailing in silence, as brave men wail,
    An army of lovers around her stands,
With fierce bitten lips and brows all pale,
    With broken swords and with manacled hands![13]

Orator and editor Henry W. Grady traveled to Boston and New York in the 1880s to paint the same benign picture of the emerging New South that filled his editorials in the Atlanta *Constitution*. Central to the peace and order of the awakened region are hallowed visions of pure wife and noble mother who inspire men of the South on their mission.[14] Similarly, Thomas Nelson Page's novels celebrate radiant maidens who grace old mansions and symbolize continuity with the best of the antebellum world.

Thomas Dixon goes a step further in *The Clansman*, extending standard maternal and maidenly associations for the South to embrace all "Anglo-Saxon civilisation" by the end of the novel. *The Clansman* is Dixon's attempt to convince a national audience that Reconstruction unleashed a rapacious horde of emancipated Negroes upon the South whose "wounded people lay helpless amid rags and ashes under the beak and talon of the Vulture." As "An Historical Romance of the Ku Klux Klan," the story seeks to justify vigilante action as a chivalric crusade to save white civilization personified in the women of the South. Leslie Fiedler argues that here Dixon revived the archetypes of Spotless Maiden and Holy Mother which Harriet Beecher Stowe had used so successfully in *Uncle Tom's Cabin*, but for very different didactic purposes. Whereas Stowe had associated the violation of pure females with the oppression of Negro slaves, Dixon's "anti-Tom" novel reiterates the traditional Southern insistence on exclusively white and aristocratic connections for the ancient mother/daughter pair and emphasizes their status as white male property.[15]

The climactic turn in Dixon's plot comes when a mother and daughter who represent the most radiant qualities of antebellum life commit suicide to escape the shame of the daughter's rape by a black man. Marion Lenoir, though only sixteen, carries the knowledge of her defilement with courage and resolution. She rallies her stunned mother to their joint duty, leading her "down the dim cathedral aisles of the woods" to a cliff called Lover's Leap above the river. Dixon presents their death as a *liebestod*.

> A fresh motionless day brooded over the world as the amorous stir of the spirit of morning rose from the moist earth of the fields below.
>
> A bright star still shone in the sky, and the face of the mother gazed on it intently. Did the woman-spirit, the burning focus of the fiercest desire to live and will, catch in this supreme moment the star's Divine speech before which all human passions sink into silence? Perhaps, for she smiled. The daughter answered with a smile; and then, hand in hand, they stepped from the cliff into the mists and on through the opal gates of death. [p. 308]

When the white male leaders of the town learn of the event, they see it as the ultimate degradation of their culture. The novel's hero, Ben Cameron, scion of the town's leading family who has just recovered from his Civil War wounds, discovers evidence of the suicide atop Lover's Leap and knows that the fate of Mrs. Lenoir and Marion involves all white society. "Now, Lord God, give me strength for the service of my people!" he prays (p. 310). He hurries to acquaint his father with "the hell-lit secret beneath the tragedy" and to assemble the local Klan members and apprehend the rapist. The symbolic importance of the rape is so great that Dixon repeats the scene at a huge nocturnal Klan gathering in a cave, by having Ben's father, Dr. Cameron, hypnotize the black prisoner so that he can enact the crime again. What follows is a cherished Southern nightmare.[16]

> Gus rose to his feet and started across the cave as if to spring on the shivering figure of the girl, the clansmen with muttered groans, sobs and curses falling back as he advanced. He still wore his full Captain's uniform, its heavy epaulets flashing their gold in the unearthly light, his beastly jaws half covering the gold braid on the collar. His thick lips were drawn upward in an ugly leer and his sinister bead-eyes gleamed like a gorilla's. A single fierce leap and the black claws clutched the air slowly as if sinking into the soft white throat.
>
> Strong men began to cry like children. [p. 323]

These men dedicate themselves to revenge in a strange ritual substituting the blood of the dead women and the water of the local river for the blood of Christ. A boulder in the cave serves as altar, and Dr. Cameron places upon it a crude cross, a candle, and the silver cup of blood and water. Lifting the cup, he says, "Brethren, I hold in my hand the water of your river bearing the red stain of the life of a Southern woman, a priceless sacrifice on the altar of outraged civilisation" (p. 325). This sacrifice rouses the assembled host to execute justice upon the rapist and ultimately to restore order and virtuous prosperity to the region. The novel ends with Ben Cameron's exultant claim that "Civilisation has been saved, and the South redeemed from shame" (p. 374).[17]

Such a close association of the South's integrity with that of white women continued to nourish the regional imagination until fairly recently. As Kolodny reminds us, the Southern Agrarians saw their filial duty to be the defense of their region's female honor against the harsh masculine industrialism of the North which threatened to destroy traditional virtues.[18] John Crowe Ransom was explicit about the distinction in *I'll take My Stand*.

> The masculine form is hallowed by Americans, as I have said, under the name of Progress. The concept of Progress is the concept of man's increasing command, and eventually perfect command, over the forces of nature; a concept which enhances too readily our conceit, and brutalizes our life. I believe there is possible no deep sense of beauty, no heroism of conduct, and no sublimity of religion, which is not informed by the humble sense of man's precarious position in the universe. The feminine form is likewise hallowed among us under the name of Service. The term has many meanings, but we come finally to the one which is critical for the moderns; service means the function of Eve, it means the seducing of laggard men into fresh struggles with nature. It has special application to the apparently stagnant sections of mankind, it busies itself with the heathen Chinee, with the Roman Catholic Mexican, with the "lower" classes in our own society. Its motive is missionary. Its watchwords are such as Protestantism, Individualism, Democracy, and the point of its appeal is a discontent, generally labeled "divine."[19]

By now most readers probably find *I'll Take My stand* archaic in tone and reactionary in purpose, but the attitudes expressed by Ransom, Tate, Warren, Davidson, and the others were common among traditional Southern families during the childhoods of Eudora Welty, Carson McCullers, and Flannery O'Connor. Muted echoes continue to be heard in the writing of Southern journalists like Russell Kirk (whose books Flannery O'Connor had in her personal library) and James Kilpatrick.

However sentimental or extreme the traditional Southern veneration of woman may have been, however much at odds with the actual hardships and unromantic responsibilities which Anne Firor Scott shows to have been the realistic lot of most Southern women, the worshipful stereotypes remained the standards by which women were ultimately measured. Scott demonstrates how difficult they were to emulate. Southern women's diaries and letters of the nineteenth century were full of self-deprecation, prayers for greater purity of spirit, and admonitions to live up to all the ideals their men held for them.[20] Unlike other ideals of behavior which have all been impossible to achieve, however, this one was undercut by a sort of moral and political schizophrenia. It was extreme, socially elite, the creation of a patriarchy whose power was far less secure than it pretended.

Though Professor Edwin Mims of Vanderbilt University urged the Randolph-Macon graduating class of 1915 to preserve the "social charm and the pious devotion which come to us from a former generation," he did admit one of the obvious limitations of the ideal. Mims quotes fellow Southerner Walter Hines Page, then ambassador to England, on "The Forgotten Woman" of the South.

> Both the aristocratic and the ecclesiastical systems made provision for the women of special classes—the fortunately born and the religious well-to-do. But all other women were forgotten. Let any man whose mind is not hardened by some worn-out theory of politics or of ecclesiasticism go to the country in almost any part of the State (North Carolina)—to make a study of the life of the women. He will see them thin and wrinkled in youth from ill-prepared food, clad without warmth or grace, living in untidy houses, working from daylight till bedtime at the dull round of weary duties, the slaves of men of equal slovenliness, the mothers of joyless children—all uneducated if not illiterate. . . . Some men who are born under these conditions escape from them; a man may go away, go where life offers opportunities, but the women are forever helpless.[21]

The image of the Southern lady was thus perceived early in the century by some observers to be hopelessly inappropriate for any but the privileged, who of course were white. Most women in the

South were not members of the fortunate group; as far as the myth of Southern culture was concerned, they did not exist.

Even for the "aristocratic" women who were acknowledged to participate, the patriarchal focus of their culture made their exalted position ironic. Educated and propertied white men were of course the chief architects of Southern patterns of life and thought; they wielded direct political and economic power. All the declarations we have see of reverence for Southern womanhood, and the original fictional embodiments of the type, came from them. Women were the *objects* of worship, the muses or guiding saints for these men who saw themselves as having established a chivalric and cultured world. Their patriarchal vision, legitimized by Protestant reliance on the Old Testament and the teachings of St. Paul, dominated nineteenth-century Southern discussion of regional social patterns,[22] and Richard King's recent study of the so-called Southern Renaissance of the 1930s and 1940s continues to assume the patriarchal structure of plantation life and of the traditional culture which grew from it. King attributes the blossoming of Southern literary and intellectual life after World War I to the ferment caused by an Oedipal struggle between the sons of the New South and the heroic traditions of their fathers and grandfathers. The Southern imagination as revealed in the writings of the Agrarians, William Faulkner, Thomas Wolfe, James Agee, and William Alexander Percy is thus dominated by a patriarchal family romance in Freudian terms, a myth centered on the father. No matter how important the Southern lady might be in fact, "she was distinctly subordinate in the romance to the powerful and heroic father." As time separated the Civil War heroes from their descendants, the heroes grew in stature to legendary proportions impossible to emulate. "Further, though many Southerners embraced the gospel of progress in the post-Reconstruction years, this optimistic stance was shadowed by the strong suspicion that the age of heroes lay in the past. Decline was an integral part of the Southern family romance."

King marshals compelling evidence for the obsession with paternal heritage expressed by Southern writers of the "renaissance." He seems to have accurately interpreted their view of the past and its debilitating grip on Southern intellectuals of the 1930s and 1940s. Theirs was the same culture, however, which had elevated white woman to sainthood for a century and continued to pay lip service to her veneration. King has trouble explaining this paradox.

> If the Southern family romance placed the father-son relationship at its center, the white woman was expected to play the role of the mother. As mistress of the plantation she was the lady bountiful, caring for the wants and needs of her family, both white and black. . . . The Southern woman was caught in a social double-bind: toward men she was to be submissive, meek and gentle; with the children and slaves and in the management of the household, she was supposed to display competence, initiative, and energy. *But she remained a shadowy figure, always there and ever necessary, but rarely emerging in full force. She was "queen of the home."* [my emphasis][23]

Not only is there a contradiction in the qualities expected of the Southern woman, as King recognizes, but there is also a logical problem in the movement of his description He begins with the mother as "lady bountiful" but ends by calling her a shadowy figure whom he tries to revive by the final epithet of "queen of the home." Presumably, home is the scene of family life, yet in a cultural myth centered in the family, the queen does not really exist. Something is askew.

The truth is that the patriarchy of the South never really liked or fully believed in its custom-made goddess. The white Southern male might offer her ecstatic toasts or use her as a divine reference point, but he also betrayed a paradoxical condescension which sometimes revealed hostility or contempt. The chinks in his chivalrous armor are already visible in antebellum days. George

Fitzhugh seems to protest too much when he demands weakness and frivolity of the Southern lady in 1854: "So long as she is nervous, fickle, capricious, delicate, diffident and dependent, man will worship and adore her. Her weakness is her strength, and her true art is to cultivate and improve that weakness. Woman naturally shrinks from public gaze, and from the struggle and competition of life.... A husband, a lord and master, whom she should love, honor and obey, nature designed for every woman.... If she be obedient she stands little danger of maltreatment."[24] The whole statement is an implied threat. If the Southern woman were the paragon her men claimed in their paeans, she would need no such coercion. Furthermore, if the lordliness and mastery of the husband required that she cultivate and improve her weakness, there must have been serious danger of feminine strength.

A series of articles that appeared in the *Southern Review* (Baltimore) from 1869 to 1872 is even more revealing. The journal was written almost single-handedly by Albert Taylor Bledsoe, a former University of Virginia professor who dedicated his publication to "the despised, disfranchised, and downtrodden people of the South." In order to elevate their spirits and instill new strength for the rebuilding of their land, Bledsoe vigorously defended the Lost Cause and argued against Yankee civilization in agrarian terms that anticipated the position of the Vanderbilt Fugitives in the next century. Bledsoe also sought to encourage Southern intellectual life by reviewing important current books in science, philosophy, art, literature, and politics. Although his journal lasted only eleven years (for two years after Bledsoe's death in 1877 it was edited by his daughter Sophia), it is an important voice expressing the tenaciously cherished values which would seduce the entire nation by the time of Woodrow Wilson's presidency. In a four-year period during which his review treated Darwin, "Recent Researches in Geography," German philosophy and an anthology of Southern verse, four essays are devoted to the subject of woman. Is one to suppose that he wrote them out of chivalrous veneration? He claims to entertain it, as, for instance, when he begins an article on "The Education and Influence of Woman" with an attack on "those poor forlorn misogynists" who attempt to elevate themselves by insulting the gentler sex. In defense of women, he ends by quoting St. Paul's familiar assertion that "the head of the woman is the man," but goes on to produce another declaration from the same epistle, that "The woman is the glory of the man," because she embodies love, the major attribute of God, "In conclusion, then, man is the superior animal, and also the superior intelligence, but woman is the superior being, 'the cunningest pattern of excelling nature,' the paragon of all God's works."

More specifically Bledsoe examines woman's capacity for friendship and for artistic achievement, pronouncing her too personal and concrete in her responses, too weak in intellect, for either. "She must have a personal God, a personal religion, a personal honor, and a particular love, which are her own, to touch, to hide, to lock up, it may be, for her own private uses and enjoyment." Generous but not liberal, she "can give but does not know how to share." This renders her incapable of friendship.

On the question of artistic achievement, Bledsoe begins with characteristic gallantry toward the fair sex, intending to make a serious attempt to recover neglected geniuses. Men have always been willing to hope for female art, he says, for

> even in the darkest periods of woman's history, there has been instinctive recognition of the apparent relation between her chaste, flexuous, subtile organism, and the delicate grades and refinement of art-work, and no less an eager appreciation of all that she has done or tried to do in that regard. Even in this hypercritical and skeptic age we are always ready and ardent to welcome a poem by a woman, whether it be poetry or not, as if

there was a certain consciousness at the bottom of our minds that the poet *ought* to come from that side of the house, whether he will or not.

Such phrases as "apparent relation," "all that she has done or tried to do," and "whether it be poetry or not" erode Bledsoe's assertions, and, most telling of all, he uses the masculine pronoun "he" to refer to the poet who *ought* to emerge from the distaff side of the house. Whether Bledsoe is unaware of his condescension or means to be snide, it is clear that he does not seriously expect art to issue from female hands. His researches lead him reluctantly to conclude that the whole sex is defective in the artistic sense, and in the strength necessary to sustain an aesthetic or moral idea. "The man, having reserved forces and discretion . . . can go to the mountain top and return safely; the woman, out of breath at the start, must abide at a low level, or succumb from exhaustion in an atmosphere too rare and chill. Hence, her art-work is almost invariably petty, inadequate, mean."[25]

Despite the certainty in Bledsoe's assertion of woman's innate inferiority, in his 1871 article on "The Mission of Woman," he acknowledges a problem which turns out to have been threatening on the Southern male horizon since around the middle of the nineteenth century. Anne Scott describes the slow growth of the suffrage movement in the South after the Seneca Falls Declaration in 1848, suggesting that male opposition below the Mason-Dixon Line betrayed deep fears.[26] Even before the Civil War, Southern men felt the need to defend themselves from "strong-minded" Northern women in the Abolition and Temperance movements. In 1853 John Hartwell Cocke, liberal Virginian, friend of Thomas Jefferson, and advocate of the emancipation of slaves, described the struggle for power at the World Temperance Convention in New York, where the "strong-minded" women asserted themselves. He bragged that the men "gained a perfect triumph, and I believe have given a rebuke to this most impudent clique of unsexed females and rampant abolitionists which must put down the petty-coats—at least as far as their claim to take the platform of public debate."[27] His self-congratulations were premature, for after the Civil War the disease crept South, at first in secret but gradually moving more into public awareness.[28]

Already in 1871 Bledsoe sensed the danger, fearing "the great and increasing multitudes" of strong-minded Northern women whose emancipation would bring Anglo-Saxon civilization to collapse, just as the independence of Roman matrons destroyed the grandeur of the Empire two thousand years before. There is still hope, however. "Our Southern woman have, thank God! shown, as yet, but little taste for such forbidden fruit" but instead still grace "their own hallowed sphere" and thus remain sacred and inspirational. his essay concludes with a stirring exhortation:

> Be this your glory, then, O ye blessed and beautiful women of the South!—not that you can vote, or beat a negro for Congress, but that you can point to your sons as *your* jewels, and as the ornaments of the human race. Be this your glory, not that you are "the head," but that you are "the glory," of the man. Be this your glory, not that you can equal man in the might and the majesty of his intellectual dominion, but that you can surpass him in the sublime mission of mercy to a fallen world.

Women are further urged to soften and subdue man's rugged nature with Christian meekness, "to enchant the home circle" with their loveliness, and "mould the future Washingtons, and Lees, and Jacksons of the South, to protect and preserve the sacred rights of woman as well as of man."[29] Bledsoe is a representative spokesman for the traditional Southern point of view, as Scott's survey of responses to the suffrage movement shows.[30] Southern men wanted their women kept in cages, peripheral, submissive, inert. Any movement towards independence was grimly opposed.

Regardless of male resistance, more and more Southern women of the privileged class were feeling sympathy for the "strong-minded" activists in the North and beginning to seek glory outside the "hallowed sphere" of the home. The disruption of normal life during the Civil War and Reconstruction necessitated Southern women's active participation in areas formerly the exclusive preserves of men, but as the patriarchy gradually reestablihed itself in the hands of the war's survivors, most of these women receded into domestic life. The old habits of deference to men were diminished, however, partly because of the recent experiences of responsibility, partly because "the Lost Cause lost a great deal of its lustre upon close observation of the ex-heroes," and partly because of pressures for change from the North and from Europe.[31] Two exemplary cases are those of Mrs. Cornelia Phillips Spencer of North Carolina and Mrs. Caroline E. Merrick of New Orleans, both born in 1825 and both beginning with traditionally deferential attitudes toward male superiority but ending in defiance. Mrs. Spencer treated the issue of suffrage in the Young Ladies' Column of the *North Carolina Presbyterian Standard*, gradually evolving from strong opposition to sympathy in the 1890s. After conforming for most of her life to masculine dominance, Mrs. Merrick grew flippant by the 1850s and became an active worker for the equality of women. Her answer to chivalry is the following parody of 1881:

> Lest they should feel overlooked and slighted, I will say a word to the men. God bless them. Our hearts warm towards the manly angels—our rulers, guides and protectors, to whom we confide all our troubles an on whom we lay all our burdens. Oh, what a noble being is an honest, upright, fearless, generous, manly man. How such men endear our firesides, adorn and bless our homes. How sweet is their encouragement of our timid efforts in every good word and work, and how grateful we are to be loved by these noble comforters, and how utterly wretched and sad this world would be, deprived of their honored and gracious presence. Again I say, God bless the men.[32]

Times were changing. Professor Mims described the emergence of vigorous new economic and intellectual life in *The Advancing South* (1926). In a chapter called "The Revolt Against Chivalry" he chronicles the liberating descent of Southern ladies from their pedestals, he advocates higher education for women, and he heralds their entry into the professions. But even he is ambivalent about the kind of independence expressed in the radical intellectual life of Frances Newman, with her brash championing of Freud, Joyce, and Sherwood Anderson. He praises her learning, her acquaintance with the most challenging modern literature, and the incisiveness of her criticism, but he ends by saying, "Miss Newman has certainly gone a long way from Georgia! Too far, I am inclined to think."

Mims closes his chapter by evoking the same comforting scene he had used ten years earlier to end his Randolph-Macon commencement speech. He describes the exemplary life of a cultured Southern matron who lives among books in a country home "of the Elizabethan type" surrounded by huge oaks and pastures full of sheep. Here is a cultured mecca for the fortunate in the neighborhood who are invited to afternoon garden parties. The husband is a prominent lawyer of intellectual habits, and the woman herself, "a social leader in her younger days, is president of the Drama League and the friend of every cause that promotes the culture of the community." She is mother of four children: "three boys, who are honour graduates of the university, and a daughter, who is a student at Bryn Mawr." This new image of the Southern lady reminds him of the best of antebellum life.[33]

Although Mims champions women's education, he seems happiest in thinking its product will be an elegantly cultured Southern matron. In this preference he is really not terribly far from Bledsoe's notion of the proper destiny for Southern white women. Evidence that Southern men in general did not go even as far as he comes from his own criticism of the refusal of men's colleges and universities to support coeducation.[34]

What distinguishes the Southern attitude from the wider, Western European chivalric heritage of reverence for women is the complicated relationship of the Southern white woman to blacks. As William R. Taylor observes, the first published appearance of antebellum plantation myths "coincided not only with the appearance of militant abolition in the North but also, and I think just as significantly, with the first stirrings of the movement for women's rights, which occurred at about this time and appealed to—as well as alarmed—many of the same people."[35] Traditional defenses of slavery were intimately intertwined with declarations about the veneration and protection of white women. Yet these women in fact shared inferiority and powerlessness with blacks as subjects of the ruling patriarchs. "There is no slave, after all," commented Mary Chesnut with some bitterness in 1861, "like a wife." Throughout her diary Mrs. Chesnut sympathizes with the slaves and connects their sufferings with the plight of women. She describes the Southern gentleman as jovial and courtly when in a pleasant mood but ultimately "as absolute a tyrant as the czar of Russia, the khan of Tartary—or the sultan of Turkey." Under such masters African slaves must certainly suffer, and with them, all women, for "all married women, all children, and girls who live on in their father's [sic] houses are slaves."[36] When the suffrage movement became a serious political force, white male leaders resisted it in terms which support Mary Chesnut's connection of sexual and racist subordination. In Alabama, for instance, while suffragists prepared for the 1915 legislative session, a defensive pamphlet circulated around the state, warning of the chaos that would result from enfranchisement of women: "It is the avowed purpose of leaders among Northern advocates to break the 'Solid South' by means of votes of Negro women and break down race and sex distinction. Is this in keeping with the traditions and civilization of the south?"[37]

Southern white men—many of them—had been breaking down these distinctions from the beginning, but their picture of the graceful plantation world never betrayed the miscegenation which blighted their pretensions of Anglo-Saxon purity. The illicit recourse of white men to black women was far more frequent than is commonly acknowledged, and it had understandably painful effects. Black men and white women shared the deepest kind of sexual humiliation, and black women were denied control of their own bodies and forced into concubinage. Black women were somehow able to retain a sense of wholeness despite these conditions, perhaps because their essential identity was never denied. They knew themselves to be sexually potent and desirable, and they were the hyper-mothers of the South, nursing not only their own children but also those of their white masters and mistresses. The strength of popular stereotypes testifies to their power; though the 1960s banished the Mammy from popular view, she remains in the national imagination, and other strong black female images have convincingly taken her place in television specials chronicling the lives of Miss Jane Pittman, Wilma Rudolph, and Harriet Tubman.[38] Black men have proven themselves in national culture as the supermen of sports, seeming to fulfill the worst fears of white Southern folklore which had compensated for political (and sometimes literal) emasculation by fantasizing heroic black virility.

All along, the white Southern lady had been left in chilly isolation on her pedestal, for the facts of miscegenation spelled rejection and rendered chivalric tributes a painful lie. In 1941 W. J. Cash stressed the depth of this betrayal, though he described it primarily from the white male perspective of shame in the presence of white women: "And even though she feigned blindness, as the convention demanded she should—even if she actually knew or suspected nothing—the guilty man, supposing he possessed any shadow of decency, must inexorably writhe in shame and an intolerable sense of impurity under her eyes." And so Cash agrees with the 1924 assertion of Frank

Tannenbaum's *Darker Phases of the South* that the idealization of white women was an unconscious compensation for male frailties. Lillian Smith claims that this behavior created a sexual schizophrenia in white men and made the lives of white women "only a shameful sore."[39]

Lest these reactions seem excessive, let us gauge the accuracy of the charges. The facts of racial mingling were evident to anyone in the South who chose to recognize them. Even an innocent young visitor from the North could not help noticing, as Lucius Verus Bierce did on his walking tour of the South following college graduation in 1822. Pausing for three months in Waxaw, South Carolina, to earn money teaching school, Bierce had occasion to observe the social life of the community. His diary describes the disparity between the lives of the planter class and the demoralized lower class of whites, comments on the layout of the plantations, and then describes the character of the inhabitants. "The virtues of the higher order," he writes, "are a love of liberty, hospitality, charity, and a nice sense of honor. The vices are drunkenness, indolence, and *among all classes of males, an indiscriminate connexion with the female negroes. This evil has extended so far that more than one half of the slave population are mixed with the whites*" (my emphasis).

Later, in Alabama, Bierce finds even more riotous habits and hears a remarkable story about a former governor of the state.

> The country around here is delightful, but the people devilish. Duelling and fighting the chief diversions, Gambling and drinking pastimes, *and an uninterrupted, common intercourse with the negroes the virtue of all the men.* . . . Governor Pope, of Huntsville, a wealthy respectable man of a family, formerly Governor, notoriously kept a mulatto girl with whom he associated as freely as with his wife. His wife finding them in each others embraces made so much fuss about it that he sent the girl on to his plantation near to Mooresville where he then spent more of his time than he did at home. His wife complaining of his neglect, and knowing the cause, would consent to nothing short of the girls being sent to New Orleans and sold, which was done, when a merchant of Mooresville sent to his agent in Orleans, purchased the girl, and brought her back to Mooresville for himself. This but a specimen of manners in that respect. [my emphasis][40]

Reports of this kind were vigorously denied by Southerners, especially when Abolitionists began using them to prove the immoral consequences of slavery. But in a modern study of slavery, historian Kenneth Stampp concludes that "sexual contacts between the races were not the rare aberrations of a small group of depraved whites but a frequent occurrence involving whites of all social and cultural levels." Members of the slave-holding class could be expected to have superior advantages. "Indeed, given their easy access to female slaves, it seems probable that miscegenation was more common among them than among the members of any other group." Even though Eugene Genovese assumes the greatest frequency of interracial intimacy to have been in the cosmopolitan cities and slave-trading centers rather than on plantations and farms, he agrees that miscegenation "had a profound and in some respects devastating effect on southern life." *Roll, Jordan, Roll* richly documents the complexity of the problem. Nevertheless, Southern denials of "mongrelizing," as Southerners liked to call it, continued to appear even after the Civil War had put an end to the slaveholders' free use of their human property. Professor Robert L. Dabney refers to the problem in 1867. "It is the delight of abolitionists to impute to slavery a result peculiarly corrupting as to sins of unchastity," Dabney admits, but he challenges both the factual basis of the charge and its psychological probability. Temptations of the flesh between young men and female domestics are greatly diminished by racial differences, "while the very sentiment of superior caste would render the intercourse more repulsive and unnatural." Dabney recommends the example of white women as further evidence of Southern morality in domestic affairs. "If then, slavery is morally corrupting, Southern ladies should show the sad result very plainly. But what says fact? Its testimony is one which fills the heart of every Southern man with grateful pride; that the Southern lady is proverbially eminent for all that adorns female character."[41] We return to chivalric rhapsodies upon the familiar feminine theme.

But suppose Dabney had phrased his appeal a little differently, asking "What say the ladies?" to Abolitionist charges of unchastity among their men? Plenty of Southern ladies had ready answers, as Anne Scott shows, but most kept them within the pages of private letters and diaries. Mary Chesnut's voluminous running commentary on life in the social and political center of the Confederacy is especially outspoken. She would probably have answered Dabney to his face if he had tried to deny the hypocrisy which so disgusted her. In March 1861 she reports taking opium to quiet her nerves and then releases a flood of bitter indignation.

> I wonder if it be a sin to think slavery a curse to any land. [Charles] Sumner said not one word of this hated institution which is not true. Men and women are punished when their masters and mistresses are brutes and not when they do wrong—and then we live surrounded by prostitutes. An abandoned woman is sent out of any decent house elsewhere. Who thinks any worse of a negro or mulatto woman for being a thing we can't name? God forgive us, but our is a *monstrous* system and wrong and iniquity. Perhaps the rest of the world is as bad—this *only* I see. Like the patriarchs of old our men live all in one house with their wives and their concubines, and the mulattoes one sees in every family exactly resemble the white children—and every lady tells you who is the father of all the mulatto children in everybody's household, but those in her own she seems to think drop from the clouds, or pretends so to think. Good women we have, *but* they talk of all *nastiness*—tho' they never do wrong, they talk all day and night of [erasures illegible except for the words "all unconsciousness"] my disgust sometimes is boiling over—but they are, I believe, in conduct the purest women God ever made. Thank God for my countrywomen—alas for the men! No worse than men everywhere, but the lower their mistresses, the more degraded they must be.

Mrs. Chesnut then recalls her mother-in law's veiled references to the mulatto children of her own husband, a subject to which she returns in a later entry of similar exasperation.[42] I quote her comments at such length because she explicitly draws together many of the themes I have been stressing: the connection between slavery and the position of women, black and white; the morality of white women and its relation to the behavior of white men; and the effect of miscegenation upon the interior lives of white women.

If white men's dalliance with slave women evoked this irate intensity in Chesnut's mind, it must have been so common that upper-class women all over the South suffered more terrible private anguish. Mary Chesnut, after all, was remarkably cosmopolitan for her region, gender, and era, so that she was not shocked by the normal quotient of vice and corruption she was around her in the Confederate capital. She read widely in French and English literature and was a lively participant in the most intellectually sophisticated circles of Southern society. Few subjects in her diary excite the kind of passion this one does; miscegenation was worse than ordinary failings she assumed human nature to exhibit, because it violated the central racial caste system of her culture and it deprived the patriarchal authorities of honor in the domestic relations to which they claimed such pious allegiance.

One of Mary Chesnut's contemporaries, Laura Clay of Kentucky, expressed similar sentiments in 1874. "When I consider the unspotted chastity, the temperance, the unselfishness, the daily ruling of life by duty of women, and compare it to the sensual and selfish lives of men it seems to me marvellous that their virtue should be overlooked by the world and all the great revolutions in the moral world should be imputed to men."[43] And Katherine Anne Porter records a similar response to the situation in "The Old Order," as the matriarch of a Texas family in old age recalls her struggle as a widow to raise her children after her husband's death from a Civil War wound.

> Miss Sophia Jane had taken upon herself all the responsibilities of her tangled world, half white, half black, mingling steadily and the confusion growing ever deeper. There sere so many young men about the place, always, younger brothers-in-law, first cousins, second cousins, nephews. They came visiting and they stayed, and there was no accounting for them nor any way of controlling their quietly headstrong habits. She learned early to keep silent and give no sign of uneasiness, but whenever a child was born in the Negro quarters, pink, worm-like, she held her breath for three days, she told her eldest granddaughter, years later, to see whether the newly born would turn black after the proper interval. . . . It was a strain that told on her, and ended by giving her a deeply grounded contempt for men. She could not help it, she despised men.[44]

Upper-class white women's entanglement in these problems continued in the New South, because white men's involvement with black women did not stop with Reconstruction. Lillian Smith makes a strong case for the natural attraction between the races by appealing to the emotional bonds formed in those whites brought up by black nurses who provided the formative experience of warmth and love.[45] No doubt there is considerable truth in this Freudian explanation, but the simple force of social traditions also played a strong part. Sociologist John Dollard found the old-fashioned erotic habits still very common in the anonymous town he surveyed in *Caste and Class in a Southern Town* (1937). His data are dispassionately presented, in the context of the universal human tendency to underestimate departures from public morals. Nevertheless, he lost all his friends in the town when his book was published. Dollard had violated the taboo he described as still surrounding the image of the white lady.

> This ideal image is passionately and even violently defended, and the danger of soiling it is one of the threats which brings out the fullest hostility of southern men. . . . It seems possible that this idealization has an effect on the erotic behavior of white men toward their own white women, and produces perhaps a feeling that they are untouchable, that sexual sentiments are unbecoming in relation to them, and that sexual behavior toward white women must take place, though, of course it does take place, only against a personal sense of guilt. . . . It seems possible that the image of the white woman is in part conserved against sexual thought and allusions, whereas the Negro woman tends to draw the full burden of unsublimated sexual feeling.

Thus many white Southern boys began their sexual experience with black girls, and many continued finding solace in later life with prostitutes or mistresses of the other race, sometimes fathering children whose resemblance to them was cause of gossip and humiliation for their white wives.[46]

By the time Dollard published his study of small-town Southern life, Eudora Welty and Carson McCullers were young women in their twenties, and Flannery O'Connor was just entering adolescence. The troubled racial and sexual relations of the South were enveloped in a cloud of charming fraud through which these young women had to grope their way to maturity. Certainly all traditions of courtesy involve deceit of a graceful kind and for generous purposes, but a profound betrayal yawned behind the special privileges for girls of their backgrounds. The old-fashioned ideal of the lady made demands of them, though in fainter terms than it had for their mothers, and theirs was still an apparently patriarchal world. But girls like Eudora Alice Welty and Lula Carson Smith and Mary Flannery O'Connor were too perceptive not to sense the emptiness of its pretensions. The men who claimed to worship white women secretly preferred their darker sisters in many ways, so that their chivalry masked guilt, and serious intelligence in women was a terrible threat because it might probe through the sentimental facade. The Southern world provided only a dishonest basis for a girl's identity as she grew into a woman, and dishonest grounds for relations with men.

Ellen Glasgow seems to have been the first Southern writer to consciously understand the problem, though she was never fully able to transcend it.[47] She wrote in her autobiography, "I hated—I had always hated—the inherent falseness in much Southern tradition." As a beginning writer she vowed to write "as no Southerner had ever written, of the universal human chords beneath the superficial variations of scene and character. I would write of all the harsher realities beneath manners, beneath social customs, beneath the poetry of the past, and the romantic nostalgia of the present."[48] In *Virginia* (1913) she achieved her first clear success. Not only does the heroine stand for the vanishing (and actually irrelevant) type of the Southern lady, but as Anne Jones remarks, "the state takes the body of a woman."[49] By extension the beautiful Virginia Pendleton, who is betrayed and abandoned at the end of the novel, represents the whole South, abandoned by her men in search of the almighty Yankee dollar. Glasgow even alludes to the problem of miscegenation, though by very careful implication. Cyrus Treadwell, the typical grasping new Southern industrialist, has managed to achieve an obliviousness to poverty and injustice in his single-minded pursuit of money, just as more old-fashioned citizens use what Glasgow ironically calls "idealism" to avoid seeing ugly realities. Early in the novel Treadwell looks out over the town from his bank office, toward his factory, ignoring the squalid view of poverty beneath his building. "Nearer still, within the narrow board fences which surrounded the backyards of negro hovels, under the moving shadows of broad-leaved mulberry or sycamore trees, he gazed down on the *swarms of mulatto children;* though to his mind *that problem*, like the problem of labour, loomed vague" (my emphasis).[50]

Later, in his own home, he absentmindedly greets "a coloured washerwoman, accompanied by a bright mulatto boy" as he goes up to see his embittered wife (p. 87). Taken together, these few details could easily refer to the intimate crimes of white men, perhaps even Mr. Treadwell's engendering of an illegitimate son. Indeed, later the identity of the father is revealed, in a stroke that is bold for Glasgow to make in such a fastidious age, but which she can hazard behind the veil of genteel and delicate understatement. Treadwell chances to meet the tattered washerwoman some weeks later in the garden, and casual conversation about her age moves into dangerous territory. We learn that Mandy had come to work for the Treadwells eighteen years earlier at the age of fifteen, that Cyrus's wife had discharged her before a year passed, and that a month or two later the mulatto boy Jubal was born. When Mandy tries to play on the past for a bit of sympathy by reminding Cyrus Treadwell of what a "moughty likely gal" she had once been and asking for a slight raise in wages from her four dollars a month so that she can raise her son, Treadwell is outraged at her effrontery. He refuses and orders her to get out. When she has gone, he congratulates himself for having resisted blackmail. "It's a pretty pass things have come to when men have to protect themselves from negro women," he thinks indignantly. Then he turns his thoughts to his legitimate white nephew's need for a job. Treadwell decides to offer the young man a position because "even if the boy's a fool, I'm not one to let those of my own blood come to want" (pp. 172–75).

In a much later chapter entitled "The Problem of the South," we learn that Jubal has murdered a policeman in a nearby town and will probably be lynched. Again his mother appeals to his father for help.

"You ain' done furgot 'im, Marster. He 'uz born jes two mont's atter Miss Lindy turnt me outer hyer—en he's jes ez w'ite ez ef'n he b'longed ter w'ite folks."

But she had gone too far—she had outraged that curious Anglo-Saxon instinct in Cyrus which permitted him to sin against his race's integrity, yet forbade him to acknowledge, even to himself, that he bore any part in the consequence of that sin. Illogical, he might have admitted, but there are some truths so poisonous that no honest man could breathe the same air with them.

Treadwell hands her a fifty-dollar bill and orders her not to come whining around him any more. "Black or white," he says, "the man that commits a murder has got to hang for it" (pp. 367–68).

Glasgow has not explicitly defined Treadwell's sin, and she has made only three widely spaced references to it in the novel where even Cyrus Treadwell is a peripheral character. In this chapter Jubal's dilemma is deliberately merged with the larger racial issue, replaced in the foreground by the gentle old Episcopal minister's defense of an innocent black man. Gabriel Pendleton, Virginia's father, has been on his way to help Jubal when he comes upon an innocent man being beaten by drunken whites. In a battle with the drunks, the black escapes, and then the old man has a heart attack and dies, returning us urgently to the central plot involving the personal tragedies in Virginia's life. But for the attentive reader, Ellen Glasgow has placed an unmistakable burden of guilt on the Southern white man, and it is an important part of her exposure of the cruel ironies surrounding the old-fashioned ideal of the lady.

Another subtle but important emphasis Glasgow makes in this novel is Virginia's association with plants and the landscape. She continually identifies or contrasts Virginia's moods with the seasons and the growing trees, flowers, and crops of her native state. In the days of her courtship, for the young man who will become her husband, "the thought of Virginia lay always like an enclosed garden of sweetness and bloom. To think of her was to pass from the scorching heat of the day to the freshness of dewwashed flowers under the starlight." When he goes to her in her parents' garden the June night he proposes, "her breath left her parted lips as softly as the perfume detached itself from the opening rose-leaves" (p. 181). This is the traditional Southern habit of associating the white lady with the landscape, which we have seen originating with the first English colonists and running through the nineteenth-century mind. But Ellen Glasgow embodies the tradition in a new perspective in the early years of our century—the perspective of the woman herself who, like the land, has been beloved, exploited, and then abandoned. Anne Goodwyn Jones sees Virginia as representing, like the roses, "nature radically shaped by civilization," but also as inappropriately desiring "to stay in an eternally springlike Eden."[51] But the proper place for a rose is exactly such a paradise. The problem is that Eden is a mythological garden of continual spring. All the flowers which Glasgow associates with Virginia should make us see that, like the land, she flowers in the real world of changing seasons. Her delicate beauty is short-lived unless it is cultivated artificially, one supposes, by a doting husband. Virginia obviously does not have such a husband. He abandons the garden he found in her, because it begins to stifle him. His being cannot endure enclosure, while Virginia's thrives on it. When she turns her absorbed attention from him to the fruit of their love—to their children—he withdraws and eventually leaves the South to become a successful playwright in New York.

Virginia's husband Oliver refuses to face unpleasantness or the process of aging. In his own way he is as romantic as Virginia, but, unlike her, he is selfish. Where she lives in a dreamworld of loving sacrifice, he seeks comfort and pleasure. he ceases to love her when she loses her youthful beauty, and he goes North to pursue the success and money which keep him youthfully vital. While Virginia is at the mercy of the seasons and the passage of time, Oliver stands outside organic nature and uses it for his own pleasure. Glasgow certainly means him to represent the dashing Southern gentleman in many respects, the white male who loved but betrayed his region's honor. He knows his guilt in abandoning Virginia, but his shame can be forgotten in a new life.

Southern writers in our own age have continued to emphasize the relation of woman to land, but most of them have been men. Thus through their writing we have been exposed primarily to Oliver's point of view rather than Virginia's. In 1941 Wilbur J. Cash expressed the ambivalence in the male perspective when he described the influence of the Southern climate and land upon the regional mind as "a sort of cosmic conspiracy against reality in favour of romance."

> The country is one of extravagant color, of proliferating foliage and bloom, of flooding yellow sunlight, and, above all perhaps, of haze. Pale blue fogs hang above the valleys in the morning, the atmosphere smokes faintly at midday, and through the long slow afternoon cloudstacks tower from the horizon and the earth-heat quivers upward through the iridescent air, blurring every outline and rendering every object vague and problematical. I know that winter comes to the land, certainly. I know there are days when the color and the haze are stripped away and the real stands up in drab and depressing harshness. But these things pass and are forgotten.
>
> The dominant mood, the mood that lingers in the memory, is one of *wellnigh drunken reverie*—of a hush that seems all the deeper for the far-away mourning of the hounds and the far-away crying of the doves—of such *sweet and inexorable opiates as the rich odours of hot earth and pinewood and the perfume of the magnolia in bloom*—*of soft languor creeping through the blood and mounting surely to the brain* . . . it is a mood, in sum, in which *directed thinking is all but impossible*, a mood in which the mind yields almost perforce to drift and in which the imagination holds unchecked sway, a mood in which nothing any more seems improbable save the puny inadequateness of fact, nothing incredible save the bareness of truth. [my emphasis]

Cash is partly in jest when he says the land is part of a romantic cosmic conspiracy. But he has chosen to abandon himself in the same overripe language of seduction we saw earlier in Robert Beverley's description of colonial Virginia. Still, Cash does not trust the drunken reverie, the opiates which subdue the rational mind. Violence lurks beneath the surface, ready to explode. "But I must tell you that the sequel to this mood is invariably a thunderstorm."[52]

It is William Faulkner, however, as so often in the affairs of the Southern heart, who gives this complex of problems its definitive expression. *Absalom, Absalom!* came out in 1936 and *Go Down, Moses* in 1942. Together these books provide the most astute embodiment of the guilty web of traditional relations between the white man and the land, white women, native Americans, and blacks. Isaac McCaslin is, of all of Faulkner's characters, the most fully conscious that the white man has violated the land by trying to tame it and control it and rape it for its riches. The ledger section of "The Bear" shows that in a parallel way the white man has corrupted the Indians by implicating them in the improper exploitation of the land, and has violated black women while betraying those of his own kind. The races are fatally entangled in blood kinship whose taint only the blacks are strong and virtuous enough to survive.[53] As a child, Isaac had accompanied his mother on a visit to her bachelor brother and witnessed the response of outraged Southern womanhood when she encountered her brother Hubert's black mistress. Hubert Beauchamp's moral dereliction is further symbolized by the state of the gift he gave his nephew at birth. When Isaac finally opens the burlap lump at the age of twenty-one, instead of the original silver cup filled with gold coins, all he finds is a tin coffeepot full of IOUs from his uncle and a few copper pennies. Hubert Beauchamp passed on a debt rather than anything of credit, just as all white men handed their moral debt to their heirs. Because Ike has been initiated by the Indian Sam Fathers to the knowledge that no man has a right to own the land, and because he and his cousin McCaslin Edmonds have understood their inherited guilt by reading through the history of their family in the ledger entries of two hundred years at the commissary store, Ike repudiates his claim to their patrimony—ownership of the family lands. The feminine qualities of this land become apparent near the end of "The Bear" when Ike McCaslin's young wife tries to force him to claim it. For the first time in their marriage, she shows herself to him fully naked. She seems to him not the woman he has known, "but composite of all woman-flesh since man that ever of its own will reclined on its back and opened," and this archetypal female demands that he promise to settle on the land before he can claim his right to her naked body. She is the land, despite McCaslin Edmonds's description of "their ravaged patrimony, the dark and ravaged fatherland still prone and panting" (p. 298). It is a motherland, traditionally as we have seen in the Southern imagination, and specifically here in the symbolic terms of Faulkner's story. Ike's passion overcomes his resolve on the one afternoon in his rented room, and he answers "Yes" to his wife's demand for a promise to claim his heritage, the family farm. The ecstatic sexual epiphany which follows is to be his last. His wife laughs cruelly with her back to him, "And that's all. That's all from me. If this dont get you that son you talk about, it wont be mine." (p. 315). She knows he did not mean his promise, that he will never commit himself to the land. Thus no child can come from their union. Connection with the land is fraught with guilt, but it is necessary for both human and agricultural fertility.

Faulkner himself reveals confusion here, for Ike McCaslin's wife seems to be an evil creature who is trying to corrupt a saint. She is Eve to his Adam, enticing him to fall. Saintliness is associated with celibacy in the characterization of Sam Fathers too, and the only great good place in *Go Down, Moses* is an all-male hunting camp in the heart of the virgin wilderness reminiscent of Eden before Eve, Andrew Marvell's "happy gardenstate,/While man there walked without a mate." The object of the hunters is to live as prelapsarian boys in noble innocent fellowship upon her bosom, hunting for the meat they eat but never defiling the wild spirit of the place, which is oddly represented by great male creatures—first a huge magical stag in "The Old People" and then Old Ben in "The Bear."

Leslie Fiedler points out Faulkner's ambivalent attitude toward the female attributes of the land in *Love and Death in the American Novel* when he discusses the suggestive names of Faulkner's women. Dewey Dell and Lena Grove and Temple Drake are ultimately horrifying characters, Fiedler believes; "Faulkner's dewiest dells turn out to be destroyers rather than redeemers, quicksands disguised as sacred groves." Why is Faulkner horrified as well as fascinated by these associations? Is it because white Southern men are guilty of abusing woman and land, or is it because women in any form are too dangerous to approach with security? Fiedler inclines to the latter explanation, asserting the Freudian/Jungian view that "the themes of self-punishment and self-destruction are inseparable (in the West at least) from the worship of the Female, who represents the dissolution of consciousness as well as poetic vision, the blackness of extinction as well as that of ecstasy."[54] This sounds very close to Cash's comment on the romantic influence of the Southern physical world, whose sensuous opiates drown the rational mind in dreamy bliss but will be followed by a thunderstorm of violence. Fiedler also thinks Faulkner is revolted by Southern woman's betrayal of her traditionally submissive role. I think Faulkner shares these views of the female but he also quite consciously blames his own white patrimony for its sins.

Faulkner could never untangle the snarl of his love, his guilt, his fear, and his disgust for his Southern heritage, but he does explore and dramatize the bitter side of the Southern lady in *Absalom, Absalom!* In this novel an implacable old maid is the repository of her family's honor and its guilty history. Miss Rosa Coldfield, her very name suggesting forbidding and barren earth which should have flowered, is the only surviving white remnant of a family representing the Southern aristocracy in its questionable origins and its inevitable decline. She has remained inviolate, but her sister Ellen has been exploited in marriage by reckless Thomas Sutpen, Faulkner's archetypal "Southern gentleman." Sutpen in fact had tried to use Miss Rosa as he had her sister, but his dynastic ambitions fell into ruin because be abused land and woman alike as objects in his grand design. Furthermore, he is guilty of miscegenation more than once, repudiates a mulatto wife and son, and then refuses to acknowledge his paternity when the son appears again as a grown man. The mulatto son's name, Charles Bon, suggests that he is good enough to receive equal treatment from his father, but Sutpen will never accept him, and the ensuing tragedy of fratricide and incest between pure white and mulatto offspring destroys Sutpen's fortune and family.

This is Faulkner's intended point in the novel, but less often explored is the text's tremendous ambivalence about women. On one hand he describes the eternal female as "the eternal Who-suffers," and presents her almost reverentially as wiser and far older than infantile man.[55] But then he speaks of the dread and fear of females which men draw in "with the primary mammalian milk" (p. 265) and describes Charles Bon's nearly hysterical flight from his octoroon wife as escape "from that massy five-foot-thick maggot-cheesy solidarity which overlays the earth, in which men and women in couples are ranked and racked like ninepins; thanks to whatever God for the masculine hipless tapering peg which fits light and glib to move where the cartridge-chambered hips of women hold them fast" (p. 312).

At the end of the novel we are left with destruction presided over by two women and a spellbound adolescent Quentin Compson, white scion of the town's other prominent family. Quentin's father says Sutpen's mistake was a fatal innocence, but Miss Rosa doesn't agree. She sees him as Satanic destroyer, a cold-blooded Bluebeard who only uses women to produce offspring and abandons them if they are unsatisfactory. Miss Rosa, who successfully withstood his seduction, and Clytie, his illegitimate mulatto daughter, are triumphant witnesses to the burning of the family plantation, while the only male descendant to survive is a mulatto half-wit and grandson of Charles Bon rather than offspring of Sutpen's legitimate son Henry. These survivors, in other words, represent those whom Sutpen abused. They are all sterile, and only the women have their wits intact.

The novel ends with Quentin hoping some satisfaction can come from the tragedy—"that the one [Sutpen] cannot escape the censure which no doubt he deserves, that the other [the women and blacks he wronged] no longer lack the commiseration which let us hope (while we are hoping) that they have longed for" (p. 377). Quentin hopes for new life to arise in this blasted Southern land, but he seems unable to convince himself that he does not hate it as his college friend accuses him of doing. His masculine heritage has doomed itself, and he has to take the side of outraged womanhood. In *The Sound and the Fury* Quentin is finally unable to bear the burden of his past; he commits suicide, leaving behind an idiot castrated brother and his sister Caddy. She is the new woman of the South, soiled but fertile and defiant, having rejected the hollow code of her patriarchal culture. If Caddy represents new life, it is not the kind Quentin hoped for or Faulkner himself desired. Caddy produced a daughter named Quentin, who debases herself even more than her mother had and blames her only white male relative, her embittered and sterile uncle Jason.

Faulkner concurs with the female Quentin's charge, yet he seems to have been unable to think of a way to compensate the Southern woman for the betrayal she suffered. For one thing, as we have seen, he was profoundly disturbed by women's power. But he did give Quentin Compson's heritage to the women of the family, even sealing the bequest with the scion's Christian name. The male voice of the archetypal Southern family is dead, leaving the women to carry on and to speak for themselves.

They had begun telling their side of the story in letters and diaries before Mary Chesnut's time. Anne Firor Scott has recovered their testimony, C. Vann Woodward has edited a full edition of Chesnut's diaries, and Anne Goodwyn Jones has provided a close study of seven fiction writers, from Augusta Jane Evans in the mid-nineteenth century to Margaret Mitchell in the third decade of our own, who began a more public but subtly artistic exploration of the feminine experience in the Southern heritage. In general, Jones concludes, "the masks they wear as authors, the personae they create, half reveal and half disguise the truth within their fictions. Yet perhaps their ambivalence should be forgiven; it is quite a magician's trick, after all, to make a marble statue live and move, and then to make it speak."[56] Ellen Glasgow's self-sacrificing Virginia Pendleton and Margaret Mitchell's cynically capable Scarlett O'Hara are two contrasting examples of Southern women writers' indictments of the idea which had proved such an illusory example for their lives. The next generation of writers in the tradition would provide a deeper and more direct examination of the feminine self in the Southern landscape.

Notes

1. Wyatt-Brown, *Southern Honor*, 228.
2. Anne Firor Scott surveys the historical situation of upper-class Southern women in *The Southern Lady: From Pedestal to Politics*, 1830-1930, and in *Tomorrow Is Another Day* Anne Goodwyn Jones presents a catalog of historical trends and recent theories of their causes in her explanation of attitudes toward women which must have affected those in the South who became writers between 1859 and 1936. Since Scott and jones have paved the way so thoroughly, I need not repeat their exhaustive documentation. Instead I shall emphasize what seem to me the crucial problems in Southern cultural ideology about women.
3. Mims, "The Southern Woman: Past and Present," 3.
4. Cash, *The Mind of the South*, 86-87.
5. See Paul Gaston, *The New South Creed*, 40-41; Lawrence J. Friedman, *The White Savage*, 61; and Rolin G. Osterweis, *The Myth of the Lost Cause*, 24-29.
6. See Friedman, *The White Savage*, 171-72, and Leslie Fiedler, *The Inadvertent Epic*, 43-57.
7. Dixon, *The Clansman*, 362. All further citations of this work will be from this edition; page numbers will be indicated parenthetically in my text.
8. See, for example, Leo Marx, *The Machine in the Garden*, and Annette Kolodny, *The Lay of the Land*.
9. Barlowe, quoted in Richard Hakluyt's *The Principall Navigations of the English Nation*, 728; Rolfe, *A True Relation of the State of Virginia*, 3; Bradford, *Of Plymouth Plantation*, 62.
10. Quoted in Annette Kolodny, " 'Stript, Shorne and Made Deformed': Images on the Southern Landscape," 58-59.
11. See Marx, 75-88.
12. Beverley, *The History and Present State of Virginia*, 296-97.
13. Simms, quoted in Kolodny, " 'Stript, Shorne and Made Deformed,' " 67; Dabney, *A Defence of Virginia*, 5; anonymous poem from *Southern Voices*, quoted in the *Southern Review* 11 (July 1872): 44.
14. Grady, *Orations and Speeches of Henry W. Grady*.
15. *The Inadvertent Epic*, 45-49.
16. See Jacquelyn Dowd Hall's recent analysis of the rape complex *Revolt Against Chivalry: Jessie Daniel Ames and the Women's Campaign Against Lynching*, 145-57.
17. This connection between the rape of white women and the destruction of civilization during Reconstruction was also made by the popular novels of Thomas Nelson Page. See Friedman, *The White Savage*, 67.
18. " 'Stript, Shorne and Made Deformed,' " 55.
19. Ransom, *I'll Take My Stand*, 10-11.
20. Scott, 4-14.
21. Quoted in "The Southern Woman," 6-7.
22. Scott, 16-21.
23. King, *A Southern Renaissance*, 34-35.
24. Quoted in Scott, 17.
25. *Southern Review* 8 (October 1870): 406, 418-19; 8 (July 1870): 52; 5 (April 1869): 303, 315.

26. See Scott, chapter 7, "The Right to Vote."
27. Quoted by Clement Eaton, in "Breaking a Path for the Liberation of Women in the South," 187.
28. Scott, 170-209.
29. *Southern Review* 9 (October 1871): 94—42.
30. See also William R. Taylor's excellent discussion of the fear of insubordination which underlay the sentimental plantation myth in *Cavalier and Yankee*, 165-76, and Marie Stokes Jemison, "Ladies Become Voters," 48–59.
31. Marjorie Stratford Mendenhall, "Southern Women of a 'Lost Generation,' " 351. See also Scott, 98–102.
32. Quoted in Mendenhall, 353.
33. Mims, *The Advancing South*, 254–56.
34. *The Advancing South*, 233–34.
35. Taylor, 165.
36. Chesnut, *Mary Chesnut's Civil War*, 59, 261–62, 279; see also 15, 23, 29–30, 172, 180–81.
37. Jemison, 53-54.
38. See Leslie Fiedler's "Uncle Tom as White Mother," in *The Inadvertent Epic*, 29–41, for a provocative bit of reconstructive surgery which bears on this issue.
39. Cash, 85-86; Tannenbaum, *Darker Phases of the South*, 33; Smith, *Killers of the Dream*, 119–34, 138–39.
40. Bierce, *Travels in the Southland*, 78, 99-100.
41. Stampp, *The Peculiar Institution*, 350-57; Genovese, *Roll, Jordan, Roll*, 413-31; Dabney, *A Defense of Virginia*, 281, 285.
42. Scott, 52-54; Chesnut, 30-31, 72. See Mrs. Chesnut's argument with British journalist William Howard Russell of the London *Times* on the subject, pp. 168-70, and the story she reports "a la Stowe," pp. 347-48. See also C. Vann Woodward, *American Counterpoint*, 72-77.
43. Quoted by Clement Eaton, "Breaking a Path," 193.
44. Porter, *The Collected Stories of Katherine Anne Porter*, 337.
45. Smith, 114–37.
46. Dollard, *Caste and Class in a Southern Town*, 136–37, 138–43.
47. See Anne Jones's discussion of Glasgow's life and work, pp. 225–70.
48. Glasgow, *The Woman Within*, 97-98.
49. Jones, 230.
50. Glasgow, *Virginia*, 83. All further citations of the novel are from this edition; page numbers will be indicated parenthetically in my text.
51. Jones, 245–47.
52. Cash, 46–47.
53. Faulkner, *Go Down, Moses*, 294. All further citations of this work are from this edition; page numbers will be indicated parenthetically in my text.
54. Fiedler, *Love and Death in the American Novel*, 51, 320, 321.
55. Faulkner, *Absalom, Absalom!*, 114. All further citations of this work will be from this edition, and page numbers will be indicated parenthetically in my text.
56. Jones, 362.

Voices of Color

"All of us had something to prove, and it might be called our right to share the American dream."

from *They Call Me Moses Masaoka* by Mike Masaoka

V
Native-Americans

"They made us many promises, more than I can remember, but they never kept but one; they promised to take our land, and they took it."

anonymous Indian

17
Black Elk Speaks

Black Elk was born in 1863 into one of the most powerful branches of the Sioux family, the Oglala tribe. He was related to Chief Crazy Horse and well acquainted with Sitting Bull and Red Cloud. Both his father and several brothers were medicine men; as a result Black Elk was well instructed in all the sacred traditions of his people. Black Elk's impressive life spanned the good years, the years of war and ultimately the defeat of his people. The following excerpts are from his autobiography as dictated to Flaming Rainbow in his final years on the Pine Ridge Reservation in South Dakota between 1930–31.

Early Boyhood

I am a Lakota of the Ogalala band. My father's name was Black Elk, and his father before him bore the name, and the father of his father, so that I am the fourth to bear it. He was a medicine man and so were several of his brothers. Also, he and the great Crazy Horse's father were cousins, having the same grandfather. My mother's name was White Cow Sees; her father was called Refuse-to-Go, and her mother, Plenty Eagle Feathers. I can remember my mother's mother and her father. My father's father was killed by the Pawnees when I was too little to know, and his mother, Red Eagle Woman, died soon after.

I was born in the Moon of the Popping Trees (December) on the Little Powder River in the Winter When the Four Crows Were Killed (1863), and I was three years old when my father's right leg was broken in the Battle of the Hundred Slain.[1] From that wound he limped until the day he died, which was about the time when Big Foot's band was butchered on Wounded Knee (1890). He is buried here in these hills.

I can remember that Winter of the Hundred Slain as a man may remember some bad dream he dreamed when he was little, but I can not tell just how much I heard when I was bigger and how much I understood when I was little. It is like some fearful thing in a fog, for it was a time when everything seemed troubled and afraid.

I had never seen a Wasichu[2] then, and did not know what one looked like; but every one was saying that the Wasichus were coming and that they were going to take our country and rub us all out and that we should all have to die fighting. It was the Wasichus who got rubbed out in that battle, and all the people were talking about it for a long while; but a hundred Wasichus was not much if there were others and others without number where those came from.

I remember once that I asked my grandfather about this. I said: "When the scouts come back from seeing the prairie full of bison somewhere, the people say the Wasichus are coming; and when strange men are coming to kill us all, they say the Wasichus are coming. What does it mean?" And he said, "That they are many."

When I was older, I learned what the fighting was about that winter and the next summer. Up on the Madison Fork the Wasichus had found much of the yellow metal that they worship and that makes them crazy, and they wanted to have a road up through our country to the place where the yellow metal was; but my people did not want the road. It would scare the bison and make them go away, and also it would let the other Wasichus come in like a river. They told us that they wanted only to use a little land, as much as a wagon would take between the wheels; but our people knew better. And when you look about you now, you can see what it was they wanted.

Once we were happy in our own country and we were seldom hungry, for then the two-leggeds and the four-leggeds lived together like relatives, and there was plenty for them and for us. But the Wasichus came, and they have made little islands for us and other little islands for the four-leggeds, and always these islands are becoming smaller, for around them surges the gnawing flood of the Wasichu; and it is dirty with lies and greed.

A long time ago my father told me what his father told him, that there was once a Lakota holy man, called Drinks Water, who dreamed what was to be; and this was long before the coming of the Wasichus. He dreamed that the four-leggeds were going back into the earth and that a strange race had woven a spider's web all around the Lakotas. And he said: "When this happens, you shall live in square gray houses, in a barren land, and beside those square gray houses you shall starve." They say he went back to Mother Earth soon after he saw this vision, and it was sorrow that killed him. You can look about you now and see that he meant these dirt-roofed houses we are living in, and that all the rest was true. Sometimes dreams are wiser than waking.

And so when the soldiers came and built themselves a town of logs there on the Piney Fork of the Powder, my people knew they meant to have their road and take our country and maybe kill us all when they were strong enough. Crazy horse was only about 19 years old then, and Red Cloud was still our great chief. In the Moon of the Changing Season (October) he called together all the scattered bands of the Lakota for a big council on the Powder River, and when we went on the warpath against the soldiers, a horseback could ride through our villages from sunrise until the day was above his head, so far did our camp stretch along the valley of the river; for many of our friends, the Shyela[3] and the Blue Clouds,[4] had come to help us fight.

And it was about when the bitten moon was delayed (last quarter) in the Time of the Popping Trees when the hundred were rubbed out. My friend, Fire Thunder here, who is older than I, was in that fight and he can tell you how it was.

Walking the Black Road

Then we moved on down stream to a sacred place where there is a big rock bluff right beside the water, and high up on this bluff pictures used to appear, foretelling something important that was going to happen soon. There was a picture on it then, of many soldiers hanging head downward; and the people said it was there before the rubbing out of Long Hair. I do not know; but it was there then, and it did not seem that anybody could get up that high to make a picture.

We moved over to the Tongue River and camped a little while. When we were there, scouts came in and said that a big fire-boat[5] had come up the Yellowstone with a load of corn for the soldiers' horses, and that it was piled on the other side of the river. Some of our young men went to see, and one of them, Yellow Shirt, got killed by the fireboat's soldiers over there. But the others brought corn home and they gave us some. We parched it, and it was good.

About this time, in the Moon of Black Cherries (August), the scattering of the people began, because by now we learned that the soldiers were coming again. Dull Knife and the Shyelas went over to Willow Creek in the Big Horn Mountains. Many of the Lakotas stole away in small parties and started for the agencies. The rest of us, still a great many, started east, and the soldiers of Three Stars followed us. Our people set fire to the grass behind us as we went, and the smoke back there was wide as the day and the light of the fire was wide as the night. This was to make the soldiers' horses starve.

Then it began to rain, and it kept on raining for days while we traveled east. Our ponies had to work hard in the deep mud, and it must have been bad for the soldiers' horses back there with nothing to eat.

Sitting Bull and Gall with some people left us and started for Grandmother's Land (Canada), and other people were going away from us all the time, but Crazy Horse would not leave the country that was ours.

In the Moon of the Black Calf (September) we were camping near the head of the Grand River when American Horse with many tepees had a fight with the soldiers of Three Stars by the Slim Buttes on Rabbit Creek.[6] They fought hard there in the rain, and the soldiers killed American Horse and chased the women and children out of their homes and took all the papa (dried bison meat) that they had made to feed themselves that winter. Then Crazy Horse went over there with a band of our warriors and chased the soldiers through the rain. They fled southward toward the Black Hills, and many of their horses died in the deep mud. He followed them a long way and made them fight as they fled.

Wherever we went, the soldiers came to kill us, and it was all our own country. It was ours already when the Wasichus made the treaty with Red Cloud, that said it would be ours as long as grass should grow and water flow. That was only eight winters before, and they were chasing us now because we remembered and they forgot.

After that we started west again, and we were not happy anymore, because so many of our people had untied their horses' tails[7] and gone over to the Wasichus. We went back deep into our country, and most of the land was black from the fire, and the bison had gone away. We camped on the Tongue River where there was some cottonwood for the ponies; and a hard winter came on early. It snowed much; game was hard to find, and it was a hungry time for us. Ponies died, and we ate them. They died because the snow froze hard and they could not find the grass that was left in the valleys and there was not enough cottonwood to feed them all. There had been thousands of us together that summer, but there were not two thousand now.

News came to us there in the Moon of the Falling Leaves (November) that the Black Hills had been sold to the Wasichus and also all the country west of the Hills—the country we were in then.[8] I learned when I was older that our people did not want to do this. The Wasichus went to some of the chiefs alone and got them to put their marks on the treaty. Maybe some of them did this when they were crazy from drinking the minne wakan (holy water, whiskey) the Wasichus gave them. I have heard this; I do not know. But only crazy or very foolish men would sell their Mother Earth. Sometimes I think it might have been better if we had stayed together and made them kill us all.

Dull Knife was camping with his band of Shyelas on Willow Creek in the edge of the Big Horn Mountains, and one morning very early near the end of the Moon of Falling Leaves the soldiers came there to kill them.[9] The people were all sleeping. The snow was deep and it was very cold. When the soldiers began shooting into the tepees, the people ran out into the snow, and most of them were naked from their sleeping robes. Men fought in the snow and cold with nothing on them but their cartridge belts, and it was a hard fight, because the warriors thought of the women and children freezing. They could not whip the soldiers, but those who were not killed and did not die from the cold, got away and came to our camp on the Tongue.

I can remember when Dull Knife came with what was left of his starving and freezing people. They had almost nothing, and some of them had died on the way. Many little babies died. We could give them clothing, but of food we could not give them much, for we were eating ponies when they died. And afterwhile they left us and started for the Soldiers' town on White River to surrender to the Wasichus; and so we were all alone there in that country that was ours and had been stolen from us.

After that the people noticed that Crazy Horse was queerer than ever. He hardly ever stayed in the camp. People would find him out alone in the cold, an they would ask him to come home with them. He would not come, but sometimes he would tell the people what to do. People wondered if he ate anything at all. Once my father found him out alone like that, and he said to my father: "Uncle, you have noticed me the way I act. But do not worry; there are caves and holes for me to live in, and out here the spirits may help me. I am making plans for the good of my people."

He was always a queer man, but that winter he was queerer than ever. Maybe he had seen that he would soon be dead and was thinking how to help us when he would not be with us any more.

It was a very bad winter for us and we were all sad. Then another trouble came. We had sent out scouts to learn where the soldiers were, and they were camping at the mouth of the Tongue.

The Messiah

There was hunger among my people before I went away across the big water, because the Wasichus did not give us all the food they promised in the Black Hills treaty. They made that treaty themselves; our people did not want it and did not make it. Yet the Wasichus who made it had given us less than half as much as they promised. So the people were hungry before I went away.

But it was worse when I came back. My people looked pitiful. There was a big drouth, and the rivers and creeks seemed to be dying. Nothing would grow that the people had planted, and the Wasichus had been sending less cattle and other food than ever before. The Wasichus had slaughtered all the bison and shut us up in pens. It looked as though we might all starve to death. We could not eat lies, and there was nothing we could do.

And now the Wasichus had made another treaty to take away from us about half the land we had left. Our people did not want this treaty either, but Three Stars[10] came and made the treaty just the same, because the Wasichus wanted our land between the Smoky Earth and the Good River. So the flood of Wasichus, dirty with bad deeds, gnawed away half of the island that was left to us. When Three Stars came to kill us on the Rosebud, Crazy Horse whipped him and drove him back. But when he came this time without any soldiers, he whipped us and drove us back. We were penned up and could do nothing.

All the time I was away from home across the big water, my power was gone, and I was like a dead man moving around most of the time. I could hardly remember my vision, and when I did remember, it seemed like a dim dream.

Just after I came back, some people asked me to cure a sick person, and I was afraid the power would not come back to me; but it did. So I went on helping the sick, and there were many, for the measles had come among the people who were already weak because of hunger. There were more sick people that winter when the whooping cough came and killed little children who did not have enough to eat.

So it was. Our people were pitiful and in despair.

But early that summer when I came back from across the big water (1889) strange news had come from the west, and the people had been talking and talking about it. They were talking about it when I came home, and that was the first I had heard of it. This news came to the Ogalalas first of all, and I heard that it came to us from the Shoshones and Blue Clouds (Arapahoes). Some believed it and some did not believe. It was hard to believe; and when I first heard of it, I thought it was only foolish talk that somebody had started somewhere. This news said that out yonder in the west at a place near where the great mountains (The Sierras) stand before you come to the big water, there was a sacred man among the Paiûtes who had talked to the Great Spirit in a vision, and the Great Spirit had told him how to save the Indian peoples and make the Wasichus disappear and bring back all the bison and the people who were dead and how there would be a new earth. Before I came back, the people had got together to talk about this and they had sent three men, Good Thunder, Brave Bear and Yellow Breast, to see this sacred man with their own eyes and learn if the story about him was true. So these three men had made the long journey west, and in the fall after I came home, they returned to the Ogalalas with wonderful things to tell.

There was a big meeting at the head of White Clay Creek, not far from Pine Ridge, when they . . . us started on the war-path to find them. My mother tried to keep me at home, because, although I could walk and ride a horse, my wound was not all healed yet. But I would not stay; for, after what I had seen at Wounded Knee, I wanted a chance to kill soldiers.

We rode down Grass Creek to Smoky Earth, and crossed, riding down stream. Soon from the top of a little hill we saw wagons and cavalry guarding them. The soldiers were making a corral of their wagons and getting ready to fight. We got off our horses and went behind some hills to a little knoll, where we crept up to look at the camp. Some soldiers were bringing harnessed horses down to a little creek to water, and I said to the others: "If you will stay here and shoot at the soldiers, I will charge over there and get some good horses." They knew of my power, so they did this, and I charged on my buckskin while the others kept shooting. I got seven of the horses; but when I started back with these, all the soldiers saw me and began shooting. They killed two of my horses, but I brought five back safe and was not hit. When I was out of range, I caught up a fine baldfaced bay and turned my buckskin loose. Then I drove the others back to our party.

By now more cavalry were coming up the river, a big bunch of them, and there was some hard fighting for a while, because there were not enough of us. We were fighting and retreating, and all at once I saw red Willow on foot running. He called to me: "Cousin, my horse is killed!" So I caught up a soldier's horse that was dragging a rope and brought it to Red Willow while the soldiers were shooting fast at me. Just then, for a little while, I was a wanekia[11] myself. In this fight Long Bear and another man, whose name I have forgotten, were badly wounded; but we saved them and carried them along with us. The soldiers did not follow us far into the Badlands, and when it was night we rode back with our wounded to the O-ona-gazhee.

We wanted a much bigger war-party so that we could meet the soldiers and get revenge. But this was hard, because the people were not all of the same mind, and they were hungry and cold. We had a meeting there, and were all ready to go out with more warriors, when Afraid-of-His-Horses came over from Pine Ridge to make peace with Red Cloud, who was with us there.

Our party wanted to go out and fight anyway, but Red Cloud made a speech to us something like this: "Brothers, this is a very hard winter. The women and children are starving and freezing. If this were summer, I would say to keep on fighting to the end. But we cannot do this. We must think of the women and children and that it is very bad for them. So we must make peace, and I will see that nobody is hurt by the soldiers."

The people agreed to this, for it was true. So we broke camp next day and went down from the O-ona-gazhee to Pine Ridge, and many, many Lakotas were already there. Also, there were many, many soldiers. They stood in two lines with their guns held in front of them as we went through to where we camped.

And so it was all over.

I did not know then how much was ended. When I look back now from this high hill of my old age, I can still see the butchered women and children lying heaped and scattered all along the crooked gulch as plain as when I saw them with eyes still young. And I can see that something else died there in the bloody mud, and was buried in the blizzard. A people's dream died there. It was a beautiful dream.

And I, to whom so great a vision was given in my youth,—you see me now a pitiful old man who has done nothing, for the nation's hoop is broken and scattered. There is no center any longer, and the sacred tree is dead.

Notes

1. The Fetterman Fight, commonly described as a "massacre," in which Captain Fetterman and 81 men were wiped out on Peno Creek near Fort Phil Kearney, December 21, 1866.
2. A term used to designate the white man, but having no reference to the color of his skin.
3. Cheyennes.
4. Arapahoes.
5. Steamboat.
6. The Battle of Slim Buttes, September 9, 1876.
7. Left the war-path.
8. The treaty was signed in October, 1876.
9. Colonel Mackenzie attacked the Cheyenne village as stated on November 26, 1876.
10. General Crook headed the commission that arranged the treaty of 1889.
11. A "make-live," savior.

18
Chief Joseph

In 1877 the Nez Perce Indians led by Chiefs Joseph, looking Glass and White Bird struggled and fought across thirteen hundred miles of Indian territory. They were a day's march from the Canadian boarder when they were attacked by the Seventh Cavalry. Chief Joseph surrendered on the fifth day of the siege. The following excerpt is from his surrender speech given on October 5, 1877 in the Bear Paw Mountains. In time this was to become one of the most quoted of all Native-American speeches.

Tell General Howard I know his heart. What he told me before I have in my heart. I am tired of fighting. Our chiefs are killed. Looking Glass is dead. Toohoolhoolzote is dead. The old men are all dead. It is the young men who say yes or no. He who led on the young men [Ollokot] is dead. It is cold and we have no blankets. The little children are freezing to death. My people, some of them, have run away to the hills, and have no blankets, no food; no one knows where they are—perhaps freezing to death. I want to have time to look for my children and see how many of them I can find. Maybe I shall find them among the dead. Hear me, my chiefs! I am tired; my heart is sick and sad. From where the sun now stands I will fight no more forever.

19
Black Hawk

In 1833, Black Hawk dictated his autobiography to Antonie LeClair. In it appears his dedication to Brigadier General H. Atkinson, the ''White Beaver''—''the great war chief who commanded the American army against my little band'' leading to Black Hawk's surrender.

    I am now an obscure member of a nation, that formerly honored and respected my opinions. The path to glory is rough, and many gloomy hours obscure it. May the Great Spirit shed light on yours—and that you may never experience the humility that the power of the American government has reduced me to, is the wish of him, who, in his native forests, was once as proud and bold as yourself.

Black Hawk

10th Moon, 1833.

VI
Hispanic Americans

20
Rudolfo A. Anaya

Rudolfo A. Anaya, author of several books, including *Bless Me, Ultima* and *Heart of Astlan*, was born and raised in New Mexico. A graduate of the University of New Mexico he is currently living in Albuquerque and teaching creative writing at the University. The first essay entitled *An American Chicano in King Arthur's Court* was presented in Tucson in October in 1984 as part of the lecture series for the writers of the Purple Sage project. The second paper, *Requiem for a Lowrider*, was the commencement speech to the Albuquerque High School class of 1978.

An American Chicano in King Arthur's Court

A variety of voices comprise the literature of the Southwest. Writers from each of the cultural groups write from their particular perspective. Eventually these different perspectives will form the body of work we call Southwestern Literature. I say eventually, because as of now the contemporary writings of the Chicano and Native American communities—while they are flourishing—have not yet been widely disseminated and have not yet made their final impact on the region.[1]

It is understood that whenever cultural groups as different as the Anglo American, the Chicano and the Native American exist side by side, cultural sharing takes place; but also each group will develop a set of biases or stereotypes about the other groups. This is unfortunate, but it is a substantiated historical fact. The problem is compounded, of course, when one of the groups holds social, political and economic power over the other groups. Then prejudices will affect in an adverse manner the members of the minority groups.

How do we make the literature of the Southwest a truly multicultural literature which informs the public about the variety of voices which reflect the cultures of the Southwest? Can our different voices which reflect the cultures of the Southwest? Can our different literatures help to lessen the negative effect of cultural stereotypes?

I am an American Chicano, and I have titled my essay 'An American Chicano in King Arthur's Court.'' For me, King Arthur's Court represents an archetypal time and experience in

From *The American Self: Myth, Ideology, and Popular Culture*, Sam B. Girgus, ed. Copyright © 1981 by University of New Mexico Press, Albuquerque, New Mexico. Reprinted with permission.

English memory, an archetype transplanted onto American soil by the first English colonists. It is an archetype which is very much alive. (Remember the Kennedy administration reviving the dreams of Camelot?) In other words, King Arthur's Court represents a "foreign" archetype that is not indigenous to the Native American memory.

There is no judgmental value attached to what I have just said. King Arthur's Court has a right to exist in the communal memory of the British and the Anglo Americans. It is part of their history, part of their identity. And communal memory is a force which defines a group. Camelot and King Arthur's Court are "real" forces in as much as they define part of the evolution of this group's eventual world view.

In 1846, King Arthur's Court moved to what we now call the Southwest United States. During the war with Mexico the United States occupied and finally took Mexico's northern territories. In so doing the United States acquired a large population of Native Americans and Mexicanos. Suddenly a very different social, economic and political system was placed over the social system of the Mexicanos. The Mexicanos became Mexican-Americans. A different world view with its particular archetypes was imposed over the communal memory of the Mexicanos. In the area of artistic impulse and creation, this element of the Anglo culture would cause as many problems for the Mexicanos as did the new language and value system with which they now had to contend.

The Mexicano of the Southwest had his own vision of the world when the Anglo Americans came. The view was principally Hispanic and Catholic, but it was also imbued with strains of belief from the Native American cultures. The culture was HIspanic, but in its soul and memory resided not only Western European thought, Greek mythology, and the Judeo-Christian mythology and religious thought, but also the thought and mythology of Indian Mexico. The Mexicano was, with few and isolated exceptions, a mestizo population. Therefore, its world view was biased by the memory of the indigenous, American cultures.

Since 1848, King Arthur's Court has been the social and legal authority in the Southwest. It has exercised its power, not always in a fair and judicious way. My concern here is to explore how the Anglo-American value system affected the artistic impulse of the Mexicano. Did it impede and stifle the creative impulse of the Mexicano, and if so, did it interfere in the Mexicano's self identity and artistic impulse?

The artistic impulse is an energy most intricately bound to the soul of the people. Art and literature reflect the cultural group, and in reflecting the group they not only deal with the surface reality, but with that substratum of thought which is the group memory. The entire spectrum of history, language, soul, voice, and the symbols of the collective memory affect the writer. A writer becomes a prism to reflect those elements which are at the roots of the value system. We write to analyze the past, explore the present, and anticipate the future, and in so doing we utilize the collective memory of the group. We seek new visions and symbols to chart the future, and yet we are bound to mythologies and symbols of our past.

I remember when I started writing as a young man, fresh out of the university, my mind teeming with the great works I had read as a student. I was affected, as were most of my generation, by the poetry of Dylan Thomas, Eliot, Pound, Wallace Stevens. I had devoured the works of world authors, as well as the more contemporary Hemingway, Faulkner, Steinbeck, and Thomas Wolfe, and I felt I had learned a little about style and technique. I tried to imitate the work of those great writers, but that was not effective for the stories I had to tell. I made a simple discovery. I found I needed to write in my voice, of my characters, using my indigenous symbols. I needed to write about my culture, my history, the collective experience of my cultural group. But I had not been prepared to explore my indigenous., American experience; I had been prepared to deal with King

Arthur's Court. I discovered that the underlying world view of King Arthur's Court could not serve to tell the stories about my communal group.

I suppose Ultima saved me. That strong, old curandera of my first novel *Bless Me, Ultima*, came to me one night and pointed the way. That is, she came to me from my subconscious, a guide and mentor who was to lead me into the world of my native American experience. Write what you know, she said. Do not fear to explore the workings of your soul, your dreams, your memory. Dive deep into the lake of your subconsciousness and your memory, find the symbols, unlock the secrets, learn who you really are. You can't be a writer of any merit if you don't know who you are.[2]

I took her kind and wise advice. I dove into the common memory, into the dark and hidden past which was a lake full of treasure. The symbols I discovered had very little to do with the symbols I knew from King Arthur's Court—they were new symbols, symbols I did not fully understand, but symbols which I was sure spoke of the indigenous American experience. The symbols and patterns I found connected me to the past, and that past was not only my Hispanic, Catholic heritage; that past was also Indian Mexico. I did what I had never been taught to do at the university. I got in touch with myself, I explored myself, and found I was a reflection of that totality of life which had worked for eons to produce me.

Each writer has to go through the process of liberating oneself and finding one's true stream of creative energy. For Chicano writers it has been doubly difficult because in the formative years we were not presented with the opportunity to study our culture, our history, our language.

My generation will receive at least some thanks from the future, if only because we dared to write from the perspective of our experience, our culture. Of course a steady stream of Southwestern Hispanic writers had been producing works all along. Before and after 1846, poetry, novels and newspapers were produced, but those works were never part of the school curriculum. The oral tradition was alive and well, and its artistic impulse was invigorating to those of us lucky enough to grow up in its bounty. But by the 1960's the Hispanic culture had reached a crisis point. Not only were the old prejudices affecting us adversely, but the very core of the culture was under threat.

The Mexican American community needed economic and political justice in the 1960's. It also needed an artistic infusion of fresh, creative energy. We had to take a look at ourselves and review a world view which had permeated the culture for hundreds of years. This is precisely what the Chicano Movement in the 1970's and '70's did. The Chicano Movement of those decades fought battles in the social, economic and political areas, and in the artistic camp. Taking up pen and paint brushes, we found we could joust against King Arthur's knights and hold our own. In fact, we often did extremely well because we were on our soil, we knew the turf. Quite simply, what we were saying was that we wanted to assert our own rights, we wanted to define ourselves, we believed that our world view was as important as any other in terms of sustaining the individual and the culture.

We engaged actively in large-scale production of creative literature. We insisted that the real definition of our community was in the arts, in poetry and stories. A wealth of works was produced which was labeled the Chicano Renaissance. This view of the writers working from within the Chicano community helped to dispel some of the old stereotypes and prejudices. We could think, we could write, we did honor parents and family, we did have a set of moral values, we were as rich and as complex a cultural group as any other group in the country, and so the old, one-dimensional stereotypes begin to crumble.

We explained to the broader "mainstream" culture that we are American Chicanos; we are an inherently American, indigenous, people. We are Hispanic from our European heritage, we are Native American from our American heritage. We are heirs to the mythologies and religions and philosophic thought of Western civilization, but we are also heirs to the mythologies, religions and thought of the Americas. A renewed pride in our American heritage defined us.

Out of the Native American world flowed a rich mythology and symbology which the poets and writers began to tap and use. We confronted our mestizo heritage and proudly identified with this New World person. The idea of an original homeland, typified by the concept of Aztlan, became a prevalent idea. The homeland was indigenous, it was recorded in Native American legend. For the Chicano consciousness of the '60's it provided a psychological and spiritual center. One of the most positive aspects of the Chicano movement was its definition of a Chicano consciousness. Spiritually and psychologically the Chicano had found his center, he could define his universe with a new set of symbols, new metaphors. He had tapped once again into his native experience and recovered the important, archetypal symbols of his experience.

That consciousness which was defined in the art, poetry and stories of the Chicano writers continues to exist not just as a historical phenomenon that happened in the '60's and '70's. It continues to define the Chicano collective memory. The power of literature, the power of story and legend is great. True, the Chicano Movement has wanted in social action, but the renewed consciousness born in the literature of those decades survives in art, writing, history , and in the language and the oral tradition of the people. In a broader sense, its humanistic principles of brotherhood its desire for justice, its positive cultural identification, its definition of historic values, and its concern for the oppressed continue to be guiding principles in the thought and conduct of American Chicanos. Chicano consciousness continues to center us, to instruct us and to define us.

The evolution of Chicano consciousness created a new perspective in humanistic philosophy. It took nothing away from our Hispanic European and Mexican heritage, it took nothing away from other Western influences; on the contrary, it expanded the world view of the Americas. But we are still involved in the struggle to define ourselves, to define our community. Evolution is a slow process. Once the definition of Chicano consciousness has worked itself into the society, then we will not have to be so sensitive about the Edenic concept of King Arthur's Court. After all, we understand its right to exist as a mythology, we understand it as part of the definition of a particular group. The challenge for us, for the writers of the Southwest from all cultural groups, is to understand and accept those views which define groups and the individuals from all communities.

Part of our task is to keep reminding each other that each cultural community has an inherent right to its own definition, and Aztlan does define us more accurately than Camelot. Hildalgo and Morelos and Zapata are as valuable as Washington, Jefferson and Lincoln. The mythology of Mesoamerica is an interesting and informing as Greek mythology. Mexico's settlement of her northern colonies is as dramatic and challenging as the settlement of the thirteen United States colonies. As American Chicanos, we have a multi-layered history on which to draw. To be complete individuals we must draw on all the world traditions and beliefs, and we must continue to understand and strengthen our own heritage. We seek not to exclude, but to build our base as we seek to understand the interrelated nature of the Americas. Our eventual goal is to incorporate the world into our understanding. But in the span of world time, the Chicano community is a young community. It is still growing, still exploring, still defining itself. Our history has already made valuable contributions to American thought and growth and we will continue to make more. What we seek now, in our relationship to the broader society, is to eliminate the mindless prejudices which hamper our evolution, and to encourage people of good will who do not fear a pluralistic society and who understand that, as a group of people define themselves in a positive way, the greater the contribution they make to mankind.

For a century American Chicanos have been influenced by the beliefs imposed by a King Arthur's Court scenario. We have learned the language, we have learned the rules of the game. We have adopted part of the cultural trappings of Arthur's Court, but we also insist on keeping true to our culture. The American Southwest is a big land, a unique land. It has room for many communities. It should have no room for the old, negative prejudices of the past. When we, each one of us, impede the fulfillment of any person's abilities and dreams, we impede our own humanity.

Notes

1. This presentation was given in Tucson in October 1984 as part of a lecture series for the Writers of the Purple Sage project. Mr. Anaya's talk at the OLD SOUTHWEST/NEW SOUTHWEST Conference, "The Voice of the Chicano in the New Southwest," continued this theme.
2. Rudolfo A. Anaya, *Bless Me, Ultima* (Berkeley, California: Tonatiuh-Quinto Sol International, 1976).

Requiem for a Lowrider

La ConFloencia Ed. Note: "Requiem for a Lowrider," Rudolfo Anaya's commencement speech to the Albuquerque High School class of 1978, moved the audience to applause and tears. We think La Confluencia readers will also find it moving. Even The New Yorker has caught on to lowriding, as defined by Calvin Trillin, July 10, 1978:

> In California, it is common for a young Mexican-American to lower his car to within a few inches of the ground, make it as beautiful as he knows how both inside and out, and drive it down the street very, very slowly. The custom is called lowriding.

In New Mexico and other parts of the Southwest, we've known about, observed, enjoyed, been caught behind lowriders for a long time. Rudolfo Anaya, didn't need to tell his audience how to define lowriding: surely almost everyone in the 1978 graduating class has cruised Central, up and down and up again. Anaya, in telling us the story of Jessie, characteristically looks at the moral questions behind the social custom.

Your graduation night has caused me to reflect on my own graduation from Albuquerque High School. In 1956, on a night much like tonight, I stumbled up to the stage and received that piece of paper which says: YOU DID IT! Look out world, here I come! I'm an AHS graduate, a Bulldog, and proud of it!

Oh, it was a time for feeling high. And I don't mean just from the elation of receiving my diploma. We had already had a week of partying and there was more to come that night. At least for a few days we felt as if we owned the world. And very few of us were worrying about the really heavy things, like getting a job, planning our future, deciding on more education, or whether to get married or wait awhile . . . the same important decisions facing you in your lives.

But that's not what I really want to talk about tonight. What has been on my mind is the fact that your graduating class tonight and mine in 1956 are a generation apart. (Ain't it funny, the way time slips away . . .) And so I have been forced to ask myself what we have in common. What is it that we can talk about across this span of time which marks a generation? We were the generation of the 50s, of be-bop, rock-n-roll, sock hops . . . those of us who were to be writers were later called a part of the "beat generation." Yours is the time of hard, acid rock, disco, you've been through Watergate, so in a sense you're more cynical.

We were post-Korean war; you are post-Viet Nam. We faced the poor times and recession of the late 50s, and you face the issues of inflation and high unemployment. So we have, I think, more in common than might appear on the surface.

But what is the *one* thing that can really help us communicate with each other? I've kept asking myself that question, and my mind keeps coming back to Jessie. I keep thinking about him because we went to Albuquerque High School together. He was one of my best friends . . . but he didn't graduate. He was one of the original lowriders, a crazy cruiser with a customized 48 Ford . . . he spent more time cruising around the school on Broadway and Central than in it. But he was one of the kindest and brightest persons I have ever known, and in thinking of him I think I discovered the one element we most have in common. In different times, you and I are a generation of lowriders. We spent four years in high school just cruising. We developed lowriding and cruising to an art.

And thank heaven for cruisers and lowriders, right? Just think how many lowriders it has taken to make this country what it is today. Christopher Columbus was one of the original lowriders! That's right, I think old Chris was just kicking back, cruising around the Atlantic, and by accident he happened to bump into the Americas. And most of us wouldn't be here today if he hadn't gone cruising that Sunday.

But what is cruising all about?

When you say, "Hey Dad," or "Oye Jefito, I'm going cruising . . ." The typical response is: "Where are you going?"

And the typical answer is: "I don't know, just cruising . . ."

Just cruising . . . huh, that's the question which keeps turning in my mind when I think about Jessie.

"We have a big assignment in history," I'd say to him, "let's go hit the books at the library . . ."

And he would smile and put his arm around my shoulder and say, "Hey, let's go cruising, man. You only live once. You take life too seriously . . . Just cool it . . ."

Cool it. In the 50s it meant kick back, take it easy . . . and that's another thing I've discovered as I compare our generations, the words change . . . language fads come and go . . . but deep down inside we all still have to deal with the real gut issues which life presents us. You're going to have to make choices. You're going to have to think about cruising as I have.

Because what is it that we're looking for when we go cruising? Let me suggest to you that we are looking for excitement to put in our lives. We go cruising to meet a friend, we hope that that special someone we like is also out there . . . just cruising. We turn up streets randomly, we follow the crowd . . . if there's a wreck or a fight or a party everybody shows up, looking for the action, looking for some excitement. In short, we're all waiting for an accident to happen.

That's what Jessie was doing. I know now. He was dissatisfied. He cruised around waiting for something to happen. In a round about way he taught me that life requires a little more planning than goes into just cruising.

But everybody loved him. Duck-tailed, baggy pants, hair slick with pomade, swinging like a pachuco, he'd come dancing down the hall, snapping his fingers, looking the girls over . . . He was Mr. Cool! He was crazy but he treated everybody with respect. Even the teachers liked him . . . that is when he was in class long enough for them to get to know him.

"Hey, Rude!" he used to say, "let's go cruise around before class. We can smoke a few tokes and be back in time for third period."

Life was easy for him when he was cruising and smoking up, looking for that excitement he needed.

By his senior year he was beyond just drinking beer and smoking mota. I still remember the first night I saw him loaded with heroin. We were going to a dance at the Heights Center, and he came to pick me up. He was really loaded, and I knew it was on heavy stuff. Carga, horse, smack, call it what you want, the words change, the junk remains the same beneath.

I cried. "Hey, Jessie, what are you doing to yourself? Do you know what you're getting into?"

I don't want to sound moralistic. I had done a lot of the things he had done. We were young men and we were growing up, bumping into accidents and new excitement every day was a part of our lives. All I tried to tell him was that there was other excitement to life. I tried to tell him that sometimes I got my high from some of the books I was reading, and that . . . yes . . . even some of the ideas the teachers kicked around in class were exciting. It wasn't all sheer boredom. I didn't give him a lecture. I talked to him as a friend. I was concerned for him because I loved him as a friend . . . and I knew he was on the wrong road.

"Easy, Rude, easy daddy-o," he smiled, "I'm okay . . . I know what I'm doing . . . Hey, this is a great high. I can handle it. Come on, let's go dancing!"

And he was a great dancer. The girls loved him. We all loved him. The only people who could have cared less about him were the ones he had run into while cruising . . . the ones who sold him the junk.

After awhile his habit was daily. He dropped out of school. We drifted apart . . . went our separate ways. I stayed in school, hoping there was something there that would help me solve the complexity of my own life; Jessie began to run with a new crowd. But he was no longer the happy-go-lucky lowrider I once knew. He was running scared.

We talked once, but it didn't do any good. "You take life too serious," he told me, "it's only a slow cruise . . . so take it easy. Look, I'm not busting my ass on books, and I've got a car, plenty of bread, everything I need." And he smiled.

But we both knew it wasn't Jessie who had those things, it was the monkey on his back who owned everything . . . and the monkey was growing, sitting by Jessie as they cruised up and down the barrio streets.

The last time I saw him was graduation night . . . on a night like tonight . . . 22 years ago; it almost seems like yesterday. I was graduating; he wasn't. I wanted him to be with me and share whatever this small accomplishment meant. "I wouldn't miss it for the world," he smiled. "I may not be getting my little piece of paper, but I'm glad you're getting yours. Hey, you keep getting those things and you're going to be a big vato someday . . ." We laughed.

How could any of us be mad at him? He was a lovable guy. We could only hurt for him. There was a gang of us that had gone through high school together, and Jessie was the only one not graduating.

But he was there to wish us luck, and he came to the party afterwards. And for a few moments we were all happy and things seemed to be the way they used to be. We joked and we laughed and we talked about what we were going to do now that we owned the world.

I could go on to tell you how each one of us . . . each member of that small gang . . . went on to develop his potential and live a worthwhile life. But this is not our story. It's Jessie's story.

He was really high that night, and he was desperate He mentioned once that he needed money, that he had big debts to pay, and then the party got loud and crowded and I lost track of him for a while. Later, when I asked for him, somebody told me that some of his "new" friends had taken him outside. I ran outside, but his car was gone. Jessie had gone on his last ride.

The following morning his brother called me and told me Jessie was dead. They had dumped him down by the river that night. He had paid his debt. When I got to the mortuary his family was already there. It was a sad time. Nothing to say or do I could only promise him that someday I'd tell his story, that maybe it would make sense to someone. And now, 22 years later, I'm telling it to you. This is Jessie's story, it's my **Requiem for a Lowrider.**

And why have I told it, when tonight should be a time of celebration for you and for your families who have helped you through school? It's a time of celebration for the teachers and the counselors who have helped. Now you've made it, and it's your time. So it is a proper time to remember the help you received, the encouragement when you were down, the love when you thought things were hopeless. And because we share our lives with many brothers and sisters, it's also a time to remember that we, too, can give help. Maybe we didn't give Jessie enough help, maybe we didn't give him enough love . . . maybe we saw too late that he was drifting into an accident from which there was no return. . . .

I sincerely believe that there is a time in life for drifting. There is a time for sitting back and getting in touch with yourself. Some of our most interesting illuminations and ideas will come when we take time to reflect, time to kick back and cruise awhile. . . . But there's also a time for planning and a time for more active participation in life. You can't cruise forever. The gas is running out . . . you're older, and at a new stage of life. Your lives will be very complex, and there will be many friends like Jessie who will need your help. So I ask you, engage life actively! Embrace it and love it! And help make it an adventure where there are fewer tragedies like the one I have told you tonight.

VII
Afro-Americans

21
Langston Hughes

Langston Hughes was born in Joplin, Missouri, in 1902. He received his B.A. from Lincoln University in Pennsylvania in 1929. He was awarded various fellowships throughout the 1930s and 40s. From 1926 until his death in 1967, Langston Hughes devoted his time to writing and lecturing. He wrote poetry, short stories, song lyrics, essays, plays and an autobiography. Two of his short poems are included here *Merry-go-round* and *American Heartbreak*.

Merry-Go-Round

Colored child at carnival:

Where is the Jim Crow section
On this merry-go-round,
Mister, cause I want to ride?
Down South where I come from
White and colored
Can't sit side by side
Down South on the train
There's a Jim Crow car.
On the bus we're put in the back—
But there ain't no back
To a merry-go-round!
Where's the horse
For a kid that's black?

Copyright 1942 by Langston Hughes and renewed 1970 by Arna Bontemps and George Houston. Reprinted from SELECTED POEMS OF LANGSTON HUGHES, by Permission of Alfred A. Knopf, Inc.

American Heartbreak

I am the American heartbreak—
Rock on which Freedom
Stumps its toe—
The great mistake
That Jamestown
Made long ago.

Copyright 1951 by Langston Hughes. Reprinted from SELECTED POEMS OF LANGSTON HUGES, by permission of Alfred A. Knopf, Inc.

22
Black Rage, Black Identity
Edwin L. Coleman II

Dr. Edwin L. Coleman II is a Professor at the University of Oregon where he currently teaches Afro-American literature, and is director of the Ethnic Studies program. Besides his teaching schedule he is widely published in American folklore and Afro-American journals. The following paper, ''Black Identity in the American Cultural Context and Elsewhere,'' Discusses the alienation felt by many Afro-Americans today.

Introduction

Establishing ethnic identity can be multi-dimensional in scope. In a society like ours, where there are may diverse cultures and one that is dominant, the social consequences are even more complex when the process of assimilation is added as an important factor. One of the consequences has been the attempt to ''Anglo-Saxonize'' the different cultural and ethnic strains that make up our country. This has created an identity crisis not only for Black Americans but for other groups throughout our history. It has given the dominant Anglo Saxon ethnic communities a distorted sense of their cultural roots. In a positive sense our ethnic diversity has been a source of strength when it draws from the various ethnic heritages those lessons which broaden men & women's understanding of their roots. When narrow ethnocentrism intrudes itself into our social fabric, as it has done, it breeds division within society as well as inside ethnic communities.

To some extent the dominance of Anglo Saxon culture in American society has contributed to this narrow ethnocentrism through its control over the channels of communication. Actually it has been a *political process* that has introduced this divisiveness rather than Anglo Saxon culture *per se*, except that one cannot separate the political features from other segments of the cultural dynamic. The politics of ethnicity can emerge in many different forms. Within the American context it has been through the framework of Federalism which was supposed to contain factionalism but really did not. The linkages between the political processes and other facets of Americans culture are still being explored by historians, sociologists, writers of fiction, and others.There is an interaction that takes place between the political processes and other forces within the cultural milieu, sometimes manifested in subtle forms. In other instances, it is a more forceful interplay.

For purposes of this (paper) I would like to limit this discussion to some of the political-psychological factors which seem to contribute to the identity crisis as it impacts on Black Americans and in turn the rest of society. I will also briefly comment on the British scene in terms of some similarities and differences, i.e., Black-White relations. This central thrust, however, will be on the American experience. The pivotal elements of this identity crisis are the false perceptions of one another that are held by Blacks and Whites.

The Political-Psychological Dimensions of the Identity Crisis

Nathan Huggins's comments are appropriate to mention at the outset because they tend to focus on one important sociological aspect related to our country's historical roots. Unfortunately his observations are not altogether outdated:

> ... the black/white relationship has been symbiotic; blacks have been essential to white identity (and whites to blacks). This interdependence has been too profound to be measured by the simple meeting out of respective contributions to American culture. Whites have needed blacks as they have needed the black face minstral mask—a guise of alter ego. And blacks sensing this psychic dependency—have been all too willing to join the charade hiding behind the minstral mask, appearing to be what the white man wanted them to be.[1]

Part of what Huggins refers to has its social-political impetus in the kind of environment that Blacks have been forced to live in until recently. The word "forced" applies to the majority of Black Americans although one can find many individual cases where some Blacks chose to identify with their oppressors for varied reasons. It must be remembered from a historical standpoint that the slave uprisings of the early 1800s were, as often as not, betrayed by Blacks. Furthermore, many Black leaders of the late 19th century gave their moral sanction to the worst features of segregation, and there are those today who would not hesitate to sell themselves and their people for "thirty pieces of silver" or less. This is one of the central facets of the political context to which I referred earlier. Conflict within ethnic groups often has a class dimension, an ideological dimension, and a psychological impact at the individual level. Sometimes, as history documents, the internal conflict that takes place within ethnic communities may be caused by forces outside the community, as Native Americans in particular have experienced. All of these factors are a part of the political-psychological level of the identity crisis.

A Brief Look at the British Experience, and the Identity Crisis as Dealt With in American Literature

While the Black experience in the United States has some features that set it apart, there are elements that transcend our national borders. For example, the rage felt by Black Britons today is not limited to the British Isles. It is part of a larger and more global historical process. White Brittania is only beginning to learn the lessons of its colonial policies.

In the American context, and with differing historical roots, it holds true for Blacks in the British Isles, smoldering anger is a part of the Black psyche. As recent events have clearly shown, such smoldering can burst forth with devastating consequences. The Black American stores anger from seeing brothers and sisters harassed by the police, from knowing that Blacks cannot take revenge on White rapists, from watching Black fathers leave home because they cannot get jobs and their families can get welfare *only* if they go. Sometimes this anger may not be directly expressed or may in fact be turned inward. This partially explains the high crime rate in Black communities, especially assault and aggravated assault. Rage results from the repression of violent anger, or it may add self-hatred to the reservoir of anger. Black rage, in the American context, issues from hundreds of years of oppression, from the dehumanization and raping of souls. In the British context it unfolds through a history of colonialism which has come to roost with the large influx of West Indians and Africans into the British Isles since the end of World War Two. White Englishmen can no longer sit back with their false sense of "America's Race Problem." The colonial "chickens" have come home.

There exists a literary tradition of Black rage, of the minstrel mask tradition with all of its social-political implications, and if there is a correct interpretation to be made of it, it is to be found in the works of Black American authors.

Although Black writers have for years been offering accurate images of Black life in this country, particularly novelist-essayists like Langston Hughes, Richard Wright, John Killens, Maya Angelou, and James Baldwin, their works have often been misread by Whites—and what is more, by some Blacks. Sometimes the works of these writers have been interpreted as quaint entertainments or embarrassing special cases, for example, calls to knee-jerk action. The findings of behavioral scientists like William H. Grier and Price Cobbs in *Black Rage*, 1968[2], are much validated in Black literature. At the same time, some of their work offers a guide to improved understanding of the literary work in its aspect as definition and description of Black experience, concepts that must be thoroughly examined before action can produce substantially greater equity for Blacks in America. Definition and description are two different phases in the analytical process. Many novels adequately describe social conditions without necessarily defining, that is to say, examining the social mechanisms that create those conditions. The extent to which a literary work can perform both functions is a matter for continuing discussion.

The identity crisis for Blacks and Whites is one of the more important themes in American literature. It is a social issue with many sociological-political ramifications. One example in literature, which in this instance draws from real life, is Langston Hughes's play *Mulatto*. Bert, the main character, exemplifies one of the chief obstacles in the search for Black identity: the White problem. Bert is half White and so does not understand why he cannot partake of the advantages enjoyed by White people. He is ambivalent about his Black heritage: "I'm no nigger anyhow, am I Ma?" "I'm half White!" "I might stay here awhile and teach o-darkies to think like men" ". . . but no more bowing down to White folks for me."[3] Unwilling to accept the status imposed upon him as a Black man, Bert is caught between his deep hatred for all Whites and the feeling that he is entitled to everything Whites have since he is *half White*. Bert is physically mature, but psychologically incomplete. In Freudian theory, Bert must identify with his father to reach manhood; yet he cannot identify with his White father because that is forbidden.

Ironically, Bert has inherited stubbornness and pride from his father. When they confront one another, Norwood breaks down because he cannot bring himself to kill his own son. But all of his life Bert has been denied a relationship with Norwood, that of father and son; so when he kills Norwood, he is not lashing out against his father, but against a *White man* who has dehumanized him and who has denied him existence as a member of his family. For a time after Bert kills his father, he is free and has control over his destiny, or so he feels. He freely chooses to kill himself before he is lynched. The extent of "free choice" that Bert engages in given the social political context is, it would seem, a central theme or issue. That is to say, he can choose to die at the hands of the lynchers or by his own hand. Furthermore, his relationship with his father is largely dictated by the dominant Anglo Saxon social mores. In other words, he and his father are victims of society in a direct sense because society has made them adversaries. Obviously not every father-son relationship has such deep sociological ramifications, but certainly Bert and Norwood's is a classic example of the identity crisis under discussion.

The action of *Mulatto* can, of course, be read as a parable of the Black American quandary: White America, or at least a powerful segment of it, is responsible for the existence of Black America and has established the rules for it to live by. With the rejection of healthy fathering, galling paternalism is all that remains, its jealous restrictions hampering normal growth and fostering rebellion. "For the Black man in this country, it's not so much a matter of acquiring manhood as it is a struggle for its possession."[4] In the British context, the Black experience unfolded from a more overt colonial context which has many of the same characteristics as the Black American's except that current events, e.g., 1945 to the present, have thrust Blacks more directly onto the British scene. Before this period they were far across the seas and the effects of racist policies were easier to ignore.

Richard Wright's *Native Son* centers on Bigger Thomas's attempt to achieve manhood, a sense of who he is, and what his purpose is on this earth. The historical backdrop of the story is Chicago during the 1930s. The thomas family is forced by circumstances (it is the middle of the American depression) to live in a rat-infested tenement house. The tenements are owned by a rich White slum landlord. Bigger doesn't understand, at least at the beginning of the story, why other people have control over his live, and he has a constant fear of Whites.

Events take an ironical twist when Bigger kills the daughter of the slum landlord, Mary Dalton, and it's (landlord's) girlfriend, Bessie Mears. The murder of Mary is an act of striking out at the system which oppresses him and his family. Wright's comments in his essay "Why Bigger Was Born" place Bigger in an international context in terms of the Black experience as well as in a social class context:

> But why did Bigger revolt? No explanation based upon hard and fast rule of conduct can be given. But there were always two factors psychologically dominant in his personality. First, through some quirk of circumstance, he had become estranged from the religion and the folk culture of his race. Second, he was trying to react to and answer the call of the dominant civilization whose glitter came to him through the newspapers, magazines, radios, movies, and the more imposing sight and sound of daily American life. In many respects his emergence as a distinct type was inevitable.[5]

The following additional passage from Wright's essay points more directly to the social, psychological, and political dimensions. These dimensions include the issue of class conflict because the "glitter" of affluence embittered Bigger as well as many Whites—or, as Wright observed:

> During this period the shadings and nuances which were filling in Bigger's picture came, not so much from Negro life, as from the lives of whites I met and grew to know. I began to sense that they had their own kind of Bigger Thomas behavioristic pattern which grew out of a more subtle and broader frustration.[6]

The link between social environment and the individual is sometimes subtle in nature. During periods of political instability or economic dislocation, as was the case in the 1930s, the impact of the social environment on individual personality can be as traumatic as Wright observed in his essay. There is ample evidence of this in numerous behavioral studies as well as in literature.

Problems of identity in Black writing in the 1960s involve no greater obstacles to the reader than did those in earlier works, but these issues are often more complicated than the desire to exist, to stand up and be counted. Though one still finds classic tragic heroes like Bert and Bigger Thomas, there are more flawed heroes, though not necessarily the lovable rogues sometimes associated with Langston Hughes. One reason for the complication is the illusion of greater promise for Black Americans that is part of the heritage of civil rights reforms, that is, some of the contemporary heroes begin their quest for identity just where previous heroes hoped to finish. There is then the problem of rising expectations which often fuels politically volatile situations when the expectations are not met or when the American dream becomes a nightmare. For West Indian Blacks moving to England after World War II there were the same rising expectations that turned sour during the 1950s and 60s with violent repercussions. In a related sense the identity crisis is linked to the problem of social alienation which often leads to feelings of rage or despair.

The work of Swedish sociologist Ulf Hannerz (*Soulside: Inquiries into Culture and Community*, New York, 1969) can help to schematize more clearly our examination of rage as motive power in Black fictional lives, that is, in literature which reflects the Black experience. The point cannot be over-emphasized that literature, especially protest literature, can only generalize the experiences of groups. It cannot, except within a limited framework, speak to individual experiences within groups. This point is sometimes overlooked by critics. Keeping this point in mind, Hannerz' comments seem relevant to note here.

Hannerz reports three defense mechanisms employed by Black youths in their attempt to reduce the self-doubt imposed upon them by a dehumanizing White society. One is to attempt to live up to the mainstream's norms, those set by White society. Another is to assert that the barriers set by society are impermeable, and so, in a sense, to give up trying to live freely. The third is to set up alternative ideals and create their own Black standards, as is manifest in the creation of the "Black consciousness" and what Hannerz terms the "rhetoric of soul." Black psychologists have quarreled wholeheartedly with Hannerz's first mechanism, both on the point of its being productive merely of further grief and self-doubt and on the question of the desirability of those standards for any life that purports to be humane. The second method explains the development of the pseudo-pathological systems and means of escape labeled "adaptive" by Grier and Cobbs—while adapting to a sick and faithless society in order to survive, one may appear to be sick and faithless. This withdrawal-or-escape attitude enables us to categorize and comprehend a range of behaviors that may seem simply deviant or inferior to readers; such behaviors comprise not only the quietism of actual retreat into an uncapsulated society but also the escape provided by drug abuse, including alcohol, violence and sometimes, religion. Fictional characters who exhibit these kinds of behavior accurately assess their world: they *are* powerless, at least in terms of acting against the society at large except in a fashion that would inevitably lead to their destruction, as happened to Bigger Thomas.

Escapism often becomes another mechanism for those who feel they are alienated from society as well as those who are in fact alienated because of social factors such as race or ethnicity. This distinction is, I believe, an important one to make because behavior that appears similar often has different origins. Trying to ascertain the causes of alienated behavior can be a complex process. This paper is concerned primarily with the alienation that has its roots in a racist society. The origins of certain kinds of behavior, drug use being one prime example, are multi-dimensional. For Blacks the primary, but by no means the only, motivating factor in drug use is social, stemming from a racist society.

Drug use effectively reduces existential rage by diverting the user's attention from the larger world to his own intrapersonal demands. The concern about drug use in certain political quarters of American society would be far less pronounced if it were not for the fact that drugs have spread into

White middle and upper class suburbs. Ironically, the drug problem has finally crossed racial, class, and ideological lines for the first time in decades. This appears to be the case, for now, in the United States. This is not to say that certain elements in our political leadership here in the United States are above promoting drug use if it could be limited to certain segments of society and if it would advance their own agenda. In a larger sense, then, the drug problem as such is not only a social issue but has political overtones as well, since people are far more easily controlled or dealt with if they can be reduced to human vegetables without endangering the favored few in the process. There is not much difference in terms of moral attitude between significant segments of the American corporate elite and their "soul brothers" among the dope dealers.

Though fictional accounts of drug use or violence are frequently exploitative, Claude Brown in his fictionalized autobiography, *Manchild in the Promised Land* (1965), gives a moving account of a view of Harlem street life that Langston Hughes did not often present—the side of death and destruction.* Although Brown, who may be identified with the character Sonny, finds a better way out of the ghetto (education), the predominant mode of life he portrays involves drugs, stealing, rape and murder.

One can draw many parallels between West Indian Blacks in England and their American cousins, regarding many of these issues. The chief difference between the two groups is important to note. The West Indians in England are recent arrivals on the British scene which in itself has different social effects. Depending on the direction British society takes during the coming decades, these new arrivals may be more easily assimilated into society—assuming they can retain their cultural heritage. Alternatively, the two cultures (Anglo Saxon and West Indian) may assimilate parts of each other's heritage. American Blacks, on the other hand, are alienated from a society that they helped to build, which has created an alienation similar in character to that of the West Indians in England, but far more intense in tone. In the past, assimilation between two cultures or multi-cultures has taken years to accomplish and the process has been rocky. However, our scientific-technological revolution may force us to accomplish this process in a far shorter time frame.

There are other forms of escapism to be considered. Violence can be a form of escape under certain circumstance: if it is random or aimless, if it is directed inward at oneself, drug abuse being a classic case in point. Certain kinds of environments promote this sort of violence more than other environments may. Alternatively, revolutions to overthrow oppressive governments represent one example of violence being employed in a positive sense, if it is organized with clearly defined goals with some kind of constraints on the use of the violence. The violence of Bigger Thomas was clearly self-destructive in the end.

Religion, too, may be a form of escapism, as it was for Bigger's mother. But religion cannot be dismissed *merely* as escape, for it pervades our culture and can bring meaning to life as well as comfort. Whether religion is escape is a matter of degree. It also depends upon how one chooses to interpret religious doctrine. In the play, *Tambourines to Glory*, for example, Langston Hughes uses religion as a readily understandable framework in which to discuss the issues of morality, God and the Devil, good and evil. The Devil is manifest in Buddy, who constantly attempts to lure the other characters, especially Laura, into his evil trap. Essie, with all her complexities, clearly represents goodness and there is a constant struggle between her and Buddy. Laura is torn between her devo-

---

*This is not to say that Hughes was unaware:

"Harlem, the Black Mecca, a potent symbol of Blackness. All roads lead to Harlem. It is the enslaved sharecropper's dream of freedom; it is the dark spawning place of invidious urban ills. Harlem is disillusionment and desperation and crime. It is opportunity. It is home. It is a place where the brothers and sisters converge and pool their strengths and joys and sorrow."[7]

tion to Essie and the temptation of Buddy, but the end of the play brings the destruction of evil and the triumph of good. Penetrating the mask of his characters, Hughes seeks out and exposes human weakness, but he also shows human strength. Though he does not deny the value of religion as a means of coping, as a means of asserting one's identity, he does not propose that it ought to be man's sole occupation. Man may find his own identity through sources other than religious belief.

Hannerz's third option, mentioned earlier, is the creation of "Black consciousness." This point returns us to our discussion of the politics of ethnicity and the question of Black identity within the American cultural context. Where the development of Black pride is strong and positive, it would not seem to deserve the label "defense mechanism." But where it is too defensive or reactive, a point not always easy to ascertain, there is danger of its moving into Hannerz's second category, withdrawal or escape. Grier and Cobbs caution: "Many Black men who today preach blackness seem headed blindly toward self-destruction uncritical of anything "black" and damming the white man for diabolical wickedness."[8] Ethnocentrism may, then, be either positive or negative in terms of its impact on society, depending upon the overall philosophical-political context in which it flourishes.

Notes

1. Nathan Huggins, *Harlem Renaissance*, New York: Oxford University Press, 1971, p. 84.
2. Grier and Cobbs, *Black Rage*, New York: Bantam Books, 1968, p. 49.
3. Langston Hughes, "Mulatto," *Five Plays by Langston Hughes*, ed. Webster Smalley, Bloomington: Indiana University Press, 1963, p. 25.
4. Grier and Cobbs, p. 49.
5. Richard Wright, "How Bigger Was Born," in *Native Son*, New York: Harper and Row Publishers, 1966, p. xiii.
6. Richard Wright, p. xvi.
7. Eugenia Collier, "A Pain in His Soul: Simple as Epic Hero," *Langston Hughes: Black Genius*, ed. Therman B. O'Daniel, New York: William Morrow and Co. Inc., 1971, p. 121.
8. Grier and Cobbs, p. 169.

VIII
Asian Americans

"The inability among many to understand that a native-born person does not have to be white to be an American is a problem that has remained with [us] to this day."
from *They Call Me Moses Masaoka* by Masaoka

23
Jeanne Wakatsuki Houston

Jeanne Wakatsuki Houston a Japanese American was born in Englewood, California. *Farewell to Manzanor* is her story, written in collaboration with her husband James D. Houston, and retells the fears, humiliations, and hopes of those Japanese-American families put into relocation camps during World War II. Currently, the Houstons' are living in Santa Cruz, California, with their children where James Houston teaches at the University of California.

Ten Thousand Voices

As I came to understand what Manzanar had meant, it gradually filled me with shame for being a person guilty of something enormous enough to deserve that kind of treatment. In order to please my accusers, I tried, for the first few years after our release, to become someone acceptable. I both succeeded and failed. By the age of seventeen I knew that *making it*, in the terms I had tried to adopt, was not only unlikely, but false and empty, no more authentic for me than trying to emulate my Great-aunt Toyo. I needed some grounding of my own, such as Woody had found when he

From FAREWELL TO MANZANAR by Jeanne Wakatsuki and James D. Houston. Copyright © 1973 by James D. Houston. Reprinted by permission of Houghton Mifflin Company.

went to commune with her and with our ancestors in Ka-ke. It took me another twenty years to accumulate the confidence to deal with what the equivalent experience would have to be for me.

It's outside the scope of this book to recount all that happened in the interim. Suffice to say, I was the first member of our family to finish college and the first to marry out of my race. As my husband and I began to raise our family, and as I sought for ways to live agreeably in Anglo-American society, my memories of Manzanar, for many years, lived far below the surface. When we finally started to talk about making a trip to visit the ruins of the camp, something would inevitably get in the way of our plans. Mainly my own doubts, my fears. I half-suspected that the place did not exist. So few people I met in those years had even heard of it, and those who had knew so little about it, sometimes I imagined I had made the whole thing up, dreamed it. Even among my brothers and sisters, we seldom discussed the internment. If we spoke of it at all, we joked.

When I think of how that secret lived in all our lives, I remember the way Kiyo and I responded to a little incident soon after we got out of camp. We were sitting on a bus-stop bench in Long Beach, when an old, embittered woman stopped and said, "Why don't all you dirty Japs go back to Japan!" She spit at us and passed on. We said nothing at the time. After she stalked off down the sidewalk we did not look at each other. We sat there for maybe fifteen minutes with downcast eyes and finally got up and walked home. We couldn't bear to mention it to anyone in the family. And over the years we never spoke of this insult. It stayed alive in our separate memories, but it was too painful to call our into the open.

In 1966 I met a Caucasian woman who had worked for one year as a photographer at Manzanar. I could scarcely speak to her. I desperately wanted to, but all my questions stuck in my throat. This time it was not the pain of memory. It was simply her validation that all those things had taken place. Someone outside the close community of Japanese Americans had actually seen the camp, with its multitude of people and its swarm of buildings on the plain between the mountains. Something inside me opened then. I began to talk about it more and more.

It was April 1972, thirty years almost to the day, that we piled our three kids into the car and headed out there. From where we live now, in the California coast town of Santa Cruz, it's a full day's drive. We started down 101 to Paso Robles, crossed over the hummocky Diablo Range to the central valley, skirted Bakersfield, and climbed through Tehachapi Pass into the desert.

At Mojave we turned north onto the same road our bus had taken out from Los Angeles in April 1942. It is the back road to the Sierras and the main route from southern California to Reno and Lake Tahoe. We joined bikers and backpackers and the skiers heading for Mammoth. The traffic through there is fast, everyone but the bikers making for the high country. As we sped along wide roads at sixty and seventy, with our kids exclaiming at the sights we passed and our car loaded down with camping gear, it seemed even more incredible to me that a place like Manzanar could have been anywhere within reach of such a highway, such a caravan of pleasure-seeking travelers.

The bikers peeled off at Red Rock Canyon, a gorgeous bulge of pink cliffs and rusty gulches humping out of the flatlands. After that it was lovely desert but nothing much to stop for. In a hundred miles we passed two oases, the first at Olancha, the second around Lone Pine, a small, tree-filled town where a lot of mountain bluffs turn off for the Mount Whitney Portal.

A few miles out of Lone Pine we started looking for another stand of trees, some tall elms, and what remains of those gnarled pear orchards. They were easy to spot. Everything else is sagebrush, tumbleweeds, and wind.

At its peak, in the summer of '42, Manzanar was the biggest city between Reno and Los Angeles, a special kind of western boom town that sprang from the sand, flourished, had its day, and now has all but disappeared. The barracks are gone, torn down right after the war. The guard towers are gone, and the mess halls and shower rooms, the hospital, the tea gardens, and the white buildings outside the compound. Even the dust is gone. Spreading brush holds it to the ground. Thirty years earlier, army bulldozers had scraped everything clean to start construction.

What you see from the road are two gatehouses, each a small empty pillbox of a building faced with flagstones and topped, like tiny pagodas, with shingled curving roofs. Farther in, you see the elms, most of which were planted by internees, and off to the right a large green building that was once our high school auditorium, now a maintenance depot for the Los Angeles Power and Water District, who leased the land to the government during the war and still owns it.

Past the gatehouses we turned left over a cattle guard and onto a dirt perimeter road that led to the far side of the campsite. About half a mile in we spotted a white obelisk gleaming in the distance and marking a subtle line where the plain begins gradually to slope upward into the alluvial fan that becomes the base of the mountains. It seemed miraculous, as if some block of stone had fallen from the peaks above and landed upright in the brush, chiseled, solitary, twelve feet high.

Near it a dozen graves were outlined in the sand with small stones, and a barbed-wire fence surrounded them to keep back the cattle and the tumbleweed. The black Japanese script cut into the white face of the obelisk read simply, "A Memorial to the Dead."

We were alone out there, too far from the road to hear anything but wind. I thought of Mama, now seven years gone. For a long time I stood gazing at the monument. I couldn't step inside the fence. I believe in ghosts and spirits. I knew I was in the presence of those who had died at Manzanar. I also felt the spiritual presence that always lingers near awesome wonders like Mount Whitney. Then, as if rising from the ground around us on the valley floor, I began to hear the first whispers, nearly inaudible, from all those thousands who once had lived out here, a wide, windy sound of the ghost of that life. As we began to walk, it grew to a murmur, a thin steady hum.

We turned the kids loose, watched them scamper off ahead of us, an we followed what used to be an asphalt road running from the back side of the camp a mile out to the highway. The obelisk—built in 1943—and the gate-houses are all that have survived intact from internment days. The rest of the place looks devastated by a bombing raid.

The old road was disintegrating, split, weed-sprung. We poked through the remains of hospital foundations, undermined by erosion channels. We found concrete slabs where the latrines and shower rooms stood, and irrigation ditches, and here and there, the small rock arrangements that once decorated many of the entrance-ways. I had found out that even in North Dakota, when Papa and the other Issei men imprisoned there had free time, they would gather small stones from the plain and spend hours sorting through a dry stream bed looking for the veined or polished rock that somehow pleased the most. It is so characteristically Japanese, the way lives were made more tolerable by gathering loose desert stones and forming with them something enduringly human. These rock gardens had outlived the barracks and the towers and would surely outlive the asphalt road and rusted pipes and shattered slabs of concrete. Each stone was a mouth, speaking for a family, for some man who had beautified his doorstep.

Vegetation gets thickest toward the center of the site, where the judo pavilion once stood and where rows of elms planted as windbreaks have tripled their growth since the forties. In there we came across the remains of a small park. A stone-lined path ran along the base of a broad mound of dirt above five feet high. Stones had been arranged on the mound, and some low trees still shaded it and made an arch above the path. For a moment I was strolling again, finding childish comfort in its incongruous design.

But after ten feet the path ended in tumbleweeds. The trees were dry and stubby, the mound was barren, and my attention was arrested by a water faucet sticking two feet out of the sand, like some subterranean periscope. One of these had provided water for each barracks. They stuck up at intervals in every direction, strangely sharpening the loneliness and desolation, sometimes the only sign of human presence in an acre or two of sand.

My mood had shifted. The murmur turned to wind. For a while I could almost detach myself from the place and its history and take pleasure in it purely as an archeological site. I saw the outlines, patterns this city must have taken. I imagined where the buildings stood, almost as I once did nosing around Old Roman villas in Europe. We saw a low ring of stones built up with cement and wondered who the mason was who knelt there and studied the shapes before fitting them together. We moved around the ring a few feet to find out. this was the old flagpole circle, where the stars and Stripes were hoisted every morning, and the inscription scratched across the top said, BUILT BY WADA AND CREW, JUNE 10 1942. A.D.

The A.D. made me shiver. I knew that the man who inscribed it had foreseen these ruins and did not want his masonry identified with the wrong era. His words coming out of the stone became a voice that merged with all the others, not a murmur this time, but low voices muttering and chattering all around me. We were crossing what used to be a firebreak, now a sandy field devoid of any growth. The wind was vicious there, with nothing to break it, and the voices grew. The firebreak was where we had talent shows and dances and outdoor movies in the summer, and where the kids played games. I heard the girls' glee club I used to sing in, way off from the other side of camp, their tiny grade-school sopranos singing, "Beautiful dreamer, wake unto me." I closed my eyes and I was ten years old again. Nothing had changed. I heard laughter. It was almost dusk, the wind had dropped, and I saw old men squatting in the dirt, Papa and some of his cronies, muttering and smoking their cigarettes. In the summertime they used to burn orange peels under gallon cans, with holes punched in the sides, to keep the mosquitoes away. Sometimes they would bring out their boards to play *gob* and *bana*. The orange peels would smolder in there, and the men would hunker down around the cans and watch the smoke seep out the holes.

From that firebreak we cut across toward the first row of pear trees, looking for what might remain of Block 28. There wasn't much to guide us but the trees themselves and a view I remembered of the blunt, bulky Inyo Range that bounds the eastern limit of the valley. When we were close enough to smell the trees we stopped. They were stunted, tenacious, thought the way a cactus has to be. The water table in that one area has kept them living through all these years of neglect,and they were ready to bloom at any moment. The heady smell was as odd in that desert setting as the little scrap of park had been, as odd yet just as familiar. We used to picnic there in blossom time, on weekends, if we got a wind-free day.

The wind blew it toward us now—chilled pear nectar—and it blew our kids around a high stand of brush. They came tumbling across the sand, demanding to know what we were going to *do* out here. Out twins were five years old at the time, a boy and a girl. Our older daughter had just turned eleven. She knew about "the evacuation," but it would be a few more years before she absorbed this part of the family history. For these three the site had been like any wreck or ruin. They became explorers, rushed around hoping the next clump of dusty trees or chunk of wall might reveal the treasure, the trinket, the exotically rusted hinge. Nothing much had turned up. The shine was wearing off the trip. Their eyes were red and their faces badly chapped. No place for kids.

My husband started walking them back to the car. I stayed behind a moment longer, first watching our eleven-year-old stride ahead, leading her brother and sister. She has long dark hair like mine and was then the same age I had been when the camp closed. It was so simple, watching her, to see why everything that had happened to me since we left camp referred back to it, in one way or another. At that age your body is changing, your imagination is galloping, your mind is in that zone between a child's vision and an adult's. Papa's life ended at Manzanar, though he lived for twelve more years after getting out. Until this trip I had not been able to admit that my own life really began there. The times I thought I had dreamed it were one way of getting rid of it, part of wanting to lose it, part of what you might call a whole Manzanar mentality I had lived with for twenty-five years. Much more than a remembered place, it had become a state of mind. Now, having seen it, I no longer wanted to lose it or to have those years erased. Having found it, I could say what you can only say when you've truly come to know a place: Farewell.

I had nearly outgrown the shame and the guilt and the sense of unworthiness. This visit, this pilgrimage, made comprehensible, finally, the traces that remained and would always remain, like a needle. That hollow ache I carried during the early months of internment had shrunk, over the years, to a tiny silver of suspicion about the very person I was. It had grown so small sometimes I'd forget it was there. Months might pass before something would remind me. When I first read, in the summer of 1972, about the pressure Japan's economy was putting on American business and how a union in New York City had printed up posters of an American flag with MADE IN JAPAN written across it, then that needle began to jab. I heard Mama's soft, weary voice from 1945 say, "It's all starting over." I knew it wouldn't. Yet neither would I have been surprised to find the FBI at my door again. I would resist it much more than my parents did, but deep within me something had been prepared for that. Manzanar would always live in my nervous system, a needle with Mama's voice.

24
Ruthanne Lum McCunn

Ruthanne Lum McCunn lives in San Francisco, California, the place of her birth. As a child she was taken back to China. Educated in both English and Chinese schools she returned to California to teach and become a librarian. She is the author of several reference books and *Thousand Pieces of Gold*. This beautifully written and well researched work tells the true story of Polly Bemis, a Chinese pioneer woman in the old west.

For Polly, Charlie's cabin with its glowing stove and two chairs pulled close, the dresser made of packing crates, and the bed they shared had always been a refuge. Now, as Charlie lit a lamp and the room flared into light, she saw it as simply another shack.

Charlie wrapped his arms around Polly. His belt buckle dug unto her, and she felt a wave of disgust as his body quivered with the same drunken exhilaration she had detected in Hong King after a big win. But she did not move. Even if he were not her new master, she could not stop him. He was to big. Too strong.

"Hey, you're supposed to be happy." he said, taking Polly's face in both his hands and kissing her full on the lips.

She flinched.

"Okay, so I don't rate a hallelujah chorus, but what about a simple thank-you?" he said.

A thank-you? For what? For humiliating her? For forcing her to break her promise that when she left Hong King it would be as a free woman. Or for teaching her that a slave had no right to make promises, especially to herself.

He took the pins out of Polly's bun. Her hair rippled down her back, a sheet of black silk.

"Tonight I ruined a man for you."

"Not for me. For the game. Because you gambler."

"It was the only way to free you."

"That what you believe. Just like Jim believe I better off if I not know Hong King sell me. Maybe Jim right. Or maybe you right. But this my life. Not Jim life. Not yours. Mine."

Charlie strode over to the dresser and poured himself a drink, downing it in a single swallow. "All right. What would you have done?"

"I shoot him." she said, knowing even as she heard the words out loud that she could never have done it, knowing that was not the point, the reason for her anger.

From *One Thousand Pieces of Gold* by Ruthanne Lum McCunn. Copyright ©1981 by Ruthanne Lum McCunn. Reprinted by permission of Beacon Press.

"There are more ways to kill a man than with a gun," Charlie said, setting his glass down. "Hong King's lost so much face, he'll have to leave camp. For you, for us, he's the same as a dead man,"

Polly slumped onto the bed. Again he had not understood, had not seen beyond her words. "You could have lost," she said tiredly.

"I didn't."

"And when you play again?"

Charlie lifted Polly off the bed and hugged her to him. She felt the worn flannel of his shirt against her face, soft as a caress.

"I would never stake you," he said, his voice surprised and hurt.

She kept her back taut. "I your slave. You can do anything."

He stood back, holding her at arm's length. "I didn't win you from Hong King so you could be my slave. You're free."

She looked down at his arms.

He dropped his hold, but the marks from his grip remained, deep red purple like the bruises from Jim when he had shaken her, demanding she face a reality neither one of them was able to confront. Rubbing the tender new bruises, she thought regretfully of the rich promise her first days with jim had held, a promise unrealized in part because of circumstances, but more because, for all their talk, they had kept too much hidden from each other, from themselves. Was she to suffer the same loss again? And for the same reason?

In front of her, she could see Charlie, shoulders slumped, his head tossing back as he downed yet another drink. And in the mirror above the dresser, she could see his hands clasping bottle and glass. But she could not see his face, for he had lowered the mirror long ago to a height appropriate for her. Suddenly, all around her, Polly notices similar instances of Charlie's thoughtful concern, the curtains nailed up to shield her from prying eyes, the second chair made smaller, the shelves and hooks lowered, and she found herself wondering if he had indeed forced the final bet to win her freedom and not the game.

Tonight, and the night before, she had been hurt by his apparent betrayals, angry because he could not understand her. But did she understand him? From the day she had ridden into Warrens, he had protected her, and she had accepted his help without question, as though it were her due. Now, for the first time, she asked herself why he had come to her rescue in the saloon. Had he interceded out of some strange sense of Western chilvary? Or pity? Or because he was Jim's friend. And after Jim's death, had he continued to protect her out of loyalty to Jim, or because he had come to care for her, or simply to keep her in his bed?

She did not even know how or why he and Jim had become friends. Like a frog at the bottom of a well, she had seen nothing beyond the small circle of blue sky that meant freedom, concentrating all her thoughts, all her energies toward piling up the gold she needed to reach it, never once considering it might be gained another way. And now she could lose that freedom which Charlie had put within her grasp, and with it, Charlie.

Searching for words that would clear away the misunderstandings, she began haltingly. "Charlie, sometimes I angry with you and you with me. But I know anger is only because you and I not understand, not believe the same way. Please, try understand this." She paused, waiting for acknowledgment.

He did not speak, but she saw his hands on bottle and glass freeze, breaking the steady drinking. Taking heart, she continued, "All my life I belong someone. My father, the bandits, Hong King. And I promise myself when I free of Hong King, I belong no man, only myself.

"You know I have gold I save to buy myself from Hong King. I want use that to build a house, start my own business. A boarding house like Mrs. Schultz."

Charlie poured another drink, gulped it. "You can't."

"You worry I not know how to cook? I watch Mrs. Schultz and I learn plenty quick."

"It's not that," he mumbled.

"Then what?" Polly demanded. "Because you think I not wife like Mrs. Schultz, not respectable, people say it bawdy house? You see, I show them they wrong."

Charlie turned to face her. "A Chinaman can't own land," he said, so softly she could barely hear him.

"But you say America have land for everyone. That people from all over the world come for the land. Rich. Poor. All the same. Anyone can have land. You said."

"Any American. You're from China."

She opened her mouth to shout denial, but the pain in Charlie's face told Polly his words had cost him too dearly to be negated by mere anger, and she sank silent onto the bed. She must think carefully, make sense out of Charlie's contradictions, her own confusion.

She knew the Chinese in Warrens did not own the stories and laundries where they worked, but she had thought that was because they planned to return to China as soon as they made enough money. Weren't the ones who came to Hong King's saloon always complaining about the loneliness of lives without wives and children, the brutish manners of white men, unfair taxes, and harsh laws? And didn't they always end their grumbling with talk of home, their eagerness to return to families left behind? But she had no family, no one to go home to.

Of course. That was it. Charlie didn't realize that she intended to remain in America. She would become an American and buy the land for her house. Land that would keep her free and independent always.

She leaped up, ran to Charlie, and crooked her arm through his. "You not understand. I never go back to China. I become American."

He pulled away. His fists clenched and unclenched. He took his pipe out of his pocket, rotated it in his hands, studying it, then tossed it onto the bed, and reached for the bottle.

Polly grabbed his arm. "What is it? What wrong?"

"The only way a Chinaman can become an American is to be born here."

She laughed. A short bitter laugh. Here or in China, slave or free, it was the same. She needed a protector. She rubbed her hands across Charlie's back, unknotting the tight muscles. He turned. Mechanically she began unbuttoning his shirt.

He took her hands in his, holding them still. "Polly, I meant what I said. You're free. Let me be your China herder and build a house for you. You can do whatever you want to in it, invite anyone, refuse anyone. It's yours, I promise you." he smiled weakly. "You don't even have to have me."

"I . . ."

His fingers brushed her lips, gently silencing. "And yes, you can pay for it too."

She laughed, a joyous peal clear as ringing bells. Hearing it, Charlie's smile grew stronger, deepening into laughter that became one with Polly's. And suddenly, within the circle of their laughter, she felt finally, wonderfully free.

25
John Okada

John Okada was born in 1923 in Seattle, Washington. While he served in the U.S. Army during World War II, his parents were held in a relocation camp. *No-No Boy*, published in 1957, is an account of the hardships faced by Japanese-Americans during World War II. John Okada died at the age of 47 of a heart attack in February, 1971.

Swinging around on the stool, he surveyed the crowd and acknowledged a number of greetings and nods.

I've got a lot of friends here and they know and like me.

Jim Eng, the slender, dapper Chinese who ran the place, came out of the office with a bagful of change and brought it behind the bar to check the register. As he did so, he grinned at Kenji and inquired about his leg.

Even the management's on my side. It's like a home away from home only more precious because one expects home to be like that. Not many places a Jap can go to and feel so completely at ease. It must be nice to be white and American and to be able to feel like this no matter where one goes to, but I won't cry about that. There's been a war and, suddenly, things are better for the Japs and the Chinks and—

There was a commotion at the entrance and Jim Eng slammed the cash drawer shut and raced toward the loud voices. He spoke briefly to someone in the office, probably to find out the cause of the disturbance, and then stepped outside. As he did so, Kenji caught sight of three youths, a Japanese and two Negroes.

After what sounded like considerable loud and excited shouting, Jim Eng stormed back in and resumed his task at the register though with hands shaking.

When he had calmed down a little, someone inquired: "What's the trouble?"

"No trouble," he said in a high-pitched voice which he was endeavoring to keep steady. "That crazy Jap boy Floyd tried to get in with two niggers. That's the second time he tried that. What's the matter with him?"

A Japanese beside Kenji shouted out sneeringly: "Them ignorant cotton pickers make me sick. You let one in and before you know it, the place will be black as night."

"Sure," said Jim Eng, " sure. I got no use for them. Nothing but trouble they make and I run a clean place."

"Hail Columbia," said a small, drunken voice.

Reprinted by permission of the University of Washington Press from *No-No Boy* by John Okada.

"Oh, you Japs and Chinks, I love you all," rasped out a brash redhead who looked as if she had come directly from one of the burlesque houses without changing her make-up. She struggled to her feet, obviously intending to launch into further oratory.

Her escort, a pale, lanky Japanese screamed "Shut up!" and, at the same time, pulled viciously at her arm, causing her to tumble comically into the chair.

Everyone laughed, or so it seemed, and quiet and decency and cleanliness and honesty returned to the Club Oriental.

Leaving his drink unfinished, Kenji left the club without returning any of the farewells which were directed at him.

He drove aimlessly, torturing himself repeatedly with the question which plagued his mind and confused it to the point of madness. Was there no answer to the bigotry and meanness and smallness and ugliness of people? One hears the voice of the Negro or Japanese or Chinese or Jew, a clear and bell-like intonation of the common struggle for recognition as a complete human begin and there is a sense of unity and purpose which inspires one to hope and optimism. One encounters obstacles, but the wedge of the persecuted is not without patience and intelligence and humility, and the opposition weakens and wavers and disperses. And the one who is the Negro or Japanese or Chinese or Jew is further fortified and gladdened with the knowledge that the democracy is a democracy in fact for all of them. One has hope, for he has reason to hope, and the quest for completeness seems to be a thing near at hand, and then . . .

the woman with the dark hair and large nose who has barely learned to speak English makes a big show of vacating her bus seat when a Negro occupies the other half. She stamps indignantly down the aisle, hastening away from the contamination which is only in her contaminated mind. The Negro stares silently out of the window, a proud calmness on his face, which hides the boiling fury that is capable of murder.

and then . . .

a sweet-looking Chinese girl is at a high-school prom with a white boy. She has risen in the world, or so she thinks, for it is evident in her expression and manner. She does not entirely ignore the other Chinese and Japanese at the dance, which would at least be honest, but worse, she flaunts her newly found status in their faces with haughty smiles and overly polite phrases.

and then . . .

there is the small Italian restaurant underneath a pool parlor, where the spaghetti and chicken is hard to beat. The Japanese, who feels he is better than the Chinese because his parents made him so, comes into the restaurant with a Jewish companion, who is a good Jew and young and American and not like the kike bastards from the countries from which they've been kicked out, and waits patiently for the waiter. None of the waiters come, although the place is quite empty and two of them are talking not ten feet away. All his efforts to attract them failing, he stalks toward them. The two, who are supposed to wait on the tables but do not, scurry into the kitchen. In a moment they return with the cook, who is also the owner, and he tells the Japanese that the place is not for Japs and to get out and go back to Tokyo.

and then . . .

the Negro who was always begin mistaken for a white man becomes a white man and he becomes hated by the Negroes with whom he once hated on the same side. And the young Japanese hates the not-so-young Japanese who is more Japanese than himself, and the not-so-young, in turn, hates the old Japanese who is all Japanese and, therefore, even more Japanese than he . . .

And Kenji thought about these things and tried to organize them in his mind so that the pattern could be seen and studied and the answers deduced therefrom. And there was no answer because there was no pattern and all he could feel was that the world was full of hatred. And he drove on and on and it was almost two o'clock when he parked in front of the grocery store.

The street was quiet, deathly so after he had cut the ignition. Down a block or so, he saw the floodlighted sign painted on the side of a large brick building. It said: "444 Rooms. Clean. Running Water. Reasonable Rates." He had been in there once a long time ago and he knew that it was just a big flophouse full of drunks and vagrant souls. Only a few tiny squares of yellowish light punctuated the softly shimmering rows of windowpanes. Still, the grocery store was brightly lit.

Wondering why, he slid out of the car and peered through the upper half of the door, which was of glass. He was immediately impressed with the neatness of the shelves and the cleanness of the paint on the walls and woodwork. Inevitably, he saw Ichiro's mother and it gave him an odd sensation as he watched her methodically empty a case of evaporated milk and line the cans with painful precision on the shelf. he tried the door and found it locked and decided not to disturb her until she finished the case. it was a long wait, for she grasped only a single can with both hands each time she stooped to reach into the box. Finally, she finished and stood as if examining her handiwork.

"I want six," he said, hating the man.

"All at one time?" the old man questioned unbelievingly.

"The sixth floor, pop." The hotness in his face was hotter still with the anger inside of him.

"Sure," he said, bringing the elevator to an abrupt halt, "that's good. I thought you meant you wanted six of them. That is good."

The old man was chuckling as Ichiro stepped out of the elevator and headed toward his room.

"Filthy-minded old bastard," he muttered viciously under his breath. No wonder the world's such a rotten place, rotten and filthy and cheap and smelly. Where is that place they talk of and paint nice pictures of and describe in all the homey magazines? Where is that place with the clean, white cottages surrounding the new, red-brick church with the clean, white steeple, where the families all have two children, one boy and one girl, and a shiny new car in the garage and a dog and a cat and life is like living in the land of the happily-ever-after? Surely it must be around here someplace, someplace in America. Or is it just that it's not for me? Maybe I dealt myself out, but what about that young kid on Burnside who was in the army and found it wasn't enough so that he has to keep proving to everyone who comes in for a cup of coffee that he was fighting for his country like the button on his shirt says he did because the army didn't do anything about his face to make him look more American? And what about the poor niggers on Jackson Street who can't find anything better to do than spit on the sidewalk and show me the way to Tokyo? They're on the outside looking in, just like that kid and just like me and just like everybody else I've ever seen or known. Even Mr. Carrick. why isn't he in? Why is he on the outside squandering his goodness on outcasts like me? Maybe the answer is that there is no in. Maybe the whole damned country is pushing and shoving and screaming to get into someplace that doesn't exist, because they don't know that the outside could be the inside if only they would stop all this pushing and shoving and creaming, and they haven't got enough sense to realize that. That makes sense. I've got the answer all figured out, simple and neat and sensible.

And then he thought about Kenji in the hospital and of Emi in bed with a stranger who reminded her of her husband and of his mother waiting for the ship form Japan, and there was no more answer. If he were in the tavern, he would drink another double with a beer for a chaser and another and still another but he wasn't in the tavern because he didn't have the courage to step out of his room and be seen by people who would know him for what he was. There was nothing for him to do but roll over and try to sleep. Somewhere, sometime, he had even forgotten how to cry.

In the morning he checked out of the hotel and drove to the hospital. Visiting hours were plainly indicated on a sign at the entrance as being in the afternoons and evenings. Feeling he had nothing to lose by trying, he walked in and stood by the registration desk until the girl working the switchboard got a chance to help him.

"What can I do for you?" she asked sweetly enough and then, prodded into action by the buzzing of the board, pulled and inserted a number of brass plugs which were attached to extendible wire cords. Tiny lights bristled actively as if to give evidence to the urgency of the calls being carried by the board.

"I've got a friend here. I'd like to find out what room he's in."

"Sure. His name?"

"Kanno."

"Kanno what?"

"Kenji. Kanno is the last name."

"How do you spell it?" She consulted the K's on the cardex.

"K-A-N—"

"Never mind. I've got it." Looking up, she continued: "He's in four-ten but you'll have to come back this afternoon. Visiting hours are posted at the entrance. Sorry."

"I'm on my way out of town. I won't be here this afternoon."

"Hospital rules, sir."

"Sure," he said, noticing the stairway off toward the right, "I understand."

The board buzzed busily and the operator turned her attention to the plugs and cords once more. Ichiro walked to the stairs and started up. Between the second and third floors he encountered two nurses coming down. When they saw him they cut short their chattering and one of them seemed on the point of questioning him. Quickening his pace, he rushed past them purposefully and was relieved when he heard them resume their talking.

Up on the fourth floor, no one bothered him as he set out to locate Kenji's room. Four-ten wasn't far from the stairway. A screen was placed inside the doorway so that he couldn't look directly in. He went around it and saw the slight figure of his friend up on the high bed with the handle of the crank poking out at the foot.

"Ken," he said in almost a whisper though he hadn't deliberately intended to speak so.

"Ichiro?" His head lay on the pillow with its top toward the door and Ichiro noted with a vague sense of alarm that his hair was beginning to thin.

He waited for Kenji to face him and was disappointed when he did not move. "How's it been with you?"

"Fine. Sit down." He kept looking toward the window.

Ichiro walked past the bed, noticing where the sheet fell over the stump beneath. It seemed to be frighteningly close to the torso. His own legs felt still and awkward as he approached the chair and settled into it.

Kenji was looking at him, a smile, weak yet warm, on his mouth.

"How's it going?" he asked, and he hardly heard his own voice, for Kenji had aged a lifetime during the two days they had been apart. Exactly what is was he couldn't say, but it was all there, the fear, the pain, the madness, and the exhaustion of mind and body.

"About as I expected, Ichiro. I should have been a doctor."

Kenji had said he was going to die.

"You could be wrong. Have they said so?"

"Not in so many words, but they know it and I know it and they know that I do."

"Why don't they do something?"

"Nothing to be done."

"I shouldn't be here," he said, not knowing why except that it suddenly seemed important to explain. "They told me to come back this afternoon but I came up anyway. Maybe I shouldn't have. Maybe you're supposed to rest."

"Hell with them." said Kenji. "You're here, stay."

It was quiet in the hospital. He'd heard someplace a long time ago that visitors ware not allowed in the morning is hospitals because that's when all the cleaning and changing of beds and mopping of floors were done. There wasn't a sound to be heard. "Quiet here," he said.

"Good for thinking," said Kenji.

"Sure, I guess it is." He wished Kenji would move, roll his head a little or wiggle his arm, but he lay there just as he was.

"Go back to Seattle."

"What?"

"Go back. Later on you might want to come to Portland to stay, but go back for now. It'll turn out for the best in the long run. The kind of trouble you've got, you can't run from it. Stick it through. Let them call you names. They don't mean it. What I mean is, they don't know what they're doing. The way I see it, they pick on you because they're vulnerable. They think just because they went and packed a rifle they're different but they aren't and they know it. They're still Japs. You weren't here when they first started to move back to the Coast. There was a great deal of opposition—name-calling, busted windows, dirty words painted on houses. People haven't changed a helluva lot. They guys who make it tough on you probably do so out of a misbegotten idea that maybe you're to blame because the good that they thought they were doing by getting killed and shot up doesn't amount to a pot of beans. They just need a little time to get cut down to their own size. Then they'll be the same as you, a bunch of Japs."

He paused for a long time, just looking and smiling at Ichiro, his face wan and tired. "There were a lot of them pouring into Seattle about the time i got back there. It made me sick. I'd heard about some of them scattering out all over the country. I read about a girl who's doing pretty good in the fashion business in New york and a guy that's principal of a school in Arkansas, and a lot of others in different places making out pretty good. I got to thinking that the Japs were wising up, that they had learned that living in big bunches and talking Jap and feeling Jap and doing Jap was just inviting trouble. But my dad came back. There was really no reason why he should have. I asked him about it once and he gave me some kink of an answer. Whatever it was, a lot of others did the same thing. I hear there's almost as many in Seattle now as there were before the war. It's a shame, a dirty rotten shame. Pretty soon it'll be just like it was before the war. A bunch of Japs with a fence around them, not the kind you can see, but it'll hurt them just as much. They bitched and hollered when the government put them in camps and put real fences around them, but now they're doing the same damn thing to themselves. They screamed because the government said they were Japs and, when they finally got out, they couldn't wait to rush together and prove that they were."

"They're not alone, Ken. The Jews, the Italians, the Poles, the Armenians, they've all got their communities."

"Sure, but that doesn't make it right. It's wrong. I don't blame the old ones so much. They don't know any better. They don't want any better. It's me I'm talking about and all the rest of the young ones who know and want better."

"You just got through telling me to go back to Seattle."

"I still say it. Go back and stay there until they have enough sense to leave you alone. Then get out. It may take a year or two or even five, but the time will come when they'll be feeling too sorry for themselves to pick on you. After that, head out. Go someplace where there isn't another Jap within a thousand miles. Marry a white girl or a Negro or an Italian or even a Chinese. Anything but a Japanese. After a few generations of that, you've got the thing beat. Am I making sense?"

"It's a fine dream, but you're not the first."

"No," he uttered and it seemed as if he might cry, "it's just a dream, a big balloon. I wonder if there's a Jackson Street wherever it is I'm going to. That would make dying tough."

Ichiro stood and, walking to his friend, placed his hand on the little shoulder and held it firmly.

"I'm going to write to Ralph," said Kenji.

"Ralph?"

"Emi's husband. I'm going to write him about how you and Emi are hitting it off."

"Why? It's not true, but what they're doing to each other is not right. They should be together or split up. If I tell him about you and how you're hot for her, it might make him mad enough to come back."

Understanding what Kenji meant, Ichiro working up a smile. "Seems like I'm not so useless after all."

"Tell her I've been thinking about her."

"Sure."

"And I'm thinking about you. All the time."

"Sure."

"Have a drink for me. Drink to whatever it is I'm headed, and don't let there be any Japs or Chinks or Jews or Poles or Niggers or Frenchies, but only people. I think about that too. I think about that most of all. You know why?"

He shook his head and Kenji seemed to know he would even though he was still staring out the window. "He was up on the roof of the barn and I shot him, killed him. He wasn't the only German I killed, but I remember him. I see him rolling down the roof. I see him all the time now and that's why I want this other place to have only people because if I'm still a Jap there and this guy's still a German, I'll have to shoot him again and I don't want to have to do that. Then maybe there is no someplace else. Maybe dying is it. The finish. The end. Nothing. I'd like that too. Better an absolute nothing than half a meaning. The living have it tough. It's like a coat rack without pegs, only you think there are. Hang it up, drop, pick it up, hang it again, drop again . . . Tell my dad I'll miss him like mad."

"I will."

"Crazy talk?"

"No, it makes a lot of sense."

"Goodbye, Ichiro."

His hand slipped off his friend's shoulder and brushed along the white sheet and dropped to his side. The things he wanted to say would not be said. He said "Bye" and no sound came out because the word got caught far down inside his throat and he felt his mouth open and shut against the empty silence. At the door he turned and looked back and, as Kenji had still not moved, he saw again the spot on the head where the hair was thinning out so that the sickly white of the scalp filtered between the strands of black. A few more years and he'll be bald, he thought, and then he started to smile inwardly because there wouldn't be a few more years and as quickly the smile vanished because the towering, choking grief was suddenly upon him.

It was almost seven hours later when Ichiro, nearing the outskirts of Seattle, turned off the highway and drove to Emi's house.

He pressed the doorbell and waited and pressed it again. When no one appeared, he pounded on the door. Thinking, hoping that she must be nearby, he walked around to the back. With a sense of relief, he noted that the shed which served as a garage housed a pre-war Ford that looked fairly new. It probably meant that she hadn't driven to town. He tried the back door without any luck and made his way around to the front once more.

Tired and hungry, he sat on the step and lit a cigarette.

26
Carlos Bulosan

America Is in the Heart is the autobiographical story of the Filipino poet Carlos Bulosan. First published in 1946, it has since become a classic in its graphic and often brutal portrayal of Filipino itinerant laborers on the West Coast.

I walked from Main Street to Vermont Avenue, three miles away. I returned to town by streetcar and went to First Street again. A Filipino poolroom was crowded, and I went inside to sit on a bench. The players were betting and once in a while they would give the table boy a dime. I waited until the men started coming in groups, because their day's work was done.

I was talking to a gambler when two police detectives darted into the place and shot a little Filipino in the back. The boy fell on his knees, face up, and expired. The players stopped for a moment, agitated, then resumed playing, their faces coloring with fear and revolt. The detectives called an ambulance, dumped the dead Filipino into the street, and left when an interne and his assistant arrived. They left hurriedly, untouched by their act, as though killing were a part of their day's work.

All at once I heard many tongues speaking excitedly. They did not know why the Filipino was shot. It seemed that the victim was new in the city. I was bewildered.

"Why was he shot?" I asked a man near me.

"They often shoot Pinoys like that," he said. "Without provocation. Sometimes when they have been drinking and they want to have fun, they come to our district and kick or beat the first Filipino they meet."

"Why don't you complain?" I asked.

"*Complain?*" he said. "Are you kidding? Why, when we complain it always turns out that *we* attacked them! And they become more vicious, I am telling you! That is why once in a while a Pinoy shoots a detective. You will see it one of these days."

"If they beat me I will kill them," I said.

The Filipino looked at me and walked away. As the crowd was beginning to disperse, I saw the familiar head of my brother Macario. He was entering the poolroom with a friend. I rushed to him and touched his hand. He could not believe that I was in America.

"Why didn't you write that you were coming?" he asked.

"I did not know I was coming, brother," I said. "Besides, I did not know your address. I knew that I would not stop traveling until I found you. You have grown older."

"I guess I have, all right," he said. Then suddenly he became quiet, as though he were remembering something. He looked at me and said, "Let's go to my hotel."

I noticed that he did not speak English the way he used to speak it in the Philippines. He spoke more rapidly now. As I walked beside him, I felt that he was afraid I would discover some horror that was crushing his life. He was undecided what to do when we reached Broadway Street, and stopped several times in deep thought. He had changed in many ways. He seemed in constant agitation, and he smoked one cigarette after another. His agitation became more frightening each minute.

"Why was the Filipino shot?" I asked, pretending not to notice his mental anguish.

"Someday you will understand, Carlos," he said.

Carlos! He had changed my name, too! Everything was changing. Why? And why all this secrecy about the death of one Filipino? Were the American people conspiring against us? I looked at my brother sidelong but he said nothing. Suddenly I felt hungry and lonely and tired.

We turned to the north and came to a hotel near the Hall of Justice building. We took the slow elevator to the fifth floor. My brother knocked on a door and looked at me. There was a hunted look in his face. I heard many voices inside. A patter of feet, then the door opened. The strong smell of whisky brought tears to my eyes. It was so strong it almost choked me. I knew at once that there was a party. I saw three American girls in evening gowns and ten Filipinos. I was amazed at their immaculate suits and shoes.

"Friends," my brother announced, "this is my kid brother—Carlos! He has just arrived from the Philippines."

"More than six months ago," I corrected him. "I went to Alaska first, then came down to Los Angeles. I think I like it here. I will buy a house here someday."

"Buy a house?" a man near me said, his face breaking a smile. But when he noticed that my brother was looking hard at him, he suddenly changed his tone and offered me a glass. "Good, good!" he said. "Buy all the houses you want. And if you need a janitor—" He turned around to hide the cynical twist of his mouth.

Then they rushed to me. All at once several cocktail glasses were offered to me. The girls pulled me to the table, tilting a glass in my mouth. The Filipinos shouted to me to drink.

I looked at my brother, ashamed, "I don't drink." I said.

"Go on—drink!" a curly-haired boy prodded me. "Drink like hell. This is America. We all drink like hell. Go on, boy!"

He was only a boy, but he drank like a man. I watched him empty three glasses, one after the other. My brother came to me.

"This is a wedding party," he whispered.

"Who got married?" I asked, looking around.

"I think that one," he said, pointing to a woman. "That is the man. I think he is twenty years old."

"She is old enough to be his mother," I said.

"What is the difference?" the curly-haired boy said to me. "They know what they want, don't they?" He winked at me foolishly and emptied another glass.

I gripped the glass in my hand so hard that it nearly broke.

It was now the year of the great hatred: the lives of Filipinos were cheaper than those of dogs. They were forcibly shoved off the streets when they showed resistance. The sentiment against them was accelerated by the marriage of a Filipino and a girl of the Caucasian race in Pasadena. The case was tried in court and many technicalities were brought in with it to degrade the lineage and character of the Filipino people.

Prior to the *Roldan vs. The United States* case, Filipinos were considered Mongolians. Since there is a law which forbids the marriage between members of the Mongolian and Caucasian races, those who hated Filipinos wanted them to be included in this discriminatory legislation. Anthropologists and other experts maintained that the Filipinos are not Mongolians, but members of the Malayan race. It was then a simple thing for the state legislature to pass a law forbidding marriage between members of the Malayan and Caucasian races. This action was followed by neighboring states until, when the war with Japan broke out in 1941, New Mexico was the nearest place to the Pacific Coast where Filipino soldiers could marry Caucasian women.

This was the condition in California when Jose and I arrived in San Diego. I was still unaware of the vast social implications of the discrimination against Filipinos, and my ignorance had innocently brought me to the attention of white Americans. In San Diego, where I tried to get a job, I was beaten upon several occasions by restaurant and hotel proprietors. I put the blame on certain Filipinos who had behaved badly in America, who had instigated hate and discontent among their friends and followers. This misconception was generated by a confused personal reaction to dynamic social forces, but my hunger for the truth had inevitably led me to take an historical attitude. I was to understand and interpret this chaos from a collective point of view, because it was pervasive and universal.

From San Diego, Jose and I traveled by freight train to the south. We were told, when we reached the little desert town of Calipatria, that local whites were hunting Filipinos at night with shotguns. A countryman offered to take us in his loading truck to Brawley, but we decided it was too dangerous. We walked to Holtville where we found a Japanese farmer who hired us to pick winter peas.

It was cold at night and when morning came the fog was so think it was tangible. But it was a safe place and it was far from the surveillance of vigilantes. Then from nearby El Centro, the center of Filipino population in the Imperial Valley, news came that a Filipino labor organizer had been found dead in a ditch.

I wanted to leave Holtville, but Jose insisted that we work through the season. I worked but made myself inconspicuous. At night I slept with a long knife under my pillow. My ears became sensitive to sounds and even my sense of smell was sharpened. I knew when rabbits were mating between the rows of peas. I knew when night birds were feasting in the melon patches.

One day a Filipino came to Holtville with his American wife and their child. It was blazing noon and the child was hungry. The strangers went to a little restaurant and sat down at a table. When they were refused service, they stayed on, hoping for some consideration. But it was no use. Bewildered, they walked outside; suddenly the child began to cry with hunger. The Filipino went back to the restaurant and asked if he could buy a bottle of milk for his child.

"It is only for my baby," he said humbly.

The proprietor came out from behind the counter. "For *your* baby" he shouted.

"Yes sir," said the Filipino.

The proprietor pushed him violently outside. "If you say *that* again in my place, I'll bash in your head!" he shouted aloud so that he would attract attention. "You goddamn brown monkeys have your nerve, marrying our women. Now get out of this town!"

"I love my wife and my child," said the Filipino desperately.

"*Goddamn* you!" The white man struck the Filipino viciously between the eyes with his fist.

Years of degradation came into the Filipino's face. All the fears of his life were here—in the white hand against his face. Was there no place where he could escape? Crouching like a leopard, he hurled his whole weight upon the white man, knocking him down instantly. He seized a stone the size of his fist and began smashing it into the man's face. Then the white men in the restaurant seized the small Filipino, beating him unconscious with pieces of wood and with their fists.

He lay inert on the road. When two deputy sheriffs came to take him away, he looked tearfully back at his wife and child.

IX
Jewish-Americans

27
Mira Rothenberg

Mira Rothenberg was born in Wilno, Poland, and came to the United States as a young girl. She was educated at Brooklyn College and Columbia University. Mira is a certified clinical psychologist, a teacher and cofounder of Blueberry Treatment Centers. Her adult life has been spent helping the alienated—the emotionally disturbed minority children in America. She is the author of numerous essays and *Children With Emerald Eyes*; the following essay is her account of coming to the United States. It is written from the heart and through the eyes of a child. Because of this, the editors have chosen not to edit out grammatical errors and let the story stand as written.

"You have problems with loss?" Someone said to me wisely. "You're darn right, I thought, you would too." I knew "America" as I called it and saw it in my child's mind as a place where there is gold in the streets, where everybody wears eye glasses and where the buildings are made of concrete and they kidnap children.

America and the U.S.A were interchangeable to me. I did not want to come to America, I loved my own country, Poland, it was big and beautiful, the earth smelled good, the rain was clean, the sun shone bright, the grass was green, and it was mine.

I was to be saved. I did not want to leave my country, I did not want to be saved. I had a right, a right to belong to, to stay where I was born. A right to my land, to my mountains, to my trees, to my earth. A right. A right to the graves of my Father, my Cousins, my Grandparents and Stefcia. A right. But they did not want me, they did not recognize this right. They wanted me out. One way or another. Dead or alive, but out. And that was most incomprehensible to me, my earth, my country, the place of my birth and all my ancestors.

World War II, everybody dead, all, all my relatives who stayed in Poland. All my friends. Dead, all gone, all taken away from me, all lost. No, I do not take loss well, I came here, it was winter and there was snow on the ground, that was familiar.

I came alone, alone and terribly lonely. My Uncle who was to come and pick me up at Ellis Island was late. I was the last one there. The officials were kidding me and said no one will come claim me. I was terrified. Terrified of the sounds of this strange language, terrified of the smells, unfamiliar. Terrified of sitting on these long benches in that huge room in Ellis Island, alone, forever, Forever alone.

Finally, he came, this Uncle of mine, whom I've seen only twice in Poland, when he came to visit. I did not know him. We took the subway "home." I sat there deaf and dumb and so isolated. I had never seen black people before, except in paintings and sculptures, beautiful men in bronze. In the subway they were sitting opposite me and around me. I had to know, see that they were real. I moved across the subway isle and touched one. My uncle, surprised, grabbed me. They were real, here the men of bronze were real.

I saw mouths moving in constant rhythmic motion (in that subway), and I could not understand it, they chewed and chewed and chewed and never swallowed. Chewing "gum" my Uncle explained. I did not understand. If it is not food why don't they swallow it? If it is not why do they keep it in their mouths, they chew it.

When I got "home," an apartment in the Bronx, I lost all my feelings, I walked around like an automation from room to room, looking for something familiar. I found there my Brother and my Sister, my Mother, who I have not seen for a long, long time, (physically and psychologically), they were strangers to me. I found my Aunt whom I've seen twice in my life, and oh, wonder of all wonders, I found the bathroom. It was so white, so clean, so large and there was in the medicine cabinet chocolate. Bitter sweet chocolate. The kind of chocolate we had in Poland, at home. Strange country, they eat here in the bathroom. And I proceeded to devour this bar of chocolate. It's name was "Ex-Lax" and the results were more bitter than sweet.

I tried, and tried, and tried to get used to it, this new home, but could not. They laughed here and made merry while people, my people in my country were getting killed.

A strange country, America. A lot of people did wear glasses. There was more concrete in the streets than I thought possible. I felt trapped, closed in, choking. A lot of noise around me, noise of words I could not understand, smells, new smells, unfamiliar, unacceptable, sights and lack of sights, incomprehensible.

They travelled under the ground. Like moles, they spent their time for a large part of the day under the ground. No sun, no moon, no sky. Subways. Horrible. Someone said that not only were they under the ground, but also in places, under water. My God! I got a nickel and decided to try it, to see what it felt like to travel under the water and in the bowels of the earth. I got lost. I rode the subway from an afternoon into the night. Back and forth, back and forth, back and forth. It was the line that starts in the Bronx and leads to Brooklyn. I had a piece of paper with my address and telephone number written on it, but since I could say only "wine," "bread," and "love you" in English I could not ask anyone.

A conductor spotted this "young person" as he put it later, riding back and forth on the subway. He talked to me, but I did not answer as I did not know his tongue. Nor did I show him my piece of paper since he wore a uniform. And I knew better than to say anything to anyone in a uniform. He looked helplessly around and then came back with a policeman. The policeman tried to talk to me. But I knew better than to talk to a policeman. Which Jew in my country would talk to a cop? It mean danger, trouble, horror and possible death. They think I am so dumb, I thought to myself, that I would show a cop anything. Did they think that the ruse of a friendly smile would make me trust him? Just so he can then kill me? No way!

My Aunt sent out an alarm for me. I guess she must have said I could only speak Polish and Russian. In came a conductor who spoke to me in Polish. I refused to answer. Who says the Poles are to be trusted. After what they were doing to Jews in my country. When he told me where I lived and that my Aunt was worried and that all he wanted was to take me home, I started to bolt out of the subway door. He caught me, told me not to be afraid, he would not hurt me, nobody would. "This is a different country, they don't hurt Jewish kids."

He, the cop, took me "home." I was sure that they were taking me someplace to be killed. But at that point it was "no matter." I was too tired. And I did not like this country any how, and I desperately had to go to the bathroom. When they did bring me home, my whole family was asking me why I did not show the policeman or the conductor the slip of paper with my address. I thought that my family had gone mad. Did they think I was that stupid and I'd trust a policeman? Did they forget the dangers? And all of them were very sad, including the policeman and conductor, they all sat and drank tea together and the cop said "It is awful to do that to a kid in the old country." But I did not fall for any of it. I knew better. You do not talk to a cop. You do not talk to anyone in a uniform.

As I was getting more and more settled in, I began to feel terribly claustrophobic, New York, I was a caged in animal, trapped in a zoo, pacing back and forth. I needed room. I needed space. I needed trees, trees and more trees. I needed mountains and no concrete. I needed sculptures in the churches and on houses, not in museums. I needed my trees and my mountains. Spring came and still only concrete and me crowded within the walls of this concrete city. I would not breathe. I thought every day spent without seeing trees and mountains will be my last one and yet they spread endlessly.

I set out to look for trees, green grass and earth. I began to walk immense distances to find trees, mountains and earth. But did not find them. I began to walk on roofs of tall buildings to feel space, to get a better view in the hope of finding the country. No luck, the roofs were tiny, tarred, hot and black. Finally, I found a park. I think it was Bronx Park. I spent whatever time I had in the Park, covering the whole Park, every nook and cranny of it, while I was learning to say the "th". After a while I've gotten used to my concrete cage a bit. But only superficially so. Because whenever I am with the earth in the country, amongst trees and mountains I feel better. My Polish mountains, rivers and forests are in my blood and in no way can they be forced out of there.

About a year later I began to study the Constitution of the U.S.A. My Uncle being a historian wanted me to understand democracy well. Democracy, that was a big joke. What do you mean people elect a president? Of the people, by the people, for the people, it was a fairy tale. For anyone who comes from a dictatorship, any totalitarian system. Freedom? Ha! I was indoctrinated well by the Polish system. Being a cynic through circumstances and a quick learner by nature, I knew well that there was no such thing as democracy.

A Bill of Rights? Whose rights? The right of the dictators and the master race. Congress? House of Representatives? I remember these, a joke. Supreme Court? I've heard of Judges who are pawns of the government, who say right is wrong and wrong is right. Who say that killing you or raping you is okay, because you are inferior.

People vote for all these people, the Representatives, Congressmen, President, etc., etc., etc. Hog wash. They are told how to vote. All men are created equal, ha! Which ones are the equal ones. The Constitution, who is fooling whom. My Uncle drilled me on all that was written, but he as well as I, knew only too well that I did not believe any of it, could not accept any of it. Could not even imagine the possibility of any of it.

Then there was this presidential election and my Uncle was going to vote. The debates on the radio by all the contenders for the job of the President were going on. As controversial as they were, they were going on and nobody got shot for it. Nobody got carted away to a camp.

Then I met Norman Thomas, a friend of my Uncles, who was once a contender for the presidential job. He was so very kind and nice and gentle, and asked me to believe "even though you can not yet, try to believe that the Constitution is there of the people for the people and by the people . . ." And told me a lot about Washington, Lincoln and Jefferson. Then there was a Judge. A very, very old, wise and wonderful Judge from the Supreme Court. He explained about the American system of justice and the Bill of Rights. He was so gentle, so patient, and loving with me. That one day it suddenly hit me. My God, it is true. People do elect a president. There is a Constitution and a Bill of Rights, there are other ways of governing than through a dictatorship. A way that I always secretly wished for and dreamed of, hoped for and so desperately wanted.

Democracy. Freedom. No concentration camp, no killings for disagreeing. That this country is made of Refugees of people just like me. Refugees, fleeing from persecutions, being thrown out because they were different. The Irish, the English, the Jews, the Haitians. . . . And that this wonderful land accepts and shelters all of them. That all men are created equal and there is no super race. That was the miracle to me, the miracle of America.

The concrete did not matter so much any more. The many people in eyeglasses did not matter so much any more, the underground subways did not matter so much any more. It was a country, a free country, a beautiful country, where no one puts people into concentration camps. Where nobody kills people because they are "inferior" where nobody in the name of Christ and the government and race exterminates a race. Unbelievable.

And yet, still when I see mountains on the sun set with its wonderful glow warming the ocean. Or the moon playing hide and seek amongst the trees, or meadows of grass, or fields full of wheat, potatoes, onions. Or trees, cherry trees, apple trees, pear trees, I remember the mother earth that spawned me and miss the country that I came from, the country that did not want me.

I never went back to Poland. Yet, once I was invited to the Soviet Union to diagnose and possibly treat one of their children. I went to some Polish government office to find out if I could stop and see Wilno, the city of my birth. The most elegant Polish gentleman greeted me there. He asked me to go back to Poland and stay there, work with their disturbed children. He said that I "owed them" that allegiance, to the country of my birth. I said I could not live there, I'd be walking on the blood of my relatives and friends. And he said "don't worry, we washed it all off." he had a crystal ink well on his desk. I grabbed it to throw it at him. He smiled, smacked his lips and said "How nice a Jewess with a temper." Still the inferior race. I did not throw the ink well, he was not worth it.

I never went to Poland, yet, I do not miss my country any more. Except . . . when May appears and Spring is in full swing, I smell lilacs. I smell them everywhere, where there are any and there aren't any. That was the month for lilacs where I came from.

Except . . . when winter comes and I walk amongst snow covered mountains here, I feel my mountains "over there." Ponary under the soft deep white blanket of snow with the proud fir and pine tree looking up.

But then I must remember that all my Aunts, Uncles, Cousins, friends' parents, and friends, were taken there, made to dig their own graves and shot to death. Those were the mountains where I once walked, looked and loved.

Except . . . when summer comes and I look for wild strawberries and sometimes even find them, pick cherries and apples in the orchards. The way I used to there.

Except . . . when autumn comes and the horse chestnut trees shed their precious fruit and I collect them and take them from the beautiful shiny nut out of its prickly green cradle, the way I used too.

Then I remember with my memory, my gut, my whole body, my origins.

Except when . . .

X
Epilogue
28
The American as Radical Outsider
Sam B. Girgus

The following is a chapter from *The New Covenant: The Jewish Writer and the American Idea* by Sam B. Girgus (Chapel Hill: University of North Carolina Press, 1984).

Although E. L. Doctorow is not the same kind of public personality as Mailer, the quality of his commitment to the role of the New Jeremiah in the tradition of the New Covenant is as strong and as significant as Mailer's. Like Mailer, Doctorow writes from the perspective of a moral consciousness to reexamine the meaning of the American experience and to revivify our moral imagination. His concern for the relevance of America as a myth and ideology has led him to write a form of "metahistory" that builds upon the poetic and linguistic origins of historical understanding.[1] Moreover, it can be argued that as metahistory, in Hayden White's sense of the term, Doctorow's work can be compared with Nietzsche's philosophy of history. According to White, Nietzsche attempted "to translate history into art." Doctorow shares Nietzsche's interest in, as White says, returning "consciousness to the enjoyment of its Metaphorical powers."[2] Much of Nietzsche's discussion in *The Use and Abuse of History* of the objectives and responsibilities of the historian could serve as a model for Doctorow. Nietzsche insists that the "real value" of history "lies in inventing ingenious variations on a probably commonplace theme, in raising the popular melody to a universal symbol and showing what a world of depth, power and beauty exists in it." To achieve such a level of creativity, the historian, Nietzsche argues, must function and think like an artist. The historian, he says, must develop "above all a great artistic faculty, a creative vision from a height, the loving study of the data of experience, the free elaborating of a given type."[3] Based on this artistic theory of rendering history, Nietzsche goes on in *The Genealogy of Morals* to establish something like guidelines for an approach to history that emphasizes openness and invention.[4]

The elements of myth and symbol, as well as art and invention, are the important factors in Nietzsche's thinking about history that elucidate Doctorow's work. For Nietzsche, myth and symbol constitute the heart of a culture and its history and must, therefore, be contrasted with the fictions derived from ordinary history. History and culture without myth turn man into an abstraction. Man's loss of myth, Nietzsche writes in *The Birth of Tragedy*, leads to "abstract man stripped of myth, abstract education, abstract mores, abstract law, abstract government; the random vagaries of the artistic imagination unchanneled by any native myth; a culture without any fixed and con-

From Sam B. Girgus: *The New Covenant: Jewish Writers and the American Idea*, Copyright © 1984 by University of North Carolina Press, Chapel Hill, North Carolina. Reprinted by permission.

secrated place of origin, condemned to exhaust all possibilities and feed miserably and parasitically on every culture under the sun." In contrast to such abstraction, Nietzsche hopes to return culture to its "mythic home, the mythic womb."[5] He associates the power of myth to define the essence of culture with the power of music to stimulate men to operate and think beyond their usual capacities. Both myth and music come together for him in a truly exciting culture. Through the revivification of the metaphoric consciousness, he seeks to establish in cultural history "the mythopoeic power of true music."[6] Nietzsche's understanding of history in terms of myth, metaphor, and music is, as White says, the "notion of historical representation as pure story, fabulation, myth conceived as the verbal equivalent of the spirit of music."[7] *Ragtime* represents the most obvious example of Doctorow's attempt to develop the narrative structure of the historical novel in what can be described as a Nietzschean mode that uses music as the metaphor to best dramatize an era and a people. Thus, Doctorow indicates his interest in the idea of history as, in White's words, "pure story, fabulation, myth" when he says of *Ragtime* that "there's no more fiction or nonfiction now, there's only narrative. All the nonfiction means of communication employ narrative today."[8]

However, there are also major differences between Nietzsche and Doctorow. Most importantly, Doctorow rejects the nihilistic implications of Nietzsche's philosophy. As White indicates, in Nietzsche's "conception of history, the prospects of any *community* whatsoever are sternly rejected." "In Nietzsche," White says, "no historical grounds exist for the construction of any specific *political* posture except that of antipolitics itself. Thought is liberated from responsibility to anything outside the ego and will of the individual, whether past, future, or present."[9] Although certainly aware of such implications in contemporary thought, Doctorow remains committed to community and politics, to a moral vision that includes individual responsibility, and to history itself, meaning a belief in the necessity of trying to understand the past as a means for attempting to deal intelligently with the present and future. Such humanistic concerns also put Doctorow in opposition to a modern school of apocalyptic writers. Harry Henderson's list of these writers includes Nathanael West, John Barth, Joseph Heller, and Thomas Pynchon. Henderson believes that these writers have an "apocalyptic historical imagination" that entertains the "idea of an apocalyptic Day of Doom, an end to history that is foreshadowed by the exhaustion of the historical imagination that their parody signifies."[10] Although the ending to Doctorow's first novel, *Welcome to Hard Times*, resembles this kind of apocalyptic catastrophe, the spirit of the hero and narrator suggests a hope for human communication, truth, and love that characterizes Doctorow's literature and philosophy in general.

Welcome to Hard Times also indicates Doctorow's important interest in working with universal figures and classic motifs in a mythic pattern. In the novel Doctorow places classic western types in a traditional setting and narrative. The absence of surnames for the characters reenforces their universality. They clearly are intended to stand for general personality types that fit into the mythic scheme of "the Western." For example, the stock figure of the bad man who destroys the town of Hard Times and massacres its residents is cast simply as the Man from Bodie. The hero is know as Blue, depicting the low key, almost maudlin, mood of the piece. He is also called mayor since he assumes a kind of clerical and administrative responsibility for the town. From being a record keeper of sorts, he eventually achieves a judicial and prophetic role. His consciousness and vision make the town a community. Condemning himself for his initial cowardice in failing to stand up to the bad man, he restores the town and establishes something of a family. However, he finds himself forced to confront the return of the Bad Man from Bodie, who once again destroys everything. The mayor blames himself. He says, "I can forgive everyone But I cannot forgive myself. I told Molly we'd be ready for the Bad Man but we can never be ready. Nothing is ever buried, the earth rolls in its tracks, it never goes anywhere, it never changes, only the hope changes like morning and night, only the expectations rise and set. Why does there have to be a promise before destruction?"[11]

However, even in the face of the evil and the destructiveness of the Bad Man, Blue cannot surrender his humanistic priorities, which include at the top of the list the need to conclude his history. In spite of his awareness of what we can call the epistemological difficulties and uncertainties entailed in attempting to know and transmit the truth, Blue feels compelled to complete his project. The only meaning the events can have will be provided by Blue as the historian whose work will make them part of human consciousness. Rather than confirming the nihilism of the apocalyptic vision, the destruction of Hard Times seems to demand of Blue just the opposite of a concession to death. In spite of his fears and self-doubts, Hard Times for Blue requires a reassertion of his individual moral responsibility. He says, "And now I've put down what happened, everything that scares me that it may show the truth." Blue admits that he cannot be sure of the final meaning of his account given the difficulty of figuring out "which minutes were important and which not." He asks, "Does the truth come out in such scrawls, so bound by my limits?"[12] His actions, however, along with his fulfillment of the obligation to record history, stand as the moral judgment upon Blue. Thus, as he takes his last look upon the destruction of the town, he notes that wood for reconstruction remains available. He says, "And I have to allow, with great shame, I keep thinking someone will come by sometime who will want to use the wood."[13] So, even in death, he continues to be the builder, the pioneer, the American.

Blue's questions concerning his dilemma about being caught up as a man, a citizen, and a historian in the making and writing of his own history achieve brilliant elaboration and discussion in Doctorow's most successful and important novel to date, *The Book of Daniel*. Issues about history, myth, human values, and individual moral responsibility that are suggested in *Welcome to Hard Times*, and to a lesser degree in *Big as Life*,[14] reach maturity in *The Book of Daniel*, a largely neglected work that may yet receive deserving recognition as a major work of contemporary literature. There are reasons for this neglect. First of all, with the important exception of Stanley Kauffmann in the *New Republic*, most reviewers have failed to see much beyond the novel's most obvious intention of dramatizing the story of Julius and Ethel Rosenberg, who were convicted and executed by electrocution as spies for stealing atomic secrets for the Russians in the early 1950s. In the novel the names of the Rosenbergs are changed to Paul and Rochelle Isaacson, and the story is told through the consciousness of their son, Daniel Isaacson.[15] In addition, other novels in the Doctorow canon, especially *Ragtime*, have received far more critical attention from major reviewers and scholars. Doctorow's dazzling insertion of real characters in the fictional setting of *Ragtime* and his experimentation in that novel with a kind of verbal and imagistic syncopation have intrigued both popular and critical audiences, but it has also distracted them from much of the inventiveness and originality of *The Book of Daniel*, which also experiments with the form of the historical novel. In terms of sparkle and glitter, *The Book of Daniel* cannot compete with *Ragtime's* use of such figures as Evelyn Nesbit, J. P. Morgan, Freud, Houdini, and Emma Goldman. As Barbara Foley indicates, *Ragtime* departs radically from the historical novel's practice of dealing only plausibly with historical figures. Foley writes, "Events so audaciously 'invented' as Freud's and Jung's trip through the Tunnel of Love at Coney Island of Emma Goldman's massage of Evelyn Nesbit clearly violate this canon of historical decorum. Doctorow is doing something quite different here: he is utilizing the reader's encyclopedic knowledge that a historical Freud, Jung, Goldman, and Nesbit did in fact exist in order to pose an open challenge to the reader's preconceived notions about what historical 'truth' actually is. Asked on one occasion whether Goldman and Nesbit ever really met, Doctorow has boldly replied, 'They have now!' "[16] Other critics such as Leonard Kriegel and John Seelye also have expressed their great admiration for the cleverness of Doctorow's technique in *Ragtime*. Kriegel considers the novel "intriguing" and says, "In Dos Passos' great trilogy, the biographical is used as a counterweight to the fictional. In Doctorow, the study of J. P. Morgan is, indeed, the stuff of fictional life." Also relating *Ragtime* to Dos Passos, Seelye notes that "perhaps Doctorow's most significant borrowing is from continental, not American literature, namely, his use of Heinrich von Kleist's historical novel *Michael Kohlhous*." Seelye further states that *Ragtime* "manages to syncopate materials borrowed from other radically oriented novels of the '30s, including Roth's *Call It Sleep* and George Milburn's forgotten *tour de force, Catalogue*."[17]

The experimentation in *The Book of Daniel* is one of a more traditional sort than in either *Ragtime* or the more recent *Loon Lake*. In *The Book of Daniel*, Doctorow, like Philip Roth, develops the idea of the self-consciousness of modern literature and art so that the process of creativity and production becomes a subject in itself. However, while Roth writes fiction about writing fiction, Doctorow writes fiction about writing history. At the beginning of the novel, we learn that Daniel Isaacson is writing his history dissertation at Columbia University and that we will be watching him watching himself as he progresses on it. In fact, Daniel's history will take the form of the very book in our hands. We also see that Doctorow, through the persona of Daniel, really writes a special kind of history that imbues Daniel's prophetic narration with the rhetoric of the jeremiad in a linguistic achievement that projects a vision of justice and truth upon American culture. In effect, then, Doctorow demands of himself a literary work of initiation that includes the stories of Daniel and his family and, for want of a better term, Daniel's inner spirit or sense of being; an intellectual and social history that establishes the ideals, values, trends, and mores of America from the period of the depression until the era of the Great Greening of America in the late 1960s; a political study of modern radical movements and thought; a moral history that lives up to the rhetorical tradition of the jeremiad. Putting all of this together—Daniel's own story plus the story of his people and their times in America—Doctrow, by adhering consistently to the complex consciousness and multi-dimensional point of view of his young Columbia graduate student, writes one of the great Jewish novels of our times.

Two figures are especially important examples to Daniel in his effort to write such a history—Edgar Allen Poe and the Prophet Daniel. Our Daniel—Daniel Isaacson—sees Poe as an important literary and cultural model of the power of the alienated artistic consciousness to instigate a revolution in the values and thought of his time. In Poe, art and alienation go hand in hand. Thus, Daniel calls Poe "the archetype traitor, the master subversive Poe, who wore a hole into the parchment and let the darkness pour through" by virtue of his drinking, his relationship to his thirteen-year-old cousin, and his poetry.[18] He says, "A small powerful odor arose from the Constitution; there was a wisp of smoke which exploded and quickly turned mustard yellow in color. When Poe blew this away through the resulting aperture in the parchment the darkness of the depths rose, and rises still from that small hole all these years incessantly pouring its dark hellish gases like soot, like smog, like the poisonous effulgence of combustion engines over Thrift and virtue and Reason and Natural Law and the Rights of Man. It's Poe, not those other guys. He and he alone. It's Poe who ruined us, that scream from the smiling face of America" (*BD*, pp. 193–94). Daniel believes that Poe would understand him as a complex and divided consciousness who has been trained by his parents to be "a small criminal of perception" and "a psychic alien" (*BD*, pp. 41, 45), meaning someone whose point of view and ideas of reality always will be difficult and multidimensional. Daniel also believes that Poe provides an original lesson in American culture of the cost of such a complex consciousness. Poe demonstrates how an alien vision becomes a double edged sword. Though a complex consciousness allows Daniel to function with great perspicacity and imagination on many different levels and through many creative forms, it also can be a self-destructive and nonproductive force in the manner of much of modern nihilism. The tendency in art to carry such alienation to its nihilistic extreme interests Daniel and becomes an ideology in itself. Daniel finds a symbol for the nihilistic potential of his own perspective in the mutilation of a woman's eye in "a classic surrealist silent film by Buñuel and Dali" (*BD*, p. 72). In the movie a man brings his straight razor toward a woman's face and her eyeball. Daniel says, "And just as you, the audience, have settled for this symbolic mutilation of the woman's eye, the camera cuts back to the scene, and in closeup, shows the razor slicing into the eyeball" (*BD*, p. 73).

The counterpart to Daniel's psychological and aesthetic alienation as represented by Poe is the moral alienation of the prophetic and righteous visionary in a corrupt land as embodied in the biblical story of Daniel. The biblical Daniel stands as a symbol, or a "type" in the Puritan sense of the word, for the Daniel in the novel. His moral vision and his story establish a standard and a pattern for our Daniel. Through Daniel the Prophet, the novel attempts to transcend historical limitations and extends itself to a higher realm of moral authority. However, the psychological credibility for the moral consciousness of Daniel and his sister derives from the abrasive onslaught of continuous preachings from their parents. The obsessive moralism of their parents' left-wing politics, values, and views has taught Daniel and Susan to see even ordinary matters as ultimate moral issues. Moreover, Daniel recognizes important parallels between his own situation and that of the biblical Daniel, of whom he says, "It is a bad time for Daniel and his co-religionists, for they re second-class citizens, in a distinctly hostile environment. But in that peculiar kind of symbiosis of pagan kings and wise subject-Jews, Daniel is apparently able to soften the worst excesses of the rulers against his people by making himself available for interpretation of dreams, visions or apparitions in the night" (*BD*, p. 21). Similarly, as Jews and Communists, Daniel's parents consider themselves to be second-class citizens, and Daniel also feels like an alien in his own country. In addition, he sees an existential connection between himself and the biblical Daniel. As someone who inherits an awesome guilt and loss through his parents, Daniel can sympathize and identify with the biblical Daniel's feeling of having been chosen. God, according to Daniel, "enlists the help of naturally righteous humans who become messengers, or carriers of his miracles, or who deliver their people. Each age has by trial to achieve its recognition of Him—or to put it another way, every generation has to learn anew the lesson of His Existence. The drama of the Bible is always in the conflict of those who have learned with those who have not learned" (*BD*, p. 20). The biblical Book of Daniel, therefore, operates as a moral metaphor for our Daniel's history.

Daniel's moral vision achieves additional depth and specificity through the character of Susan, who functions as an alter—or more precisely a super-super—ego for Daniel, forever torturing him with ever increasing moral demands. Their intimate relationship as almost a single mind or psyche becomes solidified when circumstances unite them against the world. This special relationship emerges after the arrest and the death of their parents. Thus, she becomes capable of sending a "signal" to him "from the spasm of soul." He says, "Susan and I, we were the only ones left" (*BD*, pp. 40–41). At times he tries to treat her moral intensity facetiously, but in fact her moral authoritarianism operates as a kind of tourniquet upon his personality. He says that she has become "a dupe of the international moralist propagandist apparatus" and has been made into a "moral speed freak" (*BD*, p. 20). Significantly, her moral position is heavy with political content because she identifies ferociously with her parents and vehemently maintains a radical ideology. She attacks Daniel for defaming the memory of their parents and argues that his decision to attend graduate school is an act of cowardice and of treason against them and the left. "'What did they die for?'"

she exclaims as a curse against Daniel (*BD*, p. 94). He, of course, assumes the guilt and responsibility for her eventual breakdown and death. "There is," he says, "some evidence that she was driven finally to eradicate him from her consciousness by the radical means of eradicating her consciousness" (*BD*, p. 95).

Whereas Susan radiates radical moral righteousness, Daniel usually responds to situations with the defensive detachment of a student of radicalism. In contrast to Susan, whose radicalism recoils against herself, Daniel vents his frustration in his writing. The scattered inclusion of Daniel's interpretations of history, politics, and thought within *The Book of Daniel* is one of the novel's major accomplishments. Doctorow presents a relatively traditional Marxist historical methodology and perspective within the broader concept of history represented by the book in its entirety. By expanding upon the studies and ideas of established radical and revisionist historians such as William Appleman Williams, Daniel develops an interesting framework through which to interpret history in terms of class oppression, organized violence, bourgeois control of society's institutions, and capitalist domination of the means of economic production and distribution.[19] Daniel expounds upon this point of view in a series of statements dealing with diverse periods and events in diplomatic, political, and social history, all of which ultimately contribute to and explain the background and meaning of his parents' execution. Some of Daniel's leftist disquisitions include an explanation and justification of Stalin's leadership based on E. H. Carr's interpretation of the dictator's role in revivifying Russian nationalism (*BD*, p. 65); an argument that all men are inherently both victims and enemies of all governments because "the final existential condition is citizenship. Every man is the enemy of his own country" (*BD*, p. 85); a revisionist argument entitled "A True History of the Cold War: A Raga" that maintains that the cold war was initiated by America in the hope of using atomic weapons as a means for controlling Russia and that the Truman Doctrine and the Marshall Plan were thinly veiled disguises to protect and advance American capitalistic interests (*BD*, pp. 248–54); and a belief "that the basis of all class distinctions in society is corporal punishment. Classes are created by corporal punishment, and maintained by corporal punishment" (*BD*, p. 144). Daniel develops the latter argument along classic Marxist lines. He writes, "As societies endure in history they symbolize complex systems of corporal punishment in economic terms. That is why Marx used the word 'slavery' to define the role of the working class under capitalism" (*BD*, pp. 144–45). Daniel's obsession with the authoritarian power and brutality of the state motivates his dramatic history of civic and governmental torture and punishment that includes drawing and quartering, smoking, knouting, and burning at the stake, which he offers to strengthen the argument for the martyrdom of his electrocuted parents (*BD*, pp. 86, 122, 143, 144).

On the other hand, Daniel's personal experiences with people on the left and his proclivity to temper his radicalism and Marxism with self-criticism and pragmatic intellectualism tend to challenge Susan's ideological rigidity. Although he identifies with the left, he frequently views it ironically and critically. From his perspective the left seems more pathetic than ominous. In fact, it appears to be a danger only to those people like his parents who let their belief in it become a new kind of orthodoxy that inflates their sense of importance, disguises their vulnerability, and encourages a kind of moral myopia, which confuses immediate self-interest, personal status, and convenience with universal truth and justice. The novel offers innumerable examples of the failure of thought and character by members of the left, many of them most powerfully dramatized by his parents and their friends. His parents are filled with an enormous sense of their own importance and knowledge. They believe their access to historical truth makes them part of a psychological, moral, and intellectual elite. Ironically, such self-elevation puts them in opposition to the very masses they are supposed to serve. The fact of their political irrelevance and impotence in the face of such reputed power contributes to a sense of frustration that further increases their feeling of internal weakness and ineptitude. Thus, Daniel remembers how mixed motivations inspired the idealism of his parents. Daniel writes, "They rushed after self-esteem. If you could recognize a Humphrey Bogart movie for the cheap trash it was, you had culture. If you discovered the working class you found the roots of democracy. In social justice you discovered your own virtue. To desire social justice was a way of living without envy, which is the emotion of a loser. It was a way of transforming envy into constructive outgoing hate" (*BD*, p. 43).

Unfortunately, such hatred became a characteristic way of being in the world for his parents. He writes, "The thing about the Isaacson family, the thing about everyone in our family, is that we're not nice people"(*BD*, p. 37). The wife of the lawyer who lost his health in his tireless efforts on their behalf understandably resents the impact of the Isaacsons upon her own life. "'I have no love for the memory of your parents,'" she tells Daniel. "'They were Communists and they destroyed everything they touched'" (*BD*, p. 232). Accusing his parents of being unkind to everyone, she also feels that "'they were not innocent of permitting themselves to be used. And of using other people in their fanaticism'"(*BD*, p. 232). Furthermore, during the trial his own mother comes to recognize many harsh facts about the left and the people in it. She ironically fails, however, to see similarities between herself and her friends. She thinks, "My God how I hate them all, how I despise their pompous little egos and their discussions and resolutions and breast-beating; with their arrogance as they delivered to us each week the truth, the gospel according to 11th Street. Always they treated Paul like a child and with his mind! A mind so fine, so superior to theirs except in the grubby self-serving politics of the Party. He was always being censured, he was never quite in step. All he did was slave for them, believe for them. Communists have no respect for people, only for positions. . . . You blind them with your ideals and while they are looking up you stab them in the belly for the sake of your ideals" (*BD*, pp. 219–20). Thus, for Daniel, the major lesson of the left in America as rendered by his parents was self-destruction, partly through self-delusion. "But you see," he says, "I was learning. I was learning how to be an Isaacson. An Isaacson does things boldly calculated to bring self-destructive results" (*BD*, p. 222).

One of Daniel's most bitter accounts of the contrast between his parents' sense of self-importance as radicals and the reality of their pathos concerns the search of his home and the arrest of his father by the Federal Bureau of Investigation. As the FBI empties the house of its miserable belongings, Daniel sarcastically warns the reader to be alert to the scene "so that you may record in clarity one of the Great Moments in the American Left. The American Left is in this great moment artfully reduced to the shabby conspiracies of a couple named Paul and Rochelle Isaacson" (*BD*, p. 125). The extent of their real power and contribution to the left probably is best summarized by a *New York Times* reporter, who tells Daniel that they "'had to have been into some goddam thing. They *acted* guilty. They were little neighborhood commies probably with some kind of third-rate operation that wasn't of use to anyone except maybe it made them feel important. Maybe what they were doing was worth five years. Maybe' " (*BD*, p. 230).

Daniel's understanding of the complexity of his parents' relationship to the old left influences his perception of the people and program on the new left. When his sister proposes to use a trust fund that had been established on their behalf to advance a "New Left" cultural revolution, Daniel seems uncertain. Later in the book he thinks, "THEY'RE STILL FUCKING US. . . . The Isaacsons are nothing to the New Left" (*BD*, p. 169). Moreover, as a product of the more conventional moralism of the old left, Daniel feels basically uncomfortable with certain new left character types who live a kind of self-centered existence. The superiority such people express over the previous generation of Isaacson radicals further alienates Daniel from them. They render an easy view of the failures of the past that are part of Daniel's own personal history. Thus after receiving a beating on the historic 1967 Washington march on the Pentagon, he assures his wife that the wounds are not major. He says, "'It looks worse than it is. There was nothing to it. It is a lot easier to be a revolutionary nowadays than it used to be' " (*BD*, p. 274).

In their attitude toward his parents, many of those Daniel encounters on the new left simply share the so-called dominant culture's disdain for his parents. In a sense, the Isaacsons were born guilty. They are guilty of being losers, guilty of being poor Jews, guilty of not being quite smart enough or powerful enough to escape or transcend the limitations of their environment, guilty of being used and of using others. At the same time, their attitude in death gives them a moral strength that elevates them above their enemies both on the right and the left. For Daniel, they achieve a quality of martyrdom and sacrifice that rises above their political and personal causes and failures. Daniel says, "But they stuck to it, didn't they, Daniel? When the call came they answered. They offered up those genitals, didn't they, Dandan? Yes, they did. There were moments when I thought he would crack, I had my doubts about him. But I knew she would take it finally, to the last volt, in absolute selfishness, in unbelievably rigid fury" (*BD*, 43). In order for Daniel to find a meaning and significance for their death, he must go beyond its political context. He puts their death, as we shall see, in a Jewish framework. As a Jew, he finds a structure through ritual to express and contain his grief, his morning, his sense of inadequacy, and his guilt as an heir to the pain and burdens of the past.

Throughout the novel, Daniel thinks of his parents as representatives of a lower-middle-class Jewish subculture of radicalism. Their backgrounds, values, life-style, behavior, thought, language, tastes, and opinions epitomize the particular world view of the Jewish left in New York that developed early in the century, reached its peak during the depression and the war years, and quickly declined during the late 1940s and early 1950s. As Stanley Kauffmann says, "The novel faces up squarely and intelligently to the Jewishness of its subject."[20] Jewish identity provides an important frame of reference to help Daniel comprehend his history and the tragedy of his family. The symbol for Daniel of his Jewish past as both a burden and dynamic heritage can be found in his grandmother, Rochelle's mother. She stands for him as an exuberant and eccentric life force. She appears early in the novel as the neighborhood's crazy woman whose story is told in part through the Bintel Brief, or "Bundles of Letters" section of the *Jewish Daily Forward*, which served as both an outlet for expression and a rare source of comfort and advice to thousands of immigrants. The strengths, dedication, deprivation, and psychological trauma in the immigrant generation are evoked in her character. Daniel conjures up a vision of her during which she reminds him that " 'this placing of the burden of the children is a family tradition. But only your crazy grandma had the grace to make a ritual of it' " (*BD*, p. 83). During this ghostly visit, she reminds Daniel that he inherited from her the "'shimmering fullness of stored life which always marks the victim. What we have, too much life in each of us, is what the world hates most. We offend. We stink with life. Our hearts make love to the world not gently. We are brutal with life and our brutality is called suffering. We scream into our pillows when we come' " (*BD*, p. 82).

However, the Jewish experience in America as presented in this novel includes more than insights into Jewish radicalism and portrayals of the immigrant generation. The novel deals with the meaning of America to the Jews, and one of the novel's deepest ironies concerns the significance to Daniel's family and people of the idea of America. Nothing represents the hold of the American Way more dramatically than Paul Isaacson's belief, almost until his last breath, in the principles, ideals, and purposes of the American idea to displace dissent by directing it into a framework of the ideology's own terms. Isaacson typifies Sacvan Bercovitch's thesis that the rhetorical structure of the myth and ideology of America integrates opposition into a consensus of belief in the very ideals and values that comprise the American Way. Thus, Isaacson internalizes the ideology of America even while fighting it. The depth of his bitterness about America makes him a target of its legal system. As a Communist, he oppugns the validity of the American idea. Nevertheless, he believes in America. "It's screwy," Daniel says as he describes how his father's generation of Communists could both challenge and believe so desperately in America. He says, "Lots of them were like that. They were Stalinists and every instance of Capitalist America fucking up drove them wild. My country! Why aren't you what you claim to be? If they were put on trial, they didn't say *Of course, what else could we expect*, they said *You are making a mockery of American justice!* And it was more than strategy, it was more than Lenin's advice to use the reactionary apparatus to defend yourself, it was passion" (*BD*, p. 51). In other words, in terms of the New Covenant, even Paul cannot dissociate himself from the rhetoric of the jeremiad in his radical politics. His Americanism helps to drive him toward a foreign ideology in order to achieve those things he believes to be most American. Daniel remembers his father "eating [his] heart out" while listening to Radio Town Meeting of the Air because the program so perfectly exemplified the failure of American democracy to live up to itself. "He used to turn that on at home," Daniel says. "It would make him furious" (*BD*, p. 50). Daniel insists that "the implication of all the things he used to flagellate himself was that American democracy wasn't democratic enough. He continued to be astonished, insulted, outraged, that it wasn't purer, freer, finer, more ideal" (*BD* p. 51). In a sense, Paul's belief in America follows the pattern of the family's drive toward self-destruction. It could be argued that his undiminished belief in those American ideals that his more "patriotic" and "American" persecutors defame and corrupt leads to his electrocution as a traitor and spy. In the Death House at Sing Sing he says to his children, who a moment before had hysterically insisted upon being searched by a guard before the visit, "'You cannot put innocent people to death in this country. It can't be done'" (*BD*, p. 265).

Daniel's life as an Isaacson represents only one phase of his life and one aspect of the Jewish experience in America. It gives him roots in the radical and immigrant-based subculture of the Jewish left. That phase culminates for Daniel when this mother says that her execution should serve as a bar mitzvah, or day of initiation into manhood, for him. At the time of her execution, she says, "Let my son be bar mitzvahed today. Let our death be his bar mitzvah'" (*BD*, p. 314). Considering the significance of the bar mitzvah in Jewish life, as well as Daniel's general helplessness at the time, the words amount to a curse on his head. They are an act against the living that helps propel her son into a life of anguish. The mother's words also conclude what had been a period od devastation for the children, including the arrest of the father, the steady isolation of the family, the horrible failure of the mother to return home one day after saying good-bye to them because she also has been arrested, the sense of abandonment that leaves the children with almost no emotional support and love, the loneliness of living with an inept and grotesque aunt, and the nightmare of a public shelter in which Susan screams at night and recedes into old habits like wetting the bed. At one point during this period, Daniel from his own place in the shelter believes that he can hear his sister scream from another part of the building. He soon masterminds their escape, and they return to their old house as though believing that everything can be made normal and safe in the old surroundings. Instead, of course, they find nothing and in turn are found alone in the house by the Isaacson's lawyer, a stream of the girl's urine on the floor.

Following the execution, a new phase begins for the Isaacson children with their adoption by a liberal law professor and his wife. However, since the novel defies traditional chronological plot development, we know from the beginning that this new phase marks just a temporary reprieve for the children. Their new parents are ideal in conventional middle-class terms. They can give the children a new life, but they cannot rewrite the history the children already have had. Nevertheless, in terms of the Jewishness of the novel and its success in rendering the meaning of the story of the Jews in America, the new parents, Robert and Lise Lewin, are vitally important. While Paul Isaacson believes devoutly in the aspect of the American idea that relates to social justice and equality, Robert Lewin adheres with comparable vigor to another view of the American idea. Together, for Daniel, they move his book closer toward presenting a total view of the relationship between the Jews and America. Daniel directly addresses the question of Lewin's significance as a bond between Judaism and Americanism in a comment about a letter he receives from him. Daniel writes, "It is interesting to note, aside from everything else, the operating pressure of fatherhood in Robert Lewin's letter. He wants to stabilize me with responsibility. That is a true blue american puritan idea. In that idea is the fusion of the Jew and America, both of them heirs of the ancient seafarers: you ride the sea best with lead in your keel. My lawyer father is no accident, and it is no accident that he loves American Law, an institution that he constantly loves, like a bad child who someday in his love will not fail, stabilized with responsibility" (*BD,* p. 171).

The marriage between the Jews and America that Lewin represents is further developed through the character of Jacob Ascher, the defense counsel for the Isaacsons and the law partner of Lewin's father. Ascher served as the children's only real friend and companion throughout the period of the trial. Daniel writes, "Ascher was a pillar of the Bronx bar. He was not brilliant, but his law was sound, and his honor as a man, as a religious man, was unquestionable. He was an honest lawyer, and was dogged for his clients. I picture him on Yom Kippur standing in the pew with his homburg on his head, and a tallis around his shoulders. Ascher could wear a homburg and a tallis at the same time" (*BD,* p. 132). The symbols of the tallis, or Jewish prayer shawl, and the homburg combine to form one symbol of the union between the American Way and the Jewish Way in thought and life-style. Daniel writes, "Ascher was not a political man, you could imagine him voting for anyone he found morally recognizable, no matter what the party. If anything, he was conservative. He perceived in the law a codification of the religious sense of life. He was said to have worked for years on a still unfinished book demonstrating the contributions of the Old Testament to American law" (*BD,* p. 133).

The prominence of Ascher and Lewin in the novel emphasizes the point that *The Book of Daniel,* like its biblical model, is the story of the Jews in a foreign land. However, through them Doctorow is also able to dramatize the marriage between American and Jewish life and thought. In a sense, the novel suggests that the Jews have become the modern archetypal Americans. They are almost super Americans. Accordingly, the Isaacsons' saga in the history of America becomes literally a Jewish story of America. Isaacson himself talks of the Jewishness of the event during his trial. However, from his point of view they all have become slaves bowing before the enemy. He writes to Rochelle, "My darling have you noticed how many of the characters in this capitalist drama are Jewish? The defendants, the defense lawyer, the prosecution, the major prosecution witness, the judge. We are putting on this little passion play for our Christian masters. In the concentration camps the Nazis made guards of certain Jews and gave them whips. In Jim Crow Harlem the worst cops are Negro" (*BD,* p. 213). His hatred is particularly directed toward the Jewish judge named Hirsch and the Chief U.S. Attorney General, Howard "Red" Feuerman. "Feuerman," he writes, "in his freckles and flaming red hair, this graduate of St. John's, the arch assimilationist who repressed the fact that he could never get a job with the telephone company—Feuerman is so full of self-hatred HE IS DETERMINED to purge us. Imperialism has many guises, and each is a measure of its desperation" (*BD,* p. 213). As told in this part of the novel through Paul's perspective, his judgment upon these two lawyers seems just. He thinks, "Hirsch has heard more cases brought by the government in the field of subversive activities than anyone else. He is Jewish. He wears a striped, ivy league tie, the knot of which can be seen under his judicial robe" (BD, p. 201). It is commonly believed, he reports, that the judge hopes his role in the trial will earn him a place on the Supreme Court. The insensitivity and vulgarity of Hirsch and Feuerman do not diminish the moral authority of either Ascher or Lewin. Nor do they weaken the Isaacsons' passion for justice. However, they do round out the Jewishness of the story in a way that avoids sentimentality. *The Book of Daniel* does not turn all Jews into American heroes, but it does dramatize the significance of their role in American culture.

To adequately tell this story of the marriage between two cultures required Doctorow to untie in one form history, literature, and moral prophecy while he wove into a single web stories of initiation, crime and punishment, self-destruction, courage, and moral triumph. In a sense, the whole story turns the Jews into a prophetic tribe of Daniels casting multiple perspectives on the totality of the American experience. The result is an ingenious reconstitution of the myth of regeneration in America. Daniel is ultimately rescued and saved. Moreover, he gives himself three choices of how to dramatize his regeneration. The first two endings deal with Daniel's ability to confront and transcend his past and express a form of reconciliation. In the first suggested ending, he returns to the old house in the Bronx that was the scene of his youth. As he observes a family of strangers in the house, Daniel seems able to leave, finally, that part of his life. The second ending proposes two funerals. In the first funeral, both he and Susan bury their parents. In the second Daniel and his new parents bury his sister. In this scene, which recalls the command of his grandmother to remember the dead, Daniel initiates one of the most important rituals in the Jewish religion, a Mourner's Kaddish, or prayer for the dead. The moment reveals Daniel's sense of himself as a Jew as well as his ability to use Judaism as a way to confront his experience. It thereby becomes an act of integration of his Jewish and American selves as part of a reconciliation between his sense of the past and his hope for the future. At his sister's grave, he dismisses "the company rabbi" (*BD* p. 317) but calls together the other Jews at the cemetery—the kind of souls who make their living as Jews by praying for a fee for other Jews—and they say Kaddish. Daniel suddenly becomes part of this community of mourners, and, as they pray, he finds himself forcing them to continue. Throughout the entire novel Daniel has had to be a rock. however, in this graveside scene he turns into a human. He writes, "The funeral director waits impatiently beside his shiny hearse. But I encourage the prayermakers, and when one is through I tell him *again*, this time for my mother and father. Isaacson. Pinchas. Rachele. Susele. For all of them. I hold my wife's hand. And I think I am going to be able to cry" (*BD*, p. 318).

Both endings suggest freedom for Daniel, but the third ending discusses the subject of freedom itself. In this ending, Daniel is in the library at work on *The Book of Daniel* and trying to conceive of an ending for it. Suddenly a man interrupts Daniel's work to order him to leave because the students are closing the library as part of their protect against the university. The intruder shouts, " 'Close the book, man, what's the matter with you, don't you know you're liberated?' "(*BD*, p. 318). Daniel feels compelled to smile at this announcement of his new freedom by a stranger. "It has not been unexpected." he writes (*BD*, p. 318).

Daniel us free. Not because of the student rebellion but because of his ability to complete his book, he achieves a form of liberation. He has freed himself from the task of the book. He has written a book of freedom—a lesson in freedom—because through it he gives everything of himself to fulfill his obligations to his parents and his sister, to his present, and to his hopes for the future. He liberates his life by humanizing it through the exertion of his moral and historic consciousness. Not just an animal or a victim, he overcomes his mother's cry and achieves his own form of bar mitzvah by initiating himself into the realm of those willing to accept moral responsibility for themselves. It is as though Daniel has been striving to achieve a degree in humanity and finally receives it. He writes, "DANIEL'S BOOK: A Life Submitted in Partial Fulfillment of the Requirements for the Doctoral Degree . . ." (*BD*, p. 318). The final words in the book are in italics and come from the biblical Book of Daniel (12:1–4, 9). They say that Daniel has done all that he can for his own deliverance and for the deliverance of his people: *"and there shall be a time of trouble such as never was since there was a nation . . . and at that time the people shall be delivered, everyone that shall be found written in the book. . . . But thou, O Daniel, shut up the words, and seal the book, even to the time of the end. . . . Go thy way Daniel: for the words are closed up and sealed till the time of the end"* (*BD*, p. 319).

In *The Book of Daniel* and in his subsequent novel *Ragtime*, Doctorow achieves a level of literature that fits Warner Berthoff's category of the mythic. But to be a mythmaker, to move toward myth, is not simply to invent new fictions, including exploratory or ironic reconstructions of famous individual myths. It is rather to compose by way of continuously refreshing the substance of what people characteristically say in each other's presence up and down the whole range, or some great part of it, of purposeful human utterance."[21] Both novels are attempts to relate fiction to myth in Berthoff's sense of transforming the language and thought of an era into an art form that reflects and touches all aspects of culture. Doctorow again endeavors in *Loon Lake* to develop and modernize "famous individual myths" for the purpose of capturing the essence of American culture.

In *Loon Lake*, Doctorow elaborates upon the mythic, historical, and cultural significance of a fictional geographic landmark in a way that attempts to re-create and modernize the relationship between the landscape and the American imagination. He invents a geographic region to demonstrate how such a space becomes a region of the mind. The physical space functions as a means of cultural self-identification only to be corrupted by the culture itself, which fails to live up to the meaning it implanted into its own geography. As a fictional reenactment of this process, the novel attempts to get to the heart of the American spirit. In a Nietzschean manner we get history as a symbol. Moreover, Doctorow inhabits this region of the mind with characters and images that are themselves products of the American mythic and literary imagination. Parallels and interesting connections between *Loon Lake* and such works as *Walden, The Great Gatsby*, and *U.S.A.* abound.

Thus, in *Walden* the loons become symbolic of both Thoreau's and the pond's independence. He writes, "I am no more lonely than the loon in the pond that laughs so loud, or than Walden Pond itself. What company has that lonely lake, I pray?"[22] In another part of his narrative, Thoreau describes in detail his attempts to chase down a loon who keeps hitting the surface from flight and disappearing under the water, only to emerge again at an unexpected place in the like. The loon seems to mock Thoreau's attempts to understand him. He sends forth loud "demoniac laughter" that taunts Thoreau with its suggestion that the loon possesses some unique knowledge. Thoreau writes, "While he was thinking one thing in his brain, I was endeavoring to divine his thought in mine. It was a pretty game, played on the smooth surface of the pond, a man against a loon." The loon's ability to thrive on all three realms of the lake—above the water, on the surface, and below—demonstrates the bird's possession of special gifts. Thoreau writes, "How surprised must the fishes be to see this ungainly visitor from another sphere speeding his way amid their schools!"[23] Thoreau also notes "that loons have been caught in the New York lakes eighty feet beneath the surface, with hooks set for trout."[24] It is at such a lake situated in the Adirondacks in New York that Doctorow picks up the mystery of the loon.

As in *Walden*, the history of the meaning to mankind of Loon Lake goes back to the time of the Indians, and the story of the lake symbolizes society. In the novel, a poet named Warren Penfield functions as the consciousness who describes the meaning of the lake. Naturally, his book is called *Loon Lake* so that the physical landmark merges with the poetic and intellectual construct. Penfield writes, "All due respect to the Indians of Loon Lake/the Adirondack nations, with due respect. / What a clear cold life it must have been."[25] Penfield the poet sees the loons as symbolic of an eternal process of death and rebirth. The image of the loons connects the past of the Indians with the present. "The loons they heard were the loons we hear today," Penfield writes (LL, p. 54). The representation of the lake in the poem as the embodiment of the natural and spiritual purity of America contrasts with the current uses of the lake. Following the invasion of the Adirondacks by artists and painters who helped invent "the wilderness as luxury" business (LL, p. 46), the lake became the property of a wealthy industrialist named F. W. Bennett. Under Bennett, the wilderness of Loon Lake changes into a beautiful mountain camp where leading celebrities as well as the corrupt and the criminal are entertained. As though to dramatize the change, a loon appears from nowhere while gangsters speedboat along the lake's surface. The loon catches in midair a cigarette that the wind had "whipped out" of the mouth of one of the gangsters. "The crazy bird" seems almost trained to do it, as though they are now part of the entertainment for the corrupt company at the camp (LL, p. 47).

The novel's best example, however, of the change to the new America of industrial exploitation and waste can be found in a character named Joe who functions as the most significant consciousness in the novel. Born Joseph Korzeniowski, he is called Joe Paterson after his native city. Primarily through Joe's consciousness, we get compact, intense, and personal visions of experience that remind one of the "Camera Eye" sections of Dos Passos's *U.S.A.* A wanderer and loner, Joe also seems modeled after several Dos Passos types, especially Joe Williams, who represents in *U.S.A.* the consciousness of the common-man victim. Thus, in style and substance, Doctorow recognizes and consciously elaborates upon the mythic constructs in much of modern America literature. Joe Paterson's story, however, seems most related to that of F. Scott Fitzgerald's Gatsby. The pattern of Joe's development and metamorphosis follows the one established by Gatsby, and the cultural implications that Gatsby's story embodies are duplicated by Joe. Gatsby, of course, was born Jay Gatz and through the intervention of a wealth benefactor achieves a new life. For Gatsby, the sponsor fulfills the role of both God and father. This help enables Gatsby to create a new identity for himself based on his understanding of what success and power mean in America. Fitzgerald writes, "The truth was that Jay Gatsby of West Egg, Long Island, sprang from his Platonic conception of himself. He was a son of God—a phrase which, if it means anything, means just that—and he must be about His Father's business, the service of a vast, vulgar, and meretricious beauty. So he invented just the sort of Jay Gatsby that a seventeen-year-old boy would be likely to invent, and to this conception he was faithful to the end."[26] Similarly, Joe Paterson in *Loon Lake* achieves a new identity through the intervention of the industrialist Bennett who sees himself in certain ways as a mythic or God-like figure. Bennett adopts Joe. Joe in turn develops into the corporate, social, and political image of his new father. In a summary of his career at the end of the novel, Doctorow provides Joe with all the accoutrements of modern-day corporate and social success. His titles, organizations, positions, achievements, and memberships represent the things that Doctorow obviously detests about contemporary America. Joe's success, therefor, constitutes a political and moral failure. Along with all his achievements, including duty as "Deputy Assistant Director of the C.I.A." and an ambassadorship, Joe can call himself "Master of Loon Lake." The last title on the list indicates the ultimate betrayal in terms of the novel's values.

In *Loon Lake,* Doctorow continues to maintain a radical perspective on American culture. Imbued with the literary and mythic sensibility of an earlier radical generation, he still attacks corporate bureaucracy and capitalistic exploitation. However, like Daniel Isaacson, he embodies a new radical consciousness that reflects contemporary concerns and realities. For example, in his description of Disneyland in *The Book of Daniel (BD,* pp. 301-9), Doctorow discusses the power that enables mass culture and the entertainment media to turn our great narratives into palliatives for complacency and conformity and to undermine the existential challenge of literature. As a writer, he wants to repossess the culture's natural resources of myth and narrative in order to restore the culture and to reaffirm the values of individual freedom and responsibility. Similarly, Doctorow uses psychology to develop a new radical perspective that can offer possible insights unavailable to traditional radical politics. Thus, early in the novel, he describes the sexual relations between Daniel and his wife, Phyllis, in a way that combines physical and political terms. The description implies that in a modern radical ideology the psychological roots of oppression may be as important as the economic. Portraying Phyllis as a "sex martyr" and Daniel as a "tormentor" who makes her suffer "yet another penetration," Doctorow plays with the idea of the sexual origins of political power as Daniel "explores the small geography of those distant island ranges, that geology of gland formation, Stalinites and Trotskyites, the Stalinites growing from the top, the Trotskyites up from the bottom" *(BD,* p. 16).

The different elements that form Doctorow's political and literary vision can be discerned from the figures he quotes at the beginning of *The Book of Daniel.* The quotations are from the Prophet Daniel, Walt Whitman, and Allen Ginsberg. All three indicate Doctorow's attraction to prophets who become aliens in their own lands partly because they often speak for the values and ideals of the very cultures that ostracize them and resist their messages. They are vital and distinct landmarks in Doctorow's moral and cultural consciousness and represent major aspects of his thought and his literary and political program—Jewish, American, and radical. Although important differences separate Daniel, Whitman, and Ginsberg, they are also related elements of one moral vision. They are like the various selves that comprise the one mythic American Self for both Whitman and Emerson. Their examples encourage Doctorow to continue his effort to meld together the literary, historic, and mythic to express the meaning of America. Taken together, the figures of Daniel, Whitman, and Ginsberg dramatize how well Doctorow propels the thrust of the New Covenant. As a Jewish writer and thinker, he contributes to the development of the American idea by being at once both the most conservative and the most radical of Americans. He is the most conservative because of his concern for preserving those institutions and values of democracy that constitute the American idea. At the same time, he is the most radical because he extends and modernizes the ideology and meaning of America to make it relevant to contemporary American life, thought, and needs. Like Daniel, he brings together the social visions of both the Isaacsons and Lewins into one unified whole. Thus, because of his purposes as a writer and thinker and his philosophy of the American idea Doctorow demonstrates that he holds a position of leadership in the New Covenant tradition in America.

Notes

1. The idea of "metahistory" as used throughout this study relates to an interesting new work on "the political unconscious" that relies heavily for its theoretical basis upon such thinkers as Freud, Lacan, Althusser, and Marx. See Jameson, *The Political Unconscious.*
2. See White, *Metahistory,* p. 334.
3. Nietzsch, *The use and Abuse of History,* p. 39.
4. See Nietzsche, *The Genealogy of Morals,* p. 209.

5. Nietzsche, *The Birth of Tragedy*, p. 137.
6. Ibid., p. 106.
7. White, *Metahistory*, p. 371.
8. Quoted in Clemons, "Houdini, Meet Ferdinand," p. 76.
9. White, *Metahistory*, p. 372.
10. Henderson, *Versions of the Past*, pp. 283, 270.
11. Doctorow, *Welcome to Hard Times*, p. 214.
12. Ibid., p. 213.
13. Ibid., p. 215.
14. Doctorow's second novel, *Big as Life,* also distinguishes him from an apocalyptic vision of history and demonstrates his interest in popular myth. *Big as Life* is written in the mode of science fiction and concerns the chaotic reaction of New York to the appearance of two monsters in New York harbor. Although events in this novel approach the same kind of catastrophe that befalls Hard Times, the conclusion reaffirms Doctorow's humanistic vision as the characters after near bedlam pull themselves together in anticipation of a new beginning.
15. See Kauffmann, "Wrestling Society for a Soul," pp. 25–27; Charyn, "The Book of Daniel," p. 6; Bell, "Writers and Writing," pp. 17–18; Richmond, "To the End of the Night," pp. 627–29.
16. Foley, "From *U.S.A.* to *Ragtime*," p. 95.
17. Kriegel, "The Stuff of Fictional History," p. 632; Seelye, "Doctorow's Dissertation." pp. 22–23, 22.
18. Doctorow, *The Book of Daniel*, p. 193 (hereafter cited in the text as BD).
19. See Zins, "Daniel's 'Teacher' in Doctorow's *The Book of Daniel,*" item 16. See also a comparison between *The Book of Daniel* and *All the King's Men* in Hamner, "The Burden of the Past," pp. 55–61, and Stark, "Alienation and Analysis in Doctorow's *The Book of Daniel*," pp. 101–110.
20. Kauffmann, "Wrestling Society for a Soul," p. 25.
21. Berthoff, "Fiction, History, Myth," p. 54.
22. Thoreau, *Walden, p. 92.*
23. Ibid., pp. 157, 156.
24. Ibid., p. 156.
25. Doctorow, *Loon Lake, P. 54 (hereafter cited in the text as LL).*
26. Fitzgerald, *The Great Gatsby*, p. 99.

DATE DUE